# arizona

# arizona

by Bill Weir

National Geographic
Washington, D.C.

# CONTENTS

Pages 2–3: The Grand Canyon and Colorado River take center stage.
Opposite: Winter rains pave the way for blossom-dappled landscapes.

# TRAVELING WITH EYES OPEN

Alert travelers go with a purpose and leave with a benefit. If you travel responsibly, you can help support wildlife conservation, historic preservation, and cultural enrichment in the places you visit. You can enrich your own travel experience as well.

To be a geo-savvy traveler:

- Recognize that your presence has an impact on the places you visit.

- Spend your time and money in ways that sustain local character. (Besides, it's more interesting that way.)

- Value the destination's natural and cultural heritage.

- Respect the local customs and traditions.

- Express appreciation to local people about things you find interesting and unique to the place: its nature and scenery, music and food, historic villages and buildings.

- Vote with your wallet: Support the people who support the place, patronizing businesses that make an effort to celebrate and protect what's special there. Seek out shops, local restaurants, inns, and tour operators who love their home—who love taking care of it and showing it off. Avoid businesses that detract from the character of the place.

- Enrich yourself, taking home memories and stories to tell, knowing that you have contributed to the preservation and enhancement of the destination.

That is the type of travel now called geotourism, defined as "tourism that sustains or enhances the geographical character of a place—its environment, culture, aesthetics, heritage, and the well-being of its residents." To learn more, visit National Geographic's Center for Sustainable Destinations at *www.nationalgeographic.com/travel/sustainable*.

# NATIONAL GEOGRAPHIC TRAVELER

# arizona

## ABOUT THE AUTHOR

**Bill Weir** discovered travel while still in school and has never tried very hard to settle down. A bicycle ride across the United States with Bikecentennial in 1976 inspired the idea of the ultimate ride—a cycle tour around the world. He got started writing guidebooks on that trip in 1979 by sending suggestions to the author of the *South Pacific Handbook* while island-hopping there. That led to paid assignments with the publisher to update parts of the *Indonesia Handbook* for five cents a word. When Weir returned to Arizona after four and a half years of travel, he started thinking of places about which to write a guidebook. Realizing that the best one lay under his feet, he wrote the *Arizona Handbook*. Utah beckoned next, and Weir completed the *Utah Handbook* a couple of years later. His bicycle, Bessie, collected dust for a while, but they returned to Asia in 1995 to finish the round-the-world ride via the Middle East and Europe. He continues to explore the world, a good bit of it by bicycle, as well as enjoying Arizona travels and writing. Weir is based in Flagstaff, Arizona, but you are more likely to find him on the road or trail.

# Charting Your Trip

In every part of Arizona, Mother Earth puts on a geologic spectacle. At the Grand Canyon you'll look down on thousands of feet of colorful rock layers. Structures made by people who lived here long ago add an air of mystery, and Native American groups continue to practice centuries-old traditions. European settlers came about 300 years ago. Today's lively mix of cultures beckons.

### Traveling There & Getting Around

Phoenix's Sky Harbor Airport, in the south-central part of the state, offers regularly scheduled flights to and from other points in North America. Tucson, in Arizona's southeastern corner, offers useful connections. Amtrak's trains—running east-west across the northern and southern parts of the state—provide more leisurely travel. A car definitely gives you the greatest flexibility and convenience to explore Arizona; Phoenix and Tucson have the largest choice of vehicle rentals, including RVs. If you'd rather not drive, you can check out guided tours to the state's most popular destinations, such as the Grand Canyon, Phoenix, and Tucson.

### The Truly Great Outdoors

Stunning scenery and sunshine will give you many reasons to stretch your legs. Parks, national forests, national wildlife refuges, and other public lands cover much of Arizona—there's room to roam! For the greatest range of outdoor activities, head for Grand Canyon National Park. Here you can enjoy the thrill of white-water rafting deep in the canyon's depths, or you can hit the trails on a horse or mule, or on your own two feet. Other sections of the Colorado River offer placid expanses of water suitable for fishing, scouting for wildlife, or just relaxing.

Outdoor adventures are also fantastic elsewhere in the state. Hiking trails range from easy interpretive walks to challenging climbs such as Humphreys Peak, the state's highest summit at 12,633 feet, just northwest of Flagstaff—though most can be done as day hikes. For fly-fishing in clear flowing streams and alpine lakes, head to the forests on the White Mountain Apache Indian Reservation in the east. This tribe also has a fine ski resort, and there's more good snow up north

**Saguaro National Park near Tucson boasts grand cactuses.**

around Flagstaff and nearby Williams. Getting wet is easier than you might think in a desert state, with pools, water parks, lakes, and rivers to cool off; tubing on a section of the Salt River near Phoenix is popular in summer.

## Arizona in One Week

But not all Arizona pleasures are in the wild. Phoenix, Tucson, and the state's other multifaceted cities lure with culture, entertainment, and history still visible in vintage buildings and fine museums. This rewarding itinerary—a grand loop drive north out of Phoenix to the Grand Canyon and back around—takes in a wealth of Arizona's majestic scenery, history, and art.

On Day One from Phoenix, plan to drive 60 miles northwest to **Wickenburg** (see pp. 150–151), rich in Old West and gold-mining legacies, then turn north on Ariz. 89 and head another 60 miles into the high country around the charming town of **Prescott** (see pp. 115–117), where historic hotels and bed-and-breakfasts abound.

On Day Two, weave through hills northeast on Ariz. 89A an hour to **Jerome** (see p. 113), a mining-town-turned-art-colony perched high on a mountainside with fine Red Rock Country views. Then follow Ariz. 89A down and across the Verde Valley and past splendid red-rock monoliths on the 30-mile drive to **Sedona** (see p. 104), home of many art galleries and some of the state's finest resorts.

On Day Three, drive north on Ariz. 89A through **Oak Creek Canyon** (see pp. 106–107) with a stop for a short hike amid the wonderfully sculptured canyon walls of the West Fork of Oak Creek. A twisting climb on Ariz. 89A brings you onto the Mogollon Rim for a viewpoint and the ponderosa pine-lined drive to **Flagstaff** (see pp. 92–95), 140 miles from Phoenix, where you can stroll the historic downtown and perhaps take

## NOT TO BE MISSED:

The Grand Canyon's vast and complex depths **46–63**

Gazing across Monument Valley's iconic landscapes **76–77**

Exploring Canyon de Chelly's evocative ruins **78–79**

Walpi, a traditional Hopi village atop a narrow mesa **83**

The museum-rich mountain town of Flagstaff **92–95**

Hiking Sedona's awesome Red Rock Country **104–108**

Driving Route 66 for scenery and nostalgia **132–133**

Phoenix and the Valley of the Sun's arts and sports **144–165**

The Petrified Forest's rainbow-hued logs and Painted Desert **179–181**

Tucson's rich Spanish legacy and modern culture **196–203**

## Packing for Arizona

Expect wide temperature swings between day and night in desert climes; dressing in layers works well. Comfortable closed-toe shoes will be handy on the state's many enticing walks and hikes; add a pair of lightweight boots for longer or more rugged trails. Arizonans tend to dress informally, but you might wish to include something elegant for nights out on the town. Raingear is a good idea, though you're most likely to see precipitation only in winter and late summer/early autumn. Winter in the highlands can see temperatures dip well below freezing, so warm clothing is a must then. A good hat and sunscreen are essential year-round.

## Visitor Information

Arizona Office of Tourism provides a one-stop reference for travelers (www.arizonaguide.com) with sights, stories, events, recreation, places to stay, and travel tips. If you would like printed literature, there's a request form online. Tourism offices throughout Arizona have brochures or you can call the state office in Phoenix (tel 866/275-5816 or 602/364-3700). Painted Cliffs Welcome Center near the Arizona/New Mexico border is worth a stop if you're arriving via I-40; take the Grants Road Exit #359; the Welcome Center is open every day except holidays, 8 a.m.–5 p.m.

in a museum; this mountain town offers a huge range of accommodations and restaurants.

On Day Four, take US 89 a half-hour north from Flagstaff to the turnoff for a scenic drive through **Sunset Crater Volcano National Monument**'s pretty cinder cones and lava fields (see p. 100) and **Wupatki National Monument**'s well preserved prehistoric stone pueblos (see p. 101), with stops to walk the short trails at each site. Continue north on US 89 about 20 miles to Cameron Trading Post, a good place for lunch and shopping, then turn west on Ariz. 64, which becomes **Desert View Drive** (see p. 51) on Grand Canyon National Park's South Rim; overnight in Grand Canyon Village or Tusayan.

On Day Five, take in the sights of **Grand Canyon Village** (see pp. 48-49) and **Hermit Road** (see p. 50) before looping back the 80 miles to Flagstaff via Valle on Ariz. 64 and US 180.

On Day Six, pack a picnic for the beautiful 90-minute drive southeast from Flagstaff across the meadows and forests of the **Mogollon Rim** (see pp. 122–126) via Lake Mary Road/Forest Hwy. 3 and Ariz. 87, then drop down to nearby **Payson** (see p 122), which has a good selection of places to stay; 11 miles north of Payson you may wish to detour 3 miles west to see the dazzling **Tonto Bridge Natural Bridge State Park** (see p. 123–124).

On Day Seven, you can return to the Phoenix area on the 90-mile drive along Ariz. 87, or you take the longer and more adventurous route via Theodore Roosevelt Dam and the largely unpaved **Apache Trail** (see pp. 166–169).

### If You Have More Time

Arizona invites—and handsomely rewards—leisurely exploration as well as active pursuits. Choose a wedge of the state and immerse yourself.

## What Time Is It, Anyway?

Unique in the continental United States, Arizona does not observe daylight saving time. The state stays on mountain standard time (GMT -7) throughout the year, but there is one exception: In the northeastern part of Arizona, the Navajo Nation goes on daylight saving time because of its enormous size—it is actually located in three states. Here clocks are set ahead one hour at 2 a.m. on the second Sunday of March, then back to standard time at 2 a.m. on the first Sunday in November.

To make matters more than a little confusing, the Hopi Indian Reservation, which is completely surrounded by the Navajo Nation, remains on mountain standard time year-round.

Exhilarated boaters brave the wild waters of the Salt River in eastern Arizona.

Arizona is home to the Navajo tribe, whose lands include **Monument Valley** (see pp. 76–77), an iconic piece of the American West that is about 150 miles northeast of Flagstaff. En route, you can detour north to **Navajo National Monument** (see p. 80), with its ancient cliff dwellings. From Monument Vallley, drive southeast for about 100 miles to the mesmerizing **Canyon de Chelly National Monument** (see pp. 78–79) before continuing some 60 miles west to the atmospheric **Hopi mesa-top villages** (see pp. 81–85), which continue a long history of traditional life.

One of the West's greatest road-trip adventures, a drive on the winding 123-mile Coronado Trail (see pp. 190–191), about 200 miles east of Phoenix, would be the highlight of a leisurely loop through eastern Arizona, which could include **Petrified Forest National Park** (see p. 179) and the verdant lands of the **White Mountain Apache Reservation** (see pp. 183–184).

On the western edge of the state, explore **ghost towns** and wilderness areas in winter and splash in the **Colorado River** and its reservoirs in summer. On your must-see list should be **Organ Pipe Cactus National Monument** (see pp. 218–219), 175 miles southwest of Tucson, great for hiking, and maybe a drive on the longest remaining stretch of **Route 66** near **Kingman** (pp. 130–131), a good base for ghost-town visits.

You can drive completely around the **Grand Canyon** (about 200 miles) with detours along the way to the spectacular **North Rim viewpoints** (see pp. 58–63) and the lonely **Toroweap Overlook** (see p. 63; dirt road access only) on the north, **Lake Mead National Recreation Area** (see pp. 134–135) on the west, and the lands of the **Hualapai** and **Havasupai tribes** (see pp. 54–57) on the south.

# History & Culture

A Hopi basket sports bold detail. Opposite: Traditionally dressed dancers add to the festive spirit at the Parada Del Sol, a February event in Scottsdale, Arizona.

# Arizona Today

A heady mix of rich cultural traditions—Native American, Spanish, Mexican, Anglo—and a wealth of great natural wonders form the basis of Arizona's unique appeal. The names and pictures of such spots as the Grand Canyon, Painted Desert, and Monument Valley, however, only hint at the grandeur. These places of a lifetime really do have to be experienced to be believed.

Accounts of early explorers, amply embellished by Hollywood, provide much of the popular perception of present-day Arizona. Images come to mind of cowboys herding cattle amid scenic splendor, travelers fighting off Indians, gunfighters settling scores on the dusty streets of Tombstone, or miners seeking gold in forbidding mountains. These mental pictures have some truth, but they reflect southern Arizona—the area known to most early explorers and settlers. Lonely outposts of the Spanish Empire had reached this far, and later groups of Mexicans and Anglos preferred the region. Hostile tribes and lack of precious minerals in the northern half of what is now Arizona discouraged outsiders until well into the 1800s.

Yet it's in the north where you'll find the sparkling mountain streams, alpine meadows, snowcapped volcanoes, and the world's greatest expanse of ponderosa pine forest. Vigorous rivers in this northern high country have cut immense canyons that hold beautiful worlds of their own. Although you won't see an ocean in Arizona, the Colorado River emerges from its canyons to become the state's "west coast"—hundreds of miles of watery playgrounds and tranquil wildlife sanctuaries. Arizona's immensely varied topography creates many different natural environments and climates; you can come any time of year and find one to your liking.

> **Although you won't see an ocean in Arizona, the Colorado River emerges from its canyons to become the state's "west coast."**

Each region has something to offer. The remote Arizona Strip in the far north holds canyons, plateaus, and volcanoes in wilderness areas that many travelers have yet to discover. Just south of the Strip, the Grand Canyon's sheer size and beauty make it one of the great natural wonders of the world. You'll appreciate it best if you make time for contemplation, hiking, mule riding, or river running. Navajo lands begin on the east edge of the Grand Canyon and stretch across most of northeastern Arizona, a stunning region of rock and sky with such beautiful spots as Monument Valley and Canyon de Chelly. Within this land you'll also find the Hopi tribe, whose villages rise from the mesa tops as they have for centuries.

Moving south from the Grand Canyon and Native American lands, you'll reach Flagstaff, a mountain town with a lively university and a strong sense of the outdoors. Winter skiing, hiking, camping, boating, and fishing are all within easy reach of the town. Volcanoes in the region and farther east make up the rooftop of Arizona, with heights to 12,633 feet. Craters abound—not only volcanic cones such as Sunset Crater but also the world's best preserved impact structure, Meteor Crater. The high country finally

**The Arizona Center's landscaped grounds offer a restful retreat in downtown Phoenix.**

**So many fantastic colors: A Native American dances in traditional dress at a powwow.**

drops off in the spectacular cliffs of the Mogollon Rim, a long sweep of forests and canyons, including the red-rock country around Sedona and the less well-known Sycamore Canyon and West Clear Creek wilderness areas.

Over in the west, the Colorado River's gentle flow brings life to the hottest and driest part of the state. People come here to splash in the water during summer and soak up the sunshine in winter. Yet the harsh desert takes over just a stone's throw from the river, and here you can find ghost towns and old mines that mark prospectors' dreams of gold and silver. In the desert heart of Arizona, the skyscrapers of Phoenix celebrate the dynamic hub of the state's largest metropolitan area and a multitude of fine museums, scenic parklands, and stylish nightspots. Scottsdale's luxurious resorts and Tempe's large university add to the sophistication. Miners dug gold out of the surrounding ranges, where you can visit the old sites or perhaps even search for the mysterious Lost Dutchman Mine.

Wildly twisting roads—the Apache Trail and other highways—lead to eastern Arizona's Apache tribes, who have opened much of their scenic mountain and desert lands for outdoor recreation. Farther east, the Coronado Trail, now a paved highway through rugged hills and pretty forests, follows the route taken by Spanish explorers in 1540. In the Sonoran Desert of southern Arizona, national parklands have been set aside for stately saguaro and organ pipe cactuses. "Sky islands" punctuate the desert with alpine forests on their lofty summits and diverse wildlife within their canyons. Exceptionally clear skies in the area have attracted astronomers to study the heavens at several major observatories you can visit. The Spanish have left their cultural imprint on the architecture, religion, and language. Tucson, or the Old Pueblo, as it is sometimes called, still has historic neighborhoods reminiscent of Spanish colonial days. As Arizona's second largest city and home of a major university, Tucson offers much to see and do in the worlds of art, nature, and history.

## Arizonans

Who are they? The answers are many, because groups have migrated in and out of this area for millennia. Hopi can trace their clans back at least 2,000 years to inhabitants of ancient village sites widely scattered across northern Arizona. To the south, O'odham (AH-tomb) are thought to have descended from an early civilization that had mastered skills of irrigating crops in the desert.

Most of the tribes in western Arizona appear to have arrived many centuries ago too, though their nomadic lifestyle has left few traces. Navajo and Apache probably drifted into eastern Arizona from the east between A.D. 1300 and 1600—about the time the first Spanish explorers arrived.

The Spaniards kept mostly to the southeast corner of Arizona, especially after their missions were destroyed during revolts in Hopi country to the north and Quechan lands to the west. Spanish religion and culture did take root among some of the O'odham, who still worship at the 18th-century Mission San Xavier del Bac near Tucson. The legacy of the many Spanish soldiers, missionaries, and settlers who came to the region continued to have an influence despite the change to a Mexican flag in 1821 and finally, in 1847–1848 and 1854, to the American Stars and Stripes.

Pioneers, including many recent European immigrants, joined Mexican communities in the mid-19th century and adopted their architectural styles, foods, and customs—all well suited to this desert climate. American influence increased with the opportunities the new railroads offered to townspeople, miners, and ranchers. Finally, the advent of air-conditioning after World War II made year-round living in the desert a more attractive proposition.

A small number of blacks arrived here too. Estévan, a Moorish slave in an advance party of Fray Marcos de Niza's 1539 expedition, was probably the first non-Indian to enter Arizona. Black people of the area are remembered for their heroic service as Buffalo Soldiers with the U.S. Army from 1866—when Congress passed legislation establishing six (later consolidated to two) regiments to be made up of African Americans—until statehood.

### EXPERIENCE:
### Cheer at Spring Training

More than a dozen major league baseball teams—known as the **Cactus League**—warm up for the season in spring training camps under Arizona's sunny skies. The action takes place in the greater Phoenix area. For fans, it's a time to welcome the teams back after a long winter and watch them practice and play exhibition games. Low ticket prices and many new or renovated stadiums add to the pleasure of watching the teams begin their play. Spring training takes place in **March,** with occasional games played at the end of February or beginning of April. Look for the schedule of games—along with stories about the teams—on the Cactus League's official website, www.cactusleague.com, and **Mesa Convention & Visitors Bureau's** site, www.visitmesa.com/spring-training/.

Getting above it all: Ballooners drift peacefully past the sheer sandstone cliffs of Monument Valley.

## Arizona's Ethnic Influences

Hispanic people make up about one-fifth of Arizona's population. Family life is a central feature of their society, and they are more likely than their Anglo neighbors to stay near home. Mexican cuisine attracts fiercely loyal adherents—you're rarely far from a good enchilada. Fiestas and major events in towns with Hispanic populations bring out mariachi bands and *folklórico* dancers to entertain appreciative audiences. Mariachi, traditionally played with guitars of different sizes, violins, trumpets, and sometimes a harp, has roots that go back to 18th-century Spanish orchestras. Good places to experience Hispanic culture include the historic districts of Tucson (see pp. 196–201) and the mission of San Xavier del Bac (see p. 220).

Native American homelands cover about 27 percent of Arizona on 23 reservations. A visit to a tribal cultural center or museum is a good introduction to traditional ways of life. Also recommended are the Museum of Northern Arizona in Flagstaff (see pp. 92–94), the Heard Museum in Phoenix (see pp. 147–148), and the Amerind Museum (see p. 232) southeast of Tucson. Native artists and craftspeople create many beautiful pieces, which are sold directly or at galleries or trading posts.

Majestic scenery also draws visitors to Native American lands—the Navajo Nation, Havasupai, and Hualapai reservations all adjoin the Grand Canyon, and the Navajo lands include Monument Valley and some impressive cliff dwellings. A visit to a traditional Hopi village—hundreds of years old—is a rich experience no visitor soon forgets.

Navajo and Apache, who entered present-day Arizona about 500 years ago, have undergone a transformation from a nomadic existence to a settled one. Forests,

lakes, and mountain streams on the lands held by the Apache in eastern Arizona provide many recreation possibilities. Hopi have the longest record of Arizona's native tribes—both in their oral history and in archaeological findings. They successfully farm at high elevations with only meager sources of water. The Pai (including the Paiute, Havasupai, Hualapai, and Yavapai) traditionally lived in small family groups, practiced a little agriculture, and made seasonal migrations to hunt and gather wild foods. Today they are settled and follow a modern lifestyle. Paiute live on the Arizona Strip near the Utah border. Havasupai reside in beautiful Havasu Canyon, off the Grand Canyon, Hualapai are near the South Rim of the western Grand Canyon, and the Yavapai have several reservations in central Arizona. Yuman-speaking tribes—the Mohave, Quechan, and Cocopah—have lived and farmed along the lower Colorado River for hundreds of years. Chemehuevi relinquished their nomadic life in the early 1800s and settled on the lower Colorado; they are related to the southern Paiute.

Maricopa once lived along the lower Colorado, but they gradually migrated up the Gila River Valley to escape their aggressive Mohave and Quechan neighbors and now live with the Pima. The O'odham of southern Arizona, who farm the Gila and Salt River Valleys, call themselves Pima or Akimel O'odham (River People), while those who live in the deserts prefer Tohono O'odham (Desert People) rather than the old name of Papago. Outsiders have often wondered how the Tohono O'odham could exist in the harsh Sonoran Desert, but one member stated, "We don't think of ourselves as surviving in the desert. It is our home, we *live* here." Yaqui, fleeing Mexican persecution, began arriving after 1878 and into the 1920s. The federal government gave them tribal status in 1978, and they now live near Tucson and in the town of Guadalupe, between Phoenix and Tempe; they are noted for their Easter ceremonial dances.

**Hopi have the longest record of Arizona's native tribes—both in their oral history and in archaeological findings.**

   Most tribespeople have found a balance between tradition and modern life, working at regular jobs yet honoring the religion and customs of their ancestors. They welcome visitors who respect the privacy of people living on the reservation and follow tribal laws. You'll need to get permits or permission and pay a small fee to hike, camp, fish, hunt, or leave the paved roads. Always ask before taking a photo of someone, and be prepared to pay. The Hopi, overwhelmed by photographers in the past, now prohibit the taking of pictures, sound recordings, and even notes.

## EXPERIENCE: Cooking, Arizona Style

Southwestern cuisine has its roots in the food of Native Americans—corn, chilies, beans, tomatoes, and avocados. When Spanish colonial settlers, Mexicans, and cowboys arrived, they adopted these and contributed cheese, rice, pork, and beef to the larder. Join this long culinary tradition by learning from today's Southwestern chefs. Skilled teachers provide hands-on and demonstration classes.

In Phoenix, September through May, cookbook author Barbara Fenzl (or a visiting chef) offers a demonstration followed by a meal at **Les Gourmettes Cooking School** (6610 N. Central Ave., Phoenix, 85012, tel 602/240-6767, e-mail: barbara .fenzl@cox.net).

Not far away, in Scottsdale, variety is the spice of life in the mostly hands-on classes taught by expert chefs at **Sweet Basil Cooking School** (10749 N. Scottsdale Rd., Scottsdale, 85260, tel 480/596-5628, www.sweetbasilgourmet.com).

In Tucson, Janos Wilder shares recipes and tips at **Janos Cooking School** (3770 E. Sunrise Dr., Tucson, 85718, tel 520/615-6100, www.janos.com). Most classes take place monthly on Saturdays from October to May at Janos Restaurant, on the grounds of the Westin La Paloma Resort. For each class, Janos presents a discussion, cooking demonstration, beverage pairing, and a tasting of the items demonstrated.

Over in Yuma, Tina Clark is an enthusiastic historian and chef who leads classes in Southwestern, Sonoran, and heritage cuisine at **Tina's Cocina** (St. Paul's Cultural Center, 645 S. 2nd Ave., Yuma, 85364, tel 928/783-3530, www.stpaulsculturalcenter .com). You'll be cooking in a restored hacienda-style kitchen, complete with a cast-iron stove.

### Southwestern Cuisine

Dining reflects Arizona's heritage. Mexican food, especially that of nearby Sonora, has a large following. Cafés primarily serve old standbys, while chefs at more sophisticated restaurants strive to create new and more flavorful dishes featuring Southwestern ingredients, such as chilies, beans, corn, cilantro, tomatillos, pine nuts, and even prickly pear cactus. Cowboy fare makes a big hit with both locals and visitors—steak, ribs, chicken, or trout grilled and served with beans, biscuits, potatoes, and gravy; some places entertain with songs and skits from the range. Native Americans have their favorites too, such as fry bread, which can be a snack or—when topped with meat, beans, cheese, lettuce, and tomato—a filling meal. The Chinese have been running restaurants here since territorial days, and their cuisine can be found in almost every sizable town. International flavors, such as those from India and Japan, are becoming more common, most often in cities with universities.

### Government & Politics

A relative youngster in the Union, Arizona became the 48th state on St. Valentine's Day, 1912. Early politics tended toward populism, and the state was solidly Democratic, but during the 1950s, as many retirees and other newcomers swelled the cities, the state became increasingly Republican. Through the years, Arizonans have reflected their conservative side in Senator Barry Goldwater, their liberal aspect in Governor Bruce Babbitt, and their independent streak in Senator John McCain—all former presidential candidates. Generally, Arizonans believe they can manage fine, even on immigration issues, without being pushed around by big government, a sense of self-reliance perhaps influenced by years of frontier existence.

## The Outdoors

Experiencing Arizona's natural wonders provides some of the greatest inspiration—and perspiration—the state offers. The rewards of close encounters with the Arizona outdoors make any extra efforts worthwhile. Viewing the Grand Canyon from a roadside overlook is fine, but you'll experience it more fully on a walk into its depths. Instead of seeing it as just a giant, colorful cavity, you'll know firsthand that it's an intricate system of canyons within canyons, each with its own mix of plants, wildlife, and presence or absence of water. Other canyon, mountain, and desert regions offer their own beauties and mysteries. Your options range from easy strolls on paved trails to adventurous treks into wilderness areas. Mountain bikers can pedal down quiet lanes in a national forest or challenge daunting trails. Kayakers and rafters can take on the rapids of the Grand Canyon's Colorado River or float on placid streams and lakes.

Humans need to adapt to the different environments here just as other living things have learned to do. Hiking guides offer advice, and rangers and other backcountry travelers will suggest ideas on how to avoid the dangers of heat exhaustion, hypothermia, lightning, flash floods, and venomous reptiles and arthropods. If you're new to these outdoors, consider starting with short trips, then attempt the more challenging routes as your experience grows. ■

**The fry bread contest—a caloric highlight at the Navajo Nation Fair in Window Rock**

# History of the Land

A fortunate combination of geology and climate has made the long history of Arizona's land easily visible today. Uplift by subterranean forces and downcutting by rivers have revealed the geologic layers like an open book. The rock, usually free of vegetation, tends to break off in vertical faces if hard; sloping surfaces if soft.

The visible geologic story begins about two billion years ago with the base layer of mountain ranges, now exposed as granite, schist, and gneiss at the bottom of the Grand Canyon. Erosion wore down the mountains, and the sea moved in and out over the following millennia. Limestone and other sedimentary rocks document the history of the oceans during the Paleozoic (570–240 million years ago). The graceful lines of sand dunes once blown by desert winds lie preserved in cross-bedded sandstones. Rock layers of the Mesozoic (240–66 million years ago) record the dinosaurs and other strange creatures of their time.

During the Cenozoic (66 million years ago to the present), a massive uplift in northern Arizona created the Colorado Plateau, where the Colorado River and its tributaries began carving the Grand Canyon. Periods of volcanism occurred throughout geologic history, sometimes forming underground intrusions, erupting at other times either as furious clouds of incandescent cinders or as gentle flows of lava. Arizona's youngest volcanoes lie atop the Colorado Plateau; the newest of these, Sunset Crater, last erupted only about 700 years ago. The plateau, which extends into neighboring Utah, Colorado, and New Mexico, ends at the dramatic cliffs of the Mogollon Rim on the south and the Grand Wash Cliffs on the west. The faulting of the Earth's restless crust across the rest of Arizona has squeezed up massive blocks, helping to create the region's distinctive landscape: countless mountain ranges and plateaus interspersed with desert valleys. The highest of these ranges and plateaus exceed 9,000 feet in elevation and are known as sky islands because they support forests and wildlife now isolated by the surrounding desert. Most rivers in the state flow to the west or south and meet in the southwest at an elevation of only 70 feet.

> Arizona's skies . . .
> often blaze with stars
> at night, radiate a deep
> blue by day, and present
> memorable sunrises
> and sunsets.

## Climate

Arizona's skies above the broad horizon often blaze with stars at night, radiate a deep blue by day, and present memorable sunrises and sunsets. Don't put too much faith in what you read about the state's average temperatures: In the deserts, low humidity combined with a lack of insulating forests can cause swings of 40°F between day and night. A warm jacket will be useful even in summer for drives or hikes into the mountains. Winter storms can bring snow to the high country as late

Ancient dunes, now Navajo sandstone, form the Coyote Buttes in Arizona's far north.

as April, though they rarely last more than a few days. The sun prevails everywhere in the state, bringing warmth and brightness even in January, when the highs between storms run into the 50s in the high country and the 70s in the low deserts.

The plateaus and mountains enjoy springlike weather in summer, with highs in the 70s and 80s. Meanwhile, the desert areas bake in highs regularly topping 100°F. The desert can still be enjoyable in summer—just set your alarm clock early to be out at first light, then retire to the air-conditioning by late morning, when the sun hammers down. Many outdoor attractions in the desert, such as zoos and gardens, have early opening hours in summer. Residents and visitors cope by making bad jokes about "it's a dry heat."

Elevation greatly affects precipitation, which ranges from about 3 inches annually in the southwestern deserts to more than 30 inches in the White Mountains in eastern Arizona. Precipitation can vary considerably from one year to the next. Most arrives as gentle rain or snow during winter or as late summer thunderstorms. April, May, and June are the driest months.

## Vegetation & Wildlife

The spectrum of life zones extends from the lower Sonoran Desert of southern Arizona to alpine conditions atop the San Francisco Peaks in the northern part of the state. At low elevations, which seldom experience extended freezing conditions, saguaro cactuses and other plants of the Sonoran Desert thrive (see pp. 214–215). If winter rains come in the right amounts and at the right times, beautiful floral displays cover the desert from about February through May. The ephemerals (annuals that can complete their growth cycle very quickly) bloom first; they need to grow, flower, and produce seed before the hot sun dries them out. Cactuses and other perennials follow. The giant saguaros bloom last, around May, when spring

## Carving the Grand Canyon

It seems like a simple process—the land rose and the river cut down—yet geologists have a tough time pinpointing the age of the canyon itself. Rocks now on the rim lay at sea level 70 million years ago when the Earth's crust began a slow uplift. Sometime later the ancestral Colorado River settled in its present course and began to carve the Grand Canyon. The question is, when did this start? Too much of the geologic record is missing to know for sure. Studies of river deposits have led to conflicting theories on the canyon's birth date—it was sometime between 5 million and 70 million years ago, with many geologists supporting an age of 5 to 6 million years.

Even the river's direction of flow is in doubt, with some experts saying that the Little Colorado and ancestral Colorado Rivers once drained north, a theory supported by the angle of tributaries to the Colorado, suggesting a northward tilt of the land. Others say that the Little Colorado and Colorado once flowed south into a giant lake or the Rio Grande. Or perhaps the Colorado River once flowed in its present course, but in the opposite direction, only later to be reversed by tilting of the Colorado Plateau. Some geologists go along with John Wesley Powell (see pp. 64–65), believing the Colorado has always followed its present course. The problem with this theory is that no river deposits older than 5 million years have been found in the lower canyon.

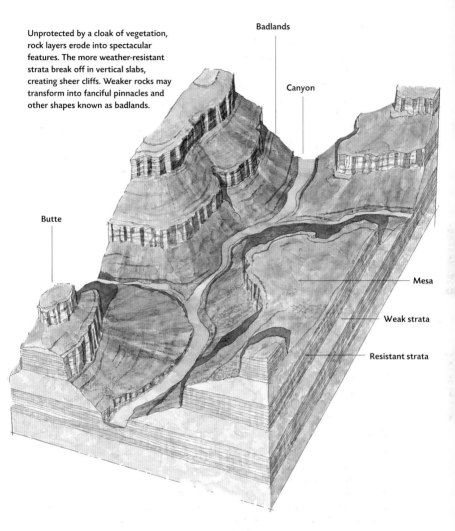

Unprotected by a cloak of vegetation, rock layers erode into spectacular features. The more weather-resistant strata break off in vertical slabs, creating sheer cliffs. Weaker rocks may transform into fanciful pinnacles and other shapes known as badlands.

Badlands

Canyon

Butte

Mesa

Weak strata

Resistant strata

gives way to summer. Higher desert areas support grasslands (a favored habitat of the speedy, antelope-like pronghorn), chaparral (a tangle of manzanita, oak, and shrubs), or woodlands (pinyon pine, juniper, and oak). Here, too, agave plants shoot up their tall flowering stalks. Sweet-smelling ponderosa pine covers much of the plateaus and mountains between 6,500 and 8,000 feet. Dense forests of aspen, spruce, pine, and Douglas and other firs cling to the cool, wet slopes of the higher mountains. In summer, meadows display colorful shows of wildflowers, such as pentstemons, lupines, daisies, and sunflowers, followed in autumn by shimmering groves of aspen turning to gold. Above about 11,500 feet, on the San Francisco Peaks, trees give way to tundra.

Opportunistic animals such as the coyote and the common raven seek food nearly everywhere, while others have adapted to specific environments. Some subspecies in

**Winter rain ushers in spring desert color at Organ Pipe Cactus National Monument.**

forest areas have been isolated atop sky islands or plateaus surrounded by desert. On the South Rim of the Grand Canyon, for example, you'll see the large Abert squirrel, with a gray body except for white on the belly and underside of the tail. The similarly sized Kaibab squirrel, which inhabits the North Rim, has a dark gray belly and a white tail. Their ancestors may have crossed from the South Rim during cool periods of the Pleistocene epoch (1.6 million–10,000 years ago), when the canyon would have had large forests.

Reptiles proliferate in the warmer regions of Arizona. They include 11 species of rattlesnake, all of which are born live and can live up to 20 years in the wild. Within the Grand Canyon you might spot the shy Grand Canyon or pink rattlesnake, a subspecies of the western rattlesnake that lives only here. The Sonoran coral snake has venom, too, but is less of a threat; it has a black head and rings of alternating red and black separated by narrower rings of yellow. Don't toy with a Gila monster either—it has razor-sharp teeth, strong jaws, and venom. The lizard reaches 9 to 14 inches in length and has a black and pink (or orange) beaded skin. Desert tortoises, which dine on grasses, herbs, some shrubs, wildflowers, and cactus fruit, can live 80 years and reach 14 inches in length; they are now threatened in southern California, Nevada, Utah, and northern Arizona but seem to be doing well in the Sonoran Desert.

The roadrunner, a comical member of the cuckoo family, sometimes flies but, like its Warner Brothers counterpart, prefers a speedy gait across the desert. In the mountains and the deserts you're also likely to encounter mule deer with their outsize ears. Elk—shy but large and imposing animals—roam the high forests and meadows. Black bears, also brown or cinnamon-colored, live in mountainous areas but are rarely seen, though you should heed warnings on signs at campgrounds and trailheads. Mountain lions live in the remotest areas; they are likelier to spot you than you are to notice them. Southeastern Arizona is famed for its birds, which congregate in the canyons and mountains during the warmer months. Of the large number of species, several are found only rarely elsewhere in the United States.

## Arizona State Parks

You can enjoy some of Arizona's most intriguing historic sites and natural areas, along with fine facilities, at its state parks. Historical parks relate the history of Pueblo Indians, Spanish colonizers, the territorial years, or mining. Nature parks include scenic desert, mountain, and canyon areas and a beautiful living cave. Recreation parks feature lakeside and riverside locations ideal for water sports. About half the parks offer campgrounds. The main office of Arizona State Parks in Phoenix has an information desk and gift shop *(1300 W. Washington St., Phoenix, AZ 85007, tel 602/542-4174 or 800/285-3703 in Arizona beyond the Phoenix area, closed Sat.–Sun., www.azstateparks.com).*

## National Parks, Monuments, & Forests

Besides the well-known Grand Canyon National Park, the National Park Service *(www.nps.gov)* looks after ancient pueblos, a Spanish mission ruin, colorful petrified wood, a volcano, Sonoran Desert regions, and other scenic and recreational areas. If you plan to visit many of these sites, ask about the America the Beautiful Pass, which gives a year of unlimited entry for a flat fee. Seniors (62 and older) and the disabled who are citizens or permanent residents of the United States can get lifetime versions of the pass.

National forests cover large areas of the high country in Arizona, offering opportunities for scenic drives, hiking, mountain biking, fishing, and camping. You can visit any of the U.S. Forest Service offices or visitor centers for maps and recreation information, or check the Internet *(www.fs.fed.us/r3).* Expect to pay a fee in the more heavily used areas.

The Bureau of Land Management Information Access Center is an excellent source of information, maps, and books for all the federal and state areas *(tel 602/417-9300, closed Sat.–Sun., www.publiclands.org).*

### High-altitude Flora

At an elevation of 7,150 feet, the Arboretum at Flagstaff (see p. 95) is the highest botanical garden in the United States engaged in horticultural research. Plant researchers study both native and non-native flora, including rare and endangered species that thrive in the cool climate of the Flagstaff area. About 2,000 species of plants grow on the 200-acre grounds despite the short (75 days on average) growing season.

## Arizona Trail

Nearing completion, this challenging 800-mile trail offers hikers, mountain bikers, and equestrians an opportunity to see Arizona up close. Unlike other major trails that follow a single feature, the Arizona Trail winds through a variety of terrain. Its south end touches the Mexican border in Coronado National Memorial, and its north end is on the Arizona Strip near the Utah border. In between lie many mountain ranges, some desert sections, plateaus, and the Grand Canyon. Contact the Arizona Trail Association *(P.O. Box 36736, Phoenix, 85067, tel 602/252-4794, www.aztrail.org).* ∎

# History of Arizona

The human story in Arizona spans at least 12,000 years of triumph and retreat as people sought new or better opportunities. Farming and water management became the means by which complex societies were able to develop in early times—and to progress to the present.

## The First Tribes

Nomadic hunters once roamed a green landscape in search of big game such as mammoth, bison, pronghorn, and camel. The bands lived along streams and lakes, leaving few traces other than projectile points and animal bones. By 8000 B.C. most large animals were extinct. This, and a drier climate, caused the tribes to rely more on gathering wild plants and hunting small game. A detailed knowledge of the land guided the people on seasonal migrations to harvest seeds, nuts, and berries. Most likely they traveled in small bands with minimal possessions and lived in caves or brush shelters. Some tribes pursued this existence into the late 1800s.

**The Hohokam ... developed extensive networks of irrigation canals to channel water from the Salt and Gila Rivers to their fields.**

## Growth of the Great Pueblos

Farming may have started as early as 3000 B.C. but did not provide a substantial part of the tribes' diet until 200 B.C. or so. People planted their fields in spring, continued their migrations in summer, and returned in autumn to harvest their crops. Cultivation of corn, beans, and squash became increasingly important over the centuries and made sophisticated cultures possible. Agricultural skills and pottery making probably originated in Mexico. By A.D. 200, tribes began building small villages of pit houses—partly underground dwellings roofed with sticks and mud—near their fields.

Three distinct farming cultures emerged, classified by archaeologists as the Anasazi (ancient Pueblo people) of the Colorado Plateau in the north, the Mogollon (MUG-gy-yon) of the eastern uplands, and the Hohokam of the southern deserts. Trade among the cultures and with Mexico brought new ideas and goods to the villages. Already skilled in basketmaking, the tribespeople also learned to grow and weave cotton. Their decorated pottery was of such high artistic quality that it is greatly admired today. Masonry and adobe houses replaced pit houses as villages grew and became more widespread between A.D. 500 and 1100. Complex religious ceremonies evolved, and kivas—underground rooms reminiscent of pit houses—served as ceremonial chambers in the uplands. The Hohokam built platform mounds and oval ball courts. These desert dwellers also developed networks of irrigation canals to channel water from the Salt and Gila Rivers to their fields. Most of their adobe structures disappeared long ago, but a huge Great House has survived at Casa Grande Ruins National Monument (see p. 171). The cultures reached their peak of craft, masonry, and agricultural skills about 1100,

**Prehistoric tribes left behind records—such as these vivid petroglyphs at Wupatki National Monument—in just about every corner of the state.**

The richly detailed interior of Mission San Xavier del Bac, near Tucson

but then a series of migrations left nearly all the villages abandoned. The Mogollon had apparently vanished by 1200, perhaps absorbed into Anasazi and Hohokam villages. By 1400 the Hohokam culture had also collapsed. Spanish explorers in the following century found the O'odham (AH-tomb), also known as Pima and Papago, living a simple existence. O'odham legends relate a revolt against oppressive villages. The Anasazi consolidated on the Hopi mesas and in pueblos to the east, where they live today. Hopi oral tradition tells of their ancestors migrating as part of a great plan. Archaeologists suspect that drought, erosion, overpopulation, disease, and dwindling food may have contributed to the large-scale abandonment. Schisms, which have occurred in modern times, likely had a role too. Navajo and Apache had begun moving into eastern Arizona about the time villages were vacated, but there is no evidence this affected the upheavals of pueblo cultures.

## Spanish Conquistadores, Missions, & Presidios

In 1539 the viceroy of Mexico, on hearing tales of the treasure-filled Seven Cities of Cíbola to the north, sent Brother Marcos de Niza to investigate. After losing some of his party to hostile Zuni Indians, Niza returned with reports of a great city of stone. The following year Francisco Vásquez de Coronado set out from Mexico with

336 soldiers and nearly a thousand Native American allies to conquer the cities. But instead of magnificent wealth, Coronado found only poor villages. His fruitless search lasted two years, and he reached the area of modern Kansas before returning to Mexico.

Despite disappointments, Coronado's expedition greatly increased knowledge of these new lands among the Spanish. A detachment under Garcia López de Cárdenas had visited Hopi villages and continued west to the Grand Canyon. Meanwhile, Hernando de Alarcón—who had sailed along the west coast and traveled a short way up the Colorado River—added this new area to the maps.

In 1629, Franciscans opened the first of several missions among the Hopi. They were reasonably successful in gaining converts until some Hopi joined the large, well-organized Pueblo Revolt of 1680 and killed or threw out the friars and many of their followers. Missionaries tried again with the Hopi in 1700, but villagers promptly destroyed the mission. In the south, Father Eusebio Francisco Kino achieved good relations with the O'odham by introducing cattle and new crops from 1691 until his death in 1711. The work that he started led to the later construction of Mission San Xavier del Bac, in which the O'odham worship today. Relations between the Spanish and the O'odham took a turn for the worse in 1751, when the tribe staged a major revolt, but the Spanish stayed on, making some reforms and establishing presidios (fortified military camps) at Tubac, Tucson, and other locations. A revolt by Quechan against the Spanish in 1781 on the lower Colorado River brought mission work there to an abrupt end. The Spanish then kept to the area around the Santa Cruz River for the rest of their time in Arizona.

## A Mexican Interlude

When Mexico won independence from Spain in 1821, mission work declined as funds were cut and foreign-born missionaries were expelled. Political instability in Mexico City resulted in a failure to uphold peace treaties with the Apache, who then besieged the unfortunate settlers. American traders and trappers, discouraged earlier by the Spanish, began to sneak in and got to know the land. Many of these mountain men, including Kit Carson, Jedediah Smith, and the unusually named Pauline Weaver, paved the way for military expeditions. Arizona came into the Union almost by accident—the Mexican War of 1847–1848 had ceded not only the desired Texas and California but also everything in between.

> Arizona came into the Union almost by accident—the Mexican War . . . ceded not only the desired California and Texas but also everything in between.

The United States government paid little attention to Arizona, which was part of New Mexico Territory after 1850. What is now southern Arizona came into American hands with the Gadsden Purchase in 1854, but for most early travelers the territory was just an obstacle to be crossed on the way to Californian goldfields. In the 1850s, gold strikes along the lower Colorado River, steamboat service, and the establishment

## How Arizona Got Its Name

We can only conjecture who bestowed this name! It first appears on Spanish records in the 1730s when prospectors and ranchers arrived, and it's likely that Basque people among them named their new home Arizona (the good oak tree). A vaguely defined area with little more than ranch operations, Arizona became well known because of the fabulous Planchas de Plata (slabs of silver) discovery nearby in 1736. Reportedly an American mine speculator picked up the name and used it to publicize and sell mining shares, and Arizona became so well known that politicians later chose it for the entire territory. Maps still show the original site, located just south of the present-day Mexican border near Nogales.

of Army posts attracted the attention of prospectors and farmers. The taking of land by the newcomers soon upset the Native Americans, who began sporadic warfare that would last three decades. The Civil War made life much worse for the settlers after Army troops headed east to fight. Residents tended to favor the Confederacy, and Rebel captain Sherod Hunter received a fine welcome at Tucson in 1862. He had hoped to ally California with the Confederacy, but that plan fell through, and he could only delay the 2,000-man Union force headed his way from California. The Battle of Picacho Pass on April 15, 1862, took place between detachments of both sides (see p. 172). The Californians lost three men, but the Confederates, knowing that Union reinforcements would soon arrive, beat a retreat back to Tucson and on to Texas.

### Territorial Years

Arizona emerged for the first time as a separate entity during the Civil War. President Abraham Lincoln signed the bill establishing the Arizona Territory on February 24, 1863. The promising mining area of Prescott became the territorial capital a year later; Tucson lost out because it had leaned too much toward the Confederacy. Although the Indian wars continued to slow development, the arrival of railroads in the late 1870s and early 1880s opened up the land to large-scale ranching, mining, and logging. People could now import material for stylish Victorian houses instead of living in adobe or log structures. The mining of gold and silver, then copper, propelled the economy.

Members of the Church of Jesus Christ of Latter-day Saints (more commonly known as Mormons) from Utah, seeking new opportunities and freedoms, arrived in 1864 at Littlefield, in Arizona's northwest corner, only to see their farms washed away in a flood three years later. Other Mormon groups pushed south, setting up Lees Ferry across the Colorado River, above the Grand Canyon, and progressing as far as St. David in southeastern Arizona. Hard work and a strong sense of community enabled most Mormon settlements to prosper, but their practice of polygamy offended their neighbors until the Mormon Church, under federal government pressure, outlawed it. Some members refused to go along and broke away from the main church; you'll see their unusually large houses on a drive past Colorado City in Arizona's far north. Many Mormon settlements in the territory became thriving cities, including Springerville (founded 1871), Mesa (1878), Snowflake (1878), and Show Low (1890).

Conflict between the Army and Native American tribes persisted. The Army ended Navajo resistance in 1863–1864 with a brutal campaign that temporarily removed the tribe to a camp in eastern New Mexico, but renegade Apache continued to attack outsiders until their leader, Geronimo, surrendered to the Army in 1886. Arizonans had lobbied for statehood since 1872, but primitive roads, outlaw and Apache troubles, and political feuds kept delaying the goal. Even though citizens largely resolved these problems by the end of the century, Eastern politicians turned a deaf ear. Admitting Arizona would have adversely affected the Easterners' preference for the gold standard (Arizona was pushing for silver) and Republican values (Arizona was Democratic).

Meanwhile, the territory's citizens had no vote in Congress nor any say in who would be appointed governor. When the country needed volunteers for the Spanish-American War, Arizonans quickly signed up to show their loyalty. Prescott's William "Buckey" O'Neil, a popular former sheriff, newspaperman, and politician, led troops into battle in Cuba, earning admiration from the press, who called his group the Rough Riders. A Spanish sniper cut him down on San Juan Hill, but he died a hero.

Surely, Arizonans felt, they would be awarded statehood now, but Washington big-wigs continued their delaying tactics. It took Congress until 1910 to pass the Enabling Act; with a constitutional convention and a little more wrangling, the statehood bill was ready to be signed on February 12, 1912. The 12th turned out to be Lincoln's birthday—a holiday—and the following day an "unlucky" 13th, so President William Howard Taft waited until the 14th to give Arizona its Valentine's Day gift. Wild celebrations broke out across the new state as soon as news arrived. One young Phoenix

An 1886 surrender: Geronimo (squatting, center left) concedes to Gen. George Crook (in helmet on right).

couple, Joe Melczer and Hazel Goldberg, had planned to have the state's first wedding. They had patiently waited, along with their three-year-old ring bearer, for the message. When it came, little Barry Goldwater presented the rings, and the couple exchanged vows.

## Statehood

On statehood day, Governor George W. P. Hunt led a trium- phant procession to the Capitol in Phoenix. Though one of the richest men in Arizona, Hunt had arrived in the territory 31 years earlier as a penniless miner. He had worked his way up to become a successful merchant, banker, territorial representative, and president of Arizona's Constitutional Convention. While Hunt was governor, his determined efforts for road building, labor, and other liberal causes earned him seven terms in office. Arizona's first state legislature gave women the right to vote in 1912—a full eight years before national suffrage—and in 1914 vot- ers elected a woman to the Arizona House and another to the Arizona Senate, the first and second in the nation to hold such offices. World War I inspired another round of patriotism with heroes such as aviator Frank Luke of Phoenix, who shot down 14 German observation balloons and four planes in 17 days. Forced down behind enemy lines, he pulled out his revolver and died fighting the German infantry.

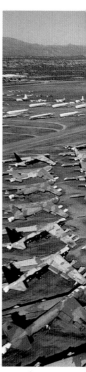

**Arizona's first state legislature gave women the right to vote in 1912—a full eight years before national suffrage.**

Relying heavily on its mining industry, Arizona, the Copper State, benefited or suffered according to the metal's price. Cotton, especially long-staple Pima, led agricultural production. New dams on the Salt, Gila, and Verde Rivers supplied the water necessary for continued growth. The Great Depression hit hard, causing crop prices to plummet and forcing many mines to close. Tourism helped in the 1920s and 1930s, when fashionable resorts opened, catering to wealthy Northerners. Dude ranches offered the romance of the Old West. The clean, dry desert air also drew "lung- ers"—people suffering from tuberculosis—to recuperate. Governor Benjamin Moore, a country doctor from Tempe, helped the state during the Depression years by slashing property taxes, adding luxury taxes to keep needed programs afloat, and holding free medical clinics for the poor.

## World War II & Postwar Boom

With the outbreak of World War II, Arizona again jumped at the chance to serve the nation. The Army Air Corps trained an estimated 60,000. General George Patton prepared his men for the invasion of North Africa by rehearsing in the demanding heat of southwestern Arizona. The desert also seemed a logical place to house prisoners of war. Its aridity was the undoing of an escape plan by German submariners from Papago Park in Phoenix: U-boat commander Capt. Jürgen Wattenberg and 24 fellow prisoners

**B-52 bombers dot Tucson's Davis-Monthan Air Force base in 1995. Most have since been scrapped.**

managed to tunnel 180 feet to freedom, only to find their plan to raft down the Salt River to Mexico thwarted by a dry riverbed. All were recaptured. The desert also became an unhappy home for thousands of innocent Japanese Americans.

Of the many Arizona heroes fighting overseas, perhaps the most unusual were the Navajo Code Talkers. The Japanese had been intercepting American radio transmissions in the Pacific and using the information to attack and confuse troops, so Navajo in the Marine Corps developed a code in their native language. The Japanese never broke it, probably saving the lives of thousands of soldiers, sailors, and marines. Ira Hayes, a Pima (O'odham), helped raise the flag on Mount Suribachi during the battle for Iwo Jima in 1945; he's the last in line with upraised hands in the famous photo.

By war's end, many servicemen and women stationed in Arizona had grown to like the state, so they settled in. Manufacturing had more than quadrupled over the war years as aeronautical and other defense industries built new factories. Most of the new industries stayed. Year-round living in Arizona became an attractive proposition, thanks to air-conditioning. Retired people, many weary of shoveling snow up north, began moving to the desert; entire cities blossomed to hold them. The state has continued to develop at a rapid pace, generating loud debate about growth and urban sprawl. Planners wonder when the supply of water will run out. Yet the career opportunities, climate, outdoor recreation, and resorts continue to attract new faces. ■

# The Arts

Arizona's natural setting influences the perceptions of nearly all who come here. The light and the way nature's hand has sculpted the landscape into wonderful forms inspire people to portray them. Art also reflects the mystique of Native Americans and cowboys, symbolizing the close relationship between humans and nature. Additional inspiration comes from the state's many historical periods.

Thomas Moran depicted the Grand Canyon in "Under the Red Wall" in 1917.

## Visual Arts

Early tribes, which had perhaps the closest connection with the land and its life, carved or painted thousands of enigmatic geometric, animal, human, and anthropomorphic designs in cliffs and boulders. The Hopi recognize some of these as clan symbols, but many others challenge us with their mysteries. Landscapes continue to delight artists and make up a large category of regional art today. Western or cowboy art stirs up both derision and admiration. Some see it as just an assemblage of stock images—the cowboy or Indian with a horse in the desert or mountains and perhaps a sunset. Others admire the painter's skill and the qualities depicted. They

feel nostalgia for a time past, when a simpler world knew self-reliance, untrammeled nature, and purity of purpose. Native American artists have extended their traditional crafts to fine jewelry, sculpture, and paintings. Tribal people have also been subjects themselves—portrayed both romantically in paintings and, perhaps more honestly, by skilled photographers.

> **Much of early Arizona's art documents 19th-century expeditions and reveals the sense of wonder the artists felt.**

To experience the work of regional, national, and international artists, visit the Phoenix Art Museum (see p. 147) and the Tucson Museum of Art and Historic Block (see p. 196). The Scottsdale Museum of Contemporary Art (see pp. 161–162) displays cutting-edge work in the fields of art, design, and architecture. Northern Arizona University in Flagstaff (see pp. 94–95) offers changing and permanent collections in Old Main and a changing gallery in the Fine and Performing Arts building. Arizona State University (see pp. 159–60) in Tempe, east of Phoenix, offers several exhibit venues, including the architecturally striking Nelson Fine Arts Center. The University of Arizona (see pp. 197–198) in Tucson features diverse collections in its Art Museum and outstanding photos in its Center for Creative Photography. The Old West lives on at the Phippen Museum near Prescott (see p. 117) and the Desert Caballeros Western Museum in Wickenburg (see p. 150). Three museums present outstanding traditional and contemporary Native American art: Flagstaff's Museum of Northern Arizona (see pp. 92–94), Phoenix's Heard Museum (see pp. 147–148), and southeastern Arizona's Amerind Museum (see p. 232). Art galleries abound in Sedona, Scottsdale, Tucson, Tubac, Jerome, Bisbee, and on Hopi and Navajo lands.

### Artists & Photographers

Much of early Arizona's art documents 19th-century expeditions and reveals the sense of wonder the artists felt. Explorer John Wesley Powell understood the importance of showing

## North American Indian Mega Project

In his 20-volume life's work, *The North American Indian*, Edward S. Curtis (1868–1952) sought to capture images of Native Americans living their traditional ways of life. The fading away of the U.S. frontier gave added urgency to his mission. Together with assistants who helped with text and other details of the immense project, he created an artistic masterpiece in a photographic essay that gave us much ethnographic knowledge. During his 30 years of work he sacrificed his health and his marriage. In 1905, President Theodore Roosevelt wrote in a letter to Curtis: "I regard the work you do as one of the most valuable works which any American could now do."

the West to people elsewhere when he invited artist Thomas Moran (1837–1926) to join him on a river expedition in 1873. Moran painted a magnificent canvas, *The Grand Canyon of the Yellowstone,* the following year. Measuring 7 feet by 12 feet, it shows the canyon bathed in light with a thunderstorm above and mists in the abysses. It hung in the lobby of the U.S. Senate in Washington, D.C., where it caught the attention not only of the public and lawmakers but also Santa Fe Railroad officials, who later promoted the Southwest as a tourist spot.

Also in the late 1800s, artist Frederic Remington (1861–1909) earned fame for his realistic portrayals of Native Americans, cowboys, soldiers, horses, and other aspects of the West in sculptures, paintings, and illustrations. In 1900, photographer Edward S. Curtis set out to record all 80 tribes active in the United States, an ambitious project that would last 30 years and produce 20 volumes (see sidebar this page). Much of his early work was done in Arizona, where Curtis lived and traveled with the tribespeople to earn their trust.

Contemporary artists continue these traditions. Howard Post (1948–) learned to rope and ride as a cowboy in southern Arizona, then began to portray range life on canvas. Robert Daughters (1929–) uses bold strokes and vibrant colors to depict the many facets of the craggy landscapes he paints in impressionistic style. Photographers strive to capture the people and land of Arizona, too; many of their best shots appear in *Arizona Highways* magazine, where you'll see the work of such artists as Jerry Jacka, Gary Ladd, Jack Dykinga, Josef Muench, and Muench's son David and grandson Marc.

### Native American Arts

Of all Arizona's tribes, the Hopi and Navajo create the most artwork, and many families rely on sales as a major source of income. You may see pieces by other tribes too, such as beadwork by the Apache, pottery and basketry by the Maricopa and Pima, and basketry by the Tohono O'odham. Some Native American artists now realize their visions in paintings, sculptures, furniture, and stained glass.

Hopi pottery reflects both a 2,000-year-old tradition and contemporary visions in its geometric patterns and figures from Hopi mythology. In the late 1800s, the Hopi craft of pottery making began to decline as modern cookware replaced the old pots. Soon only the women of First Mesa were still making and selling pots to other villages for cooking. During an excavation of nearby Sikyatki Ruin in 1895, however, one of the village men took some decorated pottery sherds back to his wife, Nampeyo, a skilled Tewa potter. She adapted the designs to her own work and, with the encouragement of trader Thomas Keams, perfected her re-creations of the old shapes and patterns. Brisk sales of her work encouraged other potters to take up the "new" Sikyatki style.

The Hopi also create fine basketry—one of the oldest Native American crafts—that displays bold patterns and colors. Cotton weaving—traditionally done by men during the winter—is an old skill, too. During the 1890s the first Hopi silversmiths learned their skill from the Zuni, who in turn had picked it up from the Navajo, and all three groups initially produced similar styles.

Staff at the Museum of Northern Arizona in Flagstaff saw the need for the Hopi to develop a unique style; they suggested that the Hopi adapt pottery and basketry designs for their silverwork by cutting the patterns in sheets of silver, then soldering

A Navajo woman, dressed in the style of a 19th-century army officer wife, cards wool for rug yarn.

them onto the main body of the piece as an overlay. The idea took off after World War II, when Hopi veterans returned and joined a G.I. training program. In 1949 the new Hopi Silvercrafts Cooperative Guild further helped the artists by providing a place to purchase supplies, work, display, and sell their work. Kachina dolls, carved from cottonwood roots, originally served to educate children about the spirits in the Hopi religion. They were usually flat or cylindrical, with just enough decoration for identification. When visitors started purchasing these dolls, artists began carving increasingly realistic representations. Some figures now boast fine detail. The Heard Museum in Phoenix devotes an exhibit to kachina dolls.

Navajo weavers, traditionally women, at first produced fine blankets using wool from sheep obtained from the Spanish and weaving skills learned from the Pueblo

A downtown Tucson statue of Gen. Francisco "Pancho" Villa, who once led raids on U.S. soil

tribes. In the late 1800s, factory-made blankets greatly reduced demand, so traders suggested making rugs instead. These became a great success , and more than a dozen regional styles have emerged across the vast Navajo Nation. Silversmiths developed distinctive wares such as the squash-blossom necklace with its horseshoe-shaped pendant.

Turquoise is the gemstone of choice for Navajo jewelry. Sand paintings of Navajo deities and symbols play a role in healing ceremonies; they are also mounted and sold.

## Architecture

Prehistoric cliff dwellings with their multi-story towers still impress people today at Montezuma Castle National Monument (see pp. 110–11) and other sites across the Southwest. A later wave of people—the Spanish—constructed Mission San Xavier del Bac (see p. 220) in the late 1700s, a great domed monument to their faith. The sheer visual impact of the ornate interior, with its many statues, murals, and decorations, was intended to make the Catholic religion appeal to the O'odham people of the time. The church's beauty and size are even more impressive in light of the fact that workers built it under the shadow of Apache raids at the edge of the Spanish Empire.

Before the railroads, Americans made do with simple adobe houses in the desert and log structures in the forested uplands. Victorian houses became the fashion in the late 1800s, adding a comforting touch of civilization to the frontier. By 1900, Arizonans sought a regional identity and went through phases of mission revival from 1900 to 1915 and the more romantic Spanish colonial revival between 1915 and 1930. City planners then decided they needed more "serious" buildings and adopted less colorful modern styles—undistinguished "boxes" with little or no ornamentation. Up at the Grand Canyon, architect Mary Colter (see sidebar below) had been designing distinctive public buildings using Southwestern themes or elaborate stories. She worked hard

## Mary Colter, Extraordinary Architect

A rarity in the male-dominated world of early 20th-century architecture, Mary Colter (1869–1958) designed many of the Grand Canyon's most memorable buildings. After her father died in 1886, she obtained permission from her mother to attend the California School of Design in San Francisco to learn skills to help support her family. After teaching mechanical drawing for awhile, she applied for work with the Fred Harvey Company, beginning a relationship that would last more than 40 years. In 1902 she obtained a contract to decorate the Indian Building, a new museum and sales gallery in Albuquerque, New Mexico. Colter's enthusiasm and research into Native American architecture led to a remarkable series of buildings along the Grand Canyon's South Rim, beginning with the Hopi House, which opened in 1905. Each of her commissions tells a story, and she took great care with the details to make sure that everything was just so. She went on to design Lookout Studio with a jagged roof that blends into the scenery, which opened in 1914, and Hermits Rest with a cozy interior that a hermit might inhabit, also completed that year. In 1922 she designed the rustic stone lodge and four cabins at Phantom Ranch in the bottom of the Canyon. The intriguing Desert View Watchtower, opened in 1932, incorporates both ancient and modern Native American themes. When building the 1935 Bright Angel Lodge, she saved the 1890s Buckey O'Neil Cabin and Red Horse Station by incorporating them into the plan; otherwise these historic structures would have been demolished. She also came up with the idea of the geologic fireplace in the lodge's History Room.

to get the details just right, even choosing the interior furnishings and colors. When called upon to design a Native American art gallery at the South Rim, she patterned the 1905 Hopi House (see p. 49) after structures in the Hopi village of Old Oraibi. Hermits Rest (1914), another tourist facility on the South Rim, was made to look and feel as if a recluse had just decamped the premises. La Posada (1930), a luxurious railroad hotel in Winslow, may have been Colter's grandest commission—a vast hacienda designed to make guests feel as though they were the personal guests of a Spanish don.

Architect Frank Lloyd Wright (1867–1959) had already achieved worldwide fame when he opened Taliesin West (see pp. 162–163) near Scottsdale in 1937 as a winter home for both his family and his school of architecture. Tours offer an introduction to Wright's philosophies and designs, in which he allowed his organic architecture to "grow" from the inside out. You'll see how his buildings fit gracefully upon the land and look different from every angle. Wright had a hand in the Biltmore Resort in Phoenix and designed the Gammage auditorium (see p. 160), one of his last major buildings, on Arizona State University's Tempe campus. Also worth seeing at ASU, the Nelson Fine Arts Center (see p. 159), built in 1989 by architect Antoine Predock, interprets the desert's sparse beauty and special qualities of light and air.

## Writers

Author Zane Grey (1872–1939) turned out so many romantic novels about the American West that he is often credited with inventing the genre. While working as a dentist in New York City, he tried his hand at writing *Betty Zane* (1903), a novel about pioneer life based on an ancestor's journal, then plunged into writing full-time and came out West. With his wife taking care of editing, marketing, and family, Grey was able to write more than 80 books. His passion for fishing, hunting, and collecting stories took him on wide-ranging travels that included Arizona. He built a lodge beneath the Mogollon Rim; here he researched some of his most popular novels. Historic events that had taken place nearby inspired *To the Last Man* (1922), his graphic depiction of the tragic Pleasant Valley War between sheepmen and cattlemen. Grey portrayed Arizona's social problems in books such as *Under the Tonto Rim* (1926), also set below the Mogollon Rim, and

**Zane Grey's stories of the Southwest form the core of some of the earliest Western movies.**

*The Call of the Canyon* (1924), which takes place in the Oak Creek Canyon area. Even if his publisher balked, he was not afraid of tackling controversial issues encountered by Native Americans: *The Vanishing American* (1925) and *Captives of the Desert* (1952) both present the difficulties faced by the Navajo people on their reservation.

Historian, folksinger, and educator Marshall Trimble (1939– ) has probably done more than anyone to make Arizona's history enjoyable. He writes in an informal storytelling style that brings to life people who walked and rode through the past. His books include *Arizona: A Cavalcade of History* (1990) and *A Roadside History of Arizona* (1986). His stories also appeared in *Arizona Highways* magazine and in the books *Law of the Gun* (1997) and the entertaining *Never Give a Heifer a Bum Steer* (1999).

Edward Abbey (1927–1989) captured the imagination of many who reveled in nature's wildness, as expressed in his iconic *Desert Solitaire* (1968). Later works, such as *The Monkey Wrench Gang* (1975) and its posthumous sequel, *Hayduke Lives!* (1989), added impetus to the environmental movement. Abbey's sharp wit and lively prose balance out his cynicism.

Arizona's landscapes, people, rivers, wildlife, and plants have inspired a great many writers to describe the natural world in books such as Ann Zwinger's *Downcanyon: A Naturalist Explores the Colorado River Through the Grand Canyon* (1995), Craig Childs' *Grand Canyon: Time Below the Rim* (1999), John Alcock's *In a Desert Garden: Love and Death Among the Insects* (1997), and Janice Emily Bower's *Fear Falls Away; and Other Essays from Hard and Rocky Places* (1997).

**Author Zane Grey (1872–1939) turned out so many romantic novels about the American West that he is often credited with creating the genre.**

## Dreamers

Italian-born architect Paolo Soleri (1919–) has lived most of his life in Arizona pursuing a dream. Not content to do the usual house and building designs, he offers ideas for futuristic cities that will provide integrated total environments to maximize beneficial social interaction while minimizing land use and damage to the environment. The ideas provide alternatives to the urban sprawl and reliance on automobiles that plague cities today, and they point toward a future in which humans can seek their full potential. His dream is now taking shape in the desert of central Arizona through an urban laboratory called Arcosanti (see pp. 120–21). Dedicated workers at the site test the ideas of "arcology," a concept of architecture and ecology working together as a single process. Success here could revolutionize the way people build their cities.

Arizona's people, living mostly in urban settings, often dream of finding a place in the natural environment, yet earlier cultures sometimes knew best how to fit in. The alcoves that sheltered their cliff dwellings gave shade in summer but let in the low winter sun—a concept reborn in the apses of Arcosanti. Adobe villages of the Pueblo tribes featured closely spaced houses that shaded each other, protecting their inhabitants from temperature extremes and maximizing the land available for agriculture. Spanish settlers introduced to the Southwest the shady walled courtyards of the Mediterranean, an architectural style worthy of a comeback. Native plants, with their beautiful shapes and colorful flowers, seem a much better alternative to lawns and gardens imported from the Midwest or East, where water is more plentiful. As Charles Bowden wrote in the book *Blue Desert:* "Here the land always makes promises of aching beauty and the people always fail the land." Thirst for water has dammed all but a handful of rivers and destroyed most of the native riparian forests. Desert grasslands are still recovering from the overgrazing of a century ago. Arizonans have responded to these challenges by setting aside natural areas as preserves and continuing to think hard about how to best meet water and land needs.

## Performing Arts

Classical music fills the halls during performances by the symphony orchestras of Flagstaff, Phoenix, Scottsdale, and Tucson. Arizona Opera and Ballet Arizona stage productions in both Phoenix and Tucson. These cities also host classical and contemporary plays staged by the Arizona Theater Company. All three universities—Flagstaff's Northern Arizona University, Tempe's Arizona State University, and Tucson's University of Arizona—host varied concerts and plays by students and visiting artists. Local tourist offices can advise on upcoming music and fine arts festivals.

## Lights, Camera, Action!

Arizona's cinematic history began in 1923 with *Robber's Roost,* based on a Zane Grey story and filmed in Oak Creek Canyon. *The Vanishing American,* another silent picture portrayal of a Zane Grey story, was filmed two years later at Monument Valley, a location that would became synonymous with Westerns. Director John Ford (1895–1973) delighted in working at Monument Valley, declaring it the "most complete, beautiful, and peaceful place on earth."

Westerns were no longer in fashion when Ford arrived in 1938, but he had a promising script about a disparate group of travelers taking a stagecoach through hostile Apache country. Local traders Harry and Leone "Mike" Goulding had made a successful sales pitch to Ford about their beloved valley and convinced him to come out and see it.

The Great Depression brought hard times for the Navajo. Many faced starvation; indeed, they needed the jobs that movie production would bring to the region. The action-packed movie *Stagecoach* was nominated for seven Academy Awards in 1939. It also transformed the career of a 31-year-old actor named John Wayne. In addition, the movie ignited a love affair between John Ford and Monument Valley that burned brightly for the rest of his life. The appreciative Navajo made him a member of their tribe, giving him the name Natani Nez— Tall Soldier. Ford made his last Western, *Cheyenne Autumn,* a sympathetic story about a Native American tribe, here in 1964, then returned one last time in 1971 to appear in the Peter Bogdanovich documentary called *Directed by John Ford.*

**Filmed in Arizona, the 1939 movie *Stagecoach* made John Wayne a household name.**

In southern Arizona, 21-year-old William Holden and 31-year-old Jean Arthur starred in *Arizona,* the 1939 epic about "bringing civilization" to the frontier. Rather than tear down the set after filming was complete, the movie company kept it as a permanent studio. Old Tucson Studios (see pp. 204–205) has hosted more than 300 films and television shows since. ∎

The Grand Canyon, a "geologic book" carved out of the colorful
rock layers of the Earth's crust by the raging Colorado River

# Grand Canyon Country

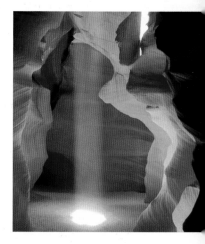

Magical landscapes of light and stone
define Grand Canyon country.

# Grand Canyon Country

**Grand indeed are the Grand Canyon's statistics. The great chasm extends 277 river miles across northern Arizona, with an average width of 10 miles. At the bottom, about a mile below the rim, the Colorado River roars through 70 major rapids in the course of its 2,200-foot descent through the canyon. Stunning figures—yet they scarcely hint at the magnificence of the spectacle itself.**

Behind the Grand Canyon's incredible geologic record are its arid climate and sparse vegetation, which have left the many layers of rock clearly visible. Lying one below another are deposits of ancient seas, rivers, sand dunes, volcanoes, and—at the very bottom—the roots of a mountain range that are more than one billion years old.

Native Americans lived here thousands of years ago, leaving behind split-twig animal figurines and stone tools. Ancient Pueblo people (Anasazi) arrived by A.D. 500 and

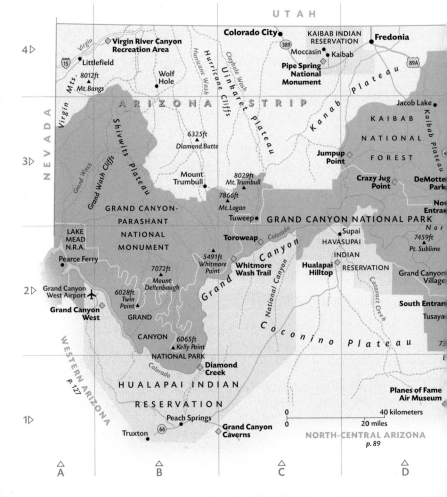

stayed until about 1200. You can still see their masonry villages and granaries. About 1300, the Havasupai moved in from the west; they have lived in Havasu Canyon—a major tributary of the Grand Canyon—ever since. You can hike in, visit their village, and view the spectacular waterfalls and travertine pools. Other tribes live near the canyon: the Kaibab Paiute to the north, the Navajo to the east, and the Hualapai to the south.

Spanish explorers first saw the canyon in 1540, when a detachment of Francisco Vásquez de Coronado's expedition arrived but could not find a way down. From the 1880s on, American

**NOT TO BE MISSED:**

Strolling on the Rim Trail for the delightful views and historic buildings  48

Exploring Hermit Road for new Grand Canyon perspectives  50

Desert View Drive's scenery, pueblo, and Desert View Watchtower  51

The beautiful panoramas on a South Kaibab Trail day hike  53

Havasu Canyon's waterfalls and blue-green travertine pools  54–55

Bright Angel Point for the view down to the Inner Gorge  58–59

Hiking the dramatic North Kaibab Trail  59

Cape Royal Scenic Drive's forests and sweeping views  60

Area of map detail

when the first train puffed in. Conservationists such as Theodore Roosevelt urged government protection of the canyon. It became a forest reserve in 1893, a national monument in 1908, and a national park in 1919.

Today Grand Canyon National Park receives about 4.5 million visitors each year. It's wise to plan ahead, especially in summer, when parking spots, accommodations, and campgrounds all fill up. You can often find solitude on Kaibab National Forest lands adjacent to the park on both rims. Relatively few visitors know about the viewpoints, trails, camping, and beautiful forests there.

The great barrier of the Grand Canyon separates the lonely country of the Arizona Strip from the rest of Arizona. People on widely scattered ranches and in a handful of small towns scratch out a living on the strip's 14,000 acres of rugged plateaus, mountains, and canyons. Historically, the region has far closer ties with Utah, whose Mormon explorers and settlers ventured here in the second half of the 19th century. ■

prospectors following old Indian trails struck silver, copper, lead, and asbestos. Getting the ore up and out of the canyon was tough work, however; many of the miners found guiding tourists more profitable. Early visitors faced an all-day stage ride from Flagstaff to the South Rim, but that changed in 1901,

# South Rim

"Do nothing to mar its grandeur for the ages have been at work upon it and man cannot improve it. Keep it for your children, your children's children, and all who come after you."

—*President Theodore Roosevelt, 1903*

Hikers enjoy the spectacle of a Grand Canyon sunset from Yaki Point on the South Rim.

**Grand Canyon National Park**

🅰 46 C3–D3

**Visitor information**

✉ P.O. Box 129, Grand Canyon, AZ 86023

☎ 928/638-7888

💲 $$$$ per vehicle for 7 days or America the Beautiful pass

www.nps.gov/grca

The Grand Canyon's easily accessible South Rim has many scenic overlooks and extensive visitor services. It lies at an elevation averaging 7,000 feet. The **South Entrance** is 58 miles north of I-40 Exit 165. Tusayan, a mile south of the South Entrance, has places to stay, a campground, restaurants, stores, and an IMAX theater. The **East Entrance,** an alternative connection with Flagstaff, is closer to the North Rim and to Navajo and Hopi lands. Desert View Drive connects the South and East Entrances. At either one, pick up a map and *The Guide*, with ranger programs, hikes, and park news.

The National Park Service offers free **shuttle service** on parts of the South Rim to alleviate congestion. *The Guide*, which can

be downloaded from the park's website, has a map of the shuttle routes, schedules, and parking info.

**Grand Canyon Village** is the heart of South Rim sightseeing. You'll see the great expanse of canyon, points, buttes, and temples—majestic remnants of canyon rims isolated by erosion. Panels outside the **Canyon View Information Plaza** show sightseeing, hiking, and program options; inside is the information desk.

For walkers, the **Rim Trail** is the ticket; it's paved and nearly level on the 3.8 miles between Bright Angel Lodge to the west and Pipe Creek Vista (first overlook on Desert View Drive) to the east. Except for the westernmost 1.5 miles near Hermits Rest, cyclists may not use the Rim Trail, but can ride roads

A free South Rim shuttle takes you to Hermits Rest, the work of architect Mary Colter. Board at one of the many bus stops.

—JONATHAN B. TOURTELLOT
*National Geographic fellow*

and paved trails farther back.

Several points of interest line the rim near **Bright Angel Lodge.** Step into the rustic lodge to see early-tourism exhibits and a geologic fireplace (made from Grand Canyon rocks layered in the same sequence as in the canyon). The 1914 stone **Lookout Studio,** just to the west, has a viewing platform and gift shop.

Next is the **Kolb Studio,** a 1904 photographic studio that now has a bookstore and temporary exhibits. Then nearby **Bright Angel Trail** (see p. 52) switchbacks down to Indian Garden and onto the Colorado River and Phantom Ranch. East along the rim you'll come to the unique example of rustic elegance that is **El Tovar Hotel,** the top lodging in the park. Visit the lobby for a look at the cathedral ceilings and log walls even if you are staying elsewhere.

**Hopi House,** just beyond, opened in 1905 for members of the Hopi tribe to live, demonstrate their work, and run a gallery. You'll find beautiful Native American art and crafts for sale. Continue along the Rim Trail, past **Verkamp's Visitor Center,** to **Yavapai Observation Station** for its geology exhibits and fine panoramas. You may wish to linger here for the sunset. ■

**Tusayan Ranger District, Kaibab National Forest**

✉ Just S of the Grand Canyon NP South Entrance (P.O. Box 3088, Tusayan, AZ 86023)

☎ 928/638-2443

**www.fs.fed.us/ r3/kai**

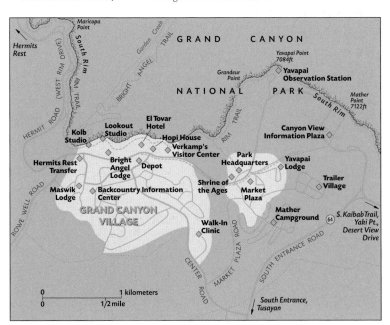

# Drive: Two South Rim Trips

These routes follow the South Rim of the Grand Canyon past a wealth of overlooks, each offering a different perspective of the canyon's spectacular scenery and geology. You can start from Grand Canyon Village, where the drives join, or at Desert View on the east end, 33 miles from Cameron.

## Drive One:
### Hermit Road (West Rim Drive)

Except in winter, most visitors use the free shuttle bus to travel this 7-mile road along the rim west from Grand Canyon Village. The bus solves parking problems, and you can hop on and off as you please. Private cars can use the road only in winter, when the bus isn't running. Disabled visitors may obtain a special permit from any visitor center. Bicyclists may ride the road but must pull off to let large vehicles pass. The **Rim Trail** parallels Hermit Road; the last 1.5 miles are paved and open to cyclists.

Besides breathtaking views of the canyon at stops along the way, you'll see the **John**

---

### NOT TO BE MISSED:

**Hermits Rest • Grandview Point • Tusayan Ruin • Desert View**

---

**Wesley Powell Memorial ❶** and **The Abyss ❷**, where the ground falls away from the rim in a 3,000-foot sheer drop. The drive ends at **Hermits Rest ❸**, a 1914 stone building named for prospector Louis Boucher, who lived in the Grand Canyon for 21 years. Nearby is the start of the **Hermit Trail,** taking walkers all the way to the Colorado River and connecting with other trails on the way.

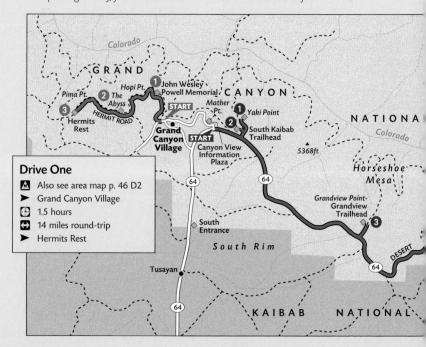

### Drive One

- 🅰 Also see area map p. 46 D2
- ▶ Grand Canyon Village
- 🕐 1.5 hours
- ↔ 14 miles round-trip
- ▶ Hermits Rest

## Drive Two:
### Desert View Drive (East Rim Drive)

This 25-mile ride begins east of Grand Canyon Village and continues to Desert View, the highest viewpoint on the South Rim and one of the most spectacular. The many overlooks on or just off the drive provide differing perspectives of the canyon. You must take a shuttle bus from Canyon View Information Plaza to visit Yaki Point and South Kaibab Trailhead. *(Disabled visitors may obtain a permit to drive.)*

Enjoy the sweeping vistas at **Yaki Point ❶**. A branch of the Yaki Point Road goes to the **South Kaibab Trailhead ❷**, where the South Kaibab Trail follows a ridge into the canyon. Cedar Ridge is a good 3-mile round-trip hike—roughly three hours.

About 8 miles farther along the drive, find the well-named **Grandview Point ❸**. From

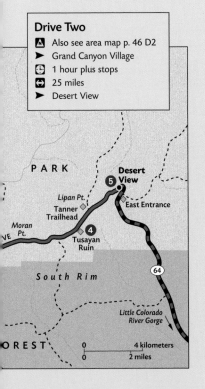

**Drive Two**

- 🅜 Also see area map p. 46 D2
- ► Grand Canyon Village
- 🕐 1 hour plus stops
- ↔ 25 miles
- ► Desert View

**INSIDER TIP:**

Atop a mule, with an outfitter, you'll experience the dramatic descent into the Grand Canyon much as early park visitors did.

—SHEILA BUCKMASTER
National Geographic Traveler *magazine editor at large*

1892 to 1907, miners worked copper deposits on Horseshoe Mesa and brought the ore up on the Grandview Trail, a former Indian route. **Tusayan Ruin ❹** marks the site of a village built by Pueblo people about 1185, according to tree-ring dating of the roof beams. For almost 40 years residents coaxed a meager living from their fields and surrounding countryside, then migrated elsewhere. Exhibits in a small museum introduce the ancient and modern peoples of this region. A short self-guided tour takes you around the plaza and foundations of living quarters, storage rooms, and kivas (ceremonial rooms). *The Guide* lists ranger walks and storytelling offered in peak season.

At **Desert View ❺**, a 70-foot stone 1932 watchtower stands on the canyon's edge like a timeless guardian. Inside, you can try to decipher hundreds of painted designs created by Hopi. The log ceiling in the adjacent gift shop is patterned after traditional Navajo hogans (traditional dwellings). The 360-degree panorama from the watchtower's viewing platform takes in the Grand Canyon to the north and west, volcanoes of the San Francisco Volcanic Field to the south, and the Painted Desert to the east. Facilities at Desert View include an information desk, snack bar, store, campground *(closed in winter)*, and service station.

Beyond Desert View, just north of the highway on Navajo land on the way to Cameron, are two **Little Colorado River Gorge** overlooks. The most popular is between Mileposts 285 and 286, with a short walk to the viewpoints; the other, between Mileposts 280 and 281, a quarter-mile-or-so walk to see the gorge.

# Inner Canyon Hiking

Traveling on foot is one of the best ways to appreciate the small details of the Grand Canyon—its wonderfully sculptured side canyons, its wildlife, its colorful flowers, its sounds, and its silences. Walking also reveals its grandeur and immense scale. Each of the canyons within the canyon has its own personality; you would need a lifetime to experience them all.

**Backcountry Information Center, Grand Canyon National Park**

✉ Located near Maswik Lodge on South Rim & at North Rim Ranger Station; P.O. Box 129, Grand Canyon, AZ 86023 (for permits)

☎ 928/638-7875 (Call Mon.–Fri. 1–5 p.m.)

**www.nps.gov/grca**

To enjoy a hike within the Grand Canyon's depths, plan ahead and bring the right clothing and gear for the season in this desert land. Pack energy foods, a hat, sunscreen, and comfortable sturdy shoes or boots. Water should be the heaviest item in your pack—reliable sources may be many miles apart. Weather can surprise you in all seasons; good raingear can make a big difference.

Spring sees wildflowers and generally pleasant hiking temperatures, though some roads on the North Rim may still be closed; good hiking conditions return in autumn. In summer the lower part of the Grand Canyon becomes an oven. Winter often brings a soft light and crisp nights. Snow and ice may make trails slushy or slippery, and roads to the North Rim will be closed.

The National Park Service publishes the free *Trip Planner* with lots of good advice, trail information, maps, and permit details; it's available in the park, by mail, and on the Internet. You won't need a permit for day hikes or if you have a reservation at **Phantom Ranch** (see Travelwise p. 241) in the bottom of the canyon, but all other overnight trips require one. Demand for backcountry permits far exceeds supply, so obtain them up to four months in advance.

It's a good idea to talk with a ranger about water sources and trail conditions. All trails entering from the rims offer good day hikes—save two-thirds of your water, energy, and time for the hike back! Park rangers recommend that first-time hikers use trails in the Corridor Zone—the **Bright Angel** (7.8 miles) and **South Kaibab** (6.3 miles) **Trails** from the South Rim and the **North Kaibab Trail** (14.2 miles) from the North Rim. All three meet at two footbridges across

**Hikers on the upper reaches of the easy-to-follow South Kaibab Trail are rewarded with superb vistas.**

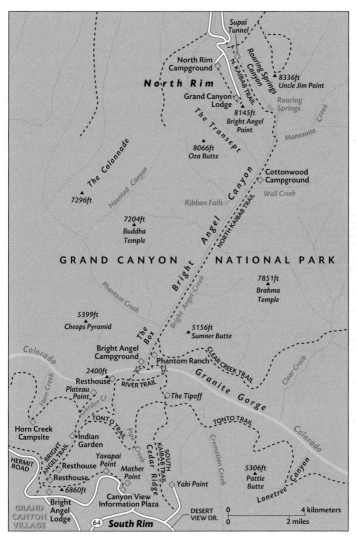

the Colorado River, near **Bright Angel Campground** and Phantom Ranch. Experienced hikers can make a great day-hike loop by descending the **South Kaibab Trail** 4.4 miles to the **Tonto Trail**, heading west and going 4.1 miles on the Tonto to **Indian Garden,** then ascending the **Bright Angel Trail** 4.6 miles back to the South Rim. **Plateau Point,** a 3-mile round-trip from Indian Garden, is a popular side-trip for hikers on the Bright Angel Trail; it features a 360-degree panorama of the canyon. A rim-to-rim hike is a grand adventure that takes three days one way; exploring side canyons and sites such as **Ribbon Falls** en route requires additional time. ■

# Havasupai Indian Reservation

A visit to Havasu Canyon—via foot or horseback—can be a transformative experience. Towering rock walls enclose Supai village and an oasis of lush vegetation, glistening waterfalls, and blue-green pools rimmed by travertine. The beauty and remoteness invoke the dawn of time.

Havasu Falls plunges into a travertine-rimmed pool in a scene reminiscent of Shangri-la.

**Havasupai Indian Reservation**

🏔 46 C2–D2

**Visitor information**

✉ Havasupai Tourist Enterprise, P.O. Box 160, Supai, AZ 86435

☎ 928/448-2141 (campground) or 928/448-2111 (lodge)

www.havasupaitribe.com

An 8-mile trail (one way), steep at first, leads from the trailhead at 5,200-foot **Hualapai Hilltop** down through spectacular canyon scenery to the village. To reach the starting point, take Route 66 (Arizona 66) northwest 28 miles from Seligman or northeast 55 miles from Kingman, then head northeast for 60 miles on Indian 18. There's no gas, food, or water along this road or at the trailhead.

Horses or mules will be waiting for you if you've made a reservation with the Havasupai Tourist Enterprise (if camping) or lodge (if staying there). The trail descends 2,000 feet between the start and **Supai** village. Carry water; in summer, avoid the heat of the day for the climb back up. The

waterfalls are too far for an enjoyable day hike, so try to stay at least two nights at the camping area or Havasupai Lodge

As you enter **Havasu Canyon** you see and hear Havasu Creek on the approach to Supai village, accessible only by trail or helicopter. About 450 Havasupai (from *havasu*, meaning "blue-green water," and *pai* for "people") live in Supai and still farm in the canyon. They welcome visitors year-round. Reserve well in advance at the **Havasupai Lodge** *(tel 928/448-2111)* or the campground 2 miles farther down.

A massive flood in 2008 destroyed Navajo Falls, leaving two new ones in its place, about a mile below the village. Half a mile farther on, **Havasu Falls** cascades a hundred feet to a large turquoise pool rimmed by travertine—an inviting spot for a swim or picnic. Continue another mile through the campground for **Mooney Falls,** the highest, with an awe-inspiring 196-foot plunge to travertine pools. In 1880 prospector Daniel Mooney tried to descend the falls via rope, but it jammed in the rock and later broke; he died on the rocks below.

Havasupai know the falls as "Mother of the Waters." A rough trail with a chain handrail winds to the bottom. A trail continues 2 miles to **Beaver Falls** and a swimming spot. Four more miles gets you to the Colorado River at the bottom of the Grand Canyon. ■

**INSIDER TIP:**

**Bring drinking water and a swimsuit (the pools are irresistible) for the hike to Havasu Canyon's waterfalls.**

—ANNE Z. COOKE
National Geographic
Traveler *magazine writer*

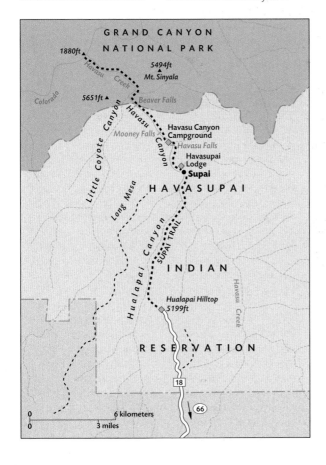

# Hualapai Indian Reservation

Relatively few people have seen the majestic panoramas from the South Rim of the lower Grand Canyon. Nor have many visitors driven Diamond Creek Road to the Colorado River at the canyon's bottom. These attractions lie on the lands of the Hualapai (Pine Tree People), Native Americans who once roamed over much of northwestern Arizona.

The glass-bottomed observation deck of the Skywalk allows travelers to gaze deep into the abyss.

**Hualapai Indian Reservation (Grand Canyon West)**

🅰 46 B1, C1
✉ 900 Route 66, Peach Springs, AZ 86434
☎ 888/868-9378 (Grand Canyon West)

www.grandcanyon west.com

See Travelwise p. 242 for Hualapai Lodge

Most of the 1,500 members of the Hualapai live in **Peach Springs,** a town lacking in charm but possessing a good motel and restaurant where you can obtain information and permits. Peach Springs sits at 4,797 feet right on Route 66 (Arizona 66), 49 miles northeast of Kingman and 34 miles northwest of Seligman.

## Grand Canyon West

The Hualapai tribe offers a tour from a remote airport terminal at Grand Canyon West to overlooks nearly 4,000 feet above the Colorado River. You can fly into the terminal from Las Vegas or drive one of four routes to get there—all of which have some dirt road. Each route takes about two hours one way. Call the reservation first to check road conditions and tour times.

The Hualapai Legacy Tour includes shuttle bus service for the 4.5 miles from the terminal to **Guano Point,** a trip that includes a fine panorama of the lower canyon. In the late 1950s, a company called U.S. Guano built a series of towers for a tramline that carried bat guano (used for fertilizer) from a cave on the north side of the canyon. The system is no longer in use, but you can visit the tower at Guano Point and see the machinery. The shuttle also stops at **Eagle Point,** and the glass-covered **Skywalk,**

INSIDER TIP:

The Hualapai live in
a most beautiful place
—a landscape photog-
rapher's dream. But
please ask before you
photograph people.

—DAWN KISH
*National Geographic photographer*

where you can step out 70 feet
from the rim and nearly 4,000
feet above the canyon bottom
*(extra fee).* Yes, Grand Canyon
West, a long detour from Grand
Canyon National Park, is touristy.
If you are looking for nature and
solitude, other portions of the
canyon, especially the North Rim,
will be more rewarding.

From Peach Springs, the best
approach to Grand Canyon West
turns north off Route 66 between
Mileposts 74 and 75 to unpaved
Antares Road, which you follow
33 miles to paved Pearce Ferry
Road; turn right (northeast) and
go 7 miles, then keep right on
Diamond Bar Road/Indian 1 for
21 miles to its end. The unpaved
first 14 miles of this road cross a
scenic area of Joshua trees, their
spare, angular branches uplifted
as if in supplication, and follow a
canyon through the Grand Wash
Cliffs. Buck and Doe Road, shorter
but rougher, can be impassable
when wet; it turns north between
Mileposts 100 and 101 on Route
66. From Kingman, you could
take the partly paved Stockton
Hill Road north to Pearce Ferry
Road and Diamond Bar Road/

Indian 1. Or from US 93 between
Kingman and Las Vegas, take the
paved Pearce Ferry Road 26 miles
to Diamond Bar Road/Indian 1.

## Diamond Creek Road

Diamond Creek Road turns north
from Peach Springs and gradually
descends into the Grand Canyon.
The earliest tourists came this way
in 1883, and from 1884 to 1889
the canyon's first hotel operated
near the confluence of Diamond
Creek and the Colorado River. The
21-mile unpaved road may require

### Hualapai Homelands

**By the peak of the United States's
western expansion in the 19th century,
the Hualapai, or "People of the Pines,"
had inhabited the tree-lined canyonlands
of northern Arizona for more than half a
millennia. The inherent conflict between
native and settler communities surged in
1867 when a mobilization of 250 Hualapai
warriors besieged Fort Mohave. After
years of such skirmishes with the military,
Hualapai resistance collapsed and the tribe
was corralled near present-day Kingman
to begin a march to a reservation in the
south. Extreme conditions bred illness and
despair, and in 1875, the remaining Hualapai fled homeward to the uplands of their
ancestors, where they remain to this day.**

a high-clearance vehicle or four-
wheel-drive after rain. Hualapai
Lodge (see Travelwise p. 242) staff
can inform you of road conditions;
they also sell permits for driving,
camping, and fishing.

To see the lower Grand Canyon
at river level, sign up for a one- or
two-day raft tour with **Hualapai
River Runners** *(mid-March–Oct.).* ∎

**Hualapai River
Runners**

✉ Office in
Hualapai Lodge
in Peach Springs
P.O. Box 246,
Peach Springs,
AZ 86434

☎ 928/769-2219
or 888/255-
9550

**www.grandcanyon
west.com**

# North Rim

Dramatic vistas of chasms and towering rock pinnacles, luxuriant forests, and wildflowers—plus cool mountain air—make the Grand Canyon's North Rim a delight to visit. If you have seen the canyon from the South Rim, it will look very different from here.

Hikers take in the view from a promontory near Bright Angel Point, on the North Rim.

**Grand Canyon National Park: North Rim**

🗺 46 D2, 47 E2

**Visitor information**

✉ P.O. Box 129, Grand Canyon, AZ 86023

☎ 928/638-7888

💲 $$$$ per vehicle; good at both rims for 7 days

www.nps.gov/grca

The southward slope of the plateau through which the Colorado River passes has caused tributary streams to cut vigorously into the North Rim and erode it far back from the river. Elevations average more than a thousand feet higher on the North Rim than on the South Rim and attract such heavy snowfall that the access road is usually closed in winter and early spring. Most facilities close mid-October, but the road is open until the first heavy snow (late November or early December). Although only 10 miles separate the rims, to get from one to the other involves a five-hour drive (see sidebar p. 63). Only about one in ten canyon visitors makes it to the North Rim, so it is much less crowded than the South Rim.

The **North Entrance** station provides a park map and a North Rim edition of *The Guide* with ranger programs, hiking tips, services, and park news. Drop in at the **North Rim Visitor Center** near Grand Canyon Lodge to learn more about activities and sights. Close by, a half-mile round-trip walk on the paved **Bright Angel Point Trail** takes you to the very tip of the point. Look into Roaring Springs Canyon on your left for the springs blasting out of the cliff below, but don't miss the equally precipitous cliffs of The Transept, on your right. Kaibab limestone, the rock exposed here and atop the South Rim, contains shells of animals that lived in an ancient sea 270 million years ago; you can see some in an outcrop just past a stone bridge. From the trail's end there is a dramatic vista down Bright Angel Canyon and across to the South Rim. The summits of the San Francisco Volcanic Field break the skyline. On the way back to the lodge, bear left and stroll the **Transept Trail,** which follows the rim to North Rim Campground (3 miles round-trip). Other options: **Widforss Trail** (10 miles round-trip), the **Ken Patrick Trail** to Point Imperial (20 miles round-trip), and the **Uncle Jim Trail,** a popular mule ride (5 miles round-trip).

Of all the Grand Canyon trails, the **North Kaibab Trail** has some of the most dramatic scenery. The complete round-trip—28 miles from the North Rim—includes a 6,000-foot descent to the Colorado River and a strenuous climb back up. Camp at either Cottonwood or Bright Angel Campgrounds or stay at Phantom Ranch (see p. 243). Good day hikes can be made along part of the trail to **Coconino Overlook** (1.5 miles round-trip), for example, to **Supai Tunnel** (4 miles round-trip), or to **Roaring Springs** (a strenuous 9.4-mile round-trip with a 3,050-foot elevation change).

## Accommodations

Grand Canyon Lodge and North Rim Campground, near Bright Angel Point, are the only developed places to stay in this section of the park, so it's best to reserve early. The campgrounds and dispersed

## EXPERIENCE: A Journey to Point Sublime

Could this North Rim viewpoint be the most memorable of all? **Point Sublime** extends far into the Grand Canyon for an awesome panorama of both rims and the Colorado River far below. You can trace the South Rim from below Bass Canyon up canyon nearly all the way to Desert View. Binoculars help you see such details as Grand Canyon Village, Hermits Rest, and the Tonto, Hermit, and Bright Angel Trails. Temples of stone rise from the depths, and you'll have a view of isolated Powell Plateau. At least half the adventure is getting here on dirt roads either from the **Bright Angel Point** area (17 miles to the east) or **De Motte Park** (27 miles north on Arizona 67). You can hike in; ride a horse, mule, or mountain bike; or drive a high-clearance vehicle. Be sure to bring water with you as none is

available once you leave pavement. You can camp at Point Sublime with a backcountry permit *(fee)* or stay in the nearby **Kaibab National Forest** *(www .fs.fed.us/r3/kai)* for free, but neither area has established sites. The roads are not always open and can be rough, so check conditions first with the information centers of the park or Kaibab National Forest. The Kaibab National Forest (North Kaibab Ranger District) map, sold at information centers, is essential to navigate the roads.

There's more. Other worth-the-trip viewpoints are **Tiyo Point** to the east with a trail, 6.3 miles one way, open only to hikers and equestrians; off to the west, you can visit **Swamp, Fire, Timp, Paris-sawampitts,** and others from West Side Road (Forest Road 22).

camping in Kaibab National Forest (see p. 62) are options; for the latter, bring water, supplies, and a shovel (to dig a latrine), and find a spot—not too close to a paved road or sole water source.

## Endangered Silence?

**Wilderness provides refuge from the ever busier world in which we live, and the space and silence in a place like the Grand Canyon make it a powerful place to spend time. Yet the silence here has come under assault from a steady stream of aircraft circling over the heart of the canyon. Pilots and passengers enjoy flying so much that they refuse to consider a ban on flights, while many proponents of peace and quiet will settle for nothing else. Only public opinion—addressed to the Park Administration and members of Congress—will determine how much silence future park visitors will experience.**

## Point Imperial & Cape Royal

Pack a picnic and spend a whole day enjoying the unforgettable panoramas of the **Cape Royal Scenic Drive.** You will soon see why John Wesley Powell remarked that "the canyon is a Book of Revelations in the rock-leaved Bible of geology."

From the turnoff 3 miles north of Grand Canyon Lodge, the paved road winds east through meadows and forests. Turn left at the junction for **Point Imperial,** at 8,803 feet the highest overlook in the park. (The road through Fuller Canyon and on to Point Imperial was heavily affected by the Outlet Fire in 2000. You will

see meadows, but much of the forested area is gone.) Views from here take in much of northeastern Arizona and the dramatic geology of the eastern Grand Canyon, where erosion and faulting have carved and tilted the rock layers into countless ridges and rock temples below. Navajo Mountain lies just across the border in Utah.

Returning to the junction and continuing toward Cape Royal (another 15 miles), you'll pass Vista Encantada, Roosevelt Point, Walhalla Overlook, and other viewpoints on the left. **Walhalla Ruins,** across the road from Walhalla Overlook, was a summer village of the ancient Pueblo people who lived in the area until about 1150. Warm air currents blowing up the canyon walls helped make agriculture possible at this 8,000-foot elevation. In winter, the villagers moved to sites such as Unkar Delta at the bottom of the canyon. Just over a mile beyond Walhalla Overlook is parking for the **Cliff Spring Trail.** This pretty hike (1 mile round-trip) takes you down a ravine, past an ancient ruin, to the spring.

**Cape Royal** extends far out into the Grand Canyon at one of its widest sections. You may feel as though you're on an island surrounded by a sea of rock temples and open space. A level, paved 0.6-mile trail takes you to the best viewpoints, while a short side trail leads out on top of **Angels Window,** a massive natural arch. Signs at Cape Royal (elevation 7,865 feet) point out some of the features in the canyon and beyond.

# EXPERIENCE: Running Grand Canyon Waters

Let the Colorado River sweep you into the wondrous depths of the Grand Canyon. The journey takes you far back in time as the river slices through one rock layer after another until you're surrounded by contorted rock more than a billion years old. Thrilling rapids alternate with long stretches of calm water mirroring the canyon scenery. Stops along the way let you explore enchanting side canyons—many with small waterfalls.

Most visitors who opt to see the canyon from the Colorado River take a commercial trip. A skilled crew does the hard work, allowing passengers to relax and enjoy the scenery. Experienced river runners can organize their own trips, but demand for permits far exceeds the supply; read the National Park Service requirements for details. For a list of commercial outfitters plus requirements for private trips, contact **Grand Canyon National Park** (*P.O. Box 129, Grand Canyon, AZ 86023, tel 928/638-7888, www.nps.gov/grca*).

Advance reservations are highly recommended, though it is sometimes possible to join a trip on short notice, especially in spring and fall or if there are just a few of you. Boat options are large motorized rafts, small oar rafts, and hard-shelled dories. Kayaks and small paddle rafts can join some raft trips. Motorized rafts travel twice as far in a day as oar-powered craft.

Nearly all trips start at Lees Ferry, just above the Grand Canyon. Some trips stop near Phantom Ranch to take on and let off hikers. Another exchange point for passengers is Whitmore Wash in the lower canyon,

Thrill-seekers ride Colorado River rapids in a raft.

Consider running the Colorado in a dory, a sleek hard-shelled flat-bottom rowboat that is graceful and quick.

—JEFF RENNICKE
*National Geographic author*

where a helicopter usually ferries people in and out. Most trips end at Diamond Creek, the only road access in the canyon, but you can continue to Lake Mead and the dramatic exit from the Grand Canyon.

Maybe a specialty trip is the one for you: **Arizona Raft Adventures** (*tel 800/ 786-7238, www.azraft.com*)

has challenging paddle trips in which you're part of a team with an experienced leader; or you might prefer the company's Natural History, Hiker's Discovery, or Yoga Discovery trips. **Canyon Explorations** (*tel 800/654-0723, www.canyon explorations.com*) offers paddle trips as well, plus the chance to hop in an inflatable kayak; hiking enthusiasts gravitate to the longer trips for extra time to trek side canyons. Dories give the liveliest ride of all, and **O.A.R.S./Grand Canyon Dories** (*tel 800/346-6277, www.oars.com*) specializes in this craft; try to go on one of their longer trips—all the way to Lake Mead, with many hiking opportunities along the way.

**Kaibab National Forest**

⚠ 46 D3, 47 E2

**Visitor information**

✉ Kaibab Visitor Center, junction of Ariz. 67 & US 89A, at Jacob Lake

☎ 928/643-7298

🕐 Closed in winter

www.fs.fed.us/r3/kai

**North Kaibab Ranger District, Kaibab National Forest**

✉ 430 S. Main St., Fredonia (P.O. Box 248, Fredonia, AZ 86022)

☎ 928/643-7395

🕐 Closed Sat.–Sun.

www.fs.fed.us/r3/kai

# Kaibab National Forest

The canyon's North Rim extends far beyond the national park to grand yet seldom visited viewpoints in Kaibab National Forest.

Although the forest roads are unpaved, some have been graded for dry-weather use by cars and small RVs. Nearly the entire forest is open for dispersed camping (except during times of fire danger), and there's always space. You can follow easy paths on the Kaibab Plateau, head down trails into the Saddle Mountain Wilderness on the east edge of the Kaibab Plateau, or descend into the Kanab Creek Wilderness on the west edge. Trails also drop into the depths of the canyon itself.

Several graded roads fan out to the east of DeMotte Park (just north of the North Rim Entrance) to reach viewpoints on the **Eastern Kaibab Plateau.** Pick up a free map with directions to

the viewpoints from the Kaibab Plateau Visitor Center at Jacob Lake or the North Kaibab Ranger District office at Fredonia. The panorama from 8,800 feet at the **East Rim Viewpoint** takes in Saddle Mountain Wilderness, the upper Grand Canyon, the Painted Desert beyond, and the Vermilion Cliffs to the north (a glowing scene at sunset and sunrise). The **Arizona Trail,** extending from the Mexican border to Utah, runs along the rim here, and other trails drop down into the canyons of Saddle Mountain Wilderness. **Dog Point,** farther north, and **Marble Viewpoint** and **Saddle Mountain Trailhead,** to the southeast, provide additional perspectives.

Points along the **Western Kaibab Plateau** offer views into the heart of the Grand Canyon. All can be reached on spur roads from West Side Road (Forest Road 22), which runs between Arizona 67 in DeMotte Park and US 89A just east of Fredonia. **Point Sublime** (7,458 feet) is possibly the best viewpoint in the Grand Canyon (see sidebar p. 59).

You can reach yet more viewpoints (Swamp, Fire, Timp, and Parissawampitts, among others) farther west from West Side Road. **Rainbow Rim Trail** (18 miles one way) connects Timp and Parissawampitts Points. **Crazy Jug Point** has the best roads for cars. **Jumpup Point** has a nearly 360-degree panorama of Kanab Creek Wilderness, an immense landscape of rugged canyons. You'll need a high-clearance vehicle for the last few miles.

*Big bird: It is not unusual to come across a handsome turkey (Meleagris gallopavo) while hiking a North Rim forest.*

## Toroweap

"What a conflict of water and fire there must have been here! Just imagine a river of molten rock running down into a river of melted snow. What seething and boiling of the waters; what clouds of steam rolled into the heavens!" John Wesley Powell's colorful description shows how the volcanic landscapes around **Toroweap Overlook** on the North Rim can capture the imagination. The sheer cliffs here plunge nearly 3,000 feet, and the narrow, steep canyon walls don't look at all like the Grand Canyon archetype.

The most reliable road to Toroweap Overlook turns off Arizona 389, 7 miles west of Fredonia, close to the state's northern boundary. A sign points the way down 61 miles of dirt road. Cautiously driven cars with good clearance can make the trip in dry weather. Watch for washouts and rough cattle guards. Take it slowly in the rocky section near the end. No supplies are available after you leave the pavement, so be sure to have water, food, and a full tank of gas. A ranger station with an emergency telephone is on the left, about 6 miles before the overlook; the campground almost a mile before the overlook sits in a scenic canyon.

On the way to Toroweap Overlook, you enter a valley flanked by dark lava flows of the Uinkaret Mountains to the west and the pale sedimentary rock layers of the Kanab Plateau to the east. It's about 140 miles by road downstream from Bright Angel Point (90 river miles). **Vulcans Throne,** a 600-foot cinder cone (formed by volcanic debris around a vent) at the lower end of the valley, is one of the youngest of area's approximately 60 volcanoes. Eruptions from volcanoes and vents lasted from about 1.2 million to 30,000 years ago. Lava even poured into the Grand Canyon, forming dams as high as 2,000 feet, now washed away.

---

### EXPERIENCE:
### Driving Rim to Rim

Although the North and South Rims sit just 10 miles apart, be prepared to take a circuitous road trip around the canyon. The five-hour, 215-mile drive passes many worthwhile sights, including two overlooks of the Little Colorado River's canyon; fine Native American art at **Cameron Trading Post;** views of the **Painted Desert, Navajo Bridge** (470 feet above the Colorado River), and imposing **Vermilion Cliffs;** and the meadows and woods atop the **Kaibab Plateau.** A short side road near Navajo Bridge leads to the **Lonely Dell Ranch** and historic buildings of the **Lees Ferry** area.

---

At Toroweap Overlook, you can peer down to see the Colorado River as it flows past **Vulcans Anvil,** an old volcanic neck rising up in the middle of the waters. Native American lands belonging to the Hualapai and the Havasupai lie opposite on the South Rim.

Don't miss the spectacle of **Lava Falls.** Just a few hundred yards' walk downstream along the rim, you can see the Colorado River explode into massive waves and foam in one of the Grand Canyon's fiercest rapids. ∎

### Toroweap
🗺 46 C2
**Visitor information**
✉ P.O. Box 129, Grand Canyon, AZ 86023
☎ 928/638-7888

# John Wesley Powell

Maps of the American West in the mid-1800s still showed large expanses of unexplored lands, and the one-armed Civil War veteran Maj. John Wesley Powell (1834–1902), born in New York to English immigrants, was destined to help fill in the gaps.

The Colorado River makes a nearly complete circle around Horseshoe Bend, near Page. You can hike out to this dizzying spot (see p. 69). Wide-angle lenses best capture the sweep of the river.

From early childhood, Powell's interest in natural history had taken him on field trips to collect plants, animals, and minerals. His strong stance against slavery influenced his decision to enlist promptly in the Union Army when President Lincoln issued a call for volunteers at the start of the Civil War. Despite a bullet wound that resulted in the amputation of his right forearm, Major Powell persevered with his duties until the war was drawing to a close, when he left the Army to become a professor of geology at Illinois Wesleyan University in Bloomington.

In 1867 he led the first of many trips to the Rocky Mountains and other areas of the West to collect specimens and carry out scientific research. His wife, Emma Dean, accompanied him and his students and became one of the first women to climb Pikes Peak. A friendly meeting with members of the Ute tribe kindled Powell's passion to study Native American customs and languages.

The idea of exploring the Green and Colorado Rivers intrigued Powell despite legends of earlier expeditions that had perished. He decided to try, selecting a hardy crew that could live off the land under the toughest conditions. On May 24, 1869, Powell set off from Green River Station, Wyoming Territory, with nine men and four boats. He knew this expedition would be an emotional ordeal when he wrote: "What falls there are, we know not; what rocks beset the channel, we know not; what walls rise over the river, we know not."

Despite fear of the unknown, near starvation, abandonment by four crew members (three never to be seen again), and raging rapids that destroyed one of the boats, the expedition emerged from the Grand Canyon and reached the mouth of the Virgin River in present-day Nevada on August 30. They had traveled more than a thousand miles, providing the first reliable reports of what lay within the canyons of the Green River and the Colorado.

Powell had hoped to undertake far more

**John Wesley Powell meets with a Paiute in the late 1800s.**

scientific research, but loss of instruments and food along with scarcity of game had limited his work. So in the spring of 1871 he returned to the original starting point with a new crew and boats on a trip that would last a year and a half. This time the expedition had photographers and a surveyor, who helped provide a splendid record of the canyons.

After this, Powell moved to Washington, D.C., where he wrote scientific reports with farsighted ideas for the federal government. In 1879 he assisted in the creation of the U.S. Geological Survey and later became its director. He also pursued his interest in Native American cultures as director of the Smithsonian Institution's Bureau of Ethnology, a post he held for the rest of his life.

In 1888, Powell helped found the National Geographic Society. He died in his 69th year and now lies buried with other Civil War heroes in Arlington National Cemetery.

## A Day in the Life: The Landscape Observed

"In one of the earlier years of exploration I stood on the summit of the Pink Cliffs of the Paunsagunt Plateau, 9,000 feet above the level of the sea. Below me, to the southwest, I could look off into the canyons of the Virgen River, down into the canyon of the Kanab, and far away into the Grand Canyon of the Colorado. From the lowlands of the Great Basin and from the depths of the Grand Canyon clouds crept up over the cliffs and floated over the landscape below me, concealing the canyons and mantling the mountains and mesas and buttes; still on toward me the clouds rolled, burying the landscape in their progress, until at last the region below was covered by a mantle of storm—a tumultuous sea of rolling clouds, black and angry in parts, white as the foam of cataracts here and there, and everywhere flecked with resplendent sheen. Below me spread a vast ocean of vapor, for I was above the clouds. On descending to the plateau, I found that a great storm had swept the land, and the dry arroyos of the day before were the channels of a thousand streams of tawny water, born of the ocean of vapor which had invaded the land before my vision."

—*The Exploration of the Colorado River and Its Canyons*, J. W. POWELL, 1895

# Arizona Strip

You can glimpse this slice of canyon country from the few highways that cross it, but to really explore the land you must leave the pavement behind. Trails and a network of back roads lead to little-visited overlooks of the Grand Canyon, high plateaus, pine-forested volcanoes, and prehistoric Native American sites.

Early travelers and ranchers passed many an evening in the parlor of Winsor Castle, fortified to protect against Navajo raids and now preserved at Pipe Spring National Monument.

**Arizona Strip**

📖 46 B3–C3

**Visitor information**

✉ Bureau of Land Management, Interagency Visitor Center, 345 E. Riverside Dr., St. George, UT 84790

☎ 435/688-3246

🕐 Closed Sun.

**www.blm.gov/az**

Wilderness designations protect many areas, as does the **Grand Canyon–Parashant National Monument,** established by President Clinton in January 2000. Expert hikers and drivers with high-clearance vehicles may go days without seeing another soul; *no services here.*

The Bureau of Land Management (BLM) administers most of the backcountry except for Grand Canyon National Park and Kaibab National

Forest. Contact the BLM at the Interagency Visitor Center in St. George, Utah, for information. The BLM's Arizona Strip map helps in navigating the back roads, most of which require a high-clearance vehicle and may need a four-wheel-drive as well.

Interstate 15 follows the deep and sheer-walled Virgin River Gorge through the extreme northwest corner of Arizona. **Virgin River Canyon Recreation Area,** just south off I-15 Exit 18, is a great spot for a picnic, hike, or camping; it's open year-round. Farther south, from the forested volcano of **Mount Dellenbaugh,** you get a 360-degree panorama of the Shivwits Plateau and the distant Grand Canyon. Continuing south, there are splendid vistas at the end of jeep roads to **Twin** and **Whitmore Points.** While traveling the back roads, you're likely to pass through the ghost town of **Mount Trumbull,** whose schoolhouse has been reconstructed and is worth a visit if it's open. **Whitmore Wash Trail,** the Grand Canyon's easiest rim-to-river hike, begins at the end of a rocky road south of the Mount Trumbull town site; you'll pass an exposure of columnar basalt and drop some 850 feet in about a mile to the river.

**Winsor Castle,** a fortified ranch building at **Pipe Spring National Monument,** dates from the precarious early days of ranching on the Arizona Strip. Mormons found the spring here in 1858; despite Navajo raids, they began ranching five years later. After the two groups signed a peace treaty in 1870, the Church of Jesus Christ of Latter-day Saints based a large cattle operation here. The pair of stone houses that went up took its name from the ranch's superintendent, Anson P. Winsor, who (despite the different spelling) was thought to be related to the British royal family. Gun slits and an enclosed courtyard gave Winsor Castle security, but it was never attacked. Arizona's first telegraph office opened in this isolated region in

1871. So many amorous couples passed through on their way to get married in the St. George Temple that the road became known as the Honeymoon Trail.

Tension between the Church of Jesus Christ of Latter-day Saints and the federal government, primarily over the practice of polygamy, led the church to sell the ranch in 1895 to a non-Mormon. In 1923, President Warren Harding proclaimed it a national monument "as a memorial of western pioneer life."

Exhibits in the museum next to the visitor center illustrate the story of the Kaibab Paiutes, the arrival of Mormon settlers, and modern-day Paiute culture.

## INSIDER TIP:

**At Nampaweap Rock Art Site, near Mount Trumbull, you can view thousands of glyphs pecked into boulders by archaic, ancestral Puebloan and Paiute tribes.**

—BILL WEIR
*National Geographic author*

You can tour Winsor Castle and the rough bunkhouses nearby. Gardening, spinning, weaving, cheese-making, and other activities in summer keep pioneer skills alive. Interpretive programs also reveal Paiute cultural traditions, such as making soap from yucca plants. The half-mile-loop **Rim Trail** climbs a ridge behind

**Pipe Spring National Monument**

✉ 14 miles SW of Fredonia on Ariz. 389
☎ 928/643-7105
💲 $
**www.nps.gov/pisp**

**Nampaweap Rock Art Site**
**www.zionnational park.com/grand-canyon-rock-art.htm**

**Glen Canyon National Recreation Area (includes Lees Ferry)**

🏔 47 E4

**Visitor information**

✉ P.O. Box 1507, Page, AZ 86040

☎ 928/608-6404 (Carl Hayden Visitor Center), 928/355-2320 (Navajo Bridge Interpretive Center)

💲 $$$

www.nps.gov/glca

the ranch to an overlook, where signs tell of the region's history and geology. A gift shop sells books, maps, and Native American arts and crafts. The Paiute tribe operates a campground nearby. *(Call 928/643-7245 or 928/643-7105 for information.)*

## Lees Ferry

Until the nearby Navajo Bridge spanned the Colorado River in 1929, a ferry provided the only direct link between the Arizona Strip and the rest of the state. The swift waters just above the Grand Canyon had forced back explorers, among them the Spanish Dominguez–Escalante Expedition in 1776 and a Mormon party led by Jacob Hamblin in 1860. But the Mormons kept trying—they needed a route for their Utah members to reach promising new areas in Arizona. In 1871, John D. Lee answered the church's call to

establish a ferry service, and he succeeded despite boat accidents and the threat of hostile Navajo. Farmers and miners came to try their hand at making a living from this remote spot but had little success.

Historic ranch buildings and mining relics recall the past. Visitors also come for the trout fishing in the clear, cold waters released by Glen Canyon Dam. The scenic Glen Canyon upstream can be explored on a rafting tour from Page (see Travelwise p. 261) or in your own boat. National Park Service rangers look after the historic sites, trails, boat ramps, and campground at Lees Ferry and the canyon upstream. Get information at the Glen Canyon National Recreation Area's Navajo Bridge Interpretive Center, near the turnoff for Lees Ferry, or at the Carl Hayden Visitor Center at Glen Canyon Dam.

The road to Lees Ferry heads north from US 89A just west of Navajo Bridge. After about 5 miles, turn left and drive 0.2 mile to see the log cabin thought to have been built by Lee at Lonely Dell Ranch in the early 1870s. Follow signs for the **Lees Ferry Historic District** to explore old buildings and mining equipment near the ferry site.

**Navajo Bridge** has now been bypassed by a new one alongside it, but you can still view the Colorado River, 470 feet below, from the old bridge. A bookstore in the visitor center *(closed in winter)* offers regional books, maps, and souvenirs. Navajo sell arts and crafts at the east end of the bridge. ∎

---

## EXPERIENCE: Exploring the Arizona Strip

Once you leave the pavement behind, you enter a vast unpopulated region of canyons, mountains, and volcanoes. A network of dirt roads leads to lofty overlooks of the Grand Canyon such as **Kanab, Whitmore,** and **Twin Points** and to wilderness areas to explore on foot. Journey back in time at **Nampaweap Rock Art Site** (see p. 67) and **Mount Trumbull School** (see p. 67). Travel here requires a high-clearance vehicle and extra caution given lack of water and remoteness. Staff at the **Interagency Visitor Center** in St. George, Utah *(345 E. Riverside Dr.)* sells the essential Arizona Strip Map and can advise on road conditions.

# Page & Glen Canyon N.R.A.

The remote desert atop Manson Mesa seems an unlikely spot for a prosperous modern town. Page sprang into existence in 1957 when workers came to build Glen Canyon Dam, a 710-foot-high concrete structure that created a 250-square-mile lake with a 2,000-mile shoreline. Today visitors find the town a handy base for discovering the dazzling canyon country all around, whether by boat on Lake Powell, by raft on the Colorado River downstream, by car, or on foot.

An aerial view reveals the otherworldly landscape surrounding Lake Powell.

The **Powell Museum** introduces the land and people of this region. Its name and that of the lake honor explorer and scientist John Wesley Powell, who made two descents of the Green and Colorado Rivers (see pp. 64–65). Exhibits tell of Powell's voyages and the area's geology, tribes, pioneers, and the construction of Glen Canyon Dam. Temporary shows illustrate aspects of the region's history and scenic beauty. Staff can arrange local tours.

Two dramatic viewpoints of Glen Canyon lie near Page. You can reach **"The Best Dam View"** by heading west from downtown on North Lake Powell Boulevard. Cross US 89 and continue on Scenic View Drive, then turn right to the viewpoint. Follow a short trail down to the best views.

The Colorado River makes a sharp turn at **Horseshoe Bend.** To reach it, go south 2.5 miles from Gateway Plaza on US 89; turn right 0.2 mile past Milepost 545 to parking. A three-quarter-mile trail leads to the overlook.

## Antelope Canyon

Many visitors are enticed by the convoluted and awe-inspiring sandstone walls of Antelope Canyon, so narrow that only

**Page & Lake Powell**

🅰 47 F4

**Visitor information**

✉ Page–Lake Powell Tourism Bureau, 647-A Elm St. (P.O. Box 332), Page, AZ 86040

☎ 928/660-3405 or 888/261-7243

🕐 Closed Sun.

💲 $$

**www.pagelakepowell tourism.com**

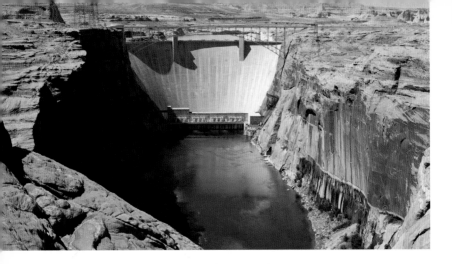

Below Glen Canyon Dam, the Colorado River glides cold and clear toward the Grand Canyon.

### Powell Museum

- ✉ 6 N. Lake Powell Blvd., Page (P.O.Box 547, Page, AZ 86040)
- ☎ 928/645-9496 or 888/597-6873
- 🕑 Closed Sat.–Sun.
- 💲 $$

**www.powell museum.org**

### Antelope Canyon Navajo Tribal Park

- ✉ P.O. Box 4803, Page, AZ 86040
- ☎ 928/698-2808 (Mon.–Fri.)
- 💲 $$$$

**www.navajonation parks.org/htm/ antelopecanyon.htm**

tiny beams of sunlight reach the canyon floor. You can visit two sections of the canyon on opposite sides of Arizona 98 southeast of Page. The more popular upper part is wider and easier to walk through; tours operate from Page, or you can take the slightly less expensive shuttle that transports visitors up to the entrance. You enter the lower section via short ladders, easily negotiated by able-bodied adults and children; the entrance is just a short walk from parking. Guided tours take you inside. Most visitors will find about an hour at either canyon sufficient; photographers may wish to stay longer.

Antelope Canyon is a Navajo tribal park with a complex and expensive system of charges involving separate fees for the park, each section of canyon, and the upper canyon's shuttle or tours. Call first for details or ask for advice at the Powell Museum or the Page–Lake Powell Tourism Bureau. Between November and February you'll need to arrange a tour in advance. Slot canyons may be just a few feet wide yet

hundreds of feet deep and are deadly during flash floods. From Page, head south on Coppermine Road or east on Arizona 98 to their junction at Big Lake Trading Post, then head east 1 mile on Arizona 98. Parking and the ticket booth for the upper canyon are on the right; those for the lower canyon are half a mile down Antelope Point Road, on the left.

## Lake Powell

This vast lake in Glen Canyon National Recreation Area reaches far up into Utah and seemingly countless side canyons. The sheer cliffs and rounded hills of sandstone create scenes suggestive of another world. The yellows and reds of the slickrock contrast with the deep blues of the lake. Most of the rock you see is Navajo sandstone—ancient sand dunes turned to stone. Weather at the lake's 3,700-foot elevation tends to be hot in summer—the most popular season for boating, waterskiing, and swimming—and freezing in winter, the quietest time. Spring and autumn are usually great for exploring the

INSIDER TIP:

**Check the weather forecast before going to water-sculpted Antelope Canyon. A sudden squall and you could be caught in a flash flood.**

—ANNE Z. COOKE
National Geographic Traveler
*magazine writer*

backcountry, though persistent winds can blow from February to May. If you don't have a boat, check out the trips and rentals at Wahweap Marina (see below).

Begin your visit at the **Carl Hayden Visitor Center,** named after a long-serving senator who strongly supported water development in the West. The center overlooks Glen Canyon Dam 2 miles northwest of Page. A detailed relief model of the recreation area gives an idea of the size and complexity of the canyon system. See if you can find Rainbow Bridge on it. Exhibits and shows introduce the wildlife, human history, recreation options, and Glen Canyon Dam. Forty-five minute tours descend into **Glen Canyon Dam** to see behind-the-scenes areas.

**Wahweap Marina,** some 5 miles north of the dam, has extensive facilities on the lake, with boat tours, summer ranger programs, lodging, restaurants, an RV park, campground, picnic area, and full-service marina. Wahweap can be very crowded, especially in summer, but less developed places

beckon nearby. Head out to **Lone Rock,** a primitive camping area and beach; follow US 89 from Page past the Wahweap turnoffs, cross the border into Utah, then turn right at the sign. **Antelope Point** has a paved boat ramp and nearby swimming areas; follow the directions to Antelope Canyon, then take paved Antelope Canyon Road 5 miles to its end; turn right for some small, sandy coves.

**Rainbow Bridge,** a national monument, spans a side canyon about 50 miles uplake from the dam. The graceful natural bridge—the world's largest—is 290 feet high and 275 feet wide. The stream below originally followed an S-bend around a narrow fin of rock; over time, erosion carved a hole, forming the bridge. You can see it on boat tours from Wahweap. Hikers can approach via trails through some of the Southwest's grandest canyon country. ∎

**Glen Canyon National Recreation Area & Rainbow Bridge National Monument**

✉ 691 Scenic View Rd., Page (P.O. Box 1507, Page, AZ 86040)
☎ 928/608-6404
$ $$$
www.nps.gov/glca
www.nps.gov/rabr

**Wahweap Marina**
✉ P.O. Box 1597, Page, AZ 86040
☎ 928/645-2433 or 800/528-6154
www.lakepowell.com

## EXPERIENCE:
## Live the Houseboat Life on Lake Powell

Imagine living in a vacation home that takes you wherever you wish to go on this large and very scenic lake. Driving a houseboat isn't any more difficult than driving a car, and marina staff will show you the ropes before you head out. The boats come in different sizes to accommodate couples, a family or two, or larger groups. The water is always just steps away for swimming or fishing, and it's easy to find your own secluded cove. **Lake Powell Resorts & Marinas** (tel 888/896-3829, *www.lakepowell.com*) has a large selection. Plan well ahead for the popular summer season.

# More Places to Visit in Grand Canyon Country

## Paria Canyon–Vermilion Cliffs Wilderness

An exceptionally beautiful hike follows the **Paria River** through a deep gorge for 38 miles between a trailhead in southern Utah and Lees Ferry (see p. 68). Even narrower side canyons and the massive Wrather Canyon Arch invite side trips. The hike takes four to six days and requires many stream crossings. **Coyote Buttes,** on top of Paria Plateau, has swirling sandstone features; it's open for day use only. For information and permits, contact the Bureau of Land Management at the Paria Information Station *(30 miles NW of Page on*

---

### Happy Trails: Way to Go

The region's mesmerizing scenery can easily entrance a hiker to forego good judgment. It's best to bring more water than you think; in hot weather, rangers recommend one gallon of water for an eight-hour hike. Healthy snacks will keep your energy up. It's a good idea to allow one-third of your strength for the descent and climb out. Although a day hike from the Grand Canyon's rim to the river and back might seem tempting, it's an exhausting trip even for very strong hikers and can be deadly for anyone in hot weather.

---

*US 89 near Milepost 21, closed in winter),* the Kanab Field Office *(318 N. 100 East, Kanab, UT 84741, tel 435/644-4600),* or the Interagency Visitor Center *(345 E. Riverside Dr., St. George, UT 84790, tel 435/688-3246, www.blm.gov/az).* Designated in November 2000, **Vermilion Cliffs National Monument**'s 293,000 stunningly beautiful acres hold a geologic treasure, including the Paria Plateau, Vermilion Cliffs, and the sheer-walled Paria River Canyon; elevations range from 3,100 to 7,100 feet above sea level. ▲ 47 E4

## Planes of Fame Air Museum

Distinguished and unusual aircraft reflect the daring and accomplishments of people in aviation history. Exhibits change as planes rotate between here and the Chino facility. A 1928 Ford Trimotor still flies; it's thought to have been a personal aircraft of Henry Ford. A Douglas AD-4N Skyraider and Messerschmitt Bf 109G represent air forces of World War II. You can climb aboard the Lockheed Constellation C-121A used by Gen. Douglas MacArthur during the Korean War. The museum is at the airport in Valle, on the way to the Grand Canyon's South Rim from Flagstaff or Williams. *www.planesoffame.org* ▲ 46 D1 ☎ 928/635-1000 💲 $$

## Tusayan District of the Kaibab National Forest

Although often overlooked, this forest near the Grand Canyon's South Rim has some good hiking, mountain biking, and cross-country skiing. Maps and information are available at the Tusayan Ranger Station, on the east side of the highway just outside the park's South Entrance Station. **Red Butte Trail** is a 2.4-mile hike up a small mountain southeast of Tusayan. It is worth the effort for the fine panorama from the lookout tower on the 7,326-foot summit. Mountain bikers can ride three interconnected loops of the **Tusayan Bike Trails** from a trailhead on the west side of the highway 0.3 mile north of Tusayan. The **Grandview Lookout,** a few miles from the South Rim, offers an aerial perspective from the top of its 80-foot tower. This is also the starting point of the 2.2-mile **Vishnu Trail;** a spur trail leads to viewpoints over the Grand Canyon. A 9.4-mile section of the **Arizona Trail** follows the top of the 500-foot cliffs of the Coconino Rim. *www.fs.fed.us/r3/kai* ▲ 46 D2 ✉ P.O. Box 3088, Grand Canyon, AZ 86023 ☎ 928/638-2443

The remote, awe-inspiring Colorado Plateau, long home to two traditional Native American tribes—the Navajo and the Hopi

# Northeastern Arizona

Fine Navajo turquoise jewelry
invariably catches the eye.

# Northeastern Arizona

The land catches the imagination here as it does in few other places in the world. Buttes and spires march across vast desert flats of sand and rock. Deep canyons reveal strange underworlds beneath the Earth's surface. Mountains reach toward the clouds. The high plateaus of northeastern Arizona provoke awe—as well as a respect for the people who have lived in this harsh landscape for generations.

Ancient sites dot the entire region, tracing the history of cultures that developed from a simple life of hunting and gathering to societies with villages of multistory masonry buildings, irrigated fields, and complex ceremonial calendars. Migrations over the centuries have left most sites in Arizona abandoned, but the Hopi continue to live in traditional villages atop three finger-like projections of Black Mesa. Today you can walk the dusty streets and catch glimpses of a life that has flourished in this land for more than a thousand years. Old Oraibi, dating from at least A.D. 1150, may be the oldest continuously inhabited village in the United States. About 10,000 Hopi still live on the reservation.

The Navajo, who call themselves Diné, entered the region between A.D. 1300 and 1600 and also became deeply attached to the land.

These seminomadic warriors had branched off from the Athapaskan tribes of what is now western Canada. Though very different from the Hopi in language, customs, and physical appearance, the adaptable Navajo learned weaving, pottery, and farming skills from

## NOT TO BE MISSED:

Monument Valley's enchanting, enduring, iconic Western landscapes  76–77

Exploring Canyon de Chelly's cliff dwellings set within stunning canyons  78–79

Navajo National Monument's large and remarkably well-preserved cliff dwellings  80

Taking a guided tour of Walpi, a centuries-old Hopi village  83

Hubbell Trading Post's authentic 19th-century marketplace  88

Lech-e
98

GRAND CANYON COUNTRY
4▷  Bitter Springs
89
NAVAJO
6520ft  Cedar Ridge
Shinumo Altar
3▷  The Gap
NATION
p. 45
Little Colorado
Willow Springs
Tuba City
Moen...
RESERVATION
64
2▷  Cameron
89
△ A
Cedar Wash

NORTH-CENTRAL ARIZONA
p. 89
1▷

Phoenix ★

Area of map detail

△ B

Pueblo groups such as the Hopi and picked up horses and livestock from the Spanish. The Navajo's habit of raiding their neighbors caused retaliatory attacks by other tribes, Spaniards, Mexicans, and Anglos. Finally, in 1863–1864, the U.S. Army forced the Navajo to surrender by destroying their livestock, crops, orchards, and food caches. The Army rounded up the Navajo and marched them on the Long Walk to the bleak camp of Fort Sumner in eastern New Mexico. An attempt at enforced domestication there failed dismally, and four years later the survivors were allowed to return to their lands in Arizona.

The Long Walk had such a profound effect on the tribe that you might hear references to the episode today. Numbering about 250,000, the Navajo Nation is the largest tribal group in the United States. At 25,000 square miles, their reservation is also the biggest: It covers most of northeastern Arizona and extends north into Utah and east into New Mexico. ■

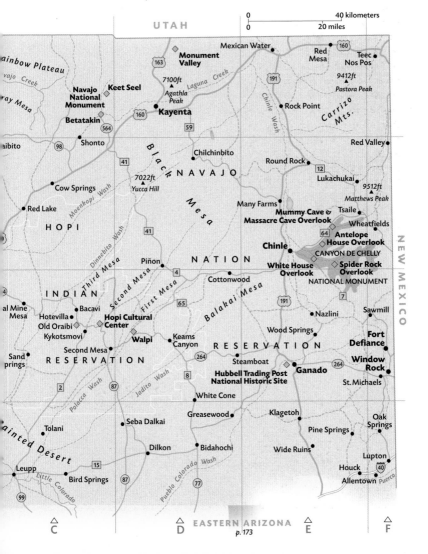

EASTERN ARIZONA p. 173

# Monument Valley

Few landscapes epitomize the American West more evocatively than the valley's grand buttes, towering pinnacles, and lonely sand dunes. Erosion sculpted sheer cliffs from sandstone and the gentle slopes below from shale. Volcanic eruptions left jagged structures of black rock. Drifting clouds, the occasional storm, and the rising and setting sun stage dramatic displays of shadow and light. The film industry's Westerns helped introduce this mysterious land to the world.

Get your motor running: The gorgeous wide-open spaces of Monument Valley free the spirit.

The Navajo have preserved Monument Valley as a vast tribal park where you can really feel the splendor of nature. Pull up near the **visitor center** for your first gaze out across the central valley's "mittens" and other buttes that rise majestically. In the visitor center, check out the options for visiting the valley and see a few exhibits. The superbly situated View Hotel, its restaurant serving Navajo/American food, is here too. A cluster of Navajo craft vendors mark the start of the 3.5-mile road to the visitor center.

You can take your own vehicle on the self-guided **Monument Valley Drive,** which drops down from the visitor center to the valley floor and makes a loop through its heart. Cyclists can ride the drive too. Enjoy a variety of sweeping vistas from overlooks and short spur roads along the way. The unpaved road is about 17 miles long and takes an hour

**INSIDER TIP:**

A Navajo sweat lodge ceremony can last up to four hours, and temperatures inside the lodge (considered a spiritual refuge) can hit triple digits.

—BERNICE NOTENBOOM
National Geographic Traveler
*magazine contributing editor*

and a half. It's normally safe for most cautiously driven cars but not for extremely low-clearance vehicles, nor for RVs over 27 feet long. Don't stop in the loose sand that sometimes blows across the road. You must stay on the designated road and not travel or hike elsewhere. No water or services are available.

## Tour the Valley

You can join one of the various vehicle, horseback, or hiking **tours** led by Navajo guides. No reservations are required—just talk with the guides to find one who offers a trip that matches your interests. Overnight excursions can be organized too; bring your own food and gear. You can arrange tours at the visitor center. The shortest trips take you along the main drive loop in an hour and a half. Longer ones venture farther into the backcountry to visit hogans, cliff dwellings, and petroglyphs; these drives take at least two and a half hours. Riding stables on the way to Monument Valley and booths outside the visitor center provide horseback and pack trips. Hikers can follow the 3.2-mile **Wildcat Trail** around the West Mitten on their own or hire a guide for other destinations. Goulding's Lodge and the tour operators in Kayenta also offer driving tours. Visit the old trading post at Goulding's Lodge to see the exhibits and period rooms. Contact the park for a list of tour operators. ■

**Monument Valley Navajo Tribal Park**

🏔 75 D4

✉ Turnoff is 24 miles N of Kayenta across Utah border on US 163 (P.O. Box 360289, Monument Valley, UT 84536)

☎ 435/727-5874

💲 $$

**www.navajonation parks.org**

**www.discovernavajo .com**

## Visiting Navajo Lands: Knowing the Ropes

Travel within Navajo lands takes some extra planning because accommodations, campgrounds, and RV parks are few and generally far between. It is important to call ahead for rooms, especially in the summer. Towns surrounding the Navajo Nation provide additional (and usually less costly) options.

Interestingly, the Navajo Nation—unlike the Hopi lands and the rest of Arizona—operates on daylight saving time, setting clocks ahead one hour from the second Sunday of March to the first Sunday of November.

As for taking pictures, the Navajo are usually agreeable to being photographed, but you should always ask first and be prepared to offer a gratuity.

Be aware that there isn't a drop of wine, beer, or spirits to drink: Alcohol became such a threat to tribal societies that both the Navajo and Hopi have banned sales and consumption on their reservations. Visitors need to respect this, because tribal laws apply to everyone. For bars and nightlife, one must leave the reservations. Yet despite the prohibition, alcohol as well as illegal drugs remain major problems here.

# Canyon de Chelly National Monument

Sheer canyon walls up to 1,000 feet high shelter both well-preserved cliff dwellings and traditional Navajo life. The national monument centers on two large canyons—26-mile-long Canyon de Chelly (pronounced de shay) and its tributary, 35-mile Canyon del Muerto. Rock art and other evidence reveal that humans have sought food and shelter here for at least 4,500 years.

White House Ruin is Canyon de Chelly's only site you can hike to without a guide.

After about 200 B.C., the canyons' inhabitants acquired corn and the agricultural skills to supplement their diet of wild foods. Over the following centuries, the tribespeople built villages with granaries, ceremonial structures, and multi-story apartments. Skilled artisans created fine baskets, pottery, and other crafts. Then, in about 1300, everyone migrated elsewhere. But some—the Hopi—remembered their old homeland, returning on pilgrimages or to look after fields of corn and other crops. Hopi visits continued over the next 400 years until the Navajo entered and settled in the canyons. Except during the four long years of captivity at Fort Sumner, Navajo have tended their farms, sheep, and horses here ever since.

Start your visit at the **visitor center,** near the mouth of Canyon de Chelly and just east of the town of Chinle. Museum exhibits introduce the archaic, ancient Pueblo, and Navajo cultures of the canyons. You can obtain advice on vehicle tours, horseback riding, hiking, and arranging for a guide. Check the bulletin board for interpretive programs and hikes. A picnic area and campground sit nearby in a cottonwood grove.

Two self-guided scenic drives begin from the visitor center. Allow at least a day to do both drives to give you time to enjoy the natural beauty and ancient pueblos—and to hike **White Rim Trail.** (Don't leave valuables in view when you park your vehicle.)

**South Rim Drive** leads to seven spectacular viewpoints on the rim of Canyon de Chelly in a 37-mile round-trip from the visitor center. You'll see Navajo farms and ancient pueblos. The canyons meet below **Junction Overlook,** from which you can see two cliff dwellings. From **White House Overlook** you get a view of a cliff dwelling and a lower ruin with about 60 rooms and four kivas (ceremonial rooms). **White House Ruin Trail** descends 500 feet and crosses the valley for a close-up look at the ancient village; allow two hours for the 2.5-mile round-trip hike. South Rim Drive ends at **Spider Rock Overlook,** where a grand panorama takes in the 800-foot rock spire named for Spider Woman, a Navajo deity who taught women how to weave.

**North Rim Drive** crosses the Chinle Wash near the visitor center and climbs to three vistas

of Canyon del Muerto in an out-and-back 34-mile round-trip. At **Antelope House Overlook,** you look almost straight down on the large pueblo and its tower. Navajo Fortress, a butte across the canyon, once served as a refuge. **Mummy Cave Overlook** takes in two cliff dwellings with more than 50 rooms in the larger alcove and about 20 in the west cave (to the right). **Massacre Cave Overlook** commemorates a bloody 1805 attack by the Spanish.

INSIDER TIP:

An air of intrigue seems to emanate from ancient Pueblo sites in the Southwest—and nowhere more so, perhaps, than Canyon de Chelly.

—R. CARLOS NAKAI
*Navajo-Ute flutist & composer*

These two drives and White House Ruin Trail are the only self-guided excursions. All others require a guide and permit—or group tour. This protects the privacy of the Navajo who live and farm here. Vehicle tours wind up in the sandy bottoms of both canyons on half- and full-day trips. With your own guide, you can go almost anywhere with a high-clearance four-wheel-drive vehicle. Riders can bring their own horses and hire a guide or go out with one of the stables. Hikers with a guide have exciting trail options on day or overnight trips. ■

**Canyon de Chelly National Monument**

🅰 75 E3

✉ P.O. Box 588, Chinle, AZ 86503-0588

☎ 928/674-5500

**www.nps.gov/cach**

# Navajo National Monument

From high in a pinyon pine and juniper woodland, you can gaze into a beautiful canyon and see one of Arizona's most impressive cliff dwellings. The 135 rooms and one kiva of Betatakin ("Ledge House") lie sheltered in a massive alcove 452 feet high and 370 feet across. Ancient Pueblo people constructed and used it for only two generations between A.D. 1260 and 1300.

**Navajo National Monument**

🅰 75 C4

✉ Take US 160 NE from Tuba City for 52 miles or from Kayenta SW for 21 miles, then turn N for 9 miles on Ariz. 564

☎ 928/672-2700

www.nps.gov/nava

The **visitor center** displays attractive examples of pottery and other crafts along with archaeological findings on diet, migrations, clothing, tools, and building techniques. The **Sandal Trail** behind the visitor center weaves through vegetation to an overlook of **Betatakin.** The paved path is 1 mile round-trip, with a descent of 160 feet to the viewpoint. Take binoculars to see details of the pueblo. **Aspen Trail** branches off Sandal Trail and then descends into the head of Betatakin Canyon, with a view of the forest on the canyon floor below. The round-trip hike is 0.8 mile, with a descent of 300 feet.

Rangers lead Betatakin hikes for a close-up look at the pueblo. The four-hour, 5-mile round-trip hike goes down and then returns on a primitive trail, strenuous because of the trailhead's 7,300-foot elevation. Check ahead for requirements and arrive early; the hike is limited to the first 25 people who sign up each day. In summer especially, take plenty of water, a hat, and sunscreen.

**Keet Seel,** one of the largest and best preserved cliff dwellings in the Southwest, has 160 rooms and four kivas. Its residents departed about A.D. 1300. Jars of corn left behind in sealed rooms indicate that the people expected to return some day. It is easy to imagine the houses and courtyards coming to life again. Potsherds still lie scattered around, as the Navajo name ("broken pottery") suggests. A 17-mile round-trip trail, including several stream crossings, leads to the site, which you can hike to with a permit; it's limited to 20 people per day and only in the summer season. Call three months ahead for a permit. The trip can be done in one day, but is most enjoyable with an overnight near Keet Seel. ∎

## At Home in a Cliff Dwelling

These natural alcoves had many advantages for the ancient Pueblo people. Residents could devote the entire canyon floor to agriculture, perhaps critical in this harsh high-altitude environment. They enjoyed warmth from the low winter sun and cool shade in summer. The natural overhang kept out rain and floods, making it easier to maintain living quarters, storage rooms, and ceremonial kivas. The steep climb to the entrance discouraged raiding parties in the area. Walls went up with mortared sandstone blocks, adobe bricks, or jacal (poles set in the ground and plastered with mud); timbers supported the flat roofs, sealed with reeds, grasses, and mud.

# Hopi Country

Life has never been easy for the Hopi. Only the hardiest corn and other crops could be coaxed to grow in the dry land. Complex social and religious obligations made many demands. Outsiders—from Spanish missionaries to federal government administrators—tried to overturn old Hopi ways. Hordes of anthropologists and shutter-snapping tourists besieged their villages. Yet the Hopi continue to follow ancient traditions while making use of new technologies.

Hopi legends tell of a long series of great migrations that eventually led them to their present-day homes atop the Hopi mesas (see pp. 82–83). Even now, clans make pilgrimages and leave *pahos* (prayer feathers) at ancestral village sites last used hundreds of years ago. Hopi social life and bonds between villages still largely revolve around the clans, which number more than 30. Each member of Hopi society has his or her own knowledge and role, depending on the person's clan, village, age group, and sex. This secrecy makes everyone important and necessary in the close-knit society. It's also the reason Hopi may be reluctant to discuss their religion with you; their knowledge may not be appropriate for a member of another clan or for a child standing nearby.

The Hopi welcome visitors to their villages and to some of their ceremonies. You'll have many opportunities to buy pottery, basketry, and silverwork (see pp. 38–41) directly from the Hopi at roadside shops and village homes—look for signs. Guides may be available to take you to rock art sites and other places of interest not normally open to visitors; ask around. Respect the privacy of residents by staying

Bessie Namoki fires classic Hopi pottery below First Mesa.

on the major streets, and never enter houses or kivas unless you are invited. To avoid offending the Hopi, take care not to hike trails without a guide, touch offerings (such as prayer feathers tied to bushes), drink alcohol, or pull out a camera. The tribe wishes visitors to receive the village life and ceremonies in their hearts—not with some gadget.

## Hopi Communities

Sheer cliffs have long protected the Hopi mesa-top villages during times of trouble, such as those following the Pueblo Revolt against the Spanish in 1680. Although the mesas are actually

### Hopi Mesas
🅰 75 C2–D2

**INSIDER TIP:**

Don't miss scenic Coal Mine Canyon, west of the Third Mesa, where, some say, ghosts appear during the full moon.

—JULIAN SMITH
National Geographic Traveler
*magazine writer*

southward-projecting fingers of Black Mesa, they are more commonly known as First, Second, and Third Mesas—the order in which the Spanish discovered them coming from the east.

Around 10,000 Hopi live on the reservation, and each of the 12 villages functions as a city-state with distinct ceremonial traditions. The Hopi Tribal Council does not rule the villages, but it helps with community services and acts as a liaison with state and federal governments. Arizona 264 between Window Rock and Tuba City passes near all the villages. You can also reach the reservation directly from Flagstaff on the paved Leupp Road (pronounced loop) or from Winslow via Arizona 87.

## First Mesa

If you arrive from the east, **Keams Canyon** will be the first community you encounter on the Hopi Reservation. It's an administrative town, not a village, but you may wish to stop at Keams Canyon Shopping Center for McGee's Indian Art Gallery, a café, and a grocery store; a picnic area is across the highway. **Polacca**

(pronounced PO-lah-kah), at the base of First Mesa, is a relatively new village; most residents hail from one of the three villages on the mesa. Turn up the steep 1.3-mile road to the top of the mesa for a visit to **Walpi** (wahl-PEE), one of the most inspiring places in Arizona. Park RVs, buses, and trailers in the large lot on your right partway up (near a water tank); from there you'll have to walk. First you'll come to **Hano,** which looks like a Hopi village but is actually settled by Tewa, a tribe from the Rio Grande area of New Mexico. They fled after an unsuccessful revolt against the Spanish in 1696 and sought refuge here. Hopi leaders agreed, with the condition that the Tewa serve as guardians of the trail to the mesa.

Despite three centuries of living with Hopi, Hano's residents still keep their own language.

You'll next reach **Sichomovi** (see-CHO-mo-vee), settled in the mid-1600s by people from Walpi when that village became too crowded. Stop here and register for a tour of **Walpi,** which lasts about one hour. With a guide, you continue across a narrow neck of land to this traditional village at the end of the mesa. You'll learn about Hopi culture and enjoy the expansive vistas. Walpi dates from about 1150, and even now its residents shun electricity and running water. Surrounded by sky, the ancient houses appear to have grown from the mesa. Bowl-shaped depressions in the rock once served to collect precious rainwater. Below, look for precipitous foot trails and remains of old fortifications and buildings. Villagers often sell kachina dolls and pottery.

## Second Mesa

At the junction of Arizona 264 and Arizona 87 just east of Second Mesa, you'll find a store, a café, and some arts and crafts shops. From here, two roads climb up to the three villages on Second Mesa—the main highway that passes near **Shungopavi** (shong-o-PO-vee) and a narrower road to **Shipaulovi** (shih-PAW-lo-vee) and **Mishongnovi** (mih-SHONG-no-vee); both roads rejoin near the Hopi Cultural Center. Shungopavi, the largest of the three villages, was moved from a site at the base

**Walpi tours, First Mesa Tourism Program**

✉ P.O. Box 260, Polacca, AZ 86042

☎ 928/737-2262

🕐 Closed for ceremonies; shorter hours in winter

💲 $$$

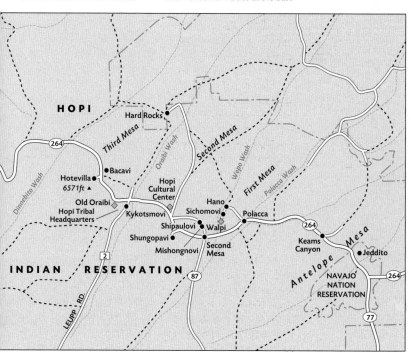

Beautiful, to be sure, yet who but the Hopi could coax corn and other crops from the soil in the desolate mesas and valleys of this unforgivingly dry high-desert country?

## Hopi Cultural Center

✉ P.O. Box 67, Second Mesa, AZ 86043

☎ 928/734-6650 (museum), 928/734-2401 (motel & restaurant)

🕐 Museum closed Sat.–Sun. late Oct.–late March

💲 $

**www.hopicultural center.com**

of the mesa to its present location after the Pueblo Revolt of 1680; there's a crafts shop on the road into the village and a few more on the highway between here and the Hopi Cultural Center. After the Pueblo Revolt, Mishongnovi was moved up to its current site at the end of an eastward projection of the mesa, and its close neighbor Shipaulovi was established. Both villages have an attractive setting and often open their plaza dances to the public.

The pueblo-style **Hopi Cultural Center** on the west side of Second Mesa has a good museum featuring Hopi history, culture, and art along with many historical photos of traditional life; there's a small gift shop, too. At its restaurant, you can sample such

Hopi foods as blue corn pancakes, paper-thin *piki* bread, *paatupsuki* (pinto beans and hominy soup), and *nöqkwivi* (lamb stew with white corn). The modern motel here, the only one on the reservation, is a good place to ask about guides and upcoming dances. Picnickers and campers can use the tables among trees just to the west. Hopi Arts & Crafts (Silvercrafts Cooperative Guild) on the other side of the campground offers a large selection.

## Third Mesa

**Old Oraibi** (o-rye-bee), atop the mesa, has stood here for nearly 900 years, probably a longer continuous stretch of time than any other community in the United States. It's worth a visit to absorb some of the atmosphere. A good place to park is the arts and crafts shop at the beginning of the village; more shops are back on Arizona 264 near the turnoff. Old Oraibi saw some hard times in the early 20th century. It had been one of the largest Hopi villages, with more than 800 people, until a dispute arose between two chiefs, You-ke-oma and Tawa-quap-tewa. Their factions fought it out with a push-of-war contest until one managed to push the other away. You-ke-oma's group lost and left to start a new village, Hotevilla, 4 miles away.

People from Old Oraibi also founded **Kykotsmovi** (kee-KEUTS-mo-vee) in 1890 beside a spring at the base of the mesa. To visit the Hopi tribal offices, store, and arts and crafts shop, drive south 1 mile on Indian Route 2 (Leupp Road) from Arizona 264.

**Hotevilla** (HOAT-vih-lah) had a difficult early history after its founding in 1906. Federal authorities demanded that villagers move back to Old Oraibi so that the children could attend school. When most of the villagers refused, the men were hauled to jail, and the schoolchildren were forced to attend a boarding school at Keams Canyon. Women and young children had to survive the winter alone in the fledgling village with little food or shelter.

**Bacavi** (BAH-kah-vee) village is another settlement that originated from the split between Hotevilla and Old Oraibi. Some of the Hotevilla people returned to the old village so their children could go to school there, but the unwelcome group found tensions unbearable and left to build its own village across the road from Hotevilla in 1909. Chief Tuba of Old Oraibi founded **Moenkopi** ("the place of running water") in the 1870s to take advantage of springs that could irrigate fields. The upper section of the village participates in the Hopi Tribal Council while the lower, more conservative part does not. Moenkopi is 48 miles northwest of Old Oraibi and near Tuba City. ∎

## Hopi Cuisine—Deliciously Sustainable

In their creation stories, Hopi tell of being left with short blue corn after other groups had chosen the corn with long ears. Corn plays a major role as a prayer object in ceremonies that seek winter snows and summer rains for crops. Indeed, farmers devote considerable time and care to its cultivation. Besides the signature blue corn, Hopi grow purple, red, yellow, white, and sweet varieties. Squash, beans, chilies, fruit, and a great many other crops also compose the Hopi diet, as does the gathering of wild plants. Nowadays hunting is mainly for ceremonial purposes: cattle provide most of the meat. On Hopi lands you may find *piki* bread—very thin layers of blue corn flour baked on a flat surface, then rolled up. The restaurant at the Hopi Cultural Center serves many traditional items that you can sample. Or do it yourself with recipes in Juanita Tiger Kavena's cookbook, *Hopi Cookery*.

# Kachinas: A Glimpse into the Hopi's Spiritual World

In the 21st century, Hopi life still closely follows the growing cycle of corn, as it has for the past 2,000 years. A richly detailed series of ceremonies summons kachinas—spirits, of which there are more than 500 types—to bring rain to nurture corn and other crops.

You may be fortunate enough to attend a kachina dance in a village plaza during the period when the crops most need rain, from April to early July. A long line of elaborately costumed and masked performers—men who actually *become* kachinas—chant while shaking gourd rattles and performing precise dance steps. Clowns, usually with painted horizontal stripes across their bodies, may appear and perform crazy antics. Ogre kachinas have been known to seek out naughty children and threaten to eat them, but the parents always manage to sweet-talk the ogres out of this punishment; the children usually behave much better afterward. You may see kachina

**Hopi carvers start with a cottonwood root.**

dolls handed out to small girls as part of their education.

The kachina season begins with the winter solstice ceremony, when the Soyala Kachina appears. At this time, Hopi begin thinking of the upcoming growing season with wishes for fertility, moisture, and harmony with nature. They express these thoughts in kachina dances, initially mostly at night in kivas (underground ceremonial chambers), and Buffalo social dances in the plazas. In April, the kachinas appear during daytime dances on the plazas in a community prayer for rain. By the summer solstice, the kachinas have completed their task and perform the Niman (Home) Ceremony. They present the first green ears of corn and offer their last dances for rain before returning to the San Francisco Peaks, their mountain home. During August, thoughts and ceremonies turn to the harvest and its celebration. In the Snake Dance (normally closed to the public), dancers hold snakes, often poisonous rattlesnakes, in their mouths, and these serve as messengers to the spirits. Young women perform the Butterfly Dance, also in August, followed by Women's Society Dances in autumn. November and December tend to be quiet months of prayer and meditation. Each village has its own set of dances, not all of which are performed every year.

Hopi dances usually take place on weekends; try asking a few days ahead at the Hopi Cultural Center or at shops on the reservation. Certain dances depend on astronomical observations, so even the Hopi have to wait for the go-ahead before setting a date. It's best to stand because seats and blankets are reserved. Not all dances are open to the public, but if

you are turned away, remember that there is plenty more to see on the Hopi lands. If you are permitted to watch, keep in mind that these are religious ceremonies; just as in a church or synagogue, visitors should dress respectfully and not ask questions during the event. And most important of all—even if no one is around—respect the strict ban on photography and all other types of recording, such as video, sound, sketching, or note-taking. Just the sight of a camera will offend some Hopi, so it's best to stow yours in the car.

Imagination, thought, and skill go into the crafting of a kachina doll.

## EXPERIENCE: Understanding the Arts & Crafts

The creativity that Navajo and Hopi artists put into their work reveals aspects of their complex cultures. Native American galleries on and off the reservations offer large selections. You'll also have the opportunity to buy directly from the maker—look for roadside stands set up by Navajo, especially on highways to the Grand Canyon, and for signs in Hopi villages. The best pieces naturally command high prices, but these can be fine mementos of a visit to Native American lands. Museums show examples of the highest quality pieces and give you an idea of what to look for; try to visit the **Museum of Northern Arizona** (p. 92) in Flagstaff and the **Heard Museum** (pp. 147–148) in Phoenix to learn more about them as well as tribal cultures.

The Navajo have long earned fame for silver jewelry and woven rugs, and you'll also see their pottery, basketry, and sand paintings. Usually women do the weaving and have developed more than a dozen regional styles. Men do much of the silversmithing, including the distinctive squash-blossom necklaces with their horseshoe-shaped pendants. The Hopi carve cottonwood roots into kachina dolls, originally used to educate children about Hopi religion, but now often made into elaborate figures from the Hopi pantheon. Hopi silversmiths commonly use an inlay technique with traditional symbols for earrings, bracelets, bolo ties, and belt buckles. Other Hopi artisans turn out beautiful pottery and baskets, as the tribe has done for centuries. Artists of both tribes create attractive paintings, prints, and sculpture with Native American motifs.

# More Places to Visit in Northeastern Arizona

## Hubbell Trading Post National Historic Site

Lorenzo Hubbell began trading with the Navajo in 1876, when they were still recovering from the trauma of the Long Walk (see p. 75). He earned the tribe's respect through his honesty, his ability to speak some of their language, and his assistance in explaining government programs. He also helped the Navajo get better prices for their rugs and

The rug room at Hubbell Trading Post invites you to admire and perhaps purchase fine wares.

silverwork by stressing the importance of high quality. Today the trading post functions much as it always has—Navajo still bring in products to trade and pick out the canned goods and other supplies they need. Visitors can choose from a great selection of Navajo rugs, jewelry, and other arts and crafts.

Hubbell's house has become a museum with an impressive collection of baskets, paintings, and rugs. In the visitor center, you're likely to see a weaver at work as well as a large selection of books on Native American cultural history and the Southwest. Scheduled tours visit Hubbell's house, and you can take a self-guided tour of the grounds and trading post. Trees shade a picnic area. The trading post is on the south side of Arizona 264, 1 mile west of Ganado between Window Rock and Keams Canyon. www.nps.gov/hutr ▲ 75 E2 ☎ 928/755-3475

## Window Rock & Vicinity

A natural arch with a circular opening averaging 47 feet across inspired the Commissioner of Indian Affairs, John Collier, to choose this site for a Navajo administration center in the early 1930s. Today Window Rock is the capital of the Navajo Nation (see www.discovernavajo.com for visitor information) with a museum, zoo, parks, and shopping for arts and crafts. You can see the "rock with a hole in it" and the Navajo Nation Veterans Memorial at Window Rock Tribal Park; the turnoff is on the east side of Indian Route 12 about half a mile north of Arizona 264. On the way in you'll pass on the left the **Council Chambers** *(tel 928/871-6417, closed Sat.–Sun.)*, which has colorful murals inside; you're welcome to visit. Inside a large attractive building, which faces east like the hogan in front, the **Navajo Nation Museum** *(tel 928/871-7941, www.navajonationmuseum.org, closed Sun.)* hosts exhibitions from the permanent collection and visiting shows; there's a gift shop too. It's in Tse Bonito Tribal Park, on the north side of Arizona 264, half a mile east of the Indian Route 12 junction. You can read more about the Navajo in a library located across the entry hall. Just north of the museum, the **Navajo Nation Zoological and Botanical Park** *(tel 928/871-6574, www.navajozoo.org, closed Sun.)* offers a close-up look at wildlife of the Southwest.

**St. Michael's Historical Museum** *(tel 928/871-4171, open daily in summer, by appt. rest of year)*, inside the original mission building, offers exhibits on the Navajo and the work of early missionaries. Head west 3 miles on Arizona 264 from the Indian Route 12 junction, then turn south at the sign. ▲ 75 F2

A region of geologic drama with a cast of volcanoes, a giant meteor crater, plateau uplifts, and canyon-carving streams

# North-central Arizona

Relics remain from the old King Mine & Ghost Town, near Jerome.

# North-central Arizona

This region ranges from searing desert to Arizona's high point—Humphreys Peak, at 12,633 feet. The cliffs of the Mogollon Rim mark the dramatic change from the Colorado Plateau in the north to the rugged hills and valleys in the south. Nature puts on a show of color and form, from Sedona's red-rock country to the golden aspen forests on the San Francisco Peaks in autumn. The university town of Flagstaff fills in with culture.

Hiking is one of the best ways to enjoy the scenery, whether climbing a volcano or strolling along a canyon. Scenic drives also lead to dramatic vistas. Lakes atop the Mogollon Rim and streams flowing out through its canyons attract wildlife and provide a challenge for anglers. Winter transforms the mountains with a blanket of snow, drawing skiers, snowboarders, and snowshoers.

Rivers and springs in the desert support beaver and other wildlife along with lush growths of cottonwood, willow, and Arizona sycamore. Cactuses dot the lower valleys, while higher desert areas see grasslands favored by antelope-like pronghorn or woodlands of juniper, pinyon pine, and oak.

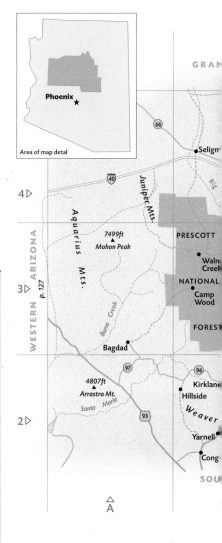

## NOT TO BE MISSED:

You might come across desert mule deer, white-tailed deer, black bear, coyote, fox, or rattle-snakes in the desert or the pine forests above. Ponderosa pines cover much of the high plateaus, along with Gambel oak and some juniper and Douglas fir. Cool forests of spruce, fir, and aspen thrive on the higher mountain slopes. Only alpine tundra can withstand the freezing temperatures and fierce winds above

timberline on the high San Francisco Peaks.

Ancient Pueblo people left behind many pit house and masonry villages as they made their migrations. Yavapai and Apache followed and still live here on a few small reservations. Mining, logging, ranching, and the railroad attracted the first Anglos in the late 1800s; these industries still flavor the personalities of many towns today. ■

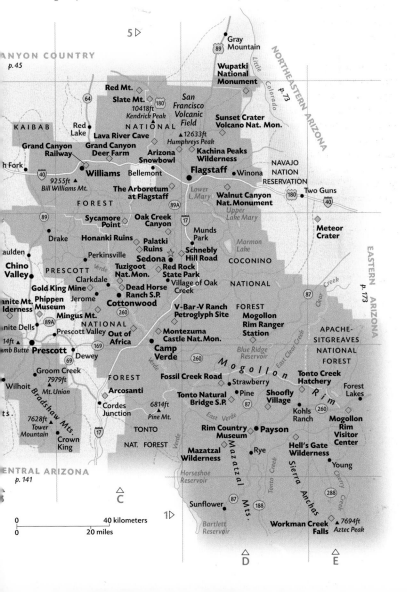

# Flagstaff

Set in the ponderosa pines below the San Francisco Peaks, Flagstaff is the largest city in the region. The town's 7,000-foot elevation can mean winter snowstorms and summer thunderstorms, but bright sunshine is likely at any time of year. Early tribes tilled fields despite the dry climate and short growing season, then left behind villages that are now preserved.

In downtown Flagstaff, many of the historic structures sport plaques that tell their stories.

**Flagstaff**

🅰 91 D4

**Flagstaff Visitor Center**

✉ 1 E. Route 66, Flagstaff, AZ 86001

☎ 928/774-9541 or 800/842-7293

**www.flagstaff arizona.org**

The threat of marauding tribes combined with the lack of both mineral wealth and good farmland discouraged Anglo settlers until 1876, when ranchers began raising sheep. The railroad arrived six years later, and a frontier town sprang up. Lumbermen set to work logging the forests, providing wealth for the community. Many fine old buildings from the early years still stand. The tourist office, in a 1926 railroad depot, is here, along with restaurants, galleries, and shops. Old Route 66 still rolls through town, carrying motorists as it has since the 1920s. You can tour museums and galleries, visit nearby archaeological sites,

or hike, horseback ride, and mountain bike nearby. Skiers can go to the Snowbowl on the San Francisco Peaks.

## On Display

One of the finest museums in Arizona, the **Museum of Northern Arizona** portrays the land and people of the Colorado Plateau from their beginnings to the present. Illustrations and fossils show how geologic upheavals created the colorful landscapes and how the environment has changed over the millennia from oceanic to tropical to high plateau. Artifacts tell the story of early peoples as they developed from nomadic hunter-gatherers to sophisticated agricultural societies. Exhibits of modern-day tribes interpret their cultures and display superb examples of their art. In the Hopi sections, you'll see kachina dolls, pottery, basketry, silverwork, a description of their ceremonial calendar, and a full-size replica of a kiva, a room used for Hopi rituals. Navajo exhibits tell of the tribe's way of life and include jewelry, sand paintings, and richly detailed rugs. Other displays reveal the heritage of the Pai (Havasu-pai, Hualapai, and Paiute), New Mexican Pueblo, and Hispanic cultures. Art galleries feature changing exhibits by tribal and other Southwestern artists.

The museum is very active in research and education. Learn more by digging into the extensive library across the highway in the

**Museum of Northern Arizona**

✉ 3101 N. Fort Valley Rd. (3 miles NW of downtown Flagstaff on US 180)

☎ 928/774-5213

💲 $$

**www.musnaz.org**

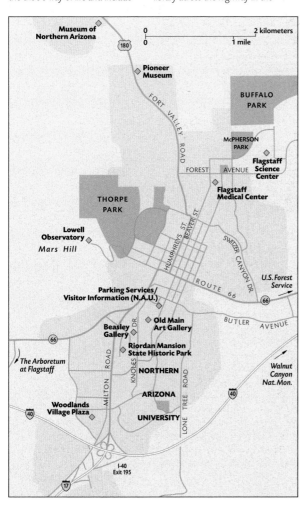

## Pioneer Museum

✉ 2340 N. Fort Valley Rd. (2 miles NW of downtown on US 180)

☎ 928/774-6272

🕐 Closed Sun.

💲 $$

www.arizona
historicalsociety.org

## Riordan Mansion State Historic Park

✉ 409 Riordan Rd.

☎ 928/779-4395

🕐 Call for tour times

💲 $$

www.azstateparks
.com

## Northern Arizona University Art Galleries

☎ 928/523-3471

🕐 Closed Sun., call for other days

www.nau.edu

Research Center, attending a lecture, or signing up for a field trip or workshop. A series of festivals, each dedicated to one Southwestern culture, provides insightful presentations, performances, activities, and opportunities to meet artists.

The **Rio de Flag Nature Trail** descends into a little canyon beside the museum on a half-mile loop; the front desk has trail brochures.

The **Pioneer Museum** tells of Flagstaff's settlers and their achievements. Changing exhibits illustrate the lives of ranchers, lumbermen, doctors, homemakers, astronomer Percival Lowell, and Grand Canyon photographer Emery Kolb. After completion in 1908, the stone building served for 30 years as the Coconino County Hospital, where elderly residents without families could live out their days; a room from that period has been preserved. Outside, you can admire the powerful 1929 Baldwin locomotive built for the logging industry and see the restored 1908 cabin that belonged to Ben Doney, a colorful character from the early

days of Flagstaff. A gift shop sells pioneer-style toys, and crafts. You could catch the Wool Festival (shearing and more, the first weekend of June), Independence Day Festival (pioneer craft demonstrations on the weekend nearest July 4), or Playthings of the Past (toys, dolls, games, and children's books during the winter holiday season).

A fascinating piece of early Flagstaff history is preserved at **Riordan Mansion State Historic Park.** Brothers Timothy and Michael Riordan arrived in the mid-1880s and became wealthy owners of the Arizona Lumber & Timber Company. They both married and in 1904 built this magnificent mansion south of downtown. Each family lived in one of the house's two wings, which were connected by the Rendezvous Room, complete with a billiard table. Architect Charles Whittlesey, who also designed El Tovar Hotel at the Grand Canyon, used a similar rustic style of stone and log slabs on the exterior. The interior has its original furniture, much of it in American arts and crafts style.

## Arts & Sciences

**Northern Arizona University,** just south of downtown, adds much life and culture to Flagstaff. The school began in 1899 as Northern Arizona Normal School and graduated its first class of four women teachers two years later. Visitors are welcome at the art galleries, concerts, sporting events, library, and many other facilities. A good place to start (and get a precious parking permit) is the **Parking Services/ Visitor Information** office at the

---

## Flagstaff's Flagpole

Although it's obvious that Flagstaff takes its name from a flagpole, the question is, which one? Of two early groups of settlers from Boston, the first claimed to have erected a flagpole in April or May of 1876, before the Fourth of July celebration held by the second group later that year. The stripped pine tree left by the second group may well have been the pole that served as the town's namesake. Later travelers referred to the spot as "the spring by the flag staff." In 1881, citizens formally chose the name Flagstaff for their little settlement.

The Riordan Mansion's Swing Room exhibits period arts and crafts style.

corner of Dupont Avenue and South Beaver Street. The 1893 Old Main building nearby on McMullen Circle has exhibits of contemporary art by local and regional artists in the **Old Main Art Gallery** on the first floor and a permanent collection of art and furniture upstairs. Paintings by Philip Curtis and Diego Rivera rub shoulders with 18th-century art, furniture, silver, and prints. On Knowles Drive, the **Beasley Gallery** in the Fine and Performing Arts Building shows works by students and faculty artists.

The large white dome of **Lowell Observatory,** atop Mars Hill just west of downtown, marks the spot where astronomer Percival Lowell searched for life on Mars. He established the observatory in 1894 and installed the 24-inch Clark refractor telescope two years later. As he peered at the red planet through the eyepiece, he thought he saw canal systems that indicated an advanced civilization. That effort proved a dead end, but other observations and research here led to discoveries such as that of Pluto. Astronomical research remains an important focus here. Daytime visitors can see the telescopes used in the study of Mars and the search for Pluto, while in the evening you can look through the Clark refractor. The visitor center has multimedia programs and interactive exhibits.

Scientists at the U.S. Geological Survey's **Flagstaff Science Center** played a major role in the Apollo moon landings between 1969 and 1972. Staff here still study the Earth and the heavens. In the Powell, Dutton, and Shoemaker Buildings (aka Buildings 3, 4, and 6), you can see photos of the planets and their moons.

About 6 miles southwest of town at **The Arboretum at Flagstaff,** you can learn about the plants of the Colorado Plateau. Gardens represent various aspects of both native and introduced flora. A passive-solar greenhouse protects the more fragile plants. Guided tours are offered daily. ■

**Lowell Observatory**
- 1400 W. Mars Hill Rd. (1 mile W of downtown on Santa Fe Ave.)
- 928/223-3211
- $$
www.lowell.edu

**Flagstaff Science Center**
- 2255 N. Gemini Dr. (on McMillan Mesa off Cedar Ave., 1.5 miles NE of downtown)
- 928/556-7000
- Closed Sat.–Sun.
http://arizona.usgs.gov/Flagstaff

**The Arboretum at Flagstaff**
- 91 C4
- 4001 S. Woody Mountain Rd. (from S. Milton Rd, turn W 1.9 miles on Route 66, then turn S 4 miles on Woody Mountain Rd.)
- 928/774-1442
- Closed Nov.–March
- $$
www.thearb.org

# Around Flagstaff

Two remarkable sites east of Flagstaff are well worth a visit. The first, Walut Canyon National Monument, gives insight into the lives and skills of the ancient peoples who made their dwellings in the sheer limestone cliffs here. The second, Meteor Crater, offers proof of the incredible impact of a meteor that fell to Earth many thousands of years ago.

**Walnut Canyon National Monument**

🗺 91 D4

✉ 7 miles E of Flagstaff on I-40, then S 3 miles at Exit 204

☎ 928/526-3367

💲 $

www.nps.gov/waca

**Meteor Crater**

🗺 91 E3

✉ 36 miles E of Flagstaff on I-40, then S 6 miles at Exit 233

☎ 928/289-2362 or 800/289-5898

💲 $$$

www.meteorcrater .com

In a beautiful canyon east of Flagstaff, **Walnut Canyon National Monument** protects about 300 ancient cliff dwellings. The tribespeople lived here from A.D. 1125 to 1250 and then moved on. A small museum in the visitor center illustrates how the inhabitants farmed, made use of wild plants and game, and traded with neighboring villages. Pottery and other artifacts show their artistry. The easy **Rim Trail** leads to canyon viewpoints, a pit house site, and a small pueblo on a three-quarter-mile loop; signs explain plant and animal life.

The more exciting and strenuous **Island Trail,** 1 mile round-trip, begins behind the visitor center and descends 240 steps for a close look at some of the cliff dwellings. On some days in summer, rangers lead hikes to

a historic cabin and cliff dwellings not on the public trails; call for the schedule.

A nickel-iron meteorite smashed into the Earth about 49,000 years ago, creating **Meteor Crater**—the world's best preserved impact crater. Measuring 4,100 feet across and 560 feet deep, it could hold 20 football fields. Museum exhibits depict the incredible forces that formed the crater. You'll also see a 1,450-pound meteorite and examples of shock-metamorphosed rock. Space exhibits honor astronauts and tell the story of the first manned flights and trips to the moon. Step outside on the viewing platforms to face the enormity of the crater. Guided hikes give you an even better feel for the crater as you follow the rim partway around. ■

---

## EXPERIENCE: Go Skiing!

**The Arizona Snowbowl** (tel 928/779-1951, www.arizonasnowbowl.com), just 14 miles northwest of Flagstaff, offers 32 runs; nearby **Flagstaff Nordic Center** (tel 928/220-0550, www.flagstaffnordic center.com) has cross-country skiing.

In eastern Arizona, the White Mountain Apache Tribe owns and operates **Sunrise Ski Park** (tel 928/735-7669 or 800/772-7669, www

.sunriseskipark.com), the largest ski area in the state with 65 runs and a popular getaway for Phoenix-area residents.

You might also enjoy the small **Elk Ridge Ski Area** (tel 928/814-5038, www .elkridgeski.com) about 40 miles west of Flagstaff near Williams and **Mt. Lemmon Ski Valley** (tel 520/576-1321, www .skithelemmon.com) in the Catalinas about 40 miles northwest of Tucson.

# San Francisco Volcanic Field

North of Flagstaff, the San Francisco Peaks soar 5,000 feet above the plateau to a height of 12,633 feet on Humphreys Peak—the rooftop of Arizona. They have great beauty year-round, whether covered by spring and summer greenery, autumn gold, or winter white.

The San Francisco Peaks stand tall as glimpsed from Bonito Lava Flow near Sunset Crater Volcano.

The volcanic eruptions that formed these mountains began about one million to 400,000 years ago. They built up an immense volcano until the center collapsed, leaving a caldera surrounded by pieces of the crater wall. During the Pleistocene (from about 1.6 million years ago to roughly 10,000 years ago), glaciers carved deep valleys into the flanks. Surrounding the peaks, the San Francisco Volcanic Field contains hundreds of volcanic peaks, cinder cones, and lava flows across 3,000 acres. Currently the volcanoes are quiet—the most recent eruptions ended in A.D. 1280 near Sunset Crater. However, there is no reason to assume that they will always be so. Periods of calm have separated eruptions all through the field's long history.

Most of the volcanoes make good day hikes, ranging from easy scrambles to the strenuous all-day climb of Humphreys Peak. Two summits are off-limits—Agassiz Peak, to safeguard its delicate tundra, and Sunset Crater, to protect the soft cinder slopes. The Peaks Ranger Station of the Coconino National Forest provides advice, maps, and trail descriptions; staffers can also suggest various camping possibilities. Be sure to take plenty of water with you on trails, as you're unlikely to find springs.

**San Francisco Volcanic Field**

◭ 91 C4–D4

**Visitor information**

✉ Peaks Ranger District, Coconino National Forest, 5075 N. Hwy. 89, Flagstaff, AZ 86004

☎ 928/526-0866

🕒 Closed Sat.–Sun.

**www.fs.fed.us/r3/ coconino**

## Exploring the San Francisco Peaks

Much of the higher ground on the peaks falls within **Kachina Peaks Wilderness,** named for the Hopi spirits who reside here for part of the year, bringing rain to the fields. The peaks also play a role in Navajo belief as one of the cardinal directions—the west—of their lands.

---

### Into the Heart of a Volcano

**Unusual erosion has dissected 740,000-year-old Red Mountain from the summit straight down to its base. Steam explosions and lava flows may have played a role in the downcutting. Most of Red Mountain is composed of soft volcanic tuff; look closely and you'll see volcanic bombs, cinders, and a variety of minerals.**

---

Just outside the wilderness, snow lovers come to glide down the runs of the **Arizona Snowbowl** *(tel 928/779-1951, www.arizonasnowbowl.com),* on the southwest side of the peaks. The Snowbowl's highest chairlift also sweeps summer visitors high up the slopes of Agassiz Peak on a **Scenic Sky Ride;** you can enjoy the views, but there's no hiking. For cross-country skiing head for the nearby Flagstaff Nordic Center.

**Humphreys Peak Trail** begins at the Arizona Snowbowl ski area, at a height of 9,300 feet, and climbs through dense forests of aspen and conifers, which diminish in size with increasing elevation until only alpine plants dot the dark volcanic rocks. This strenuous hike, 9 miles round-trip, takes about eight hours. Most years, snow blocks the way until late June and again in late September. Snow and winds can blast the summit even in summer. Lightning can be a hazard in July and August; turn back if thunderstorms threaten. To avoid damaging the alpine vegetation above 11,400 feet, stay on trails and don't make fires or camps.

If hiking downhill appeals to you, arrange a vehicle shuttle and take the **Kachina Trail** from the lower Snowbowl parking lot to a trailhead near Schultz Pass on Schultz Pass Road. This trail winds through forests on a moderate hike of 7 miles one way with a 1,300-foot drop in elevation. For another way up, follow the 5.3-mile **Weatherford Trail** from the Schultz Pass Trailhead (8,000 feet) to Doyle Saddle (10,800 feet). The trail continues to Fremont Saddle and on to a junction with the Humphreys Peak Trail in another 3.4 miles. A hike all the way to the summit would be a tough 20-mile round-trip. Another possibility is to go up the Weatherford Trail and down the Humphreys Peak Trail, with the option of making a side trip to the summit.

Around on the north side of the peaks, **Abineau** and **Bear Jaw Trails** form an enjoyable 6.5-mile loop through forests, meadows, and a little canyon. A 2.1-mile section of forest road connects the upper end of the trails to make a loop. The trailhead is off unpaved

Climbers in the San Francisco Peaks head for the summit of Humphreys Peak (far left).

Forest Road 418, which runs between US 89 and US 180.

## Other Hikes

Northwest of the peaks, **Slate Mountain** offers a fine panorama of the volcanic field and much of northern Arizona from its 8,215-foot summit. The climb, 5 miles round-trip with an 850-foot ascent, takes about five hours. Early visitors mistook the gray rock for slate, but it is volcanic rhyolite. The trailhead is 27 miles northwest of Flagstaff on US 180; turn left between Mileposts 242 and 243 onto Forest Road 191 and follow it for 2 miles.

At **Red Mountain,** the thrill is walking *into* the volcano. Erosion has cut towering pinnacles and narrow canyons into the cinder slopes, making it a great place to explore (see sidebar opposite). Head 33 miles northwest of Flagstaff on US 180, then turn left and go 0.3 mile on the dirt road opposite Milepost 247 to a parking area. Follow the trail 1.25 miles; a ladder helps hikers get over the six-foot stone dam of a former stock tank.

**Lava River Cave** leads into a volcanic underworld formed about 100,000 years ago when a lava flow began to cool and the hot core broke through, leaving this hollow tube behind. You can enter the cave through a collapse in the ceiling and explore it for 3,820 feet. Bring warm clothes and a flashlight (and a spare). The Coconino National Forest map shows the ways in. Head 14 miles northwest from Flagstaff on US 180, turn left and drive 3 miles on Forest Road 245, turn left and go 1 mile on Forest Road 171, then left about half a mile on Forest Road 171B. Another route goes 10 miles west on I-40 to the Bellemont Exit 185, turns left and runs 1 mile on the north frontage road, turns right (north) 7.5 miles on Forest Road 171, and then turns right on Forest Road 171B.

On the north edge of Flagstaff, the **Mount Elden Trail System** has many loop options in a set of mountains crowned by 9,299-foot Mount Elden. The trails, which range in difficulty, are mostly for shared use by hikers, equestrians, and mountain bikers. ■

# Sunset Crater Volcano National Monument

Yellows and reds paint the top of Sunset Crater, whose smooth, dark slopes rise a thousand feet above jagged lava flows to a height of 8,029 feet. A roar of incandescent cinders gave birth to the volcano in A.D. 1085–1090, kicking off a period of eruptions in the area that lasted about 200 years. The landscape still looks something like the surface of the moon.

**Sunset Crater Volcano National Monument**

🅼 91 D4

✉ Loop Road, off US 89 N of Flagstaff

☎ 928/526-0502

💲 $$ (includes Wupatki)

www.nps.gov/sucr

In the visitor center, rock samples and videos of volcanic eruptions introduce the forces that created Sunset Crater and its lava flows. Climbing the crater is now strictly prohibited to protect its soft flanks, but you can scramble up nearby **Lenox Crater** (7,240 feet), a cinder cone about 1 mile east of the visitor center. A short, stiff climb of some 280 feet leads to the rim, 30 to 45 minutes

round-trip. **Lava Flow Trail** begins 1.5 miles east of the visitor center and loops across the Bonita Lava Flow beside Sunset Crater. Take a trail guide and allow 30 to 60 minutes for the 1-mile walk, less for the wheelchair accessible, quarter-mile paved loop.

North of the visitor center, **O'Leary Peak** (8,916 feet) has a fantastic panorama of Sunset Crater, the San Francisco Peaks, and smaller volcanoes all around. You can climb O'Leary, weather permitting, by going a quarter of a mile west from the visitor center and turning right one-third mile on Forest Road 545A to the trailhead near O'Leary Group Campground. Continue by foot or mountain bike on the road to the fire lookout tower at the summit, 5 miles one way.

From Flagstaff, head north 12 miles on US 89, then turn right 2 miles on the Loop Road to the visitor center. The 36-mile **Loop Road,** one of Arizona's most scenic drives, continues across lava and cinder fields, swings by the base of Sunset Crater, provides views of the Painted Desert to the north and east, descends to the historic pueblos at Wupatki National Monument (see p. 101), and rejoins US 89 about 26 miles north of Flagstaff. ∎

Sunset Crater Volcano glows once more at day's end.

# Wupatki National Monument

The eruptions of Sunset Crater in the 11th and 12th centuries prompted early tribespeople to depart from the area, but after a few generations they returned and settled in Wupatki Basin. Pueblos with multistory stone buildings went up. Villagers maintained trade routes with regional tribes as far away as Mexico. Yet by A.D. 1250—a little over a hundred years later—the villages lay empty.

**Wupatki Pueblo,** with up to three stories and nearly a hundred rooms, is the largest and most impressive of the pueblos (the word pueblo means "house" in Spanish) in Wupatki National Monument. Pottery, jewelry, and other artifacts in the visitor center tell of the people who lived here.

Wupatki's centuries-old sandstone dwellings sit atop a ridge overlooking a reconstructed ball court.

**INSIDER TIP:**

At Wupatki, see how, some 850 years ago, ancestors of today's Pueblo peoples lived a "green" lifestyle, designing rain-catching roofs and east-facing homes for winter sun.

—ANNE Z. COOKE
National Geographic Traveler
*magazine writer*

A brochure for the trail through the pueblo explains construction details and archaeological findings. The reconstructed ball court is the only known masonry court in the Southwest. Players probably used a rubber or stone ball during games that were open to public view. A blowhole near the ball court connects with a system of underground cracks: Air blows out, gets sucked in, or stands still, depending on the atmospheric pressure.

**Wukoki Pueblo,** though small (only three rooms are visible today), is one of the best preserved. Drive southeast a quarter of a mile from the visitor center, then turn left and go 2.6 miles. **Citadel Pueblo** stands fortress-like atop a volcanic butte 9 miles northwest of the visitor center on the Loop Road. The trail to it passes a smaller pueblo, **Nalakihu.** The well-named **Lomaki Pueblo** (Hopi for "beautiful house") overlooks a small canyon north of Citadel Pueblo. It has two stories and contained at least nine rooms. ■

**Wupatki National Monument**

🅰 91 D5
✉ Loop Road, off US 89 N of Flagstaff
☎ 928/679-2365
$ $$ (includes Sunset Crater)
**www.nps.gov/wupa**

# Williams

This small community west of Flagstaff proudly displays its heritage. A statue of "Old Bill" Williams, the town's namesake, stands in Monument Park on the west side of downtown. This tough trapper, guide, and trader roamed the West from 1825 until he was killed by Ute in 1849. He has been credited as a skilled shot, accomplished horse thief, prodigious drinker, and preacher of profane sermons.

Like Flagstaff, Williams was founded in the 1880s with the coming of the railroad. Trains still roll in and out of the Williams station on excursions to the Grand Canyon. Local businesses thrived

**Grand Canyon Railway passengers encounter gunplay.**

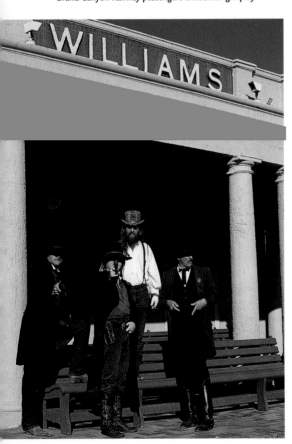

on Route 66 traffic right up until 1984, when the last segment of I-40 bypassed Williams. After weathering tough times, the town has spruced up its historic downtown and added some Old West entertainment. It's a fun place to visit and a handy stop on travels across northern Arizona.

A **Grand Canyon Railway** train departs daily from downtown Williams for the just-over-two-hour trip north across the high plains and through canyons to a log depot in Grand Canyon National Park, a short stroll from the rim. You'll ride in a restored rail car with four options: coach, first class (large reclining seats), observation dome (superlative views), and luxury parlor. Vintage diesel locomotives lead the way.

"Train robbers" have been known to provide a little excitement on the way back as they pursue the carriages on horseback and jump aboard, but "the law" always catches up with the bandits. Whether or not you're taking the train, you can head over to the Williams station in the morning, before the train pulls out, to watch a Wild West show.

Children and animal lovers will enjoy hand-feeding and walking among tame deer at **Grand Canyon Deer Farm,** 8 miles east of Williams. Other regional and

## EXPERIENCE: Follow the Keyhole Sink Trail

The **Keyhole Sink Trail** near Williams is an easy 2-mile round-trip ramble through ponderosa pines and aspen to a seasonal pool in a box canyon. On the dark basaltic rock at trail's end, you can see petroglyphs of deer and other symbols left by prehistoric Sinagua, and imagine the hunters once crouched atop the cliffs, bows drawn. You can spot birds and larger wildlife just about every month of the year along the trail. Wildflowers bloom in spring and summer, and snow attracts cross-country skiers in winter.

From Williams, head east for 8 miles on I-40 to the Pittman Valley/Deer Farm Exit 171, exit north, then continue east for 2.4 miles on an old section of Route 66; park your vehicle on the right at **Oak Hill Snowplay Area,** which features picnic tables, a warming shed, and toilets. Cross the road to the trailhead and continue north, following the blue trail markers.

exotic creatures include pronghorn, bison, reindeer, wallabies, pygmy goats, potbellied pigs, talking birds, and peacocks.

### Pure Nature

Mountains, canyons, and lakes in the scenic **Kaibab National Forest** surrounding Williams offer many recreation possibilities. Stop by the Williams Visitor Center downtown for maps and details.

A climb up **Bill Williams Mountain** (9,255 feet) reveals a panorama of the Grand Canyon to the north, the San Francisco Peaks and many other volcanoes to the east, Sycamore Canyon and the Verde Valley to the south, and vast rangelands to the west. Three moderately challenging hiking trails lead up the mountain through forests to meet at a lookout on the top. There's the 4-mile (one way) **Bill Williams Mountain Trail** on the north side, the 4.5-mile (one way) **Benham Trail** on the east, and the 2-mile (one way) **Bixler Saddle Trail** on the west. If you have a high-clearance vehicle, you can drive the mountain's unpaved road.

Winter snows close the road and trails on the mountain, but the small **Elk Ridge Ski and Outdoor Recreation Area** *(tel 928/814-5038, www.elkridgeski.com)* comes to life with skiing, snowboarding, and tubing. You can also have fun in the snow on the looping **Spring Valley Cross-Country Ski Trail** northeast of town.

Four trout lakes near Williams offer relaxation, camping, and casting: **Cataract Lake** to the west, **Kaibab Lake** to the northeast, **Dogtown Lake** to the southeast, and **White Horse Lake** farther southeast. Forest roads head southeast to **Sycamore Point,** a spectacular overlook of the Sycamore Canyon Wilderness, habitat of the bandit-masked ringtail cat. The **Perkinsville Road** features great views of the Verde Valley on a backroad drive to Jerome. Allow about three hours one way for the trip, best done in dry weather and with a high-clearance vehicle; the first 25 miles are paved, followed by 27 miles of dirt road. ∎

### Williams

Ⓜ 91 C4

**Visitor information**

✉ 200 W. Railroad Ave., Williams, AZ 86046

☎ 928/635-1418 or 800/863-0546

www.williams chamber.com

www.fs.fed.us/r3/ kai/

### Grand Canyon Railway

✉ 233 N. Grand Canyon Blvd.

☎ 928/773-1976 (Flagstaff) or 800/843-8724

Ⓢ $$$$$ train excursion; show free

www.thetrain.com

### Grand Canyon Deer Farm

✉ 6769 E. Deer Farm Rd. (I-40 Exit 171)

☎ 928/635-4073 or 800/926-3337

Ⓢ $$

www.deerfarm.com

# Sedona

Wonderfully sculptured canyon walls, fins, and great monoliths create an almost surreal setting for the Sedona area. Some people believe that powerful energies called vortexes emanate from certain natural features. Superb resorts and restaurants are among the other attractions here.

**Coffeepot Rock (center) and a wealth of other high-drama rock features overlook the magnetic town of Sedona.**

**Sedona**
🗺 91 C3
**Visitor information**
✉ Sedona-Oak Creek Canyon Chamber of Commerce (on N Ariz. 89A, 1 block N of Ariz. 179 junction), P.O. Box 478, Sedona, AZ 86339
☎ 928/282-7722 or 800/288-7336
**www.visitsedona.com**

Creative work inspired by Sedona area scenery is on view on the north edge of town in **Sedona Arts Center** (*N. Ariz. 89A & Art Barn Rd., tel 928/282-3809 or 888/954-4442, www.sedonaarts center.com*) and other galleries. Even non-shoppers will enjoy the Spanish colonial architecture, fountains, and sycamore-shaded courtyards of **Tlaquepaque** (*336 Hwy. 179, tel 928/282-4838, www.tlaq.com*), whose galleries offer

Southwestern and Native American arts and crafts.

The **Sedona Heritage Museum** (*735 Jordan Rd., tel 928/282-7038, www.sedonamuseum.org*) showcases the lives of Sedona's pioneers. Many came here in the late 1800s and early 1900s. Each room has a theme, from homemaking to farming, the U.S. Forest Service to cowboys. You can see the apple-packing shed of the 1930 Jordan farmstead.

**Airport Mesa,** one of Sedona's vortex sites (see sidebar this page), has a great panorama of red-rock country. Hikers will find some short, steep trails off Airport Road. From the airport you can take to the skies in a biplane, Cessna, or helicopter. Sunset is a magical time for a jeep tour, hike, or horseback ride (see Travelwise pp. 261–262). Also, enjoy the view from the **Chapel of the Holy Cross** (*tel 928/282-4069*). To reach the chapel, drive 3 miles south of Sedona on Arizona 179, then turn left on Chapel Road. ∎

## Sedona's Vortex Sites: Where the Magic Lies?

In the early 1980s, Page Bryant and her otherworldly guide, Albion, identified seven vortex sites in and around Sedona. Chief among these, **Airport Mesa** and **Ridge Bell Rock** are said to emanate "electric energy" that inspires and invigorates, while **Red Rock Crossing/Cathedral Rock** has a calming "magnetic energy." Are these forces real? Even if you don't sense these purported energies, the scenery will inspire you. To learn more, drop by a New Age shop in town.

# Around Sedona

The spectacular red-rock country surrounding Sedona invites you to explore its trails, back roads, and prehistoric sites. Except for two state parks, most of this region lies on Coconino National Forest lands; drop by the Sedona Ranger District office or one of the Gateway Visitor Centers for the latest information and the Red Rock Pass, which you'll need for parking in the forest.

The view of Cathedral Rock reflected in Oak Creek at **Red Rock Crossing** has long captivated photographers and filmmakers. Now part of **Crescent Moon Picnic Area** *(tel 928/203-7500)*, it has tables, grills, and swimming holes. From Sedona, head west 4.2 miles on Arizona 89A, turn left and drive 1.8 miles on Upper Red Rock Loop Road, then turn left at the sign and go 0.9 mile on Chavez Ranch Road.

Farther downstream on Oak Creek, stop at **Red Rock State Park** *(tel 928/282-6907)* to enjoy nature walks and wildlife, such as mule deer and javelina. Bird-watching is good year-round; you can pick up a list of the species found here. Rangers conduct walks and special programs.

A network of trails follows Oak Creek and climbs into the hills. From Sedona, head west 5.5 miles on Arizona 89A, turn left and drive 3 miles on Lower Red Rock Loop Road, then turn right into the park. If you're driving from Upper Red Rock Loop Road, continue 3 miles past the Red Rock Crossing turnoff; part of the way is unpaved.

Stunning scenery unfolds as you enter the Sedona area from any direction, but for sheer drama you can't beat the approach from the east along Schnebly Hill

---

**EXPERIENCE:**
## Jeep the Wilds

Many companies offer back-road adventures among Sedona's spectacular cliffs and buttes, taking you to remote areas not easily reached by private vehicles. You have a choice of serious four-wheeling or gentler rides, though drivers always take it slow and easy on the rough stuff. While all of the tours take in the scenery, some have an emphasis on archaeology, vortexes, hiking, or horseback riding. It's worth looking through websites or brochures to see what appeals most, as each company has its own perspective; Sedona's tourism website *(www.visitsedona.com)* is a good place to start.

---

Road. The unpaved, bumpy road, suitable only for high-clearance vehicles, turns off I-17 at Exit 320 atop the forested Mogollon Rim. About halfway along the 12-mile one-way trip, you'll reach **Schnebly Hill Vista** at the edge of the rim with a view of Sedona and its red-rock country. More views unfold as you bump your way down and enter a canyon. The lower end of the drive is just across the Oak Creek bridge from central Sedona on Arizona 179. Snow usually blocks the way in winter. Inquire about road conditions at the Red Rock Ranger District office. ∎

**Red Rock Ranger District, Coconino National Forest**

✉ 8375 Ariz. 179, just S of Village of Oak Creek; P.O. Box 20429, Sedona, AZ 86341

☎ 928/203-7500

**www.fs.fed.us/r3/coconino**

**Red Rock State Park**

🏕 91 C3

**www.azstateparks.com**

# Drive: Oak Creek Canyon

Oak Creek weaves through lush forests beneath high sandstone cliffs near Sedona in one of Arizona's most famous beauty spots. This drive reveals marvelous vistas on every curve, with multicolored leaves adding to the magic from mid-October to mid-November. The entire distance can be covered in less than an hour one way, but trails, picnic areas, and natural swimming holes may tempt you to linger. Try to avoid summer weekends.

No crowds: Winter can be a delightfully laid-back time to explore Oak Creek Canyon.

Before you set out, pick up travel information from the local tourist and Forest Service offices in **Sedona ❶** *(tel 928/282-7722, 800/288-7336, or 928/203-7500)*. Heading north on Arizona 89A, you could stop on the left at the far end of **Midgley Bridge,** a mile outside Sedona, to take in views of Wilson and Oak Creek Canyons. A little farther on, to the right, is **Grasshopper Point ❷**, a swimming hole at a bend in Oak Creek. Travelers can fish for their dinner (provided they pay for what they catch) a mile beyond here at **Rainbow Trout Farm** *(tel 928/282-5799)*.

At **Indian Gardens ❸** you can stop for information at the Oak Creek Visitor Center

**NOT TO BE MISSED:**

Slide Rock State Park • West Fork Oak Creek • Oak Creek Vista

and read a historic marker about a homesteader in 1876. **Encinoso Picnic Area** is soon passed on the left, followed by the turnoff to **Manzanita Campground,** along Oak Creek. The popular swimming hole at **Slide Rock State Park ❹** *(tel 928/282-3034)* is just what the name suggests—a natural waterslide in the bed of Oak Creek! (Shorts made of heavy

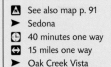

See also map p. 91
Sedona
40 minutes one way
15 miles one way
Oak Creek Vista

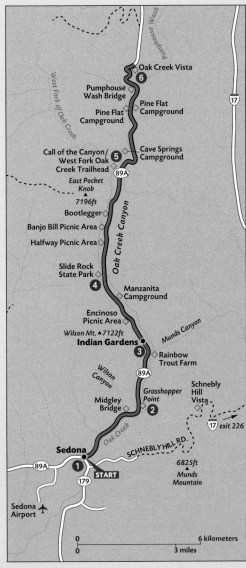

fabric work best.) The park also has an old apple orchard, picnic tables, bird-watching, and a short hiking trail.

About 7 miles from Sedona, **Halfway Picnic Area,** on the left, is on a sunny shelf with canyon views. Nearby **Banjo Bill Picnic Area,** also on the left, is down near the creek. **Bootlegger,** a few hundred yards beyond the picnic areas, is a day-use area right beside Oak Creek.

Definitely worth a stop, after another 1.5 miles, is **Call of the Canyon/West Fork Oak Creek Trailhead** ❺, to the left. Novelist Zane Grey took his inspiration for *Call of the Canyon* from the scenery around West Fork, a major tributary of Oak Creek. A 6-mile round-trip trail crosses a footbridge over Oak Creek, winds through the ruins of Mayhews Lodge, and then turns up West Fork. The walking is mostly easy, though you'll have to hop across rocks at the stream crossings.

A mile farther along the drive, **Cave Springs Campground** lies down a road to the left in a secluded setting beside Oak Creek. **Pine Flat Campground** is on both sides of the road after another mile, in a ponderosa pine forest. Soon Arizona 89A begins its steep climb out of the canyon to the rim, where it's worth stopping on the right at **Oak Creek Vista** ❻ for a panorama of Pumphouse Wash just below and Oak Creek Canyon stretching into the distance. A Forest Service information booth *(closed in winter)* offers advice, maps, and books on the area.

Arizona 89A continues north another 12 miles to Flagstaff through rolling hills forested with ponderosa pines.

# Sedona-area Archaeological Sites

The Forest Service, with the help of volunteers, has opened several cliff dwellings and rock art sites left by ancient Pueblo people. The dirt roads to the cliff dwellings are usually passable by car in dry weather and have fine scenery along the way.

**Red Rock Ranger District, Coconino National Forest**

✉ 8375 Ariz. 179, just S of the Village of Oak Creek; P.O. Box 20429, Sedona, AZ 86341

☎ 928/203-7500

www.fs.fed.us/r3/coconino

Two pueblos in a large alcove at **Palatki Ruins** *(tel 928/282-3854, reservations required, call 9:30 a.m–3:00 p.m.)* housed 30 to 50 people between about A.D. 1150 and 1300. Some of the art on the alcove wall behind and above the ruins may represent clans. The Red Cliffs—a series of alcoves a short walk to the west of Palatki—hold extensive rock art. Volunteers point out

INSIDER TIP:

**Chamber Music Sedona [*www.chambermusic sedona.org*] has Sunday "Magical Music in the Red Rocks" concerts ten times a year.**

—LINDSEY SMITH
*National Geographic contributor*

---

## EXPERIENCE:
### Biking the Red Rocks

On a mountain bike, you can enjoy unobstructed panoramas of the marvelous Red Rock Country. A host of trails interconnect for a variety of rides and loops. Most cycling is rated beginner to intermediate. Drop by one of the local visitor centers or check *www.redrockcountry.org* for lists of trails and maps. Staying on the trail is important to protect fragile desert soils and plants; also be careful not to stray into wilderness areas.

---

the different styles and periods. A former ranch house visitor center lies between Palatki and the Red Cliffs. For a less bumpy road to Palatki, follow Ariz. 89A west 9.2 miles from Sedona, turn right (north) on Forest Road 525 (5 miles), then continue north another 1.6

miles on Forest Road 795 to its end. Alternatively, head west 3.1 miles from Sedona on Arizona 89A, then turn right (north) 8.5 miles on Dry Creek Road/Forest Road 152C; curving west to Forest Road 525, where you turn right, then right again on Forest Road 795.

**Honanki Ruins** may have had 72 rooms, housing around 120 people from about A.D. 1130 to 1280. Here, you'll find rock art too. From the junction of Forest Roads 525 and 795 south of Palatki, follow 525 northwest 4 miles; high-clearance vehicles are recommended.

**V-Bar-V Ranch Petroglyph Site** *(closed Tues.–Thurs.)* contains a thousand-plus petroglyphs in 13 panels. From Sedona drive south 15 miles on Ariz. 179 to the I-17 junction, go straight for 2.4 miles and cross the Wet Beaver Creek bridge; turn right at the sign. ∎

# Camp Verde

In early 1865, knowing that the booming mining camps in the Prescott area would pay handsomely for fresh food, a group of farmers decided to grow crops along the Verde River. When raiding tribes destroyed crops and livestock, the U.S. Army built a fort and pursued the Tonto Apache and Yavapai. Although the fort closed in 1891, four of its adobe buildings still stand beside the old parade ground in the modern town of Camp Verde.

The Out of Africa experience embraces the "up close and personal."

**Camp Verde**

🄰  91 C3

**Visitor information**

✉  Camp Verde
    Chamber of
    Commerce,
    385 S. Main St.,
    Camp Verde, AZ
    86322

☎  928/567-9294

**www.visitcamp
verde.com**

**Fort Verde State
Historic Park**

✉  125 E. Hollamon
    St. (from Main
    St. in downtown,
    turn E one block
    on Hollamon
    St.)

☎  928/567-3275

💲  $

**www.azstateparks
.com**

**Out of Africa
Wildlife Park**

🄰  91 C3

✉  4020 N. Cherry
    Rd., Camp
    Verde, AZ
    86322

☎  928/567-2840

💲  $$$$$

**www.outofafrica
park.com**

Period rooms and exhibits at **Fort Verde State Historic Park** re-create life in the early territorial years. Start at the administration building to see photos and artifacts that tell the stories of enlisted men, officers and their families, Apache scouts, prospectors, and settlers. General George Crook and other commanders worked out of this building trying to end the Indian wars. A heliograph display shows how the troops beamed messages across the state with mirrors and sunlight. The three buildings of Officers' Row have been restored with 1880s furnishings. Step inside to see the quarters of the commanding officer, bachelors, and the doctor. Reenactments take place during Fort Verde Days on the second Saturday of October.

Big cats and other fauna in the **Out of Africa Wildlife Park** roam within near-natural enclosures. The animals housed in the 104-acre park reveal their behavior and personalities during "African Bush Safaris," wildlife preserve tours, and wildlife encounter demonstrations. For the exciting Tiger Splash, staffers get into a pool and coax tigers to join them and play with "prey" toys. Try to arrive early to make the most of your visit; allow at least four hours at the park. Take I-17 Exit 287, turn west and go 3 miles on Arizona 260 toward Cottonwood, then turn left at the traffic light onto Cherry Road. ∎

# Montezuma Castle National Monument

This five-story pueblo so impressed early visitors that they assumed it had been built by Aztec refugees from Mexico after their overthrow by Hernán Cortés in 1521. In fact, Montezuma Castle was constructed in the early 1100s by local Pueblo people, who built pueblos at Tuzigoot and other areas of the Verde Valley as well as in Walnut Canyon and Wupatki (see pp. 96 and 101). Archaeologists termed the culture Sinagua (Spanish for "without water") because of its ability to inhabit arid lands.

Pack sandwiches and binoculars for the drive from Phoenix to Flagstaff. Picnic at Montezuma Castle, along Beaver Creek.

—ANNE Z. COOKE
National Geographic Traveler
*magazine writer*

Year-round water in Beaver Creek below the village and fertile soil on a nearby terrace must have made this an attractive site. Wild plants, game, and salt deposits supplemented the staple crop of corn. Tribespeople may have learned masonry from groups farther north and irrigation from groups to the south.

**Montezuma Castle's** large alcove sheltered its residents from rain and summer heat yet let in warm rays of light in winter. Its location high in the cliffs provided a sense of security against attack. The 20 rooms inside remain remarkably well preserved though are too fragile to visit (see sidebar this page). The nearby **Castle A,** which towered six stories and held 45 rooms, collapsed toward the end of its occupation. The Sinagua had abandoned the Verde Valley by the early 1400s.

Visitor center exhibits interpret the daily life of the Sinagua, display artifacts, and illustrate the history of the monument. A level 0.3-mile loop trail leads to viewpoints of Montezuma Castle and the meager ruins of Castle A.

Also part of the National

Monument is **Montezuma Well,** where springs rise out of a limestone sinkhole to form a lake. A 0.3-mile loop trail climbs to a viewpoint of the lake and some pueblos. Another path drops down to the lakeshore and a few rooms in a small cave. The main trail continues along the rim of the sinkhole past foundations of a pueblo and descends along the outside wall of the sinkhole. A side trail leads to a natural drainage hole where the lake water gushes at 1,100 gallons per minute into a canal built by the Sinagua and still in use today.

The lake is 11 miles northeast of Montezuma Castle. Take I-17 north to Exit 293 and follow signs for 5 miles or, near Sedona, take I-17 Exit 298, go east for half a mile, then turn south for 3 miles on an unpaved road. ■

**Montezuma Castle National Monument**

🅰 91 C3
✉ From I-17 Exit 289, follow signs 2 miles E and N
☎ 928/567-3322
💲 $$
**www.nps.gov/moca**

## In a 12th-Century Castle

This fragile structure couldn't survive the footsteps of the more than one million annual visitors who now admire it from below. Park archaeologists provide us with a description of what's inside. There are three entrances, all requiring ladders. Centuries of soot deposited by cooking and heating fires make the rooms dark and musty. Ladders through holes in the floors connect the levels. Limestone rocks held together with clay and covered with an adobe plaster inside and out form the walls. Wooden beams support roofs and floors covered with reeds, small sticks, grass, and mud. The uppermost bit of wall forms a parapet of unknown purpose and is unique among prehistoric Southwest pueblos. Today, bats, birds, and small mammals make their home in this splendid ruin.

# Cottonwood

Named after the trees that flourish along the Verde River, Cottonwood is the focus of an area that offers an enjoyable railway trip, large ancient pueblo, and outdoor fun. Fans of early 20th-century architecture should follow signs to Old Town Cottonwood and Clarkdale (the latter built by the United Verde Company in 1912). Both towns are bypassed by Arizona 89A.

**Cottonwood**

🅰 91 C3

**Visitor information**

✉ Cottonwood Chamber of Commerce, 1010 S. Main St., Cottonwood, AZ 86326

☎ 928/634-7593

http://visitcotton woodaz.org

The **Clemenceau Heritage Museum** *(Willard St. & Mingus Ave., tel 928/634-2868, www .clemenceaumuseum.org, call for hours, donation)* shows historical and craft exhibits and has a permanent model train room spotlighting historic Verde Valley lines.

To experience the real thing, make the four-hour round-trip along the Verde River through a scenic canyon to Perkinsville and back on the **Verde Canyon Railroad** *(www.verdecanyonrr.com)*. A guide provides background

A room replica in the Tuzigoot visitor center shows how the Sinagua may have furnished their pueblo living areas.

on the area's history and Native Americans and also points out wildlife, geologic features, and historic ranches. Look for bald eagles, especially during the nesting season (late November to mid-May). Starlight tours on some Saturday evenings in summer depart in the late afternoon and come back under the full moon. Follow signs for the station in Clarkdale, 2 miles northwest of Cottonwood.

**Tuzigoot National Monument** *(www.nps.gov/tuzi)*, northeast of Clarkdale, is a massive ridgetop pueblo of the Sinagua Indians, who occupied it from about A.D. 1100 to 1400. Archaeologists discovered jewelry, stone tools, and pottery here, including offerings for 408 burials. The visitor center displays many of these artifacts and presents information on the farming, building, and craft skills of the Sinagua. A quarter-mile trail loops through the site, which was home to more than 200 people at its peak in the late 1300s.

To get a taste of the great outdoors, drive a mile north out of Cottonwood on 10th Street, following signs to **Dead Horse Ranch State Park** *(tel 928/634-5283)*. Activities here include hiking, mountain biking, horseback riding, regular and fly-fishing, birdwatching, picnicking, and camping beside the Verde River. ∎

# Jerome

A steep hillside high above the Verde Valley seems an improbable place for a town, but rich veins of copper ore lay under Cleopatra Hill. Native Americans knew of the turquoise-colored deposits and mined them for pigments and jewelry many centuries before Eugene Jerome provided the financial backing that got the mining industry going in 1883. He never visited the town named for him, missing out on its wild early days of boom and bust economic cycles.

Bordellos and riotous saloon life caused a New York newspaper to proclaim Jerome the "wickedest town in the West." Blasting in pit and underground mines shook the buildings so much that some started sliding downhill. The old jail, formerly on the uphill side of Hull Avenue, is now across the street!

Jerome's final bust came in 1953, when the mines shut down and residents began moving out. With the population down to 50 from its peak of 15,000 in the 1920s, Jerome seemed likely to fade away entirely. Then, in the late 1960s, artists and others began moving in for the town's unique character and low rents. Today's visitors come for the early-20th-century atmosphere, gorgeous setting, galleries and shops, and three museums that tell of life in the old days.

**Jerome State Historic Park** illustrates past life in the town and its mines with photos, heirlooms, and mining equipment. The 1916 adobe mansion that houses the exhibits has great views of Jerome and Little Daisy Mine on one side and Verde Valley on the other. Also on the grounds are an

Jerome's underground mines were in full swing in the late 19th century; today the town is known for its arts scene.

arrastre (primitive drag-stone mill), Chilean stone wheels (to crush the ore), and the giant stamp mill once used to grind ore to a powder before processeing. The three-dimensional mine model upstairs in the mansion shows the underground geology, mine

## Jerome
◆ 91 C3

**Visitor information**
✉ Jerome Chamber of Commerce, 310 Hull Ave. (Box K, Jerome, AZ 86331)
☎ 928/634-2900
🕐 Hours depend on staffing
www.jerome chamber.com

## Jerome State Historic Park
☎ 928/634-5381
🕐 Under major renovation; call ahead
💲 $
www.azstateparks .com

## Gold King Mine & Ghost Town
◆ 91 C3
✉ 1 mile NW of Jerome
☎ 928/634-0053
💲 $$

shafts, and work areas beneath Jerome. From Milepost 345 on Arizona 89A in the lower part of town, turn in 1 mile at the sign.

A large flywheel, its halves separated, is an eye-catching landmark for the **Jerome Historical Society Museum** (*Main St. & Jerome Ave., tel 928/634-5477*), which traces Jerome's past with paintings, photos, mining tools, and ore samples.

For a real ghost town, visit the **Gold King Mine & Ghost Town.** The town of Haynes existed from 1890 to 1914, when miners brought out modest quantities of gold and silver ore from its 1,200-foot-deep shaft instead of the rich copper ore they had hoped for. The antique sawmill runs daily and, for the cost of fuel, operators will fire up the 10,154-cubic-inch "Big Bertha" engine that once powered a local mine and town. You can enter a short prospect tunnel or visit an old schoolhouse from nearby Prescott.

Other buildings along the dusty streets include a

blacksmith shop, an assay office, and a 1930s gas station. More than a hundred historical vehicles on the grounds include a 1902 Studebaker Electric; most of them still run. To get there, turn northwest on the Perkinsville Road from the upper switchback in Jerome, drive one mile, then turn left at the sign. You'll pass a copper mine whence Jerome's smelter belched poisonous gases from 1895 to 1915. Continue on the Perkinsville Road for great panoramas of the Verde Valley.

Arizona 89A climbs above Jerome into the ponderosa pines of **Mingus Mountain.** The highway tops out at a 7,023-foot pass, where you'll find Summit Picnic Area, open during the warmer months, and Summit Snowplay in winter. Nearby attractions and services include campgrounds, hiking trails, backcountry drives, and the Woodchute Wilderness. The Prescott National Forest offices in Camp Verde and Prescott (see p. 118) offer maps and information. ∎

## EXPERIENCE: Join the Art Scene

The creative types who took note of scenic Jerome's bargain rents during the '60s and '70s brought the mile-high town back to life. Arizona artists now show their work in about 30 studios and galleries along the two main streets and in Old Jerome High School (on your left as you enter Jerome from the valley). Jerome comes alive in the evening for the monthly **First Saturday Art Walk** (*www .jeromeartwalk.com*). Musicians gather to play a wide variety of styles on weekends and during festivals. In May, the **Annual Jerome Historic Home and Building Tour** shows off the finest architectural gems, including some not normally open to the public. Drop by the Jerome Chamber of Commerce office or check online at *www.jeromechamber.com* for gallery listings and upcoming events.

# Prescott

**"Prescitt,"** as they say here, easily wins over visitors with its leafy streets and historic downtown centered on Courthouse Plaza. In 1863 the federal government chose this site for the capital of the new Arizona Territory because of its promising mineral deposits and its location far from the many Confederate sympathizers in the Tucson area.

Governor John Goodwin and his officials set up a temporary camp at Fort Whipple in Chino Valley, then moved—as did the fort—17 miles south to the present site of Prescott to be closer to the mining areas and forested land. Soldiers had to be constantly on the lookout for attacks by Tonto Apache and Yavapai as workers built the governor's mansion and other buildings. But Prescott's isolation did not appeal to all the territorial leaders, and in 1867 they moved the capital to Tucson. Ten years later they were back in Prescott; finally, in 1889, they decided that Phoenix would be the capital and departed for good.

The neatly laid-out town they left behind had taken on the appearance of a community from New England or the Midwest rather than the Spanish-flavored adobe towns of southern Arizona or the rough-and-tumble mining and logging camps in other parts of the state. Today's residents—and visitors—enjoy a rich cultural life, fine recreation opportunities, and an invigorating four-season climate.

A statue of local hero Rough Rider William Owen "Buckey" O'Neill stands in front of Prescott's Yavapai County Courthouse.

## The Culture of History

At the excellent **Sharlot Hall Museum,** you can walk through Prescott's history in a series of buildings amid parklike grounds.

Stop by the **Museum Center** to pick up a description of the exhibits and buildings, see temporary shows, and learn about Sharlot Hall (1870–1943). While other women contented themselves at home, Hall's love of the land and

## Buckey O'Neill's Last Stand

William Owen O'Neill (1860–1898) came to Arizona in 1879 seeking opportunities and adventure. He settled in Prescott and became a popular figure, taking on many roles in the community. When the Spanish-American War broke out in 1898, he petitioned Governor McCord for permission to raise "one thousand Arizona cowboys" to fight in Cuba. He succeeded, though most volunteers came from other states and territories. Newspapers dubbed his group the "Rough Riders." While standing fearlessly among his men in Cuba, he reportedly said, "the Spanish bullet is not molded that will kill me" just before a sniper's bullet cut him down.

### Prescott

◭ 91 B3

**Visitor information**

✉ Prescott Chamber of Commerce, 117 W. Goodwin St., Prescott, AZ 86302

☎ 928/445-2000 or 800/266-7534

www.prescott.org

www.visit-prescott.com

### Sharlot Hall Museum

✉ 415 W. Gurley St. (2 blocks W of Courthouse Plaza)

☎ 928/445-3122

$ $$

www.sharlot.org

people of Arizona took her on many trips down the territory's rough roads to gather stories. Herself a pioneer, having arrived in Arizona by wagon at the age of 12 in 1882, Hall served as the first territorial historian from 1909 to 1911, working to preserve important relics of the past. She wrote stories and poems and founded this museum in 1927.

Among the museum buildings is the 1864 **Governor's Mansion.** It may seem rustic today, but when new its large size and solid ponderosa pine construction must have made it the area's most impressive structure. Governor John Goodwin and Territorial Secretary Richard McCormick moved in at opposite ends of the mansion, along with other officials and family members. Today you can see the interior furnished as it was during the early years.

In the native-stone-and-log **Sharlot Hall Building** next door, completed by the Civilian

Conservation Corps in 1934, you can learn about the region's Native Americans and the people of territorial Arizona. **Fort Misery,** built as a general store in 1863–1864, is one of the oldest wooden buildings in Arizona. In the 1890s, one story goes, Judge John Howard dispensed "misery" sentences to lawbreakers here. Another report says he generously took in guests but was an awful cook.

Sharlot Hall had the **Ranch House** built in 1936 "as a tribute to early ranchers." It offers living history programs. The **schoolhouse** is a replica of the territory's first public schoolhouse, built nearby in 1867.

The 1875 **Frémont House** is an early Victorian building with a restored interior. John C. Frémont, a noted explorer of the West and Arizona's fifth territorial governor, rented this house from 1878 to 1881, but he fared badly in Arizona politics and resigned under public pressure after three years in office. Even more elegant, the 1877 **Bashford House** has some rooms restored in elaborate style, a solarium, and a gift shop.

In the **Transportation Building** are fine examples of how people got around in the late 19th and early 20th centuries. Among several gardens on the grounds, the **Rose Garden** honors pioneer women of territorial Arizona. Living history programs, talks, workshops, theater productions, concerts, and special events take place throughout the year; call or check the website to see what is on the schedule.

**INSIDER TIP:**

Along Whiskey Row
(on South Montezuma
Street) bars and res-
taurants fill buildings
frequented by Prescott
miners more than a
century ago. See what's
on at the nearby Elks
Opera House.

—LINDSEY SMITH
*National Geographic contributor*

## Native Americana

Over on the east side of downtown Prescott, at the pueblo-style
**Smoki Museum,** you'll find
treasure in the form of Native
American artistry. Excavations
near the town uncovered much
of the prehistoric jewelry, pottery,
and stone implements on display
at the museum. In addition,
exhibits of fine basketry, textiles,
pottery, and kachina dolls represent contemporary tribes of the
Southwest.

Paintings and sketches by
anthropologist and artist Kate
Cory—who lived with the Hopi
from 1905 to 1912 and helped
design this museum—offer a look
at Native American life.

Western artists, including
Native Americans, reflect their
feelings, observations, and
creative spirit in works on view
at the **Phippen Museum,** where
paintings, drawings, and some
bronzes represent both the Old
West and contemporary life in
the Southwest. George Phippen's
paintings depict the life of the
working cowboy, often with a
humorous eye. ■

### Elks Opera House
- ✉ 117 E. Gurley St.
- ☎ 928/443-8541
- www.elksopera
  housefoundation
  .org

### Smoki Museum
- ✉ 147 N. Arizona
  Ave.
- ☎ 928/445-1230
- 🕐 Closed Mon. &
  early Jan.
- 💲 $$
- www.smoki
  museum.org

### Phippen Museum
- ✉ 4701 N. Hwy.
  89 (6 miles N of
  Prescott)
- ☎ 928/778-1385
- 🕐 Closed Mon.
- 💲 $$
- www.phippenart
  museum.org

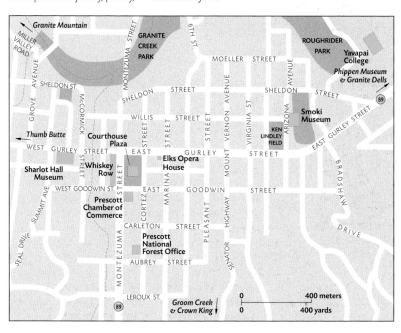

# Around Prescott

Prescott's appeal to visitors lies not only in its historic attractions. The mile-high city is also the center of an extensive area of forested mountains, lakes, and picturesque granite boulders. Several roads out of the city lead into the great expanse of Prescott National Forest, where there are enough trails, views, wildlife, and campgrounds to satisfy most outdoors enthusiasts.

Crown King Saloon, originally 5 miles down the road, was disassembled and moved here by pack mules around 1910.

**Prescott
National Forest**

🅰 90 B3

✉ 344 S. Cortez
St., Prescott, AZ
86303

☎ 928/443-8000

🕐 Closed Sat.–Sun.

**www.fs.fed.us/r3/
prescott**

Piles of smooth granite boulders line Watson Lake in **Granite Dells,** 4 miles north of Prescott on Arizona 89. **Watson Lake Park** *(tel 928/777-1121)* on the south shore offers the easiest access as well as picnicking *(year-round)* and camping *(Fri.–Mon. summer)*. **Thumb Butte** *(tel 928/443-8000)* soars high into the sky west of Prescott. A trail loops through dense ponderosa pines up to ridges covered with pinyon pine, juniper, and oak. Here two

short trails lead to vista points of Prescott and its surroundings; the 1.7-mile round-trip gains 600 feet in elevation and takes about two and a half hours. The trailhead is 3.5 miles west of downtown on Gurley Street/Thumb Butte Road.

Northwest of Prescott, **Granite Basin Lake** and **Granite Mountain Wilderness** *(tel 928/443-8000)* also feature dramatic vistas of water, forest, stone, and sky. The lake, which lies at the foot of Granite Mountain, has a picnic area and a nearby campground and trailhead. **Granite Mountain Trail** ascends gently in 1.3 miles to Blair Pass, then turns right and switchbacks 2.5 miles to an overlook at 7,185 feet; the hike is moderate to strenuous and 8.2 miles round-trip, with a 1,600-foot elevation gain, and takes about six hours. From Prescott, head west on Gurley Street, turn right and drive for 4.3 miles on Grove Avenue/Miller Valley Road/Iron Springs Road, then turn right and drive about 5 miles on Forest Road 374.

Many scenic vistas, historical sites, and hiking trails lie south of Prescott along the **Senator Highway,** also signed as Mount Vernon Avenue in town and Forest Road 52 farther south. It twists and turns through the rugged Bradshaw Mountains to Crown King, where you can follow an old railroad grade down to I-17. In the 19th century, the "highway" connected Prescott with the Senator Mine and other mining communities. Most of these have faded away, but some of the old mines and relics of that era remain. Beyond the village of Groom Creek you'll need a high-clearance vehicle with a full tank of gas, water, and most of a day to reach I-17. Check with the Prescott National Forest office in Prescott for road conditions and opportunities for hiking and camping.

Six miles south of Prescott on the Senator Highway, the **Groom Creek School Nature Trail** offers an easy quarter-mile walk on a paved loop. Back on the Senator Highway, another half-mile through the ponderosa pines takes you to **Groom Creek Trail,** which climbs to the 7,693-foot summit of Spruce Mountain and back in a 9-mile loop. This moderate-to-strenuous, six-hour hike (or horseback ride) has good panoramas of the Prescott area, Mogollon Rim, and San Francisco Peaks, with a 1,300-foot elevation gain. Equestrians can stay with their animals near the trailhead at Groom Creek Horsecamp. Drive 3.8 miles up to the lookout and picnic area atop **Spruce Mountain** (not suited for RVs or trailers) on Forest Road 52A from a turnoff 5 miles south of Prescott; you walk the last half-mile.

Past Groom Creek, Senator Highway narrows and contains some rough spots. On the highway 15 miles south of Prescott, you'll pass **Palace Station,** a former stagecoach stop.

About 36 miles from Prescott

lies **Crown King,** a small town that grew from a mining camp. The 1898 Crown King Saloon still serves food and beverages. A 1904 general store provides supplies, gas, a post office, and a phone.

From half a mile above Crown King, you can head south and east on Forest Road 52 to **Horsethief Basin Recreation Area.** Bass, catfish, and sunfish thrive in the fishing lake, while campgrounds and viewpoints beckon at the

## EXPERIENCE:
## Rodeo Action—Up Close

All across the state, cowboys and cowgirls compete for top honors. The rodeos shift between the low desert in winter and the high country in summer. Check the Internet and local visitor centers for event schedules. **La Fiesta de Los Vaqueros** (*www.tucsonrodeo.com*) runs in mid-February with rodeos and the world's longest non-motorized parade. Also in February, Scottsdale's **Parada del Sol** (*www.paradadelsol. us*) presents a rodeo along with the world's largest horse-drawn parade. Earning its billing at the start as a "cowboy tournament," held in Prescott on July Fourth, 1888, the **World's Oldest Rodeo** (*www.worldsoldest rodeo.com*) takes place in late June–early July and includes a big parade.

southern end of the Bradshaws. Trails continue into rugged **Castle Creek Wilderness.** Crown King Road, which has a dirt surface but is graded for vehicles, descends from Crown King to the desert below, where you can follow roads to I-17 via Cordes for those heading north or Bumble Bee for those going south. ∎

# Arcosanti

A strange new type of city is slowly rising from the high desert of central Arizona, 65 miles north of Phoenix. Architect Paolo Soleri envisions this urban laboratory as a place to think deeply about solving the problems of the world's cities through architecture. He calls his philosophy arcology—the joining of architecture and ecology to create a place that is both spiritually uplifting and environmentally sound.

To eliminate urban sprawl and better provide for cultural, social, and economic activities, Soleri feels cities should grow vertically. By making greater use of the third dimension, cities would no longer need freeways. People could commute efficiently by pedestrian

**Enjoy a meal at Arcosanti's light-filled café.**

walkways or elevators, giving them more time to enjoy life. Nearby land could also be preserved in its natural state.

Born in Turin, Italy, in 1919, Soleri earned his Ph.D. from Torino Polytechnico and came to the United States in 1947 for a year and a half to study with architect Frank Lloyd Wright. Soleri's work in architecture and human ecology led to the publication in 1969 of *Arcology: The City in the Image of Man.* Construction at Arcosanti began the following year.

Work at Arcosanti continues, progressing slowly as money is raised. The focus, though, is on the learning experience—the interests of Soleri and his apprentices extend well beyond "bricks and mortar." Still in an early stage, it is projected that Arcosanti could eventually house some 7,000 people—yet it would occupy only 5 percent of the land consumed by a conventional community. Those involved believe Arcosanti could become a prototype for the world's cities.

A visit is highly recommended to see Arcosanti in action. Models, drawings, and exhibits in the visitor center illustrate Soleri's ideas. Arcosanti residents lead tours for visitors, explaining some of the history and inspiration behind what you see and pointing out features such as the south-facing apses that provide shade in summer while admitting the sun in winter. A bronze foundry produces the unique wind-bells sold here and elsewhere to help fund Arcosanti.

Downstairs from the visitor center is a bakery and café. Baked goods are made with organic flours, grains, fruits, and nuts, and the coffee's good. Visitors can also stay overnight; call ahead to reserve the Sky Suite or a simple,

A tour of the indoor and outdoor spaces introduces the concepts behind Arcosanti.

inexpensive (breakfast included) room.

If you'd like to learn more, the visitor center sells books by Soleri. Better yet, workshops provide an opportunity to participate in a seminar and then join a hands-on program of building Arcosanti. The excellent website (*www.arcosanti.org*) offers information on the philosophies, construction, accommodations, and programs offered here, or you can contact the organization (*HC 74, Box 4136, Mayer, AZ 86333, tel 928/632-7135*). Arcosanti is 34 miles southeast of Prescott and 65 miles north of Phoenix; take I-17, Cordes Junction, Exit 262A, and follow the signs for 2.5 miles.

## EXPERIENCE: Arcosanti–Dive In

Would you like to explore ways to make our urban environments a better place to live? Programs offered here do just that, and you don't have to be a specialist— the workshops are open to everyone. **Seminar Week** introduces Soleri's arcology theory and how the design of Arcosanti has progressed and where it might go in the future. Tours take you inside the buildings and to the natural area surrounding the site. An optional **Second Week Program** goes deeper into the workings of Arcosanti and looks at other architectural projects in central Arizona. The **Five Week Workshop** includes these first two weeks, then dives into hands-on experiences, usually in your choice of construction, facilities maintenance, agriculture, archives, or landscaping departments. Internship programs begin with the Five Week Workshop, then run another eight weeks so that you can participate for a longer time. Arcosanti also offers a one-day program of silt casting, a technique used by Paolo Soleri since 1956; you'll make a plaster tile as you learn the basic principles of the craft. Find out more at *www.arcosanti.org*, or call the workshop coordinator (*tel 928/632-6233*).

# Mogollon Rim Country

Beneath the beautiful towering cliffs of the long escarpment known as the Mogollon Rim, cool pine forests and mountain streams entice visitors to enjoy the great outdoors. The Rim Country so entranced novelist Zane Grey that he built a cabin here in 1920 and set many of his stories in the region.

Rolling hills stretch to the distant Mazatzal Range from a Mogollon Rim overlook.

**Mogollon Rim Country**

⚠ 91 D2–E2

**Visitor information**

✉ Rim Country Regional Chamber of Commerce, 100 W. Main St., Payson (P.O. Box 1380, Payson, AZ 85547)

☎ 928/474-4515 or 800/672-9766

**www.paysonrim country.com**

**Payson**

⚠ 91 D2

## Payson

Named after Senator Louis Edwin Payson (who never visited the town) to repay a political favor, Payson got its start in 1881 with the arrival of gold miners and soon developed ranching and logging industries. Today, the many accommodations and restaurants make it a good base to explore the region.

The **Rim Country Museum** illustrates the history of prehistoric peoples, the Tonto Apache, and the pioneers. Exhibits depict mining, forestry, agriculture, and home life. The museum buildings themselves reflect the past. A 1930s forest ranger's residence houses the ticket office and a gift shop. A copy of the Herron Hotel serves as the main exhibit

hall, and a 1907 forest ranger's station has forestry displays and a library. Zane Grey's reconstructed cabin displays period furnishings along with books and memorabilia. The park surrounding the museum features picnic tables, a playground, and a lake. At the Chamber of Commerce office on Beeline Highway (Arizona 87)—the main road through town—turn west 1 mile on Main Street, turn right on Green Valley Parkway, then make the first left into the museum's parking lot.

The **Mazatzal Wilderness** southwest of Payson takes in more than 252,500 acres of rugged mountain country. The Indian name Mazatzal means "land of the deer"; you may also see piglike javelina (ha-vuh-LEE-nuh), black

Settlers built the
51-mile Highline Trail
in the 1800s; today,
hikers, equestrians,
and mountain bikers
enjoy it and its inter-
connecting trails.

—BILL WEIR
*National Geographic author*

bear, and perhaps a mountain
lion. Saguaro cactus and spiny
paloverde grow in the lower
Sonoran Desert between 2,200
and 4,000 feet. In the upper
Sonoran Desert at 4,000 to 7,000
feet, the vegetation changes to
dry grasslands and woodlands;
near the summits at 7,000 to
7,900 feet, it gives way to firs
and ponderosa pine. The Verde
River flows year-round through
the western portion, but other
water sources may not be reliable
in summer. Fourteen trailheads
provide access to the wilderness;
the Payson Ranger District office
of the Tonto National Forest *(tel
928/474-7900)* has maps and
hiking information.

## North from Payson

Just northeast of Payson, on Tonto
National Forest land, is **Shoofly
Village,** which was occupied
by Native Americans from
about 1000 to 1250. Only scant
foundations remain today, but an
interpretive trail explains the site,
which had plazas and some 80
rooms. To reach it, take Arizona 87
to the north edge of Payson, then
turn right and drive for 3 miles on
Houston Mesa Road.

A worthwhile detour off
Arizona 87, about 11 miles from
Payson, leads to **Tonto Natural
Bridge State Park.** Over the millennia, mineral springs in a pretty
canyon here have built up the
world's largest travertine bridge.
It is so big—an arch 400 feet long,
183 feet high, and up to 150 feet
wide—that you can be standing
atop the bridge without even
realizing it. Small waterfalls sparkle
brightly in the sun, supporting
wildflowers and other vegetation.
Short trails, some wheelchair
accessible, lead to overlooks at
both ends of the bridge. Other
trails descend the canyon walls,
giving close views of the waterfalls
and inside the bridge. The 0.4-mile

**Rim Country
Museum**
- 91 D2
- 700 Green
  Valley Pkwy.,
  Payson
- 928/474-3483
- Closed Tues.
- $$

www.rimcountry
museums.com

**Payson Ranger
District, Tonto
National Forest**
- 1009 E. Hwy.
  260, Payson, AZ
  85541
- 928/474-7900
- Closed Sat.–Sun.

www.fs.fed.us/r3/
tonto

**Tonto Natural
Bridge State
Park**
- 91 D2
- 11 miles N of
  Payson off Ariz.
  87 (turn left
  3 miles at the
  sign)
- 928/476-4202
- Call for hours
- $$

www.azstateparks
.com

## The Gentle Elk of the Mogollon Rim

You may encounter this imposing member
of the deer family—bulls can weigh up to
1,200 pounds—though they are quick to
shy away. Fast runners, high jumpers, and
strong swimmers, they are skilled at
fleeing. Elk like to graze in the high
country—7,000 to 10,000 feet—and only
move down to the pinyon pine and juniper
belt of 5,500 to 6,500 feet when forced to

by deep snow. Their summer coats, a rich
reddish brown, are shed for the winter
coat of dark brown and grayish brown.
Antlers of adult bulls take 150 days to
reach full size—by early August. In early
September, the bugling mating calls and
harem formations begin. Females seek out
dense cover to give birth to a single calf in
late May–early June.

Small and sweet: The log Strawberry Schoolhouse—Arizona's oldest—is just one room.

round-trip **Gowan Loop Trail** winds down from the top of the bridge to an observation deck where the creek emerges. At the observation deck, you can admire the tiny waterfall creating rainbows in the sun in front of the bridge, then walk upstream into the vast chamber beneath the bridge. Sure-footed hikers can rock-scramble along Pine Creek through the bridge (most easily done in an upstream direction) and take **Pine Creek Trail** back to the parking area about half a mile away. Another handy connector, the 500-foot **Anna Mae Trail** drops from the top of the bridge to the creek. In just 300 feet, **Waterfall Trail** dips partway down from the rim to reach a cave and a little waterfall.

A 1927 lodge, formerly part of a guest ranch, is undergoing renovation to house exhibits and a gift shop. Staffers provide lodge tours and other programs. Surrounding lawns and trees make inviting picnic spots. The last 1.5 miles of the approach to the canyon descend very steeply. You can park trailers or large RVs at the top of the grade. Rangers caution visitors to observe the speed limit to avoid overheating their brakes.

Back on Arizona 87, about 15 miles north of Payson you will reach the little community of Pine. The **Pine-Strawberry Museum** *(tel 928/476-3547, www.pinestrawhs. org, closed Sun. mid-Oct.–mid-May)* displays many pioneer exhibits in a 1917 former Mormon church. Look for a sign on your left as you head north. In another 4 miles north, you'll reach the village of Strawberry, just below the Mogollon Rim. To see the 1885 **Strawberry Schoolhouse,** Arizona's oldest, turn left at the

Strawberry Lodge and drive 1.5 miles on Fossil Springs Road. The schoolhouse interior is open on summer weekends and holidays. Scenic **Fossil Springs Road** (best suited for high-clearance vehicles) continues west into the backcountry, drops steeply to Fossil Creek, then winds up into the hills and meets Arizona 260 east of Camp Verde (see p. 109). Trails lead into Fossil Springs Wilderness to the north of the road.

Arizona 87 sweeps up to the top of the Mogollon Rim from Strawberry, then rolls through forests of ponderosa pine to the **Mogollon Rim Ranger Station** *(tel 928/477-2255, closed Sat.–Sun.)*, about 10 miles northeast of Clints Well. Here staffers offer books, maps, and information on camping, hiking trails, fishing, and exploring the back roads. Long, skinny **Blue Ridge Reservoir,** hemmed in by the walls of East Clear Creek Canyon, lies nearby, south of Arizona 87. **Forest Highway 3** runs north to Flagstaff (see pp. 92–95) on a pretty forest drive past Mormon Lake and Upper and Lower Lake Mary.

## East from Payson

At Kohl's Ranch Lodge, 17 miles east of Payson, turn north off Arizona 260 on Forest Road 289 for 4 miles to visit **Tonto Creek Hatchery** *(tel 928/478-4200).* An interpretive walk takes you past outdoor raceways (long, water-filled tanks) and lets you peer through windows into the hatchery rooms. Exhibits describe the life cycle of the rainbow and other trout species that grow up

here. The show pond is full of huge trout. You can feed them, too; buy feed at the dispenser.

After the hatchery turnoff, Arizona 260 climbs steadily up the Mogollon Rim. At the top, look on the right for the **Mogollon Rim Visitor Center** *(usually open Fri.–Sat. in summer),* which has exhibits and information on recreation in the area. Expansive views unfold behind the visitor center across countless forested mountains below the Mogollon

Rim. A series of lakes nearby offers fishing, boating, and camping in cool mountain air. Try to come midweek in summer if possible, because weekends tend to be crowded. **Forest Road 300** turns off opposite the visitor center and parallels the Mogollon Rim all the way to Arizona 87 to the northwest, passing vista points, hiking trails, and campgrounds, and coming close to three lakes. **Rim Lakes Vista Trail** is an easy

---

**EXPERIENCE:**
# Rim Lakes Vista Trail

**An easy walk along the Mogollon Rim, 3-mile Rim Lakes Vista Trail affords fine views from 7,550 feet. Much of the way is paved and wheelchair accessible. You also can make a loop of 4.2 miles along the Military Sinkhole and General Crook Trails. The season runs about May through November; steer clear if thunderstorms threaten. From Payson, drive east on Arizona 260 for about 30 miles until you reach the top of the Mogollon Rim, then turn left on Forest Road 300 and look for the signed trailhead parking on the right.**

**Black Mesa Ranger District, Apache and Sitgreaves National Forests**

✉ 55 miles E of Payson on Ariz. 260 (P.O. Box 968, Overgaard, AZ 85933)

☎ 928/535-4481

🕐 Closed Sat.–Sun.

**www.fs.fed.us/ r3/asnf**

**Pleasant Valley Ranger District, Tonto National Forest**

✉ P.O. Box 450, Young, AZ 85554

☎ 928/462-4300

🕐 Closed Sat.–Sun.

**www.fs.fed.us/r3/ tonto**

**Young**

🔼 91 E2

3-mile one-way hike along the rim between Rim and Mogollon Campgrounds, both off Forest Road 300. At nearby **Woods Canyon Lake,** you can hike around the water on an easy 5-mile loop trail, or along the half-mile loop nature trail at Rocky Point Picnic Area. Obtain recreation information year-round at the Apache and Sitgreaves National Forests' **Black Mesa Ranger District,** on Arizona 260, some 25 miles east of the Mogollon Rim Visitor Center.

## Young

Sometimes called "Arizona's last cow town," Young lies in Pleasant Valley, southeast of Payson. North of Young in the late 1800s, a range war played out between the cattlemen of the Graham clan and the sheepmen of the Tewksburys (see sidebar below). Author Zane Grey based his novel *To the Last Man* (1922) on these events.

An exceptionally scenic drive on Young Road connects Young with the Mogollon Rim to the north and the Roosevelt Lake area to the south, with great hiking, camping, and backcountry drives along the way. Sections of the drive in Young and at the south end are paved, but much of the road is gravel and is passable by cars in dry weather. Young offers a small motel as well as some rustic cafés and rental cabins. For information on the area, including the Sierra Ancha and Hell's Gate Wildernesses, contact the Pleasant Valley Ranger District office of the Tonto National Forest.

The north turnoff for Young is 33 miles east of Payson on Arizona 260 near Milepost 284, where you turn south on Forest Road 512 and drive 24 miles to Young. Only the last 4 miles are paved. Side roads lead to Colcord Lookout (7,513 feet), Canyon Creek Hatchery, historic sites of the Pleasant Valley War, and campgrounds.

South of Young, Arizona 288 weaves through the meadows and forests of the Sierra Ancha and descends to the Salt River. The drive ends 47 miles from town at the Arizona 188 junction between Roosevelt Lake and Globe; the last 13 miles are paved. About halfway (between Mileposts 285 and 284), the road crosses Workman Creek. Forest Road 487 turns east here past several basic campsites, climbs steeply (high-clearance vehicles required) to the top of 200-foot Workman Creek Falls, 3.2 miles from the highway, and continues up Forest Road 487 another 3.7 miles to the top of Aztec Peak (7,694 feet). A 250-yard walk downstream on Workman Creek from the highway leads to the "tubs," or natural swimming holes. ■

---

### Pleasant Valley War

In the late 1800s, a savage range war broke out between cattlemen and sheep herders in this valley north of Young. The trouble started when the Tewksbury clan gave protection to a band of sheep brought here in 1887. Cattle owners led by the Graham clan wouldn't tolerate "woolies" and attacked, killing a Navajo sheepherder and driving away the animals. The Tewksburys retaliated and the war was on. Efforts by lawmen to stop the feuding proved fruitless. Thirty people died, including all of the Grahams, before the fighting subsided—five years after it started.

Featuring the Colorado River, Arizona's western boundary and the lifeblood of the region and its people

# Western Arizona

Route 66—an American classic

# Western Arizona

The Colorado River's gentle current and many vast lakes lure visitors to explore backwaters in canoes or fishing boats, raft Black Canyon below Hoover Dam, skim the open waters, and cruise in houseboats. Many come simply to relax by the shore, swim, camp, and hike. Skies are normally sunny year-round; the recreation scene heats up with summer temperatures. Towns here often make national highs at well over 100°F.

The great Colorado River glides below an overlook in River Island State Park.

Small mountain ranges, seemingly lifeless from a distance, break up the desert plains. A closer look reveals hardy and adaptable life sheltered within the rocky terrain. You might see desert bighorn sheep, mule deer, coyote, desert tortoise, and Gambel's quail. The Kofas, reaching 4,877 feet, harbor California fan palms. Farther north, mountains such as the Hualapais (8,417 feet) are biological islands supporting forests of ponderosa pine, pinyon pine, oak, and some aspen and fir.

Native American groups migrated in and out of this region, depending on food availability and outbreaks of tribal warfare. Huts of brush and mud gave shelter, the river watered their crops, and the surrounding desert provided game and wild plants.

The Cocopah wound up in the lowermost part of the Colorado drainage, the Quechan upstream, and the Mohave farther upriver. The Maricopa lived here too, but warfare forced them up the Gila River to central Arizona in the mid-1800s

The Chemehuevi, a nomadic Paiute group, joined the river tribes in the early 1800s, as did some Navajo and Hopi beginning in 1945. Many now farm or work in casinos and live on reservations. You can visit tribal museums near Parker and Yuma.

The Spanish had explored the lower Colorado River as early as 1540, but they did not attempt to settle until 1780, when fears arose of Russian expansion down the California coast. The Spanish decided to open

## NOT TO BE MISSED:

The Route 66 Museum, a shrine to the era of the road trip **130**

Learning the story of northwestern Arizona at the Mohave Museum of History and Arts **133**

Driving on Route 66's longest continuous stretch **132–133**

The remarkable engineering and artwork at Hoover Dam **135**

London Bridge, an authentic piece of 19th-century England **136**

Taking a back roads trip to Swansea, the state's best ghost town **138**

Learning about life behind bars for inmates and their guards at Yuma Territorial Prison State Park **139**

an overland route to California and built two missions near present-day Yuma. Abuses by the colonizers led to a revolt by the Quechan and destruction of the missions within a year. Spanish troops ransomed the survivors and withdrew from the area. American mountain men began crossing the region in the early 1800s, followed by government explorers and forty-niners bound for California. The development of western Arizona began with the establishment of an Army camp at Yuma Crossing in 1851 and the advent of steamboats, better roads, and discoveries of valuable minerals. ■

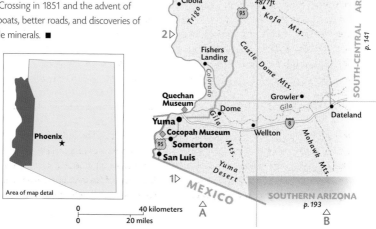

Phoenix ★

Area of map detail

| 0 | 40 kilometers |
| 0 | 20 miles |

GRAND CANYON COUNTRY
p. 45

Lake Mead

Alan Bible Visitor Center
Bonelli Landing
**Hoover Dam**
Temple Bar Resort
South Cove

NEVADA

Black Canyon
Colorado

6 ▷ LAKE
MEAD
NAT.
REC.
AREA

Dolan Springs
Red Lake
Grand Wash Cliffs
Cerbat Mts.

93
Chloride
Antares
Hackberry

Lake Mohave
**Katherine Landing**
5 ▷

68

**Kingman**
40

Black Mts.

**Bullhead City** Davis Dam

**Hualapai Mt. Park**
▲ Hualapai Peak 8417ft

95
Oatman
**Mohave Valley**
FORT MOJAVE I.R.
Yucca
Golden Shores
40
Topock

Hualapai Mts.
93

Wikieup

NORTH-CENTRAL ARIZONA
p. 89

4 ▷

95
Mohave Mts.

**London Bridge**
**Lake Havasu City**
Lake Havasu

Parker Dam
Bill Williams
Alamo Lake

CALIFORNIA

Colorado

3 ▷

**Buckskin Mt. State Park**
**Parker**
COLORADO
RIVER
INDIAN
RESERVATION

**Poston Memorial Monument**
95

Swansea Townsite
Midway

Bouse
72
Harcuvar Mts.
Wenden

**Quartzsite**
Plomosa Mts.
Vicksburg
Salome
60
Hope
10

Ehrenberg

2 ▷

Cibola
Trigo Mts.

95
Signal Peak 4877ft
Kofa Mts.

SOUTH-CENTRAL ARIZONA
p. 141

Fishers Landing
Castle Dome Mts.

Colorado

**Quechan Museum**
Dome
Gila
Growler
Dateland

**Yuma**
**Cocopah Museum**
Wellton
8
Mohawk Mts.

95
**Somerton**
**San Luis**
Yuma Desert

Gila Mts.

1 ▷ MEXICO

SOUTHERN ARIZONA
p. 193

A
B

# Kingman

Lewis Kingman worked on the survey for the Atlantic and Pacific Railroad, which opened the high desert country of northwestern Arizona in the 1880s to mining, ranching, and trade. He also gave his name to this town, today a good base for retracing historic Route 66, visiting ghost towns, and driving up into the cool Hualapai and Cerbat Mountains.

Bad guys regularly bite the dust in Oatman shootouts. Welcome to a Wild West time warp.

**Kingman**

 129 B5

**Visitor information**

✉ Powerhouse Visitor Center, 120 W. Andy Devine Ave., Kingman, AZ 86401

☎ 928/753-6106 or 866/427-7866

**www.kingman tourism.org**

For an introduction to Kingman, visit the **Powerhouse Visitor Center,** downtown in a huge 1907 building once used for power generation. Here you will find the **Route 66 Museum,** a nostalgic celebration of the "mother road," along with an information desk, theater, photo exhibits, model railroad, and gift shops.. Wide-ranging exhibits in the **Mohave Museum of History and Arts** show this region and its people from earliest times to the present. The Hualapai Indian Room has a full-size wickiup brush shelter, baskets, and pottery. Paintings of the U.S. Presidents and their wives hang on the walls. Photos illustrate the building of the Hoover Dam, and a video shows ranchers talking about their lives. The Andy Devine exhibit tells the story of the town's favorite son, a movie and TV actor. The museum has a research library and sells regional books and crafts.

The **Bonelli House** *(430 E. Spring St. & N. 5th St., tel 928/753-1413, closed Sat.–Sun., donation),* built of native tufa stone, reflects the lifestyle of a prominent local family in the early 20th century.

The forests and scenic views of **Hualapai Mountain Park** draw visitors to the high country south of Kingman for hiking, picnicking, camping, or stays in rustic cabins. Elevations range from 5,000 feet near the entrance to 8,417 feet at the summit of this county park. The mountains take their name from the Hualapai (meaning "pine tree people"), who lived here until they were relocated north near the Grand Canyon in the 1870s.

Offices at the park and in Bullhead City have checklists of birds and other animals you might see and information on hiking trails to overlooks and the summits of Aspen and Hayden Peaks. The park is open all year; snow may require chains or four-wheel-drive. A 14-mile paved road offers easy access; take any of the three I-40 Kingman exits to the junction of Andy Devine Avenue and Stockton Hill Road, then turn southeast on Hualapai Mountain Road.

Gold discovered in the western foothills of the Black Mountains in 1904 created boomtown **Oatman** *(www.oatmangoldroad. org),* 31 miles southwest of Kingman. Four roads lead here,

the two most scenic being old sections of Route 66—southwest over the Black Mountains from I-40 McConnico Exit 44 (near Kingman) or north from I-40 Topock Exit 1 (take the Oatman Highway at Golden Shores).

At its peak, Oatman had 12,000 citizens, 7 hotels, 20 saloons, and a stock exchange. The bust came in the 1930s, but the town hung on as a stop on Route 66 for a while, then as a tourist destination. Many of the old buildings survive, including the two-story **Oatman Hotel** *(tel 928/768-4408),* where Clark Gable and Carole Lombard honeymooned in 1939.

**Mohave Museum of History and Arts**

- ✉ 400 W. Beale St.
- ☎ 928/753-3195
- 🕐 Closed Sun.
- 💲 $ (includes Route 66 Museum)

**www.mohave museum.org**

**Hualapai Mountain Park**

- ✉ 6250 Hualapai Mountain Rd., Kingman, AZ 86401
- ☎ 928/681-5700 or 877/757-0915
- 💲 $$

**www.mcparks.com**

## The Oatman Tragedy

Thirteen-year-old Olive Oatman had no idea what lay ahead as she traveled with her family across what is now southern Arizona in 1850. Indians attacked and left all for dead except for Olive and her younger sister Mary Ann, whom they carried off as slaves. A group of Mohave Indians traded for the sisters and incorporated them into the tribe. Mary Ann died during a famine, but Olive later reunited with her brother Lorenzo, who had survived the massacre. News of Olive's rescue ignited intense interest in the newspapers, and citizens renamed their mining town "Oatman" to commemorate her story.

Another Oatman attraction will likely find *you:* Burros—descendants of those used by prospectors—wander down the street, hoping to be fed. It's best not to; these critters can bite. Saloons and shops provide other diversions in town. ■

# On the Road—Route 66

The "Mother Road," as writer John Steinbeck called it, beckons us to previous eras when the asphalt led to the promised land of California, when every motel and restaurant had its own identity, and when driving could be a romantic adventure. Route 66 once ran from Chicago to Los Angeles in an unbroken 2,400-mile ribbon, carrying generations of Americans to new homes and dreams and holidays.

Those times seemed to end in October 1984, when the last stretch of I-40 was paved at Williams, bypassing the old road forever. Songwriter Bobby Troup sang his "Get your kicks on Route 66" one last time in a sentimental ceremony to mark the passing of US 66 as a highway. Not everyone shed tears—gone were the long lines of traffic funneling down the narrow two-lane road.

Yet Route 66 still runs across the Arizona countryside, still goes through the old downtowns, and still passes some of the old cafés and motor courts used by early motorists. The highway can be lonely, giving its travelers a chance to contemplate the scenery and the past. Short segments in eastern and central Arizona worthwhile for history or scenery include Holbrook (I-40 Exits 285 and 289), Winslow (I-40 Exits 252 and 257), Flagstaff (I-40 Exits 191 and 204), Coconino National Forest (I-40 Exits 171 and 178), Williams (I-40 Exits 161 and 165), and Ash Fork (I-40 Exits 144 and 146).

The longest continuous stretch of Route 66 twists across 158 miles of western Arizona from a desolate junction east of Seligman (I-40 Exit 139) to near the California border (I-40 Exit 1). Take the I-40 Crookton Road Exit 139 for a gently undulating ride to Seligman, where

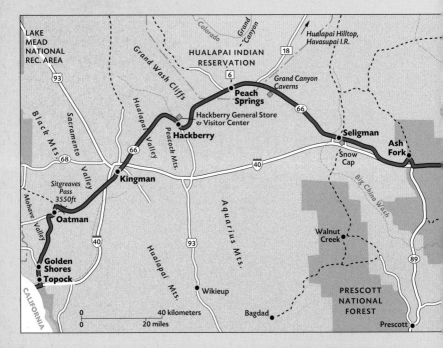

you can drop into the colorful Degadillo's Snow Cap for a soda or burger and perhaps a joke or two. Vast chambers of Grand Canyon Caverns lie underground off Route 66 northwest of Seligman. A detour to the north via Indian Route 18 leads to Hualapai Hilltop on the Havasupai Indian Reservation, where a hiking trail descends to waterfalls and pools (see pp. 54–55). On the Hualapai Indian Reservation, you can take back roads into the depths of the Grand Canyon or to overlooks on the rim (see pp. 56–57). The road skirts the south end of the Grand Wash Cliffs–the escarpment that marks the lower end of the Grand Canyon to the north–then passes the Hackberry General Store & Visitor Center. Stop at this homestead and former gas station to see its vintage cars, signs, and other Route 66 memorabilia.

After curving past the north end of the Peacock Mountains, Route 66 sweeps across the Hualapai Valley to Kingman, where it becomes Andy Devine Avenue through downtown. The road crosses the Sacramento Valley, climbs

**Old pickup trucks with rounded lines and lots of rust add to the ambience along Route 66.**

over the Black Mountains at 3,550-foot-high Sitgreaves Pass, and descends through Oatman, an old mining town (see p. 131). After a run southwest across the Mohave Valley, the old road meets I-40 Exit 1 near the Colorado River.

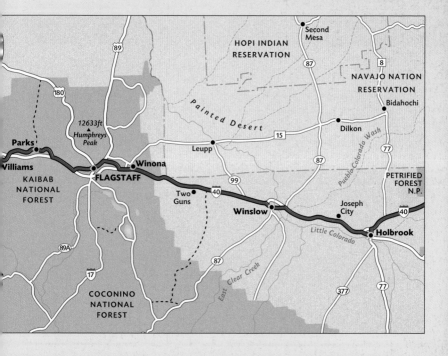

# Lake Mead National Recreation Area

Straddling the boundary between Arizona and Nevada, two giant reservoirs—Lake Mead and Lake Mohave—together form the centerpiece of this national recreation area. With the section of the Colorado River that connects them in Black Canyon, they provide many opportunities for fun. Small beaches and coves beckon. You can rent boats at the marinas and pick up supplies. Adventurous travelers can explore jeep roads and hike quiet backcountry.

Boats give access to spots tucked into the Black Canyon on the Colorado River below Hoover Dam.

### Lake Mead National Recreation Area

⚑ 129 A5–A6

**Visitor information**

✉ Alan Bible Visitor Center, Lake Mead NRA, near junction of US 93 & Nev. 166—closed into 2011; go to the admin. office: 601 Nevada Hwy., Boulder City, NV 89005

☎ 702/293-8990

💲 $$

www.nps.gov/lame

**Lake Mead** reaches into the lower Grand Canyon, where the raging rapids fade into a smooth current. After gliding smoothly beneath towering cliffs, the water emerges abruptly at the Grand Wash Cliffs into a broad desert valley.

Another major tributary, the Virgin River, feeds the lake's Overton Arm from the north. These two arms are responsible for 110-mile-long Lake Mead's roughly Y shape.

Hoover Dam holds back the reservoir—at 247 square miles, it is the largest reservoir in the United States. **Temple Bar Resort** is the

only developed area along the Arizona shores.

**Alan Bible Visitor Center** overlooks Lake Mead from the Nevada shore. It is near Boulder City, just 4 miles from Hoover Dam. A video program and exhibits tell of the area's natural and human history. Handouts include maps, places to visit, announcements of interpretive programs, and lists of plants and animals. The botanical garden outside identifies local species.

The 4.5-mile (one way) **Historic Railroad Trail,** which begins nearby, makes its way through five

huge tunnels once used to haul penstock (water) pipes and heavy equipment toward the dam.

**Hoover Dam,** an engineering and artistic landmark started in 1920 and completed in 1935, attracts some one million visitors a year. It can store up to 9.2 trillion gallons of the Colorado River in its reservoir, giant Lake Mead. The dam has 17 generators, each of which can supply electricity to 100,000 households.

Exhibits and multimedia programs in the visitor center on the Nevada side illustrate the construction of the dam. Head one floor up to hear stories of those who worked on the dam. A level higher is a viewing platform for the dam and Black Canyon.

The old visitor center across the road offers more exhibits. Tours take you 530 feet down to the Penstock Viewing Platform and the power plant's 650-foot-long Nevada Wing. The easiest

parking at the dam *(for cars only)* is a covered lot near the visitor center. Outdoor lots on the Arizona side have paid and free parking *(for cars, RVs, and trailers)*.

Rafts, canoes, and kayaks float the Colorado River through **Black Canyon** from just below Hoover Dam. **Black Canyon River Adventures** operates trips to Willow Beach (see Travelwise p. 262). Besides the memorable canyon scenery, boaters can enjoy a flooded cave, hot waterfalls, hot springs, historical sites, and sightings of bighorn sheep.

**Lake Mohave** stretches 67 miles upstream from Davis Dam but has a maximum width of only 4 miles. The dam, completed in 1953, has overlooks but no tours. Reach it by driving several miles north from either Bullhead City or Laughlin. **Katherine Landing,** 6 miles north of Bullhead City, is the largest resort on the Arizona side of the water. ■

**Hoover Dam Visitor Center**

🗺 129 A6
☎ 702/494-2517 or 866/730-9097
💲 $$ visitor center, $$$–$$$$$ including tour

**www.usbr.gov/lc/ hooverdam**

## A Surprising World of Artful Creativity at Hoover Dam

The words "dam" and "fine art" rarely appear in the same sentence, but atop Hoover Dam you'll see intriguing art deco works in bronze and stone. Flanking the flagpole, the pair of bronze "Winged Figures of the Republic" by Norwegian-born Oskar Hansen (1882–1971) reflect American ideals, what Hansen described as "the immutable calm of intellectual resolution, and the enormous power of trained physical strength, equally enthroned in placid triumph of scientific accomplishment." Hansen also made the surrounding star map of more than 200 brass disks that show how the sky looked on September 30, 1935, when President

Franklin D. Roosevelt dedicated the dam. This date is also enshrined in a Wheel of Time below the flagpole; markers represent the building of the last great pyramid, the birth of Christ, and the building of Hoover Dam. Additionally, Hansen designed the terrazzo floor below the flagpole and the bas-reliefs on the Nevada and Arizona elevator towers atop the dam. The five Nevada bas-reliefs represent the benefits of the dam—flood control, navigation, irrigation, water storage, and power. The Arizona reliefs depict "the visages of those Indian tribes who have inhabited mountains and plains from ages distant."

# Lake Havasu City

The blue waters of Lake Havasu provide a striking setting for the town and its famous London Bridge. People come to ride fast watercraft, water-ski, sail, and fish on the vast lake.

History-rich London Bridge, dedicated in 1971, serves as a landmark for Lake Havasu City boaters.

**Lake Havasu City**

🅽 129 A4

**Visitor information**

✉ Lake Havasu City Convention & Visitors Bureau, 314 London Bridge Rd., Lake Havasu City, AZ 86403

☎ 928/453-3444 or 800/242-8278

🕐 Closed Sat.–Sun.

www.golakehavasu.com

Founded on the east shore of Lake Havasu by chain-saw manufacturer Robert McCulloch in 1963, this town features a remarkable centerpiece: **London Bridge** (an old Thames span transported from England and reassembled here). English architecture, food, and shopping add to the ambience. Parks and beaches near each end of the bridge make ideal spots for a stroll, picnic, or swim. Admire the bridge from **English Village;** turn west onto London Bridge Road from Arizona 95 and make the first left into the parking lot. You'll find a tourist office *(tel 928/855-5655)* along with a bit of re-created London. Tour boats and rental boats dock nearby. You can walk south along the shore to **Rotary Community Park.** For **London Bridge Beach,** drive across the bridge on McCulloch Boulevard and turn in at either of the first two lefts to parking. ∎

## EXPERIENCE: Canoeing the Colorado

The Colorado River glides through rugged canyon country between I-40 and **Lake Havasu** with ideal conditions for canoes and other small craft. Swift currents speed your way free of rapids. You can start from **Topock,** Arizona, where I-40 crosses the river, or from **Moabi Regional Park** upriver on the California side. After about seven hours and 14 miles on the river, you pull out at **Castle Rock Bay** on the upper end of Lake Havasu. Local outfitters offer canoe and kayak rentals along with shuttle services. (See "Canoeing" in Travelwise, p. 262.)

# Parker Strip

Lake Moovalya, held back by the Headgate Rock Dam just above Parker, is better known as the Parker Strip. Resorts and parks line its shores and the Colorado River for 11 miles upstream.

Parker originally served as a trade center for the Colorado River Indian Reservation and nearby mines. Today the town is a center for agriculture and visitors who come to enjoy life on the water. Most of the Arizona development lies along Riverside Drive (Business 95), which turns off Arizona 95 several miles north of Parker and rejoins the highway at Buckskin Mountain State Park.

A **scenic drive** takes in the river and the surrounding rugged mountains on a 32-mile loop along both shores. Start by crossing the bridge at Parker, then follow Parker Dam Road north along the California shore to Parker Dam, cross the dam, and return to Parker on Arizona 95 and Business 95.

Only the top third of **Parker Dam,** which holds back Lake Havasu, is visible because its builders had to dig 235 feet below the riverbed to secure the foundations. You can park at overlooks on each end.

Facilities at **La Paz County Park** *(8 miles N of Parker at 7350 Riverside Dr., tel 928/667-2069)* include a swimming beach, picnicking, and camping; across the road is **Emerald Canyon Golf Course** *(tel 928/667-3366).* **Buckskin Mountain State Park** *(11 miles N of Parker on Ariz. 95, tel 928/667-3231)* lies on a bend in the river with a swimming beach, fishing, picnicking, camping, boat

ramp, mountain hiking, wildlife (including bobcat, gray fox, and red-tailed hawk) and a seasonal store and café. **River Island State Park** *(12.5 miles N of Parker on Ariz. 95, tel 928/667-3386)* provides similar facilities at a smaller site.

Members of the Mohave, Hopi, Chemehuevi, and Navajo tribes live south of Parker on the Colorado River Indian Reservation. Find out more about the four tribes at the **Colorado River Indian Tribes (CRIT) Museum** *(2 miles SW of Parker at 2nd Ave. & Mohave Rd., tel 928/669-9211 ext. 1335, closed Sun.).* Look for exhibits on early peoples and on World

**Parker**

🅰 129 A3

**Visitor information**

✉ Parker Area Chamber of Commerce, 1217 California Ave., Parker, AZ 85344

☎ 928/669-2174

🕐 Closed Sat. April–Oct. & Sun.

**www.parkerarea tourism.com**

In Quartzsite, the tomb of a Syrian camel driver marks the U.S. Army's attempt to use camels out West in the 1850s.

**Quartzsite**

🗺 129 A3

**Visitor information**

☎ 928/916-1090 or 888/878-2202

**www.quartzsite tourism.us**

War II Japanese relocation camps (see below).

**Poston Memorial Monument,** 13 miles south of the museum on the Parker-Ehrenberg road, commemorates the 17,867 people of Japanese ancestry who endured confinement at three camps nearby from May 1942 to November 1945. Most of the buildings have given way to farmland, but you can still see a large adobe auditorium in the distance across the road; it and other sites lie on private land. Look for a

campgrounds in the surrounding desert to socialize, soak up sunshine, and attend gem and mineral shows and swapfests.

The town of Quartzsite is 35 miles south of Parker on Arizona 95 at its junction with I-10 (Exits 17

**INSIDER TIP:**

**The one-day Yuma Airshow [www.yuma airshow.com] in March features military-plane air performances and ground displays. A gentle highlight: the Army Golden Knights Parachute Team.**

—LINDSEY SMITH
*National Geographic contributor*

---

**EXPERIENCE:**
# Driving the Back Roads to Swansea Townsite

Ruins of a large smelter and more than a dozen buildings still stand in **Swansea,** one of Arizona's best preserved ghost towns. High-clearance vehicles do best on the dirt roads to the site, 25 miles east of Parker. Built in 1909, the smelter allowed area mines to process their ore locally instead of shipping it to faraway places—such as Swansea in Wales. The town gradually faded away when the price of copper plummeted after World War I. Tourist offices have brochures with directions, as does the **BLM** (*2610 Sweetwater Ave., Lake Havasu City, AZ 86406, tel 928/505-1200, www.blm.gov/az/*).

---

and 19). **Tyson's Well Stage Station** (*just W of Ariz. 95 jct. downtown, tel 928/927-5229, www.quartzsite museum.com, call for hours, donation*) dates from 1866–1867. The adobe structure, built as a way station for travelers and their horses, houses exhibits about the area's miners and others who passed this way.

The **Hadji Ali Monument** in the cemetery on the west of town marks the resting place of a Syrian camel driver who came to the United States to help the Army conduct a camel experiment in 1856–1857. The hardy beasts showed promise as pack animals, but the Army abandoned the project during the Civil War. Hadji Ali stayed in the Southwest, becoming a prospector. ■

broken column beside the road, where you'll find the monument's information kiosk and inscriptions.

Nowhere do snowbirds descend on the desert in greater profusion than at the little town of **Quartzsite**. Their arrival takes place during the winter months. Thousands of RVers stay in vast

# Yuma

This site in Arizona's southwestern corner has long been valued as the best place to cross the lower Colorado. Native Americans, the Spanish, and early settlers left a rich heritage that you can explore at historic sites and museums. Recreation on the Colorado River and its lakes, along with shopping in nearby Mexico, makes Yuma a popular destination today.

In winter, the warm sunshine draws an estimated 80,000 snowbirds, more than doubling the town's population. An attractive pedestrian mall on a downtown section of Main Street comprises restaurants, shops, and the colorful **Lute's Casino,** a 1940s gambling hall that is now a popular spot for pool, dominoes, video games, and fast food.

Exhibits and period rooms in the **Sanguinetti House Museum** downtown give a feel for the region's Native Americans, explorers, soldiers, missionaries, miners, riverboat captains, and early settlers. The house, one of the oldest in town, dates from the 1870s. Subtropical vegetation and exotic birds thrive in a garden in back. The Adobe Annex next door sells local crafts and a good selection of historical books. The Garden Café, a pleasant spot farther back and next to the museum's gardens, serves breakfast and lunch.

In 1875 the territorial legislature awarded Yuma the funds to build a major prison. The hostile desert and the rough currents of the Colorado and Gila Rivers discouraged escape attempts. For 33 years, 29 women and some 3,000 men gazed through iron bars here. By 1909 the site proved too small; the prisoners were shipped

The 1922 St. Thomas Mission (a reproduction of the 1780 mission) stands on Indian Hill across the Colorado River.

to new quarters in Florence.

The prison is now the **Yuma Territorial Prison State Historic Park.** Step into the prison cells and imagine what life here must have been like. In the museum, photos and stories of the inmates and guards recount escape attempts, riots, and daily life. Outside, you can climb a watchtower, visit the graveyard, and walk down to the riverbank.

**Yuma Quartermaster Depot State Historic Park** vividly

## Yuma
🏕 129 A1

**Visitor information**

✉ Yuma Visitors Bureau, 201 N. 4th Ave., Yuma, AZ 85364 (at Yuma Quartermaster Depot State Historic Park)

☎ 928/783-0071 or 800/293-0071

**www.visityuma.com**

### Sanguinetti House Museum

✉ 240 S. Madison Ave.

☎ 928/782-1841

🕐 Closed Sun.–Mon.

💲 $

www.arizona historicalsociety.org

### Yuma Territorial Prison State Historic Park

✉ Giss Pkwy. & Prison Hill Rd.

☎ 928/783-4771

💲 $$

www.azstateparks .com

### Yuma Quartermaster Depot State Historic Park

✉ 201 N. 4th Ave. (before the Colorado River bridge)

☎ 928/329-0471

www.azstateparks .com

illustrates the importance of this site for early travelers. Original buildings include the restored commanding officer's quarters, which date from 1859. An office in the quartermaster depot looks as it did during the Indian wars from 1864 to 1883, when the depot supplied vital goods to posts all over the Southwest. Steamboats tied up nearby with cargo from ships docked at Port Isabel, near the mouth of the Colorado River. The goods then traveled farther upstream by steamboat or over-land on mule-drawn wagons to Army posts.

A 1907 Southern Pacific locomotive symbolizes the end of the steamboat era. A section of plank road used by early motorists to cross sand dunes dates from 1916, while a 1931 Model A truck represents the vehicles used by Dust Bowl victims of the 1930s.

The **Yuma Art Center** (254

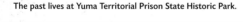

The past lives at Yuma Territorial Prison State Historic Park.

**INSIDER TIP:**

## Some 20 miles west of Yuma stretch the Imperial Sand Dunes. Portions are closed to cars but open to hikers and horse riders.

—SHEILA BUCKMASTER
National Geographic Traveler
*magazine editor at large*

S. Main St., tel 928/373-5202, www.yumafinearts.org, closed Mon.) downtown offers varied exhibits in the museum from the permanent collection and visiting shows. Plays, musicals, and concerts provide entertainment in the adjacent theater. Staff can tell you about classes and other art happenings in the Yuma area.

Two museums operated by local Native American tribes offer historical and cultural exhibits. Call before you go to check opening times.

The **Quechan Museum** (tel 760/572-0661) lies across the river from Yuma in an 1855 building of Fort Yuma. Take Fourth Avenue or I-8 to Winterhaven, turn right on S24, and follow the signs.

To reach **Cocopah Museum** (tel 928/627-1992, www.cocopah. com/cultural.html, closed Sat.–Sun.), head south 13 miles on US 95 to Somerton; go 1 mile farther, turn right and go 1 mile on Avenue G; turn left and drive about 2 miles on 15th Street, turn right after the railroad tracks, then take the next right, following signs for "West Cocopah Indian Reservation" and "Tribal Headquarters." ■

Phoenix, the geographic, governmental, and business heart
of Arizona, with an intensity unmatched in the rest of the state

# South-central Arizona

Welcome to Phoenix City Hall.

# South-central Arizona

Phoenix lies in the broad Salt River valley, whose waters, diverted by canals farther upstream, nourish both people and crops. You are likely to hear the area called the Valley of the Sun for its warm climate and average of 300 sunny days a year.

An early farming culture called the Hohokam began settling along the shores of the Salt and nearby Gila Rivers about A.D. 1. They dug canals to channel water to their fields of corn, beans, squash, cotton, and other crops. Wild plants, small game, and fish rounded out their diet. Residents lived in year-round villages of mud-walled, partly underground pit houses and later also in aboveground houses of adobe. The Hohokam created beautiful pottery and jewelry, played in ball courts, and built large platform mounds for ceremonial purposes. About 1450, less than a century before the Spanish arrived, the Hohokam culture collapsed. Legends of the

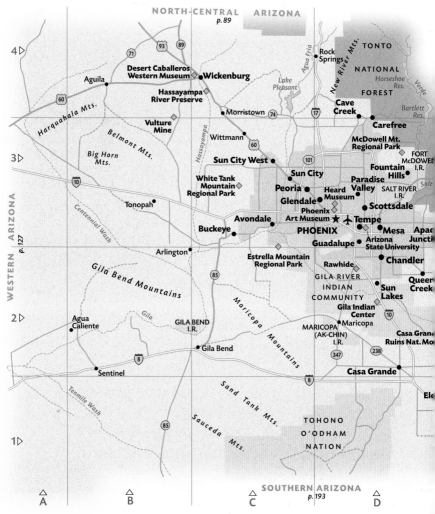

modern-day Pima and Tohono O'odham in southern Arizona trace their ancestry back to the Hohokam.

Apache tribes later roamed the Salt River Valley, preventing European settlement until the U.S. Army built Camp McDowell in 1865. Two years later, Jack Swilling, a prospector and former Confederate soldier, got some miners together and dug out the old Hohokam canals to irrigate fields. More farmers arrived and a town began to take shape. Darrel Duppa, an adventurer who could speak five languages fluently (all at once when drunk, it is said), proclaimed it "Phoenix," a city that would rise from the ancient Hohokam ruins just as the mythical Egyptian bird arose from its ashes.

By 1889, the young town had secured

## NOT TO BE MISSED:

**Visiting the restored Arizona Capitol   144–145**

**The Heard Museum's outstanding native cultures exhibits   147–148**

**A sense of the Old West at the Desert Caballeros Western Museum   150**

**The Desert Botanical Garden's displays of diverse flora   153**

**Discovering Wildlife World Zoo & Aquarium's exotic wildlife   154**

**Tonto National Monument for its two cliff dwellings   169**

**Boyce Thompson Arboretum State Park's beauty and wildlife   169**

the territorial capital and grown to become a political, business, and agricultural hub. World War II brought the rapid growth of aviation and other critical industries, boosting the population and the economy. Newcomers liked the area and stayed on—many, including retirees and snowbirds, continue to do so.

Phoenix's neighbors in the Salt River Valley include Tempe (home of Arizona State University) to the southeast, Scottsdale (renowned for its resorts and art galleries) to the northeast, Mesa (Arizona's third largest city and home of the Mormons' Arizona Temple) farther east, and Glendale (the state's antiques capital and fourth largest city) to the northwest. ■

40 kilometers
20 miles

Area of map detail

# Downtown Phoenix

Formerly staid downtown Phoenix has become a lively place thanks to a building boom that began in the 1990s, adding new museums, sports stadiums, entertainment venues, and skyscrapers. Head downtown for a look at both the past and the future of Arizona's largest city with a population of close to 1.5 million.

St. Mary's Basilica on East Monroe Street, completed in 1914, recalls a time before downtown filled with skyscrapers.

chambers to get a sense of history. A lifelike figure of George Wiley Paul Hunt presides in the governor's office. (Mr. Hunt, Arizona's first governor upon statehood, served seven terms.)

Other rooms contain exhibits illuminating Arizona's people and events. Artifacts from the U.S.S. *Arizona,* including its silver service, illustrate life aboard the battleship before its destruction at Pearl Harbor on December 7, 1941; there is also a piece of the battered ship itself. To dig deeper into the state's history, go to the research library in Room 300, where you can see a set of

## Phoenix

🅰 142 D3 & 144–145

### Visitor information

✉ Greater Phoenix Convention & Visitors Bureau, 125 N. 2nd St., Ste. 120, Phoenix, AZ 85004

☎ 602/254-6500 or 877/225-5749

🕐 Closed Sat.–Sun.

**www.visitphoenix .com**

A view west down Washington Street takes in the shiny copper dome of the **Arizona State Capitol.** Dating from 1900, the building has been well restored to the time when Arizona made the transition from a territory to a state 12 years later. Guided tours begin at 10 a.m. and 2 p.m. *(Mon.–Fri.),* or you can go around on your own. Details to look for include the 16-foot "Winged Victory" wind vane atop the dome and a state seal inlaid in the floor of the rotunda. Step into the old offices and senate and house

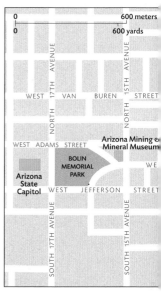

1937 murals, "Pageant of Arizona Progress." Outside in front, the many monuments in the Wesley Bolin Memorial Plaza include an anchor and a signal mast from the *Arizona.* (There is free parking on the north side of the plaza; turn in off of Adams Street.)

Glittering gold and silver plus colorful copper drew many of Arizona's pioneers. The **Arizona Mining & Mineral Museum** displays fine specimens, along with some of the tools used by early miners. Fossils reveal the history of life from cyanobacteria more than one billion years old to the dinosaurs and more recent creatures. Housed in a striking Moorish-style building, the museum is also a good place to learn of upcoming rock and mineral shows and shop for rock-hounding books, minerals, and jewelry. (Free parking behind the museum.)

The **Wells Fargo History Museum** (145 W. Adams St. bet. 1st & 2nd Aves, tel 602/378-1852, closed Sat.–Sun.) displays a 1868 Concord coach along with gold nuggets mined in the Bradshaw Mountains, a Western art gallery, antique guns, and a recreated Wells Fargo office

In Arizona's first black high school, the **George Washington Carver Museum & Cultural Center** (415 E. Grant St., 2 blocks S of Chase Field, tel 602/254-7516, www.gwcmuseumculturalcenter .org, call for hours) relates the challenges, achievements, and life of Phoenix's African-American community, along with art exhibits.

The **Arizona Latino Arts and Cultural Center** (147 E. Adams St., tel 602/254-9817, www. alacaz.org, closed Sun.–Mon.) concentrates on the colorful and energetic art of Latin America, especially Chicano and Mexican cultures. Exhibits change several times a year.

**Arizona State Capitol**

- Map p. 144 & inside back cover C2
- 1700 W. Washington St.
- 602/926-3620
- Closed Sat.–Sun. & state holidays

www.lib.az.us/ museum

**Arizona Mining & Mineral Museum**

- Map p. 144
- 1502 W. Washington St. at 15th Ave.
- 602/771-1600
- Closed Sun. & state holidays
- $

www.mines.az.gov

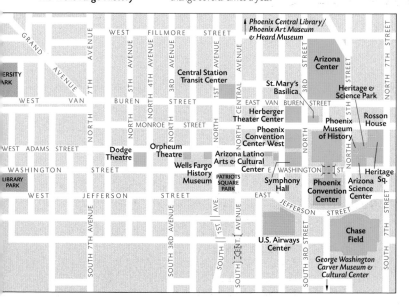

## Rosson House

- 🅰 Map p. 145
- ✉ Heritage & Science Park
- ☎ 602/262-5070
- 🕐 Closed Mon.–Tues. & mid-Aug.–Mem. Day
- 💲 $$

www.rossonhouse museum.org

## Arizona Science Center

- 🅰 Map p. 145
- ✉ Heritage & Science Park
- ☎ 602/716-2000
- 💲 $$$

www.azscience.org

You can view the last remaining residential block of the original township at the **Heritage & Science Park.** Here, in addition to some of Phoenix's earliest buildings, you will find the Arizona Science Center. (Park in the covered lot on the grounds at the southeast corner of Monroe and Fifth Streets; museums and businesses validate parking.)

The elegant 1895 **Rosson House** is the centerpiece of a group of venerable residences and shops. Not until the railroad arrived in 1887, bringing wood for construction and for firing brick kilns, did wood-frame and brick houses become practical. Before, residents had to live in adobe houses not much different from those of the early Hohokam. Tours of Rosson House tell the story of its construction and residents.

Neighboring buildings date from the early 20th century. The 1901 Stevens House is where you will find the **Arizona Doll & Toy Museum** (tel 602/253-9337, closed Mon. & Aug.). The **Bouvier-Teeter House** (1899) is now the Teeter House Tea Room (tel 602/252-4682, www.theteeterhouse.com, closed Mon. & mid-Aug.–mid-Sept.). The **Baird Machine Shop** (1929) and **Thomas House** (1909) next door house the Pizzeria Bianco (tel 602/258-8300, dinner only, closed Sun.–Mon.). The 1900 **Silva House** hosts The Rose and Crown, which serves traditional English pub fare (tel 602/256-0223).

"Have fun with science," suggests the **Arizona Science Center,** where you can choose from hundreds of hands-on experiments. Staff offer daily presentations and frequently add new exhibits to explore and celebrate such fields as the digital world, the mind, the body, the environment, optics, forces, and space. Art shows and visiting exhibits illustrate the beauty of science. Radio hams at station W7ASC show how to "work the world." A planetarium features star shows and animated journeys through the universe. Spectacular movies, some in 3D, play in the giant-screen IMAX theater. Check out the Arizona Science Center's website to see what's happening—there's a lot going on every day—and to try some online experiments.

The interactive Water Works fountain performs tricks when you activate one of the sensors that have been installed around it. Finally, the Awesome Atoms Science Store offers a large selection of educational toys and projects.

## EXPERIENCE:
## Rise Above It All

Floating in a **hot-air balloon** peacefully through the air provides new perspectives on Arizona's landscapes and a chance to see wildlife. Most flights lift off from desert regions at around sunrise; some companies also offer evening rides. You can rise into the sky year-round, depending on location, though flights may be suspended during the hot months in the lower desert. The **Phoenix, Sedona,** and **Tucson** areas are especially popular for balloon rides; drop by an information center or search the Internet for "Arizona hot-air balloon."

Elegant, clean-lined, and serene, the Phoenix Art Museum is itself a stunning work of art.

## Phoenix Art Museum

Beautiful and thought-provoking art from many ages and places appears in the spacious galleries here. Most of the temporary exhibits reside in nearby galleries on the ground floor, along with the Art of Asia Galleries.

The **Asian Collection** displays outstanding Chinese ceramics, cloisonné, bronzes, and paintings, as well as artwork from Japan, Tibet, India, and Southeast Asia.

The **Modern Art Collection** represents many of the pioneers of European and American modernism such as Pablo Picasso, Jean Cocteau, and Georgia O'Keeffe. Exciting work by top international artists turn up in the **Contemporary Collection.** The **Western American Collection** covers portrayals of Arizona exploration through the 1800s, as well as contemporary work. Nearby you will find the fascinating **Thorne Miniature Rooms,** which replicate historic European and American domestic interiors

at a charming scale of 1 to 12.

In the **Latin American Collection** you'll find portraits from Spanish colonial times, religious art, and decorative arts as well as 20th-century Mexican pieces by artists such as Diego Rivera. The museum's **American Collection,** dating from 1790 to 1930, reflects three themes: American People, Americans Abroad, and the American Landscape.

In the three galleries of the **European Collection,** look for "Salome with the Head of St. John the Baptist" by Dolci; "Madame Victoire" by Vigée-Lebrun; and "The Kiss" by Rodin.

The **Fashion Design Collection** illustrates European and American trends, with an emphasis on 20th-century American designers. Families can explore various projects in the interactive gallery.

## Heard Museum

Outstanding exhibits on the Native American tribes and lands of the Southwest are on

**Phoenix Art Museum**

🅰 142 D3 & inside back cover D2

✉ 1625 N. Central Ave.

☎ 602/257-1222

🕐 Closed Mon.

💲 $$$

**www.phxart.org**

## Heard Museum

142 D3 & inside back cover D2

✉ 2301 N. Central Ave.

☎ 602/252-8848 (recorded information & events) or 602/252-8840 (administration)

💲 $$$

**www.heard.org**

tap at this museum. The galleries in the Spanish colonial-style building take you through the centuries, from prehistoric times to the present. Courtyards with fountains and sculptures add to the enjoyment of wandering through the museum.

Native Americans express their thoughts—and music—in the audiovisual program called "HOME: Native People in the Southwest." Exhibits of jewelry, tools, pottery, weaving, and basketry all help tell the story of how the tribes adapted to and interacted with the land.

Along the way you will pass reproductions of an Apache wickiup dwelling, a Navajo hogan,

A hoop dancer at the Heard Museum shows how it's done.

and a Hopi corn-grinding room. A stunning exhibition of kachina dolls (see pp. 86–87), many from the collection of Senator Barry Goldwater, hints at the complexity of Hopi religious and ceremonial beliefs. Contemporary Native American artists express their feelings in a variety of subjects, media, and forms.

Visitors of all ages will find something of interest at the Heard. Families and small children can do projects. You can take a docent-led tour, view a variety of films, or study in the research library. Special programs are an integral part of the museum's offerings. On Saturdays there are music or dance performances, artists' demonstrations, or workshops; call or check the website for the schedule.

Several major festivals take place annually. The **World Championship Hoop Dance Contest** in early February hosts top dancers for amazing feats of agility. The **Guild Indian Market and Fair** on the first weekend in March attracts more than 700 of the finest Native American artists. Other festivals include the **Kachina Doll Marketplace** in April and the **Navajo Weavers Marketplace** and **Spanish Market** in November. The museum shop—an attraction in itself—has top-quality jewelry, art, crafts, kachina dolls, and books. (For free parking, turn east at the sign off Central Avenue.) The museum has a branch with exhibits and a shop in north Scottsdale; check the Heard Museum website or call for details. ■

# North Phoenix

Two attractions north of the city throw light on the people who lived in Arizona during two very different periods of the area's long and intriguing history: Its earliest beginnings (deep in prehistory) and the territorial years (a time of profound growth).

A superb group of more than 1,500 petroglyphs is the focus of the **Deer Valley Rock Art Center.** Here, Hohokam, Patayan, and Archaic peoples carved symbols into boulders some 800 to 5,000 years ago. Modern-day groups continue to feel a connection with the ancient designs and hold them sacred.

Visitor center exhibits and a video introduce the rock art from various perspectives: those of archaeologists, Native Americans, and physical scientists. Petroglyphs cover volcanic boulders near the end of a handicapped-accessible trail. The gift shop sells jewelry inspired by the rock art, clothing, reproductions, and books. To reach the center, take I-17 Deer Valley Road Exit 217B (about 18 miles north of downtown) and go west 2.5 miles, bearing right at the fork.

At the **Pioneer Living History Village,** visitors can stroll through a town of some 30 buildings from the state's early years—a vivid portrayal of what life was like for Arizonans between the mid-1800s and statehood in 1912. The buildings in the village are either originals that have been moved here or reconstructions built from photographs or actual plans.

Residences include the home of John Sears, one of the first wood-framed houses in Phoenix. A miner's cabin and ranch buildings recall the rough living conditions in remote corners of the state. Other buildings include the opera house, church, bank, and shops. Costumed interpreters often work in the blacksmith shop or the one-room schoolhouse. Horses and other animals bring life to the farms.

Check the website or call to find out the times of special events, such as cowboy shows, historical reenactments, and melodramas. The community celebrates Statehood Day on the weekend nearest February 14—anniversary of both the village and the state itself.

### INSIDER TIP:

While rocks take center stage at Deer Valley Rock Art Center, there are also desert plants galore.

—SHEILA BUCKMASTER
National Geographic Traveler
*magazine editor at large*

Pioneer the Past *(tel 623/465-1821)* serves meals and has a magnificent 1861 bar. You will find this spot just west of I-17 Pioneer Road Exit 225, about 26 miles north of downtown. ■

**Deer Valley Rock Art Center**
- Inside back cover C4
- 3711 W. Deer Valley Rd.
- 623/582-8007
- Closed Mon.
- $$
www.dvrac.asu.edu

**Pioneer Living History Village**
- Inside back cover C5
- 3901 W. Pioneer Rd.
- 623/465-1052
- Closed Mon.–Tues.
- $$
www.pioneeraz.org

# Wickenburg

**In 1863 the promise of gold attracted German immigrant Henry Wickenburg to the scenic hills of the Sonoran Desert, where he struck it rich. The rush was on at the Vulture Mine, but water was needed for processing, so miners hauled the ore 14 miles northeast to a site beside the Hassayampa River. Three years later the riverside mining camp had grown to become Arizona's third largest town. Indeed, Wickenburg nearly won the right to be its state capital.**

Cowboys as authentic as they come work the range and lead trail rides near Wickenburg.

Wickenburg lies 58 miles northwest of Phoenix via US 60/Grand Avenue, but the less congested route via I-17 and Arizona 74 is quicker and easier. Today, it has a Western atmosphere where you can explore a ghost town, ride the range, and stay at guest ranches (see Travelwise). A walking tour *(details available from the Wickenburg Chamber of Commerce, 216 N. Frontier St., tel 928/684-5479 or 800/942-5242, www.outwickenburgway.com)* takes in many sights downtown including the Jail Tree, a 200-year-old mesquite to which 19th-century outlaws were chained.

The **Desert Caballeros Western Museum** *(21 N. Frontier St., tel 928/684-2272, www.westernmuseum.org)* reveals the beauty of the land and the spirit of the people through its range of artistic, natural, and historical exhibits. Dioramas illustrate Henry Wickenburg's discovery of gold and the frenzied activity that followed. Downstairs, you can walk into a street scene with period rooms from the early town.

Southwestern *caballeros* (horsemen) are one major theme of the museum: The "Spirit of the Cowboy" exhibit displays old and modern

**INSIDER TIP:**

Among the Desert Caballeros Western Museum's Frederic Remington bronzes and Charlie Russell canvases is a terrific collection of handmade iron spurs—dozens of them—plus notable hand-tooled saddles.

—ANNE Z. COOKE
National Geographic Traveler *magazine writer*

cowboy gear along with rodeo, movie, and parade memorabilia. Valuable ores and precious stones gleam in the **Gem & Mineral Room,** while the **Native American Room** exhibits tribal artistry in the form of stone carvings, pottery, basketry, and kachina dolls. Paintings and sculpture by outstanding Western artists such as Frederic Remington and Charles Russell are the focus of the **Western Art Galleries.** The small park in back features "Thanks for the Rain," a life-size bronze sculpture by Joe Beeler, along with some picnic tables.

The town's riverbed is usually dry, but the river resurfaces for a 5-mile section downstream in the **Hassayampa River Preserve** (*49614 N. Hwy. 60, tel 928/684-2772, http://nature.org/ arizona; check for hours*); Hassayampa is Apache for "river that runs upside down." Managed by the Nature Conservancy, a network of trails loop through the lush vegetation to spring-fed Palm Lake, the riverbank, and across the river to a viewpoint. More than 280 species of bird live, visit, or nest in the 700-acre preserve. The huge trees provide perches for raptors such as the zone-tailed and black hawks, which fly in from Mexico to breed. Marshy Palm Lake attracts great blue heron, white-faced ibis, pied-billed grebe, and others. The riverbank is a good place to spot mule deer and javelina—plus the tracks of mountain lion, bobcat, and ring-tailed cat.

The 1860s four-room adobe that houses the visitor center has seen use as a ranch, a

stagecoach way station, and one of the state's first guest ranches. Today it is worth a stop to see the displays on local wildlife and flora, including the rare Goodding willow-Fremont cottonwood forest found here.

With dials and levers stuck in the past, this electric generator at the Vulture Mine sits idle.

## EXPERIENCE:
## Ore-of-Yore Lore

The **Vulture Mine** (*tel 602/ 859-2743, closed July–Aug.*) is an example of a mine and ghost town that have been neither destroyed nor dressed up for tourists. A self-guided tour (wear good walking shoes) takes you along dusty roads to the old head frame, where a mine shaft plunges more than 2,000 feet into the earth. It's not safe to enter the shafts, but above ground you can see the ball mill, power plant, assay office, black-smith shop, and apartments and mess hall. For safety, stay on the marked trail, keeping an eye peeled for rattlesnakes.

To visit the mine, head west out of Wickenburg for 2.5 miles on Wicken-burg Way, then turn south and drive 12 miles on paved Vulture Mine Road. The entrance is on your right

# East Phoenix

You'll find a sprinkling of major sights in and around Papago Park—on the east edge of Phoenix. The beautiful landscape of rounded hills and thriving desert vegetation led to its protection as a national monument. Today it's a city park with the Desert Botanical Garden, Phoenix Zoo, picnicking, easy hiking and biking trails, and ball fields.

Visitors can see rebuilt Hohokam homes at Pueblo Grande Museum & Archaeological Park.

### Pueblo Grande Museum & Archaeological Park

🅰 Inside back cover D2

✉ 4619 E. Washington St. (E of downtown)

☎ 602/495-0900

🕐 Closed Sun.–Mon. May–Sept.

💲 $$

www.pueblogrande.com

### Phoenix Zoo

🅰 Inside back cover D2

✉ 455 N. Galvin Pkwy. (in central Papago Park)

☎ 602/273-1341

💲 $$$$

www.phoenixzoo.org

The **Pueblo Grande Museum & Archaeological Park** reveals the life of Hohokam farmers (see pp. 142–143) through the ruins of a major village and excellent exhibits; don't miss the ceramics and jewelry. A map of an intricate canal network shows how the Hohokam brought water to their fields in the desert, and you'll see some of the tools they used to tend their waterways and crops.

The Hohokam began construction of a large platform mound atop a terrace overlooking the Salt River about 1150. Rooms for residential or religious use sat on top. Possible solstice markings suggest the tribe had a calendar to guide planting and harvesting of crops.

Signs along a short trail to the top of the mound describe layout and construction details. The trail also leads to a reconstructed pit house and adobe compound, then to a depression thought to have been a ball court. Visitors can watch a video illustrating how life may have been for the Hohokam. Children can take part in archaeology projects, and the shop sells books and Native American crafts. Ask the staff for information on hikes, tours, and special events.

A visit to the **Phoenix Zoo** brings you into contact with the exotic wildlife of the tropical rain forest, savanna, wetland, desert hills, and temperate woodland. Natural-looking enclosures are used instead of cages when possible. Animals

**INSIDER TIP:**

Lewis Carroll wrote of the boojum tree in *The Hunting of the Snark.* This odd bit of flora flourishes at the Desert Botanical Garden.

—ANNE Z. COOKE

National Geographic Traveler *magazine writer*

explore new scents and even get to forage for or chase after their food in behavioral enrichment programs. Rarely seen animals of Arizona, such as the Gila monster and mountain lion, are here too. A Safari Train (\$) with narration offers a good introduction. On the Children's Trail, young visitors can touch sculptures and pet tame animals. Schedules list the day's animal encounters, feeding times, and zookeeper talks. In summer, gates open at 7 a.m. to enable visitors to beat the heat.

Find out what it takes to be a cactus at the **Desert Botanical Garden,** a great setting to enjoy and learn about desert plants of Arizona and the world. The Desert Discovery Trail makes a 0.3-mile loop past thousands of plants, including more than half the world's cactus species. Short trails lead off to the Cactus and Succulent Galleries and to the Agave Yucca Forest. The Plants and People of the Sonoran Desert Trail interprets how Native Americans relied on the desert's resources. The Sonoran Desert Nature Trail shows the relationships between plants and wildlife, while the Herb

Garden demonstrates desert-adapted medicinal, culinary, and tea plants. On the 0.3-mile Desert Wildflower Trail you can see plants from the four deserts of the United States. The garden also has a café.

The **Arizona Historical Society Museum at Papago Park** brings the history of central Arizona to life. Enter the courtyard and follow the sound of rushing water to the outdoor exhibit about Roosevelt Dam, with displays of its stone blocks and construction machinery. Realistic scenes and interactive exhibits take you through the territorial years, agricultural accomplishments, transportation, military communities, and Phoenix's postwar boom. You'll learn about such notables as the Supreme Court's first female member, Sandra Day O'Connor. The museum hosts visiting exhibits and special events; guided tours and library access by appointment. ∎

## Fighting Fire

The Hall of Flame, near Papago Park, displays an amazingly large and well-preserved collection of firefighting equipment from all over the world. Hand- and steam-powered pumpers along with horse-drawn apparatus in the first gallery date back to the 18th and 19th centuries, while motorized trucks line up in the second gallery. Exhibits and videos commemorate the bravery of firefighters. A gift shop carries books and souvenirs with a firefighting theme.

**Desert Botanical Garden**
- Inside back cover D2
- 1201 N. Galvin Pkwy. (in northern Papago Park)
- 480/941-1225
- \$\$\$

www.dbg.org

**Arizona Historical Society Museum at Papago Park**
- Inside back cover D2
- 1300 N. College Ave., Tempe (SE corner of Papago Park)
- 480/929-9499
- Closed Mon.
- \$\$

www.arizona historicalsociety.org

**Hall of Flame**
- Inside back cover D2
- 6101 E. Van Buren St. (S of Papago Park)
- 602/275-3473
- \$\$

www.hallofflame.org

# West & South Phoenix

An exceptionally fine population of wildlife from the far corners of the world lies out in the western Valley of the Sun. To the south, Mystery Castle is a fanciful home built by a loving father.

Mystery Castle—a dream that became a reality just south of Phoenix—brims with folk art and is open for tours.

### Wildlife World Zoo & Aquarium

- Inside back cover B3
- 16501 W. Northern Ave. (Take I-10 W 18 miles to Cotton Lane/303 Loop Exit 124, then go 6 miles N)
- 623/935-9453
- $$$$$

www.wildlifeworld .com

### Mystery Castle

- Inside back cover D2
- 800 E. Mineral Rd. (7 miles S of downtown via 7th St.)
- 602/268-1581
- Closed Mon.– Wed. & June– Sept.
- $$

Many beautiful and exotic creatures live at the **Wildlife World Zoo & Aquarium,** established in 1974 as a breeding farm for rare species. You'll see ostriches (all five of the world's species), raptors, parrots, and waterfowl, and explore a walk-through aviary. Among the African animals are lion, rhinoceros, giraffe, and zebra. Oryx and other graceful antelope roam their enclosures. South America is represented by llamas, tapirs, and maned wolves. Monkeys perform their customary antics, and tigers prowl their territories. There is also an aquarium, reptile house, and small-mammal buildings.

You can get an even closer look at various small animals at the daily wildlife-encounter shows and feedings. Children also have the opportunity to enjoy five rides and an animal-petting area. The zoo also has a restaurant with aquarium views and a gift shop.

Not every little girl gets the castle of her dreams, but Mary Lou Gulley was different. As a child in Washington State, she would cry when the tide washed away her sand castles—she wanted a real one to live in! Her father, Boyce Luther Gulley, believing himself near death's door, disappeared in 1930. Unknown to his family, he had gone to the desert of Arizona and set to work on his daughter's vision. The result was **Mystery Castle.** Not until 1945 did Mary Lou discover his secret project and gift. Her father died just before sending for his family. Now Mary Lou and her assistants lead tours through this remarkable assemblage of folk art.

Call ahead to check hours. ∎

# Phoenix Out of Doors

The city parks offer plenty of room to roam, as well as a variety of scenery from grass and shady trees to the rugged landscapes and flora of the desert.

On the north side of downtown in **Margaret T. Hance Park,** monuments honor Phoenix's eight sister cities. The park's **Japanese Friendship Garden** *(tel 602/256-3204, www.japanesefriend shipgarden.org)* is open weekends and some weekdays and offers tea ceremonies (second Sat. of the month by reservation), October to May. **Phoenix Trolley Museum** *(tel 602/254-0307, www .phoenixtrolley.com),* in the park, is open Saturdays, October to May; check for hours.

**Encanto Park,** 2 miles northwest of downtown, offers greenery and a host of recreational opportunities. In the south half are picnic areas, playgrounds, a swimming pool, and courts for tennis, racquetball, volleyball, and basketball. **Enchanted Island** *(tel 602/254-1200, www.enchanted island.com, parking N of Encanto Blvd. bet. 7th & 15th Aves.)* runs a carousel, train, and other rides on weekends and some weekdays. A driving range and two golf courses are located in the park's north end.

Rock hills overlook a desert oasis at **Papago Park** in east Phoenix. Folks come to picnic, fish, and take easy hikes to the Hole in the Rock or former governor George W. P. Hunt's tomb.

For challenging hikes amid the city, head to **Phoenix Mountains Park and Recreation Area** or **Camelback Mountain,** northeast of downtown. **South Mountain Park,** 7 miles south of downtown, has a paved road to the summit, passing viewpoints, picnic areas, and trailheads. ■

## Phoenix Parks

### Visitor Information

✉ Phoenix Parks & Recreation Dept., 200 W. Washington St., 16th Fl., Phoenix, AZ 85003

☎ 602/262-6862

**http://phoenix.gov /parks**

### Encanto Park

⌦ Inside back cover C2

✉ 2605 N. 15th Ave. at Encanto Blvd.

### Papago Park

⌦ Inside back cover D2

✉ Take the Phoenix Zoo turnoff from Galvin Pkwy., then turn left to the recreation area

Encanto Park offers many recreational facilities in a verdant landscape near downtown Phoenix.

# Maricopa County Parks

Seven parks lie in scenic desert areas on the edge of the Valley of the Sun, just outside Phoenix. All have picnic areas, campgrounds, and recreation options. Lake Pleasant is the place for boating and fishing. The other parks have excellent trails for hiking, mountain biking, and horseback riding. You're likely to see birds and other wildlife, especially in the early morning and evening. Each park has maps and information for visitors; some parks have nature centers.

With more than 33 miles of trails, Estrella Mountain Park is heaven for low-carbon-footprint travel.

**Maricopa County Parks**

**Visitor information**

✉ 234 N. Central Ave., Ste. 6400, Phoenix, AZ 85004

☎ 602/506-2930

🕐 Office closed Sat.–Sun.

💲 $–$$ day use, $$–$$$$ camping

**www.maricopa.gov/parks**

Spanish explorers named the rugged mountains 26 miles southwest of Phoenix in **Estrella Mountain Regional Park** *(tel 623/932-3811)* for their star-shaped drainages. Trails lead off into the desert foothills and interconnect to make a variety of loops. Families like the park's huge grassy area with its ball fields, playgrounds, and picnic tables. You can also play on the nearby 18-hole **Estrella Mountain Golf Course** *(tel 623/932-3714)* or catch an event at a rodeo arena. To reach the park, take I-10 to Estrella Parkway Exit 126, go south for 5 miles, and then turn left half a mile.

The extensive trail system in **White Tank Mountain Regional Park** *(tel 623/935-2505),* some 30 miles west of Phoenix, climbs up canyons and high ridges. The mountains get their name from water-filled depressions that flash floods have carved in the bedrock. You can see one of these tanks in a canyon at the end of Waterfall Trail, an easy round-trip of about 2 miles; look for petroglyphs on boulders along the way.

Goat Camp, Ford Canyon, and Mesquite Canyon Trails all lead high into the mountains, where they meet. If you plan to head into the backcountry, rangers recommend that you see them for trail advisories; overnight trips require a permit. The picnic areas and campground offer magical sunrise and sunset views. To reach the park, take I-10 west 18 miles to Cotton Lane/Loop 303 Exit 124, go north 7 miles to Olive, then turn west to the entrance.

**Lake Pleasant Regional Park** (tel 928/501-1710) attracts boaters, anglers, and campers to the west shore of a 10,000-acre reservoir 30 miles northwest of Phoenix. Follow signs to Waddell Dam Overlook for the visitor center and gift shop. Nearby are a boat ramp, a marina, picnic areas, and two campgrounds. Reach Lake Pleasant from I-17 Exit 223; head west 11.5 miles on Arizona 74, turn right and drive 2.2 miles on Castle Hot Springs Road, then turn right into the park.

Trails loop through the rocky hills of an old mining area at **Cave Creek Regional Park** (tel 623/465-0431), 32 miles north of Phoenix, an equestrian favorite. Take I-17 to Exit 223, turn east and go 7 miles on Carefree Highway, then turn left and drive 1.6 miles on 32nd Street.

Many trails wend their way across the foothills and lower slopes in **McDowell Mountain Regional Park** (tel 480/471-0173), 25 miles northeast of Phoenix. Take Shea Boulevard or Arizona 87 to Fountain Hills, then turn north and drive about

5 miles to the entrance. Stop to see the town's fountain on Saguaro Boulevard; water jets to 560 feet on the hour, 10 a.m. to 9 p.m.

High cliffs of greenish volcanic ash deposits called tuff overlook **Usery Mountain Regional Park** (tel 480/984-0032), 25 miles east of Phoenix. Trails loop around the central area; the moderate Wind Cave Trail (3.2 miles round-trip) climbs to caves in Pass Mountain. The rugged Pass Mountain Trail goes 7.1 miles around the mountain. From the Superstition Freeway in Mesa, take Ellsworth Road/Usery Pass Road north about 7 miles to the entrance.

The trail network at **San Tan Mountain Regional Park** (480/655-5554), 45 miles southeast of Phoenix, offers a variety of experiences for hikers, mountain bikers, and equestrians. ■

## Javelina Lowdown

Despite their pig-like appearance, Javelina belong to another animal family, Tayassuidae. Medium size (45–90 pounds) and with poor eyesight, these critters have bristly gray hair and a white collar. Sharp tusks inspired their name, from the Spanish word for javelin. You're likely to see them running in small groups in desert and semidesert areas. You may notice their strong odor, earning them the name musk hogs. Prickly pear cactus and agave are their favorite foods, and they also search out roots, tubers, fruits, and small animals. They've even invaded the suburbs of Phoenix and Tucson to munch on garden plants. Maturity arrives by the age of two and breeding can take place year-round. Unlike true pigs, javelina cannot be domesticated.

**Estrella Mountain Regional Park**
142 C2 & Inside back cover B1–B2

**White Tank Mountain Regional Park**
142 C3

**Cave Creek Regional Park**
142 D4 & Inside back cover D5

**McDowell Mountain Regional Park**
142 C3 & Inside back cover E4–F4

# Tempe

In 1872, Charles Hayden chose this site on the Salt River's south bank for his trading post and later a ferry and a flour mill. Darrel Duppa, who had given Phoenix its name, dropped by Hayden's ferry one day and remarked that the area reminded him of the Vale of Tempe in Thessaly, Greece. The name stuck. In 1885, Arizona Territorial Normal School was established in the farming settlement, just southeast of Phoenix, and later became Arizona State University.

Local color: Downtown Tempe's Mill Avenue promises city fun, from people-watching to shopping.

**Tempe**

📍 142 D3

**Visitor information**

✉ Tempe Convention & Visitors Bureau, 51 W. 3rd St., Ste. 105, Tempe, AZ 85281

☎ 480/894-8158 or 800/283-6734

🕐 Closed Sat.–Sun.

**www.tempecvb.com**

Downtown Tempe (tem-PEE) centers on Mill Avenue, lined with restaurants, nightspots, and shops. Historic buildings include Hayden's early 1870s house (now Monti's Las Casa Vieja Restaurant) at Mill Avenue and Rio Salado Parkway, and commercial buildings dating from the late 1800s, such as the Hackett House/Tempe Bakery at 95 West Fourth Street, as well as three on South Mill Avenue: Hotel Casa Loma at No. 398, the Laird & Dines Building at No. 501, and the Tempe Hardware Building at No. 520. Tempe Town Lake has parks and boating on the Salt River just north of downtown.

The "Tempe: Distinct, Diverse, Dynamic" exhibit at the **Tempe Historical Museum** (*809 E. Southern Ave., www.tempe.gov/museum, tel 480/350-5100, closed Mon.*) dramatically stages stories of the city and explores its social, environmental, educational, and community history. Temporary shows are mounted too, and kids have their own gallery.

A visit to the 1892 **Niels Peterson House** gives insight into the lives of early settlers. Tours explain the house's evolution from Queen Anne–Victorian to 1930s bungalow. You'll also learn about the house's noted residents.

## Arizona State University

ASU has become one of the nation's biggest universities (more than 60,000 students on four campuses) with a beautifully landscaped 720-acre main campus. Highlights include the ASU Art Museum, smaller museums, cultural activities, and sporting events. ASU's website provides maps, parking information, museum and library details, campus tour schedules, self-guided tours of public art and the Arboretum (which covers the entire Tempe campus), and events. Make sure to keep an eye (and ear) out for students zipping by on scooters, bikes, and in-line skates.

The **Nelson Fine Arts Center,** built in gray-purple stucco, reflects the color of a nearby hill. This complex of geometric buildings interspersed with terraces and plazas won an award for its architect Antoine Predock. Inside, the spacious galleries of the **ASU Art Museum** hosts groundbreaking shows by contemporary artists along with works from the American, Latin American, and print collections. Outdoor terraces display sculpture. The gift shop sells many fine handicrafts and books. The Nelson center also includes a theater, dance laboratory, and performance spaces. To visit the center, turn east from Mill Avenue onto Tenth Street and look for parking at the meters or in the nearby lot at Tenth and Myrtle.

A short walk from the Nelson center, at **Northlight Gallery** (Tyler Mall, tel 480/965-6517, closed Fri., Sun., & summer) in Matthews Hall, the photographic exhibits are selected from historical and contemporary collections.

MFA (master of fine arts) students exhibit their work in the **Harry Wood Gallery** (Forest Mall, closed Sat.–Sun.) in the Art Building. Drawings and scale models illustrate the newest architectural designs in the **Gallery of Design** (Forest Mall, tel 480/965-6693, closed Sat.–Sun.), which is part of the College of Design.

The **Museum of Anthropology** (Cady Mall, tel 480/965-6224, closed Sat.–Sun.) interprets Hohokam and contemporary Native American cultures along with exhibits on archaeological techniques and anthropology.

### INSIDER TIP:

**Sip the goods at Tempe's Four Peaks Brewery (1340 E. 8th Street). Hot day? Sit down at a table under the misting system.**

—LINDSEY SMITH
*National Geographic contributor*

The university's scientific exhibits are equally varied, ranging from live rattlesnakes and other reptiles at the **Life Sciences Center** (Tyler Mall, tel 480/965-3396, closed Sat.–Sun.) to visitors from outer space in the **Center for Meteorite Studies** (Palm Walk, tel 480/965-6511, closed Sat.–Sun.), located in Room C-139 and adjacent hallways of the Physical Sciences Building.

### Niels Petersen House

- ✉ 1414 W. Southern Ave.
- ☎ 480/350-5151
- 🕒 Closed Sun.–Mon. & Fri.; last tour 1:30 p.m.

### Arizona State University

- 🗺 142 D3

**Visitor information**

- ✉ University Dr. & Mill Ave., Tempe, AZ 85287
- ☎ 480/965-5728
- **www.asu.edu**

### ASU Art Museum

- ✉ Nelson Fine Arts Center, 10th St. & Mill Ave.
- ☎ 480/965-2787 (museum) or 480/965-6447 (box office)
- 🕒 Closed Sun.–Mon.
- **http://asuartmuseum.asu.edu**

### Four Peaks Brewery

- **www.fourpeaks.com**

In the same building, star shows are staged some days in the **ASU Planetarium** *(Palm Walk, tel 480/965-6891)*.

On a more terrestrial theme, a range of equipment, including a Foucault pendulum and a seismograph, keeps tabs on planet Earth in the **R.S. Dietz Museum of Geology** *(Palm Walk, tel 480/965-7065, closed Sat.–Sun.),* also in the Physical Sciences Building (F wing). Other exhibits here showcase rocks, minerals, and fossils, along with explanations of geologic processes.

---

## EXPERIENCE:
# Sign Up for Spa Bliss

**Health seekers have journeyed to the warm, dry air of Arizona's deserts since the 1880s. Resorts in the Phoenix, Tucson, and Sedona areas provide full-service spas with massages, facials, body wraps, and salt glows. Many offer their services to day guests as well. While most resort spas offer golf and tennis along with the spa treatments, destination spas focus more on a complete program including diet and education. Each spa has a distinct personality, so it's worth checking to see which one best meets your needs. Start your search here: www.arizonaguide.com.**

---

The distinctive circular 3,000-seat **ASU Gammage** *(Mill Ave. & Apache Blvd., tel 480/965-3434 box office, 480/965-0458 tour information)* hosts a variety of performances and events. Named after a former ASU president and dedicated in 1964, it is the last major public building designed by architect Frank Lloyd Wright. Tours lasting 30–45 minutes are offered on Mondays between September and mid-May.

The **Memorial Union** *(Cady & Orange Malls, tel 480/965-5728)* is the social center of ASU. Here you will find an information desk, art collection, cafés, fast-food eateries, bowling alley, and shops.

The **ASU Bookstore** lies east of the Memorial Union. Also nearby is the **Hayden Library** *(Cady Mall, tel 480/965-6164, http://lib.asu.edu/hayden),* which houses the main collection plus holdings on Arizona, Chicano studies, East Asia, and government documents.

The **Noble Science & Engineering Library** *(Tyler Mall, tel 480/965-7607, http://lib.asu.edu/noble)* serves the nearby science and engineering departments. Hikers can get a head start and plan their trips using topographical maps. Researchers can also investigate contemporary and historical maps of Arizona, the Southwest, and Mexico here.

Enthusiastic followers of the school's Sun Devils attend football games at the 75,000-seat **Sun Devil Stadium,** basketball games at the 14,000-seat **Wells Fargo Arena,** and baseball games at the 4,500-seat **Packard Stadium.** All three sports facilities are located in the northern part of the university's campus. The **Sports Hall of Fame** *(closed Sat.–Sun.)* displays trophies and photos of ASU's sporting past in the Wells Fargo Arena, where you will also find the Sun Devils Athletic Ticket Office *(tel 480/727-0000, www.thesundevils.com).* ■

# Scottsdale

Captain Winfield Scott homesteaded here, just to the northeast of Phoenix, in the 1880s, proclaiming the land "unequaled in greater fertility or richer promise." Chances are good he would be impressed if he could see the promise fulfilled in the luxurious resorts, art galleries, fine restaurants, cultural events, and attractive landscaping that are Scottsdale today.

Revel in the genius of Frank Lloyd Wright at Taliesin West, designed for his family and apprentices.

## Downtown

The Scottsdale Civic Center Mall is home to the Scottsdale Historical Museum, Scottsdale Museum of Contemporary Art, and a library, all connected by paths in a beautiful park. Porch-fronted shops of Old Town Scottsdale, on the west side of the mall, sell Western and Native American arts and crafts.

The area's cotton fields and dairy farms are gone, but just east of the intersection of Brown Avenue and Main Street you can still step into a little red schoolhouse, now the **Scottsdale Historical Museum,** to get a feel for the old days. Photographs, artifacts, and period furniture illuminate the community's development since the little school opened in 1909.

In complete contrast, the exhibits at the **Scottsdale Museum of Contemporary Art,** a short walk to the southeast, entertain and challenge with the latest concepts in art, architecture, and design. The shows change every two or three months. The galleries are housed in the Scottsdale Center for the Performing Arts and adjacent Gerard L. Cafesjian Pavilion. There is also a sculpture garden outside. Performances and special events often take place in the center's theater,

### Scottsdale

🅰 142 D3

**Visitor information**

✉ Scottsdale Convention and Visitors Bureau, Galleria Corporate Center, 4343 N. Scottsdale Rd., Ste. 170, Scottsdale, AZ 85251

☎ 480/421-1004 or 800/782-1117

🕑 Closed Sat.–Sun.

**www.scottsdalecvb .com**

## Scottsdale Historical Museum

- ✉ 7333 E. Scottsdale Mall
- ☎ 480/945-4499
- 🕐 Closed Mon.– Tues. & July– Aug.

www.scottsdale museum.com

## Scottsdale Museum of Contemporary Art

- ✉ 7374 E. 2nd St.
- ☎ 480/874-4666
- 🕐 Closed Mon. (Mon.–Tues. in summer)
- 💲 $$, free on Thurs.

www.scottsdalearts .org

## McCormick-Stillman Railroad Park

- ✉ 7301 E. Indian Bend Rd. (SE corner of Indian Bend & Scottsdale Rds.)
- ☎ 480/312-2312
- 💲 $ (train & carousel rides)

www.therailroad park.com

## Taliesin West

- ✉ 12621 N. Frank Lloyd Wright Blvd.
- ☎ 480/860-2700 ext. 494 or 495
- 🕐 Closed Tues.– Wed. July–Aug.
- 💲 $$$$–$$$$$ (tours cost less in summer)

www.franklloyd wright.org

cinema, and amphitheater. Both the center and the pavilion have large gift shops, often with art related to current exhibits.

## Farther Afield

Rail fans will enjoy exploring the 30-acre **McCormick-Stillman Railroad Park.** You can hop aboard the Paradise and Pacific Railroad for a 1-mile loop through the grassy grounds. It's modeled after narrow-gauge trains of Colorado and has both diesel and steam locomotives pulling the passenger-carrying gondolas and other cars. You can see a standard-gauge, Mogul-type Baldwin steam locomotive, a variety of railroad cars, and seasonal museum exhibits. The Stillman Station, a copy of the depot at Clifton, sells tickets, gifts, and snacks. Another snack bar is in a caboose.

Model railroad clubs meet in the park on Sunday afternoons; you can view their layouts and working steam locomotive models. Other attractions: a 1950 carousel, playgrounds, picnic tables, and a small xeriscape arboretum.

Architecture and the desert meet at **Taliesin West,** a masterpiece by architect Frank Lloyd Wright. In 1937 he began work on the site as a winter home for both his family and his apprentices, where they could learn from nature and from one another. Apprentices still live here in tents and simple shelters, just as they did then. Wright instilled in his students ideas of how to "grow" building designs from the inside out, rather than relying on facts and figures. Wright died in 1959,

**Don't think you have to be a student of architecture to feel the creative vibes at Frank Lloyd Wright's Taliesin West, where the buildings echo the spare lines of the desert and mountains.**

—VERA MARIE BADERTSCHER
*National Geographic Traveler
· contributor*

but his school continues to train architects today, many of whom stay for three to five years.

Site tours show how Wright's architecture looks fresh and different from every angle. The one-hour Panorama Tour introduces his work with photos, a video, models, and a walk through some of the grounds and buildings; tours begin frequently during the day *(no reservations needed).*

The 90-minute Insights Tour covers the same ground but adds a visit to Wright's spacious living room; tours leave frequently daily and reservations are not required. For architecture enthusiasts, the three-hour Behind the Scenes Tour is the most detailed. It includes a meeting with Wright associates and takes in areas not on the other tours *(call for times; reservations recommended).* Desert Walks tell about the landscapes that inspired much of Wright's work. The daily 90-minute walks go at a leisurely pace; hiking shoes and reservations recommended

*(Nov.–April).* On the popular two-hour Apprentice Shelter Tour, an apprentice will show you some of the individually designed and built structures in the desert; on Saturday in winter and spring. Advance reservations recommended.

Enjoy the drama of Taliesin West at the two-hour Night Lights on the Desert tour on some Thursday and Friday evenings; reservations suggested. The Taliesin West Bookstore carries an extensive selection of Wright-related books and products.

The 600-acre site rests on the McDowell Mountain foothills 13 miles northeast of central Scottsdale. Go north 7 miles on 101 (Pima Freeway), turn right 5 miles on Cactus Road to the entrance across Frank Lloyd Wright Boulevard, then continue 1 mile on Taliesin Drive.

**Cosanti** is the home and gallery of visionary architect Paolo Soleri, who inspired the experimental city Arcosanti (see pp. 120–122). Buildings at Cosanti reflect his imaginative designs and construction techniques and date as far back as the 1950s. You'll also see exhibits, art, and the famous Soleri windbells; bronze is poured for the bells some weekday mornings. ∎

**Cosanti**

✉ 6433 E. Doubletree Ranch Rd. in Paradise Valley (N 5 miles from central Scottsdale on Scottsdale Rd., then left 1 mile on Doubletree Ranch Rd.; look for "Soleri" sign on left)

☎ 480/948-6145

**www.arcosanti.org**

---

# EXPERIENCE: Play a Round or Two of Golf

You can swing amid spectacular scenery at more than 300 courses in the state. Golf resorts, the ultimate in challenge and comforts, are concentrated in the Phoenix and Scottsdale areas, with additional options in Tucson and Sedona. Golfing in the desert attracts the greatest crowds in winter; plan well ahead. If you're willing to face summertime heat at the desert courses, benefits include lower prices and absence of crowds. Schedule a round before dawn or at twilight (some courses are lit). Or head north or east to more modest courses in the highlands. Green fees start at about $35 at public courses and go into the hundreds of dollars at the top spots.

Wildlife and the environment are benefitting from greater awareness and partnerships with the Audubon Cooperative Sanctuary Program for Golf Courses.

**Arizona Biltmore Country Club** *(tel 602/955-9655, www.arizonabiltmore.com/golf/)* in Phoenix offers the 18-hole Adobe, opened in 1928, plus the Links for a total of 36 holes. You can play at the PGA's Stadium Course, where the pros compete, at the **Players Club of Scottsdale** *(tel 480/585-4334 or 888/400-4001, www.tpc.com/scottsdale/)*. Also in Scottsdale, **Troon North Golf Club** *(www.troonnorthgolf.com)* has two 18-hole courses, Monument and Pinnacle, both with challenges amid boulders and huge saguaros. Just to the north in Carefree, giant granite rock balls and stately saguaros stand above the two 18-hole courses at the **Boulders Resort** *(tel 480/488-9028 [pro shop] or 888/579-2631 [resort], www.bouldersclub.com)*, one of the best places in the state to mix golf, luxurious living, and fine dining. Southeast in Tucson, **Ventana Canyon Golf & Racquet Club** *(tel 520/577-1400 or 800/828-5701, www.ventanacanyonclub.com)* features two 18-hole courses and the Lodge at Ventana Canyon. **Sedona Golf Resort** *(tel 877/733-6630, www.sedonagolfresort.com)* offers a traditional course surrounded by Sedona's famous Red Rock Country.

# Mesa

Arizona's third largest city after Phoenix and Tucson, Mesa spreads across a low plateau on the east side of the Valley of the Sun. The table-like site inspired the Spanish name. After arriving here in 1878, Mormon settlers built a small fort and irrigated their fields with a reworked Hohokam canal system.

The Mesa Arizona Temple sits amid tidy desert plantings.

## Mesa

🅰 142 D3 & inside back cover E2

**Visitor information**

✉ Mesa Convention & Visitors Bureau, 120 N. Center St., Mesa, AZ 85201

☎ 480/827-4700 or 800/283-6372

🕐 Closed Sat.–Sun.

**www.visitmesa.com**

## Arizona Museum of Natural History

✉ 53 N. Macdonald St. (corner of Macdonald & 1st Sts.)

☎ 480/644-2230

🕐 Closed Mon.

💲 $$

**www.azmnh.org**

Uncover mysteries of the past at the **Arizona Museum of Natural History,** where dinosaurs pose in ancient landscapes and prehistoric Native American villages look recently abandoned. You can visit the Hands-On Adventure Center.

The new **Mesa Arts Center** covers an entire block in the heart of downtown with a delightful group of galleries, theaters, and studios. Look for design elements inspired by the Sonoran Desert as you wander the landscaped grounds amid glass-walled buildings. The five galleries of Mesa Contemporary Arts offer works by emerging and internationally renowned artists. Experience Broadway-style theater, classical and pop music, dance, and family entertainment from local and visiting companies in one of the four theaters or at an outside

performance area. Professionally taught classes in the art studios let you try your hand at art or drama. The Store at Mesa Arts Center sells the work of local and national artists *(galleries & store closed Mon.).* Park in a lot off First Avenue or a garage off Sirrine Street.

Visitors are welcome to see the gardens and exhibits of the **Mesa Arizona Temple.** In the visitor center, videos and dioramas explain the beliefs of the Church of Jesus Christ of Latter-day Saints (Mormon). The temple, completed in 1927, contains elements of classical Greek architecture. Religious ceremonies are held inside *(closed to the public).* A big Easter Pageant takes place during the two weeks before Easter. A nativity scene and 750,000 lights brighten the Christmas season. To trace family roots, head across the street to check out the **Mesa Regional Family History Center** *(41 S. Hobson, tel 480/ 964-1200, www.mesarfhc.org).*

You can still see three sections of the Hohokam-built canals— later used by pioneers—at the **Park of the Canals** *(1710 N. Horne St.)* 2 miles north of downtown; the park also has a desert botanical garden. Farther north, the **Mesa Historical Museum** *(2345 N. Horne, tel 480/835-7358, www .mesahistoricalmuseum.org, closed Sun.–Mon., $$)* portrays the life of early settlers. The museum also hosts exhibits in downtown Mesa, so it's a good idea to check the website or call first for hours and locations.

Rare military aircraft undergo restoration and take to the skies at the **Arizona Wing CAF Museum.** Besides the B-17G (see sidebar below), you're apt to see a TB-25N bomber, a SNJ trainer, and a C-45 transport. To experience a vintage-plane flight, call to schedule a warbird ride. Among the exhibits: radio and navigational equipment, engines, and historical photos. To reach the museum, turn north on Greenfield Road from McKellips Road at the corner of Falcon Field.

## Chandler

Two museums offer additional historical perspectives. The **Chandler Museum** (178 E. Commonwealth Ave., tel 480/782-2717, www.chandlermuseum.org, closed Sun.-Mon.) displays archaeological findings and pioneer exhibits, and tells the story of the town's founder, Dr. Alexander J. Chandler (1859–1950), who helped transform the desert into prosperous farmland. He also built the nearby San Marcos Hotel, one of Arizona's earliest resorts. From Mesa go south on Ariz. 87 to Chandler, turn east one block on Buffalo Street, south one block on Arizona Place, then east on Commonwealth Avenue.

A 1906 steam locomotive heads up the collection at the **Arizona Railway Museum** (330 E. Ryan Rd. in Tumbleweed Park, E of Arizona Ave., tel 480/821-1108,

www.azrymuseum.org, open weekend afternoons fall–spring). Guided tours through Pullman cars recall a bygone era of rail travel.

**Rawhide Western Town & Steakhouse** (5700 West N. Loop Rd., just W of I-10 Wild Horse Pass Blvd. Exit 162, tel 480/502-5600, www.rawhide.com) re-creates an 1880s Old West town on the Gila River Indian Reservation. There's lots of activity: stunt action shows, trick and roping demonstrations, train and stagecoach rides, gold panning, and, yes, a mechanical bull. Shops sell Western gear and Native American crafts, and you can dress up for a snapshot in the photo emporium. Check the calendar for rodeo events, bull riding, and cookouts. Rawhide Steakhouse serves Western fare (check hours); at night you can dance to live country music inside and on the plaza. Most entry is free; you pay for shows and activities with tickets or an all-day pass. ∎

**Mesa Arts Center**
- ✉ 1 E. Main St. (SE corner of Main & Center Sts.)
- ☎ 480/644-6560 (galleries) or 480/644-6500 (box office)
- 🕐 Closed Mon.
- 💲 $ (galleries)

www.mesaartscenter.com

**Mesa Arizona Temple**
- ✉ 525 E. Main St.
- ☎ 480/964-7164

www.lds.org

**Arizona Wing CAF Museum**
- ✉ 2017 N. Greenfield Rd.
- ☎ 480/924-1940
- 🕐 Closed Mon.– Tues. May–Oct.
- 💲 $$

www.azcaf.org

---

## Behold *Sentimental Journey* —the B-17G Flying Fortress

When handsome *Sentimental Journey* rolled off the Douglas assembly line in late 1944, it had been designed to survive no more than a hundred missions. The plane first served in the Pacific Theater of World War II, then participated in photo-mapping, air-sea rescue, and nuclear weapon testing duties. Transferred to civilian ownership, it flew thousands of sorties against forest fires throughout the country. Now housed at the Arizona Wing CAF Museum, *Sentimental Journey* flies annual tours to thrill people with the sights and sounds of one of the most famous and rare planes in the air today.

# Apache Trail Loop Drive

To nature lover and U.S. President Theodore Roosevelt, "The Apache Trail combines the grandeur of the Alps, the glory of the Rockies, the magnificence of the Grand Canyon and then adds an indefinable something that none of the others have. To me, it is the most awe-inspiring and most sublimely beautiful panorama nature has ever created."

The Apache Trail remains one of Arizona's most scenic drives. Twisting over jagged ridges and plunging into sheer-walled canyons, it steers its wild course along the northern flanks of the Superstition Mountains, linking the Valley of the Sun and Theodore Roosevelt Lake. Native Americans walked the trail until the late 1800s, when it was upgraded to a horse trail. A

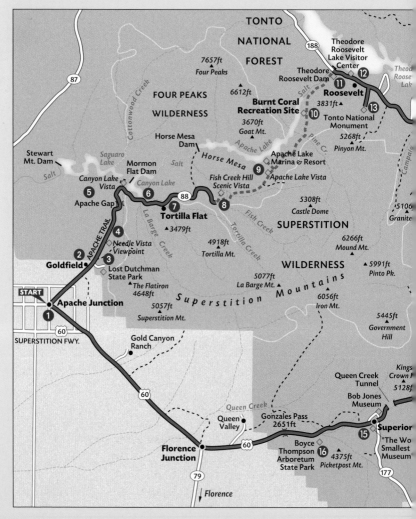

road was carved to bring in equipment to build the Theodore Roosevelt Dam. That took nearly two years; the road opened in 1905.

Though designated a state highway (Arizona 88), much of the road is unpaved—normally fine for cars and smaller RVs but not big trailers. By combining Arizona 88, Arizona 188, and US 60 via Globe-Miami, travelers can follow a 200-mile loop around the Superstition Mountains. The loop can be driven in a long day, but two or more days allow for a leisurely experience.

The reconstructed ghost town of Goldfield stages activities that carry you back in time.

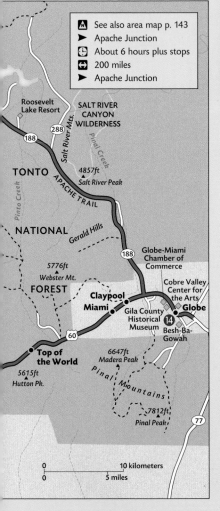

Campgrounds dot the way, and Apache Junction and Globe-Miami offer lodgings and food. The drive lies within three districts of Tonto National Forest; the Supervisor's Office *(2324 E. McDowell Rd., Phoenix, AZ 85006, tel 602/225-5200, www.fs.fed.us/r3/tonto, closed Sat.–Sun.)* has maps and information.

**Apache Junction** ❶ is a good starting point; stock up on gas and supplies. Head northeast 3.5 miles on Arizona 88 to **Superstition Mountain Museum** *(tel 480/983-4888, www .superstitionmountainmuseum.org)* for regional history exhibits. Continue 1 mile to **Goldfield** ❷

---

## NOT TO BE MISSED:

**Needle Vista Viewpoint • Tonto National Monument • Besh Ba Gowah • Boyce Thompson Arboretum State Park**

---

## EXPERIENCE: Explore a Corner of the Vast Superstition Wilderness

Trails totaling 180 miles will take you through rugged desert canyons and mountains of this 160,200-acre wilderness. You can reach all **12 main trailheads** on side roads off the Apache Loop Drive. Elevations range from about 2,000 feet along the west boundary to over 6,000 feet in the eastern uplands. Desert vegetation dominates, but a few pockets of ponderosa pine survive on the highest slopes. Wildflowers may put on colorful extravaganzas in early spring and following summer rains. Because they're so close to Phoenix, the Superstitions get unusually heavy traffic for a wilderness area, especially near the Peralta and First Water trailheads in the west. You're more likely to see javelina, desert mule deer, mountain lion, black bear, and other wildlife in the eastern part of the range. For a short hike, head in from any of the trailheads and return the same way; on longer excursions you can make loops or travel from one trailhead to another. See http://superstitionmtnhikes.com for maps and detailed hiking information.

(tel 480/983-0333, www.goldfieldghosttown.com), which sprang into existence when prospectors discovered gold in the mid-1890s. Attractions include a tour in a replica of the nearby **Mammoth Mine,** photo exhibits in the **Goldfield Superstition Museum,** the educational **Bordello Museum,** a narrated ride on the 1.5-mile **Superstition Scenic Railway,** horseback riding (tel 480/982-0133), hiking/back road tours (tel 480/982-7661), and the **Mammoth Steakhouse and Saloon** (tel 480/983-6402).

Across the highway in **Lost Dutchman State Park ❸** (tel 480/982-4485) you can hike, picnic, and camp; during the cooler months, arrive early to find a spot. **Needle Vista Viewpoint ❹** affords a view of the 4,535-foot-high pinnacle that figures in so many lost-mine legends. Heading north, **Canyon Lake Vista ❺** takes in this large reservoir on the Salt River. **Canyon Lake ❻** has a marina (tel 480/288-9233, www.canyon lakemarina.com) with boat rentals, restaurant, and campground. Budget about 90 minutes for a narrated lake tour aboard the *Dolly Steamboat* (tel 480/827-9144).

Heading east, **Tortilla Flat ❼** looks like an Old West movie set; step inside for the restaurant, curio shop, and country store. Across the highway, **Tortilla Campground**

**INSIDER TIP:**

**A paved trail behind the Tonto National Monument visitor center climbs 350 feet to the 19-room Lower Cliff Dwelling.**

—SHEILA BUCKMASTER
National Geographic Traveler *magazine editor at large*

(tel 480/610-3300, closed May–Sept.) is popular with RVers. The pavement runs out 23 miles from Apache Junction, after which it's another 2 miles to **Fish Creek Hill Scenic Vista ❽**—a good place to get a feel for the rugged beauty of this land. The descent of **Fish Creek Hill,** a 1,500-foot drop over 3 miles, is the most challenging section to drive. You can take in a panorama of the second largest reservoir on this drive at **Apache Lake Vista ❾**. A road here leads down to Apache Lake Marina & Resort (tel 928/467-2511, www.apachelake .com), where you'll find a motel, an RV park, tent areas, restaurant, store, and boat rentals. Facilities at **Burnt Corral Recreation Site ❿** on Apache Lake include camping, a picnic site, boat ramp, and beach.

The road climbs Apache Lake Gorge to **Theodore Roosevelt Dam ⓫** and two overlooks. Engineers had doubts about the masonry dam's ability to survive a moderate earthquake or major flood, so they encased it in concrete and raised the level to increase storage capacity. Theodore Roosevelt Lake covers about 19,199 acres when it's full and is the largest of the four Salt River reservoirs. The very helpful **Roosevelt Lake Visitor Center** **⑫** *(tel 928/467-3200)* houses exhibits and an information desk, and sells relevant books and maps.

**Tonto National Monument ⑬** *(tel 928/467-2241, www.nps.gov/tont)* protects two cliff dwellings constructed by the tribe known as the Salado nearly 700 years ago. A video and exhibits in the visitor center show how the tribe lived. The Lower Cliff Dwelling is a 1.5-mile walk away. You can visit the Upper Cliff Dwelling only on ranger-led tours, November through April. If your travel plans allow you to make a reservation, the 3-mile round-trip hike (with a 600-foot climb) pays off with a visit to a large and well-preserved 40-room pueblo.

Continue on Ariz. 188 to Globe-Miami at the road's end. Turn left to **Globe ⑭,** with its early 20th-century downtown and forest roads up into the Pinal Mountains. On the way into town, you'll pass the **Globe-Miami Chamber of Commerce** *(1360 N. Broad St., tel 928/425-4495 or 800/804-5623, www.globemiamichamber .com)* and, next door, the **Gila County Historical Museum** *(1330 N. Broad St., tel 928/425-7385, closed Sun.).* Downtown, the **Cobre Valley Center for the Arts** *(101 N. Broad St., tel 928/425-0884, www.cvarts.org)* shows a large collection of local art.

The Salado lived in the 200-room pueblo of **Besh Ba Gowah** *(tel 928/425-0320)* between 1225 and 1450. A museum introduces the Salado and the partially reconstructed site. To reach it, head downtown, go south on Broad Street, turn right across the bridge onto Jesse Hayes Street and continue 1 mile, then turn right up the hill.

The Globe-Miami area's history of copper mining is evident as you drive through the towns and go west on US 60. After some rugged country, the road drops into the old mining town of **Superior ⑮.** A sign on the highway indicates **"The World's Smallest Museum,"** while the **Bob Jones Museum** *(Main St. & Neary, closed Mon.–Thurs. & summer.),* in the former home of Arizona's sixth governor, stands downtown; both display historical exhibits.

Continue 3 miles west from Superior to the 323-acre **Boyce Thompson Arboretum State Park** **⑯** *(tel 520/689-2811, http://arboretum.ag.arizona.edu),* Arizona's oldest arboretum (1920s). Spring heralds an explosion of colors. Birds and other wildlife come to the desert oases at Ayer Lake and Queen Creek. The visitor center sells seeds, and plants.

An easy drive on US 60 leads back to Apache Junction, or turn south to visit the town of Florence (see p. 170) and Casa Grande Monument, a Hohokam great house.

**The Superstition Mountains host fine riding.**

# Florence

Time seems to have bypassed this old town, founded in 1866 near a ford on the Gila River. Even the 1891 Pinal County courthouse "clock" remains stuck at 11:44; funds ran out before a real clock could be installed, so workers simply painted on the hands. More than 150 buildings on the National Register of Historic Places line the porch-fronted Main Street and nearby lanes. Museums and visitor centers offer a "Historic Florence Walking Tour" handout.

**Florence**

[A] 143 E2

**Visitor information**

[✉] Florence Visitors Center, 291 Bailey St. (Florence, AZ 85132)

[☎] 520/868-4496 or 866/977-4496

[🕐] Closed Sat.–Sun.

**www.visitflorenceaz.com**

**Pinal County Visitor Center**

[✉] 330 E. Butte Ave.

[☎] 520/868-4331 or 800/557-4331

[🕐] Closed Sun. & Sat in summer

**http://pinalcountyaz.gov**

**McFarland State Historic Park**

[A] 143 E3

[✉] Main & Ruggles Sts.

[☎] 520/868-5216

[$] $

[🕐] The park underwent a major renovation; call ahead for hours

**Pinal County Historical Museum**

[✉] 715 S. Main St.

[☎] 520/868-4382

[🕐] Closed Sun. (Sat.-Sun. in summer) Donation

The 1878 adobe building in **McFarland State Historic Park** on the north side of town has seen use as Pinal County's first courthouse, sheriff's office, jail, and hospital. Exhibits illustrate these periods and tell of Florence's notable and notorious historical figures. Photos of the POW camp depict the experiences of some of the 13,000 German and Italian prisoners who spent time here during World War II. A building out back houses

### Poston's Folly

In 1863, explorer and miner Charles Poston lobbied in Washington, D.C., for a territorial government, then became one of the first Arizona delegates to Congress. He later went to India and became interested in the Zoroastrian religion. He returned to Arizona in 1877 and built a continuous fire—a temple of the sun—on a hill north of Florence. The flames died out a few months later, ending what would be called "Poston's Folly." Poston lies buried in a pyramid-shaped tomb on the summit of the hill.

exhibits and the library of Pinal County attorney Ernest McFarland (1894–1984), who went on to become a U.S. senator, Arizona governor, and chief justice of the state supreme court.

On the town's south side, the **Pinal County Historical Museum** begins with pottery and stone tools of early cultures, then portrays the lives of pioneers. An 1880s horse-drawn brougham reveals a glimpse of olden-day elegance, while the mining and household items show day-to-day existence. News clippings of silent-screen hero Tom Mix relate his fatal car accident south of town. Among the prison exhibits, you'll encounter massive prison registers and a gas chamber chair; hangman's nooses frame photos of their victims. Step out the back door to see a blacksmith shop, farm equipment, mining gear, and a homesteader's shack.

The Pima and Maricopa run the **Gila Indian Center** (tel 480/963-3981) on their land west of Florence. Exhibits in the museum interpret the archaeology and culture of Arizona's Native Americans, and you can buy jewelry, baskets, pottery, Hopi kachina dolls, and Navajo rugs in the shop. It's just off I-10 Exit 175, 26 miles southeast of Phoenix. ■

# Casa Grande Ruins National Monument

The massive and mysterious Great House built by the Hohokam looms over the desert flats near the Gila River. It dates from the early 1300s, toward the end of the culture's existence.

Many a traveler has wondered just how the Hohokam used this ancient building.

Archaeologists have speculated that the site might have been a combination temple, palace, and storehouse. Openings in the walls appear to correspond with solar and lunar events. From the roof the Hohokam could survey their extensive canal system, used for watering crops. Layers of mud (3,000 tons in all) made from caliche—a desert subsoil whose high lime content helps it dry to concrete-like hardness—constitute the walls, four feet six inches thick at the base tapering to one foot nine inches near the top. A five-foot-tall base gives the building a height equivalent to a modern four-story building.

Inside, logs once supported floors and ceilings that gave the central section three stories. In 1697, Spanish priest Father Kino recorded that the building had burned; no wood is in place today. Near the ruins look for the foundations of a wall and remnants of some of the more than 60 rooms inside the compound.

Rangers lead tours, or you can self-guide. Signs identify desert plants, and museum exhibits tell of the Hohokam's farming, trade routes, and history. Casa Grande's entrance is on the north edge of Coolidge. From Florence, head west 9 miles on Arizona 287. Turn left and drive half a mile on Arizona 87. From I-10, take any of the Coolidge exits. ■

**Casa Grande Ruins National Monument**

⚠ 143 E2
✉ Junction of Ariz. 87 & Ariz. 287
☎ 520/723-3172
$ $$

**www.nps.gov/cagr**

# Picacho Peak State Park

The volcanic spire here has served as a landmark for travelers for centuries. Anglos picked up the Spanish name, which means "peak," without comprehending it, resulting in its bilingual pleonasm "Peak Peak." Sonoran plants such as saguaro and paloverde cover the rocky hillsides. Winter rains often usher in springtime displays of such bright flowers as Mexican poppies.

Cavalry troops in full regalia gain ground during a Picacho Peak State Park Civil War reenactment.

**Picacho Peak State Park**

⚑ 143 E1
✉ 70 miles SE of Phoenix & 40 miles NW of Tucson via I-10
☎ 520/466-3183
💲 $$ day use, $$$–$$$$$ camping

www.azstateparks .com

You can walk easy loops at the base of the peak or climb 1,500 feet on a steep and challenging trail to the 3,374-foot summit—a 4-mile round-trip that takes four or five hours. Historic markers across the road from the park's entrance station commemorate the Battle of Picacho Pass, considered by historians to be the westernmost significant action in the Civil War (see sidebar this page).

Keeping this history alive, a "Civil War in the Southwest" reenactment takes place on the second weekend of March. Given the mostly unchanged nature of this land, the reenactment is eerily transporting.

The visitor center houses exhibits and a gift shop. Two campgrounds and day-use areas provide a pleasant break from travels on busy I-10. ∎

## Battle of Picacho Pass—A Fight to the Finish

During the Civil War, the Confederacy made plans to forge a link across Arizona to California, creating a coast-to-coast Rebel nation. In January 1862, Confederate Gen. Henry Sibley and his Texas army marched to Santa Fe, where he ordered men farther west to occupy Tucson.

The California plans began to unravel when Union loyalists gained full control. After an April 15 skirmish, knowing that a large Union column was on its way, the Confederates withdrew to the Rio Grande, never to return. The battle for Arizona was over.

A region where forests dominate, from the Petrified Forest National Park's rainbow-hued logs to the conifers of the White Mountains

# Eastern Arizona

A lucky someone hits the jackpot in an Apache reservation casino.

# Eastern Arizona

The lush forests and meadows that spread across the White Mountains and the Mogollon Rim will surprise anyone who thinks of Arizona as primarily desert. Here mountains and plateaus formed by geologic upheavals provide spectacular landscapes to explore.

Rock layers in Petrified Forest National Park tell not only of towering trees but also of primitive plants, giant amphibians, and fierce reptiles in a land far warmer and wetter than today's. Volcanoes on the Colorado Plateau spewed forth lava and cinders, forming lofty summits such as Baldy Peak, the state's second highest at 11,403 feet. Farther south, great blocks of the Earth's crust were thrust upward, creating the Pinaleño Mountains and other sky islands; today, these remnants of cool-climate forests stand surrounded by desert.

Phoenix ★

Area of map detail

Early tribes left behind masonry pueblos and even one made of petrified wood in Petrified Forest National Park. Around the 16th century, Apache moved in from the east and managed to hold on to their homelands in what are now the White Mountain Apache and San Carlos Apache Reservations. Tribal members maintain traditional beliefs, such as the training of medicine men and coming-of-age Sunrise Dances for young women. Cultural centers and recreation areas are open to the public on both reservations.

The arrival of the railroad in the early 1880s opened eastern Arizona up to cattle companies, which ran huge herds across the vast grasslands. Winslow and Holbrook became important ranching centers; indeed, they retain much of their Old West character even today. Spanish explorers under Francisco Vásquez de Coronado never discovered the gold and copper that lay along their trek through the mountains in 1540, but later Mexican and American prospectors found the deposits. You can watch copper miners at work in the enormous open-pit Morenci Mine.

Discover the outdoor pleasures of eastern Arizona—hiking and skiing in the mountains, fishing in the streams and lakes, rafting and kayaking the rivers, and driving through the majestic scenery. The Coronado Trail takes in some of the state's most awe-inspiring views and forests. Another great drive descends into the immense Salt River Canyon and up the other side. Or you can ascend a sky island on the Swift Trail in the Pinaleño Mountains. ∎

## NOT TO BE MISSED:

**Winslow's La Posada, a historic hotel that re-creates the vision of a grand hacienda  176**

**The Petrified Forest National Park's multi-hued petrified wood and the Painted Desert landscapes  179–181**

**The Apache Cultural Center, on the site of historic Fort Apache, for the story of this tribe  184**

**Taking a scenic drive on the twisting Coronado Trail  190–191**

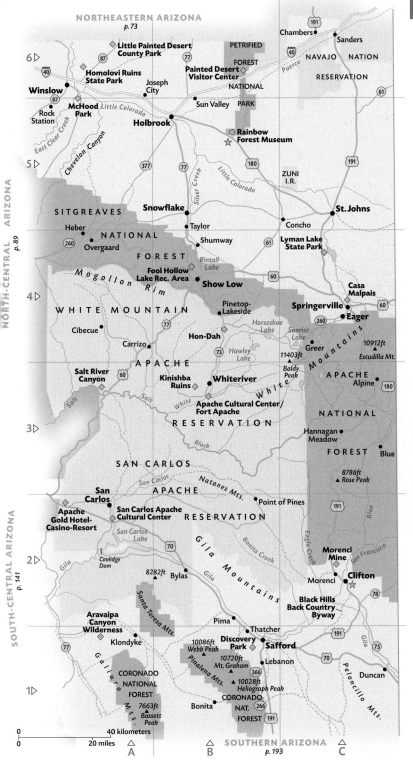

NAVAJO NATION
RESERVATION

Chambers
Sanders

PETRIFIED
FOREST

Painted Desert
Visitor Center

NATIONAL

PARK

Little Painted Desert
County Park

Homolovi Ruins
State Park

Winslow

Rock
Station

McHood
Park

Joseph
City

Sun Valley

Holbrook

Rainbow
Forest Museum

ZUNI
I.R.

St. Johns

NORTH-CENTRAL ARIZONA
p. 89

SITGREAVES

NATIONAL

FOREST

Heber
Overgaard

Snowflake
Taylor
Shumway

Concho

Lyman Lake
State Park

Fool Hollow
Lake Rec. Area

Show Low

Pintail
Lake

Casa
Malpais

Springerville
Eager

Mogollon Rim

WHITE MOUNTAIN

Cibecue

Carrizo

Pinetop-
Lakeside

Hon-Dah

Horseshoe
Lake

Sunrise
Lake

Greer

11403ft
Baldy
Peak

10912ft
Escudilla Mt.

Salt River
Canyon

APACHE

Kinishba
Ruins

Whiteriver

Hawley
Lake

White Mountains

APACHE

Alpine

Apache Cultural Center/
Fort Apache

RESERVATION

Black

NATIONAL

Hannagan
Meadow

FOREST

Blue

SAN CARLOS

San
Carlos

APACHE

San Carlos Apache
Cultural Center

RESERVATION

Natanes Mts.

Point of Pines

8786ft
Rose Peak

Apache
Gold Hotel-
Casino-Resort

San Carlos
Lake

Coolidge
Dam

Gila

8282ft
Bylas

Gila Mountains

Bonita Creek

Eagle Creek

Blue

San Francisco

Morenci
Mine

Morenci

Clifton

Aravaipa
Canyon
Wilderness

Klondyke

Santa Teresa Mts.

Pima

Thatcher

Discovery
Park

Safford

Black Hills
Back Country
Byway

Duncan

10086ft
Webb Peak

Pinaleno Mts.

10720ft
Mt. Graham

Lebanon

Galiuro Mts.

CORONADO

NATIONAL

FOREST

7663ft
Bassett
Peak

Bonita

10028ft
Heliograph Peak

CORONADO
NAT.
FOREST

Peloncillo Mts.

0
0

40 kilometers
20 miles

A            B            C

# Winslow

Named after railroad president Edward Winslow, this town began life as a rail terminal in 1882 and soon prospered with livestock and trade. Route 66 brought America to Winslow's downtown in the late 1920s. Aviator Charles Lindbergh not only designed the airport here but made the inaugural flight from it in 1930—the year the Santa Fe Railroad opened a railroad resort hotel, La Posada. Winslow, it seemed, had arrived.

"Whispering Giant," honoring Native Americans, stands downtown in First Street Pathway, off Berry Avenue.

But the good times began to unravel. Newer airplanes no longer needed to stop here, travelers had little use for passenger trains or hotels, and I-40 bypassed Route 66. Tumbleweeds seemed to outnumber visitors. Recently, however, travelers have rediscovered the romance of Route 66 in the historic buildings downtown. La Posada Hotel once again welcomes guests. A 1921 commercial building just off Route 66 downtown houses the **Old Trails Museum** *(212 Kinsley Ave., tel 928-5861, www.oldtrailsmuseum.org, closed Sun.–Mon.).* Displays include artifacts from nearby Homolovi pueblos and memorabilia of ranching, territorial doctors, Route 66, and La Posada's Harvey Girls (see sidebar opposite). The model of Brigham City shows the Mormon settlement built in 1876 just north of present-day Winslow, along the Little Colorado River; it had to be abandoned in 1881 when the river proved too tough to tame.

Architect Mary Colter (see p. 41) didn't just design **La Posada Hotel** *(303 E. 2nd St., tel 928/289-4366, www.laposada.org);* she constructed a story around it as the grand hacienda of an 18th-century Spanish don. The spot that helped put Winslow on the map has been painstakingly and lavishly

INSIDER TIP:

La Posada, originally a 1929 railway hotel, sits right on Amtrak's route. Some rooms have the old 6-foot-long cast-iron tubs.

—SHEILA BUCKMASTER
National Geographic Traveler
*magazine editor at large*

renovated; enjoy a self-guided tour (see Travelwise p. 254). More recently, the town came to the world's attention in the Eagles' 1972 song *"Take It Easy"* ("Well I'm a-standin' on a corner in Winslow, Arizona..."). The song inspired a little park at the corner of Route 66 (Second Avenue) and Kinsley, where a statue of a guitarist stands in front of a large mural illustrating the song's girl in a flatbed Ford.

For a scenic stop, try **Little Painted Desert County Park,** 15 miles north of town off Arizona 87, on the way to the Navajo and Hopi Indian Reservations. **McHood Park** *(tel 928/289-5714)* offers swimming, fishing, boating, picnicking, and camping at Clear Creek Lake. Boaters can head 2.5 miles up a pretty canyon. From downtown go south for 1.2 miles on Arizona 87; turn left and drive 4.3 miles on Arizona 99.

Ancient Pueblo people lived in the area from A.D. 600 to 1400, first in small pit house villages, then in large masonry and adobe pueblos. **Homolovi Ruins State Park** protects these sites. *(Note: For budgetary reasons, Homolovi Ruins State Park is currently closed. Check*

*www.azstateparks.com for updates.)* The pueblos are neither as picturesque nor as well preserved as those in Walnut Canyon (see p. 96) or Wupatki (see p. 101) to the west, but they are far larger. Exhibits in the visitor center tell of the people who lived here and their connection with the Hopi. **Homolovi II,** on a mesa 3 miles north of the visitor center, is the largest and most impressive of the sites. More than 1,200 rooms sheltered as many as 3,000 people between 1250 and 1400. The pueblo probably was a trade center and staging ground for migrations. A 0.25-mile trail with interpretive signs loops through the ruins. **Homolovi I** had more than a thousand rooms; it is 1.5 miles south of the visitor center.

Only the cemetery is left at the townsite of **Sunset,** where Mormon pioneers settled in 1876 and stayed 12 years, trying to irrigate crops with the silt-laden Little Colorado River. ∎

**Winslow**
🅰 175 A6
**Visitor information**
✉ Winslow Chamber of Commerce, 523 W 2nd St., Winslow, AZ 86047
☎ 928/289-2434
🕐 Closed Sat.–Sun.
**www.winslow arizona.org**

**Homolovi Ruins State Park**
🅰 175 A6
✉ From I-40 Exit 257, go N 1.3 miles on Ariz. 87, turn left & drive 2.1 miles to visitor center
☎ 928/289-4106
🕐 The park is currently closed. Check the website for updates.
💲 $
**www.azstateparks .com**

## The Harvey Girls

A partnership begun in the 1870s between Fred Harvey and the Santa Fe Railroad led to the country's first restaurant chain, providing high-quality food for rail passengers out west. Fred Harvey had troubles with his rowdy male staff, who too often showed up drunk or not at all. He solved this problem in 1883 by hiring exclusively women waitresses for his restaurants, including the one in Winslow. These "Harvey Girls" wore starched black-and-white uniforms and followed strict rules of conduct. They also had to sign a one-year contract and forfeit half their base pay should they leave early—marriage to the West's lonely bachelors tempted many away.

# Holbrook

Within a few years of the railroad's arrival here in 1881, Eastern investors had set up the nearby Aztec Land and Cattle Company (known as Hashknife for the shape of its brand). It became the third largest such company in the United States with more than 40,000 head of cattle. Hashknife cowboys would gallop through town; sheriffs had to be tough to work here. Holbrook, named for a railroad chief engineer, has preserved some of its Old West and Route 66 heritage.

**Holbrook**

🗺 175 B5

**Visitor information**

✉ Holbrook Chamber of Commerce, Old County Courthouse, 100 E. Arizona St., Holbrook, AZ 86025

☎ 928/524-6558 or 800/524-2459

**www.ci.holbrook
.az.us**

Vintage cars enhance the mood at the Wigwam Motel, a Route 66 icon.

Inside the 1898 courthouse the **Navajo County Museum** (*100 E. Arizona St.*) shows how Native Americans, pioneers, ranchers, soldiers, and businesspeople lived. Head upstairs to see the restored courtroom, with its high stamped-metal ceiling, and law library. No one escaped from the old jail in the dungeon-like basement. The Holbrook Chamber of Commerce, also in the courthouse, provides local and statewide tourist information, including a tour map.

You can't miss seeing the white stucco tepees of the **Wigwam Motel** (see sidebar this page). Stop for a closer look or spend the night in one! Of the five Mormon farming settlements established along the Little Colorado River in the 1870s, only **Joseph City** has survived. You can detour through the little community, the oldest Anglo settlement in Navajo County, 11 miles west of Holbrook between I-40 Exits 274 and 277. ∎

## EXPERIENCE:
## Sleep in a Wigwam

What kid wouldn't wish to stay the night in a teepee? The **Wigwam Motel** (*811 W. Hopi Dr., Holbrook, tel 928/524-3048*) opened for business in 1950 on Route 66. Owner Chester E. Lewis got the idea from a wigwam village he had seen in Kentucky; he worked out a deal with its owner to use the patented design. Lewis's motel operated until 1974, when business plummeted after I-40 siphoned off traffic from Route 66. His children decided to restore the wigwams, which reopened in 1988. The cozy interiors still have their original hickory furniture.

# Petrified Forest National Park

**The gentle hills of the Painted Desert contain a landscape frozen in time for more than 220 million years. Layers of soft rock, tinted in grays, whites, oranges, and reds, have worn down over the millennia to reveal colored petrified wood and animal fossils.**

Floods of that long-ago time carried fallen trees onto a plain, where minerals in the water slowly replaced the wood cells, filling the spaces between them with brilliant quartz and jasper crystals. Fossils from other plants and animals have enabled scientists to piece together a picture of the late Triassic epoch. Towering conifers grew, along with ferns and palmlike cycads. Massive phytosaurs, resembling crocodiles, and large amphibians prowled the streams and marshes. A six-inch shark searched for food in these waters too. Herds of *Placerias*—reptiles weighing two to three tons—roamed the land. Small dinosaurs scampered about, ancestors of their giant Jurassic cousins.

Nomadic groups passed through the area more than 13,000 years ago. Some later settled, farmed, and built pueblos, but all departed by about A.D. 1400. The early Native Americans left behind petroglyphs and potsherds.

In the late 1800s, when people began hauling off the wood and dynamiting logs for crystals, conservationists pushed for a bill to protect the area. Theodore Roosevelt signed the bill in 1906.

The natural landscape is still recovering from overgrazing begun in the late 1800s, but you're apt to see birds, lizards, and perhaps the speedy, antelope-like pronghorn. After sufficient rains, wildflowers blossom from March to October. ■

**Petrified Forest
National Park**

🅐 175 B5, B6

✉ S Entrance:
19 miles E of
Holbrook on
US 180;
N Entrance:
24 miles NE of
Holbrook off
I-40 Exit 311

☎ 928/524-6228

💲 $$$ per vehicle

**www.nps.gov/pefo**

A rainbow mirrors the colors of wood turned to stone at Petrified Forest National Park.

# A Drive of Many Colors: Petrified Forest National Park

A 28-mile park road connects the petrified wood areas, archaeological sites, and Painted Desert viewpoints. You could easily spend most of a day here, walking the short trails.

Newspaper Rock at Petrified Forest National Park holds many stories. Use your imagination!

Each end of the park has a visitor center with exhibits. You may wish to bring along a picnic (restaurants crop up only at the beginning and end of the drive). The road, open year-round during park hours, closes on Christmas. Dress for the bright sunshine and temperature extremes (there can be swings of up to 40°F between day and night). There are no accommodations within the park.

If you're driving across the state on I-40, save time and distance by starting at the park's south entrance on an eastbound trip and at its north entrance on a westbound one. Otherwise, you may wish to start at the south entrance, as described here, to be sure of having enough time to see the petrified wood concentrated at this end as well as the afternoon light over the Painted Desert near the north end of the drive. Hikers can walk portions of the wilderness area. Talk with a ranger for tips and to get the permit required for overnight trips.

Just inside the south entrance, 19 miles east of Holbrook on US 180, the **Rainbow Forest**

**Museum ❶** displays skeletons of the animals that once lived here and samples of petrified wood. Staff at the information desk/bookstore proffer suggestions and literature on exploring the park. A "Conscience Wood" exhibit displays stolen pieces of petrified wood returned with letters containing remorseful stories and apologies. The **Giant Logs Trail,** behind the museum, follows a half-mile loop among monster-size logs. The **Long Logs Trail ❷** provides another close look at massive logs, some more than 100 feet long, on a half-mile loop. At a trail fork, you can turn off for a 1-mile round-trip to **Agate House,** a prehistoric pueblo constructed entirely of petrified wood. The three-quarter-mile **Crystal Forest Trail ❸** leads past some of the prettiest and most abundant petrified wood. From **Jasper Forest** overlook you get a view of petrified wood that has eroded from hillsides below. A Hashknife cowboy (named after the shape of the brand of the Aztec Land and Cattle Company) once successfully rode his horse across **Agate Bridge**—a petrified log spanning a gully—on a ten-dollar bet. A side road climbs atop **Blue Mesa ❹** for views of the surrounding badlands and petrified wood; you can descend into the badlands on a 1-mile interpretive trail.

Back on the main road, the cone-shaped hills called **The Tepees** stand out, with the

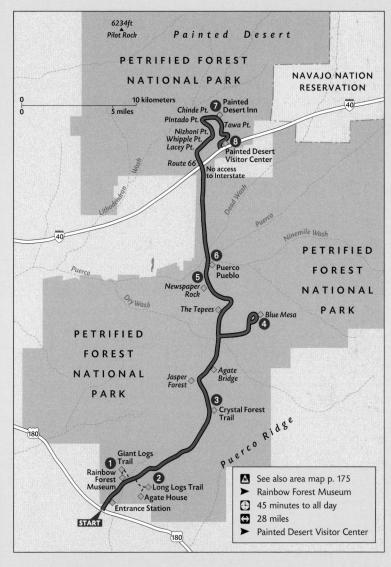

minerals forming bands of colors. Petroglyphs on boulders at **Newspaper Rock** ⑤ show designs left by early Native Americans. Dozens of rooms surround the plaza of **Puerco Pueblo** ⑥. A kiva (underground chamber) near the northwest corner suggests ceremonial life played a role here.

Each of the **viewpoints** at the north end of the drive provide panoramas of the Painted Desert's multicolored rock layers. **Painted Desert**

**Inn** ⑦, built as a traveler's stop with Indian labor and local materials, opened at Kachina Point in 1924. It later expanded into a pueblo-style building with picture windows and Hopi murals. Step inside to see the murals and other historical exhibits. A rim trail goes to Tawa Point, half a mile away. The **Painted Desert Visitor Center** ⑧, just off I-40 Exit 311 (24 miles NE of Holbrook), is near the north entrance.

# South to the Mogollon Rim

As you travel south along Arizona 77 from Holbrook, the high-desert grasslands yield to sparse pinyon pine and juniper woodlands, then to tall stands of ponderosa pine near the Mogollon Rim. Along the way there is pioneer history aplenty in Snowflake and outdoor fun (swimming boating, camping) in Show Low and Pinetop-Lakeside.

## Snowflake
🅰 175 B5

**Visitor information**

✉ Snowflake-Taylor Chamber of Commerce, 113 N. Main St., Snowflake, AZ 85937

☎ 928/536-4331

🕐 Closed Sat.–Sun.

www.snowflaketaylor chamber.org

## Pinetop-Lakeside
🅰 175 B4

**Visitor information**

✉ Pinetop-Lakeside Chamber of Commerce, 102-C W. White Mountain Blvd., Lakeside, Pinetop AZ 85935

☎ 928/367-4290 or 800/573-4031

🕐 Closed Sat.–Sun. except in summer

www.pinetoplakeside chamber.com

## Show Low

✉ 281 E. Deuce of Clubs, Show Low, AZ 85901

☎ 928/537-2326 or 888/746-9569

www.showlowcham berofcommerce.com

**Snowflake's** Mormon pioneers had fun naming their town, which honors its first leader, Erastus Snow, and a traveling church official, William Flake. Many of the buildings dating from the early decades of Snowflake, founded in 1878, still stand; some have become museums. The **John Freeman House** (closed Sat.–Sun.), corner of Main (Ariz. 77) and First North Streets, contains period (1893) rooms.

### INSIDER TIP:

**Thinking of relocating? The 35-square-mile city of Show Low has mild temperatures, six radio stations, and no property taxes.**

—SHEILA BUCKMASTER
National Geographic Traveler
*magazine editor at large*

A poker game gave **Show Low** its name. When two ranch partners found their 100,000-acre spread too small for the two of them in 1870, they decided to play a game of seven-up until one was able to "show low" by drawing the winning card—a deuce of clubs—and taking the ranch. The small **Show Low Historical Society Museum** (541 E. Deuce of Clubs, tel 928/532-7115, closed Sun.–Tues. & Nov.–mid-April; open in winter by appt. only) displays Native American and pioneer exhibits.

**Pintail Lake** attracts waterfowl and other wildlife 3.5 miles north of town on Arizona 77; turn east at the sign between Mileposts 345 and 346. For swimming, boating, picnicking, and camping, head for **Fool Hollow Lake Recreation Area** (tel 928/537-3680), just northwest of Show Low off Arizona 260, and **Show Low Lake** (tel 928/537-4126), 5 miles south of town off Arizona 260.

On the **Mogollon Rim Interpretive Trail** (tel 928/368-5111) you get a fine view of forested hills stretching to the horizon; the level, self-guided loop is about 1 mile; the first 0.3 mile is paved. The trailhead is just west off Arizona 260; drive 5.5 miles south from Show Low and turn right, or go 3 miles north from the Lakeside Ranger District and turn left.

**Pinetop-Lakeside's** name describes the pretty countryside here. On Arizona 260, staffers at the Lakeside Ranger District (2022 W. White Mountain Blvd., Lakeside, AZ 85929, tel 928/368-2100, closed Sat.–Sun., www.fs.fed.us/r3/asnf) can tell you about the lakes, hiking, and camping in the area. ■

# White Mountain Apache Reservation

Some of Arizona's prettiest country belongs to the White Mountain Apache. Their land of forests, lakes, canyons, and mountains lies between the Mogollon Rim to the north and the Salt River and its Black River tributary to the south. You'll need a tribal permit, sold at stores on and near the reservation, for recreational activities and driving on unpaved roads.

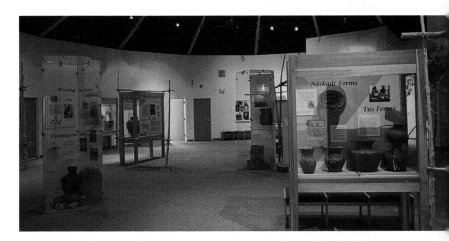

Exhibits at the Apache Cultural Center shed light on Apache beliefs and artistry.

**Hon-Dah,** Apache for "be my guest," is a tourist complex 3 miles south of Pinetop-Lakeside. In addition to a hotel, restaurants, casino, and RV park, there's **Hon-Dah Ski and Outdoor Sport** *(www.wmat outdoors.org)*—the reservation's best source of outdoors information, permits, guides, and supplies on the reservation. Most of the recreational areas lie in the high country east of Hon-Dah.

The 260-acre **Hawley Lake,** at an elevation of 8,300 feet, has a resort *(tel 928/369-1753 lodging, 928/335-7511 store, closed in winter)* with a lodge, cabins, RV park, campground, boat rentals, and store; it's 11.3 miles east of Hon-Dah on Arizona 260, then south 11 miles on Arizona 473. **Horseshoe Lake** covers 121 acres at an elevation of 8,100 feet. Facilities include a campground, summertime store, and boat rentals; head 13.5 miles east from Hon-Dah on Arizona 260, then turn south 1 mile at the sign.

**Sunrise Lake,** the largest lake at 891 acres, lies in the northeast corner of the reservation at 9,300 feet. **Sunrise Park Resort** *(tel 928/735-7669 or 800/772-7669, www.sunriseskipark.com),* 25 miles east of Hon-Dah, features both winter and summer activities. A lodge overlooks the lake, a store carries recreation permits and

**White Mountain Apache Reservation**

🅰 175 A4–C2

**Visitor information**

✉ 787 Ariz. 260, Pinetop, AZ 85935

☎ 928/369-7669 or 877/226-4868

**http://wmat.nsn.us**

supplies, and there's also a marina and ski area. Visitors—including mountain bikers—can ride a lift to the heights on summer weekends.

**Whiteriver,** the main administration town, lies 19 miles south of Hon-Dah. The tribal Game and Fish Department *(tel 928/338-4385, closed Sat.–Sun.)* provides recreation information and permits.

Navigating the Salt River's churning waters

Southwest of town and just east off Arizona 73, **Fort Apache** has buildings from the frontier days. Drop by the **Apache Cultural Center** *(tel 928/338-4625, http://wmat.us, closed Sat–Sun. except in summer,)* on the grounds of the fort to see exhibits on the Apache way of life. Fort Apache's oldest structure, the commanding officer's building, dates from 1871. Step inside for the tribal tourist office *(tel 928/338-1230, closed Sat.–Sun.)* and exhibits that illustrate the life of the Apache, their work as scouts, and how they adapted to the Army's presence. When the cavalry rode into the White River Valley in 1869, troops found peaceful Apache farmers in a garden-like setting. The Army established a camp here the following year.

**Kinishba Ruins,** about 5 miles away, consist of two pueblos built and enlarged between A.D. 1232 and 1320. Archaeologists found pottery and jewelry when they excavated and partly reconstructed the site in the 1930s. Evidence suggests that groups from the Little Colorado, central Gila, and Salt Rivers converged here. Check with the cultural center before visiting the ruins.

Farther southwest, the highway (US 60/Arizona 77) drops into the spectacular **Salt River Canyon,** 3 miles wide and 1,410 feet deep. Pullouts allow you to admire the views. To see more, obtain a recreation permit from the store north of the bridge, then drive the dirt roads downstream. In spring, rafters put in for excursions down the Salt River. ■

# San Carlos Apache Reservation

**South from the Salt and Black Rivers, the landscape gradually changes from cool mountain forests to dry woodlands and grasslands, then to a cactus-studded desert farther south. You'll find a pleasant climate any time of year.**

The administrative town of San Carlos, largest community on the reservation, lacks charm. You can get information and permits at the San Carlos Recreation and Wildlife Department, on Moon Base Road just north of US 70, about 1.5 miles east of the Arizona 170 junction. Other permit sources include the San Carlos Lake Store and businesses in towns off the reservation. No permit is needed for the paved roads, but travel on unpaved roads requires one, as do recreation activities.

Exhibits in the **San Carlos Apache Cultural Center** *(tel 928/475-2894, closed Sat.–Sun.)* tell the tribe's history from an Apache perspective. You'll learn about Apache spiritual beginnings, cultural traditions, migrations across the Southwest, confinement to reservations in the 19th century, and contemporary life. A gift shop sells local art and crafts. The cultural center is located on the north side of US 70 near Milepost 272, just east of the Arizona 170 junction. You can stay, dine, gamble, and golf at the **Apache Gold Casino Resort** *(tel 928/475-7800 or 800/272-2438, www.apachegoldcasinoresort.com)* on US 70 just 7 miles east of Globe.

**San Carlos Lake** on the Gila River attracts visitors year-round. Covering 19,500 acres when full, the lake is the largest within the

In a 1800s photo, Amos Gustina holds the violin that is now on display in the San Carlos Apache Cultural Center.

state—23 miles long and 2 miles wide. **Coolidge Dam,** dedicated in 1930, is worth a stop for the view of the dam and canyon. Paved roads to the lake branch off US 70 south of the Arizona 170 junction and near Bylas.

Soda Canyon Point Campground offers views on the northwest shore, and there's a nearby marina. The turnoff is 9.5 miles south from the US 70–Arizona 170 junction and 2 miles north of the dam. Lake levels fluctuate greatly, so call ahead if you're planning to fish or boat. ∎

## San Carlos Apache Reservation

▲ 175 A2–A3, B2–B3

**Visitor information**

✉ San Carlos Recreation & Wildlife Dept., P.O. Box 97, San Carlos, AZ 85550

☎ 928/475-2343 or 888/475-2344

🕐 Closed Sun.

www.scatrwd.com

www.sancarlos apache.com

# The Apache

**Calling themselves Indeh (The People), the Apache share a heritage with the Navajo. Ancestors of both tribes may have crossed the Bering Strait land bridge about 6,000 years ago, eventually migrating to the Great Plains, then the Southwest. By the end of the 1700s, Navajo had settled in the Four Corners region, Western Apache in the central and eastern mountains, and the Chiricahua Apache in the southeastern mountains.**

The early Apache lived a nomadic life with few possessions. The men hunted and the women foraged for wild plants. Small conical huts covered with animal skins provided shelter. Later, the tribespeople learned from their Navajo or Pueblo neighbors how to cultivate corn, beans, and squash to supplement their diet. Horses, acquired from raids on the Spanish and later on Mexican and Anglo soldiers and settlers, gave the Apache great speed and range, which they used with skill to raid other tribes, the Spanish, and the Anglos.

**An Apache woman dresses up for an 1898 portrait.**

So proficient were Apache warriors that they nearly always prevailed in conflicts. Their tenacity at holding their lands forestalled Anglo settlement long after other tribes had made peace. Only with the surrender of Geronimo in 1886 did travelers and settlers feel safe in the region. Much of the credit for the eventual success of the U.S. Army has to be given to the Apache scouts. These men voluntarily enlisted with the Army, using their traditional warrior and tracking skills to hunt down renegade bands of Apache. In exchange, the scouts received pay, horses and other valuables, and experience with a new way of life.

The federal government committed many blunders through dishonest or misguided dealings with the Apache. Attempts to force incompatible groups together on the same reservation caused friction, sparking escapes by bands who terrorized the Southwest. The Chiricahua Apache met a particularly sad fate. Unlike the Navajo, who had been allowed to return to their homeland after deportation, the Chiricahua were forced from their lands, never to return. The Western Apache fared best, retaining extensive homelands in eastern Arizona and smaller lands in central Arizona.

Today the Apache live and work like most other Arizonans, yet many of the tribe still speak Apache and follow traditional ways. Boys may train under medicine men to learn the prayers, rituals, and medicinal plants used for healing ceremonies and other rites. Young women may mark their passage to adulthood with the Sunrise Dance, a difficult ordeal that lasts four days. Apache spirit dancers, also known as crown dancers, wear masks and crowns of sticks in Sunrise Dances and other religious ceremonies as representatives of the *gaan*—friendly mountain spirits who bless and protect the Apache. Staffers at cultural centers can tell you of dances open to the public, as well as rodeos and other events.

The Apache weave very fine baskets—one of the few articles suited to an itinerant lifestyle. Women make beautiful buckskin clothing, worn at Sunrise Dances. Artists and craftspeople create paintings, crown dancer figures, and beadwork, which you'll find in galleries and cultural center gift shops.

# EXPERIENCE: Modern Adventures in the White Mountain Apache Lands

You'll find some of Arizona's prettiest forest country here in Apache country, and the pleasant summer temperatures offer cool comfort. Trout fishing is a big draw with many streams and lakes to choose from. Groups can even rent their own lake! Boaters cruise lakes or run wild rapids of the **Salt River Canyon** (see p. 184). Cabins in a few areas provide rustic luxury; you also have a choice of established campgrounds, though facilities tend to be basic. To really get away, toss on a pack and head for the backcountry. Mountain bikers can visit the heights at **Sunrise Park Resort** *(www .sunriseskipark.com)* in summer for wild downhill rides or head out on quiet forest roads. Winter snow brings skiers and snowboarders to the best runs in the state. Tribal permits are required for almost any activity, though costs are reasonable and you don't need state licenses for fishing, boating, or hunting. **Hon-Dah Ski and Outdoor Sport** *(3 miles S of Pinetop, tel 928/369-7669 or 877/226-4868)* has information, permits, and gear; also check *http://wmatoutdoors .org/* for recreation options and details.

Apache leader Geronimo (1829–1909), on the right, stands still for a photograph with some of his braves. The occasion? Geronimo's surrender on September 4, 1886.

# Safford

Farmers have long tilled the soil of the Gila River Valley—Mogollon, Hohokam, and Salado in early times and, from the 1870s through the present, Anglo colonists. Fields of cotton, together with some wheat, barley, and other crops, now cover the bottomland. The town of Safford, named for the third territorial governor, makes a pleasant base for exploring nearby mountain and wilderness areas.

The Pinaleños, "sky islands" southwest of Safford, offer a cool haven for flora, fauna, and hikers.

**Safford**

⛰ 175 B1

**Visitor information**

✉ Graham County Chamber of Commerce, 1111 Thatcher Blvd., Safford, AZ 85546

☎ 928/428-2511 or 888/837-1841

**www.visitgraham county.com**

**Kachina Mineral Springs Spa**

**www.kachinasprings .com**

Wonders of the universe are unveiled at **Discovery Park.** Gaze at an image of nearby Mount Graham projected by a camera obscura, or see the heavens at night through a telescope once used on Kitt Peak. The Polaris Space Flight Simulator takes you on a wild ride through the solar system. A wildlife sanctuary contains a variety of habitats with trails and viewing blinds. Tours of **Mount Graham International Observatory** depart Friday and Saturday from sometime in May into October, by reservation. From US 70 on the west side of town,

turn south on 20th Avenue to its end; or, from US 191 south of town, turn west on Discovery Park Boulevard and go to its end at 20th Avenue, then turn left.

Journey back in time at the **Graham County Historical Society Museum** in Thatcher, just northwest of Safford (US 70 & 4th Ave., tel 928/348-0470, closed Sun. & Wed.–Fri.). Rooms in a 1917 school suggest simpler days. In Pima, 9 miles west of Safford, the **Eastern Arizona Museum**'s collection (tel 928/485-9400, closed Sun.–Wed.) celebrates the area's Native Americans and pioneers.

**INSIDER TIP:**

Summer's too steamy, but at any other time seek out a hot soak just outside Safford at Kachina Mineral Springs Spa—nice for hike-weary muscles.

—AMY ALIPIO
*National Geographic Traveler magazine associate editor*

All that cotton in the Safford area heads to **ginning mills** during the October to December harvest. Tour one by calling ahead to the Safford Valley Cotton Growers Co-op *(tel 928/428-0714)*, just off US 191 in Safford or the Glenbar Gin *(tel 928/485-9255)* just west of Pima on US 70.

For dramatic views of the mountain ranges and valleys, hiking, picnicking, and camping, it's hard to beat the Swift Trail (Arizona 366), which climbs onto the long ridge of the Pinaleño Mountains, southwest of Safford. Start from US 191, about 7 miles south of Safford, or drive 26 miles north from I-10 Exit 352 to the start. The first 21 miles of the trail are paved, followed by a 14-mile gravel section that is generally open mid-April to mid-November.

The Pinaleños are crowned by **Mount Graham** (10,720 feet), its summit towering more than 7,000 feet above the desert. On the way up, cactus and mesquite give way to conifer forests of ponderosa pine, Douglas and white fir, and Engelmann spruce. The summit has been closed to the public to protect the Mount Graham red squirrel, which experts believe lives only in the Pinaleños. Construction of new buildings at the nearby Mount Graham International Observatory faced bitter opposition (since partly resolved) from conservationists and tribe members, who feared loss of access to this sacred area.

**Heliograph Peak** (10,028 feet), near the east end of the mountains, and **Webb Peak** (10,086 feet), farther west, provide grand panoramas. You'll normally need to walk the last 2.2 miles of unpaved road to Heliograph; likewise, you can hike the 1-mile (one way) **Webb Peak Trail** or walk the last 1.7 miles of road to Webb. Contact the Safford Ranger for details. You must obtain a permit in advance to enter **Aravaipa Canyon Wilderness,** even for day hikes. Contact the Bureau of Land Management office in Safford for directions. ∎

**Discovery Park**

- ✉ 1651 W. Discovery Park Blvd.
- ☎ 928/428-6260
- 🕐 Closed Sun., open daytime Mon.–Fri. and Sat. evening

**www.eac.edu/ discoverypark**

**Safford Ranger District, Coronado National Forest**

- ✉ 711 14th Ave., Ste. D, Safford, AZ 85546
- ☎ 928/428-4150
- 🕐 Closed Sat.–Sun.

**www.fs.fed.us/r3/ coronado**

**Bureau of Land Management**

- ✉ 711 14th Ave., Safford, AZ 85546
- ☎ 928/348-4400
- 🕐 Closed Sat.–Sun.

**www.blm.gov/az/ aravaipa**

## Flora and Fauna of Aravaipa Canyon Wilderness

The Aravaipa Creek's year-round waters ripple through the heart of the canyon, hosting the best remaining assemblage of desert fish in Arizona, with seven native species, including the threatened spikedace and loach minnow. The creek attracts more than 200 species of birds, and, with luck, you might see desert bighorn sheep, coatimundi, ring-tailed cats, black bear, or even a mountain lion. In spring, look for colorful native wildflowers such as columbine, lupine, four o'clock, and monkey flowers. You'll need a permit to visit, available from the Bureau of Land Management online or at the Safford office.

# A Drive on the Coronado Trail

The paved highway that retraces Francisco Vásquez de Coronado's epic journey in 1540 provides one of the greatest driving adventures in the West, with stellar panoramas and beautiful alpine country along the way. Many back roads, camping areas, hiking trails, mountain streams, and lakes lie near the drive, which is equally scenic in both directions. Directions here are given from the south, starting in Clifton.

Looking like toys, giant 210-ton trucks haul copper ore out of Morenci Mine.

With some 460 curves between Morenci and Alpine alone, this is not a trip for those in a hurry. Although you could travel the 123 miles in four hours nonstop, the scenery calls for a more leisurely pace. Hannagan Meadow and Alpine offer accommodations, and you'll find plenty of campgrounds. The Apache-Sitgreaves National Forest *(tel 928/333-4301, www.fs.fed.us/r3/asnf)* is

---

## NOT TO BE MISSED:

**Clifton • Morenci Mine • Blue Vista • Hannagan Meadow**

---

steward for most of the land along the way. It's best to stock up on food and gas before setting out. Snow can close the section between Morenci and Hannagan Meadow from mid-December to mid-March, when cross-country skiers come out to play.

**Clifton ❶** bears several reminders of its mining past. Stop by the Greenlee County Chamber of Commerce *(tel 928/865-3313, closed Sat.–Sun.)*, in a 1913 train depot beside US 191, for information and to see the Copper Head locomotive and old jail across the highway. Turn left up Chase Creek Street, lined with early 20th-century buildings, for exhibits on the area and its mines at **Greenlee County Historical Society Museum** *(317 Chase Creek St., tel 928/865-3115, call for hours)*.

US 191 switchbacks northwest up to the modern mining town of **Morenci,** relocated here when old Morenci got in the way of

---

## Motoring the Black Hills Back Country Byway

On this 21-mile scenic drive, you leave the pavement behind to experience the views, geology, and natural world in a way that's not possible on the main highway. A high-clearance vehicle works best for this excursion, which loops off US 191 between Milepost 139 east of Safford and Milepost 160 south of Clifton. You'll climb into the volcanic Black Mountains, where a picnic area offers fine views over the Gila River Canyon and beyond. Down near the 1918 Gila River Bridge, there's another picnic area and a nearby campground.

mining operations. Continuing higher, you'll reach an overlook on the right for the open-pit **Morenci Mine ➋.** At 3 miles wide and 6 miles long, it's one of the world's largest man-made holes. Past the mining operation, the highway enters the forest and ascends higher into the mountains. **Cherry Lodge Picnic Area,** 20 miles from Clifton on the left between Mileposts 178 and 179, is a pleasant spot to rest; a campground lies across the highway. **Rose Peak ➌** has a great panorama from a fire lookout on its 8,786-foot summit; you can hike up a 1-mile trail (one way) from a trailhead near Milepost 207.

The highway climbs up the Mogollon Rim to **Blue Vista ➍,** a 9,184-foot-high overlook from which you can see countless ridges and mountains, including Mount Graham, 70 miles southwest in the Pinaleños; the turnoff is on the left near Milepost 225. Splendid forests of spruce, fir, and aspen blanket either side of the highway in the **Hannagan Meadow ➎** area, 73 miles from Clifton. There's a year-round lodge (tel 928/339-4370, www.hannaganmeadow .com), plus campgrounds, trails, and cross-country skiing nearby.

Another 22 miles north takes you to **Alpine** (tel 928/339-4330, www.alpine arizona.com), where you'll find lodging, restaurants, and supplies. **Escudilla Mountain** (10,912 feet), a bit farther north, is Arizona's third highest summit. As US 191/180 drops to the high-desert area around Springerville, you'll pass **Nelson Reservoir,** a 60-acre lake popular for boating and fishing. **Springerville ➏** marks the end of the trail; staff at the **Springerville-Eagar Regional Chamber of Commerce** (318 E. Main St., tel 928/333-2123 or 866/733-2123, www.springerville-eagarchamber.com, closed Sun.) can suggest things to see and do in eastern Arizona (see p. 192).

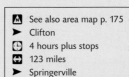

| | |
|---|---|
| 🅰 | See also area map p. 175 |
| ▶ | Clifton |
| 🕐 | 4 hours plus stops |
| ↔ | 123 miles |
| ▶ | Springerville |

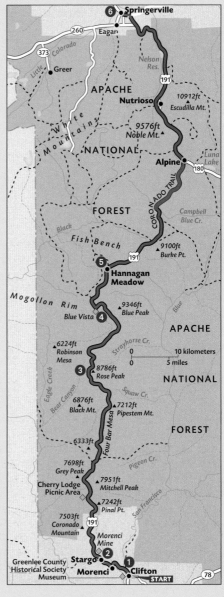

# More Places to Visit in Eastern Arizona

## Casa Malpais

Just north of Springerville, this prehistoric pueblo (whose Spanish name means "house of the badlands") boasts some unusual features. The Mogollon culture built it between A.D. 1260 and 1440 at the edge of a lava flow—and on top of more than a hundred underground cracks that once served as ritual and burial chambers. (Sacred to modern Pueblo tribes, the rooms are not open to the public.) A **Great Kiva** (ceremonial chamber) covering 62 feet by 55 feet (possibly roofed) and an enclosure that may have been an astronomical observatory reinforce the view that this pueblo was a major trade and ceremonial center. The main ruin stood two and three stories high, with more than 120 rooms. Look for rock art and unusual masonry stairways. You may enter the site only on tours, which take about 1.5–2 hours and feature a .75-mile loop walk with a climb of 125 feet. Call ahead for tour times, then meet at the **Casa Malpais Museum** in Springerville before continuing to the site. ⚠ 175 C4 ✉ Museum: 418 E. Main St., Springerville ☎ 928/333-5375 ⏱ Closed Sun. (Sun.–Mon. in winter) $ $$ (museum free)

## Greer

Evergreen and aspen forests surround this village, set in a pretty valley at an elevation of 8,500 feet in the White Mountains. It's a popular summer retreat and a winter recreation center. Trails and fishing lakes lie close at hand. When the snow arrives, people set off on cross-country skis or head for the slopes of nearby Sunrise Ski Area. Luxurious lodges, bed-and-breakfasts, rustic cabins, and campgrounds afford visitors a wide range of places to stay. Mormons settled here in 1879 and later named their community for one of its pioneers. Two extraordinary local residents, author James Willard Schultz (1859–1947) and his artist son "Lone Wolf" (1882–1970), lived in a cabin that has since become the **Butterfly Lodge Museum** (*Cty. Rd. 1126, E off Ariz. 370 0.5 mile S of the Circle B Market, tel 928/735-7514, closed Mon.–Wed. & autumn–spring*). Inside, you can learn about the elder Schultz—who married a Blackfoot woman, explored the West, and wrote 37 adventure stories—and see works by Schultz's son, who portrayed the West in paintings and sculpture. To reach Greer, head west 16 miles from Springerville on Arizona 260, then turn south and drive for 5 miles on Arizona 373. **Visitor information** *www.springerville-eagar chamber.com* ⚠ 175 C4 ✉ 418 E. Main St., Springerville (P.O. Box 31, Springerville, AZ 85938) ☎ 928/333-2123 or 866/733-2123 ⏱ Closed Sun.

**INSIDER TIP:**

There are thousands of ruins to explore in the region. What makes Casa Malpais so interesting is that folks here lived on a lava flow.

—DAWN KISH
*National Geographic photographer*

## Lyman Lake State Park

Junipers and other high-desert vegetation surround a 1,500-acre lake fed by the Little Colorado River. People come to boat, swim, picnic, and camp. Short trails lead across a peninsula to petroglyph panels. On summer weekends, rangers conduct tours to the Ultimate Petroglyph site across the lake; reservations recommended. *www.azstateparks.com* ⚠ 175 C4 ✉ 18 miles N of Springerville on US 191/180 (bet. Mileposts 380 & 381) ☎ 928/337-4441 $ $$ day use, $$$–$$$$$ camping

A rich mix of cultural heritages, where the Sonoran Desert and "sky islands" harbor a vast diversity of wildlife

# Southern Arizona

Mission San Xavier del Bac sets a
mood of serene beauty in the desert.

# Southern Arizona

A wealth of historic sights and places of natural splendor await in this sweep of the state. Across the region, rugged mountains thrust high above the desert. Isolated cool-climate forests cover the four highest ranges, all with peaks above 9,000 feet: the Santa Catalinas, the Santa Ritas, the Huachucas, and the Chiricahuas. The canyons and summits of these sky islands provide homes for a profusion of plants and animals.

A winter storm in the mountains frosts an intensely focused, elusive mountain lion.

The stately saguaro cactuses of the Sonoran Desert cover much of southern Arizona's landscape, along with many other impressive plants. Although rainfall may be scant—just 11 inches annually in Tucson, for example—it occurs during two seasons, with both winter and summer showers. The resulting greenery may come as a surprise.

Wildflowers stage a colorful show in the spring, especially when winter rains have been plentiful. So remarkable are the plants and wildlife of the Sonoran Desert that Saguaro National Park and Organ Pipe Cactus National Monument were created to help protect them.

The Hohokam settled along the rivers, channeling water to their fields of corn, beans,

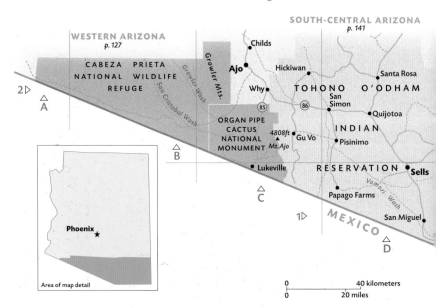

squash, and cotton. For reasons still unknown, the Hohokam's sophisticated culture collapsed sometime between A.D. 1300 and 1450. Their descendants likely became the modern O'odham (AH-tomb), who carried on life with a simpler farming existence along the rivers as the Akimel O'odham (also known as Pima) or at springs in the Sonoran Desert as the Tohono O'odham (formerly called Papago).

Spanish explorers had entered the region on unsuccessful quests for gold as early as 1539, but no attempt at a permanent Spanish presence was made until Jesuit priest Eusebio Francisco Kino arrived as a missionary in 1691. His efforts led to the founding of missions such as San Xavier del Bac, where the O'odham still worship. Presidios (fortified towns) at Tucson, Tubac, and elsewhere provided some security, but neither the Spanish nor their Mexican successors managed to subjugate the Apache, who periodically terrorized both Indian and European settlements.

Americans poured in during the late 1800s and struck silver in places such as Tombstone,

---

## NOT TO BE MISSED:

The Tucson Museum of Art & Historic Block's eclectic offerings  196–197

Arizona–Sonora Desert Museum's rare native wildlife  206–208

Mission San Xavier del Bac's wonderful folk art  220

Evoking the Old West at Tombstone  226–227

Bisbee's early 20th-century architecture  228–229

Hiking amid fanciful rock forms at Chiricahua National Monument  230

Amerind Museum for exceptional exhibits on American Indian cultures  232

---

famed for its shootout at the O.K. Corral. Vast copper deposits, still mined today, proved more valuable in the long term, giving Arizona its nickname: the Copper State. ∎

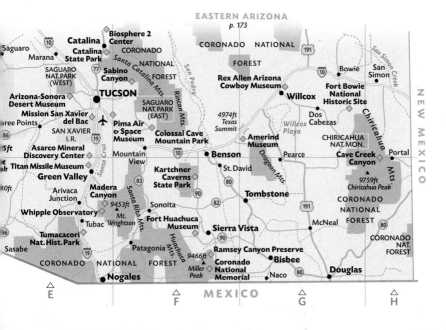

# Tucson

Arizona's second largest city, Tucson claims to be the oldest continuously inhabited settlement in the United States. Hohokam farmers had arrived here by the first century A.D. Their Akimel O'odham successors called their village Stjukshon—"spring at the foot of a black mountain." Spanish soldiers arrived in 1775 and built a presidio, adapting the name to Tucson.

Viewed from "A" Mountain, the Tucson metropolis transitions into early evening.

**Tucson**

🅰 195 E2

**Visitor information**

✉ Tucson Visitor Center, 110 S. Church Ave., Tucson, Arizona 85701

☎ 520/624-1817 or 800/638-8350

**www.visittucson.org**

Visitors to Tucson (TOO-sahn) can explore the town for quite a while before they run out of things to do. Plenty of memorable places to visit lie in the city or within an hour's drive. Nature is never far away, from alpine forests to the Sonoran Desert's saguaro cactuses and other intriguing plants. The 9,157-foot-high Mount Lemmon of the Santa Catalinas stands just to the north, offering scenic drives, challenging hiking trails, and the United States' southernmost ski area.

The "Old Pueblo," as some call the city, retains its rich and lengthy heritage. Visitors can step into old adobe buildings for a glimpse of the past, join in the lively arts scene, or explore the frontiers of science: Tucson reaches for the stars with its claim to be the "astronomy capital of the world." A good place to being is with some world-class museums.

Galleries in the main building of the downtown **Tucson Museum of Art & Historic Block** display modern and contemporary art along with visiting exhibits. Step into the 1868 Fish House to explore the **Art of the American West** collection with paintings of landscapes and cowboy life along with bronzes. Next door, the 1866 Stevens House has the **Art of Latin America** collection's Pre-Columbian, Spanish

**INSIDER TIP:**

The Lost Barrio, a strip on Tucson's South Park Avenue, is a revitalized mix of good Southwestern fun: artists, antiques, and cafés.

—CHRISTINE STANLEY
*National Geographic contributor*

colonial, and folk art; it also has a restaurant. If you walk to the street in front of the Stevens House and turn right, you'll reach the **Corbett House,** a mission revival bungalow dating from 1906–1907; you can see its arts and crafts collection on a tour or by appointment. From the central Plaza of the Pioneers, walk east to **La Casa Cordova,** an adobe dating from about 1848; it hosts the seasonal El Nacimiento, an elaborate tableau of biblical and Mexican scenes, on display from about mid-November to March.

The **University of Arizona,** east of downtown, opened in 1891 with 32 students housed and taught in a single building, now known as Old Main. The students number around 37,000 today, and the university has some excellent museums and a lively cultural life. The visitor center, just west of the campus, offers maps, tours, and listings of things to see and do. (Signs direct you to visitor parking around the edges of campus—the central area is closed to motor traffic.) The **Arizona State Museum** *(tel 520/621-6302, www.statemuseum.arizona.edu, closed*

*Sun.),* a great place to learn about Arizona's Native Americans, is on the west side of campus near University Boulevard and Park Avenue. Take time to explore the outstanding "Paths of Life: American Indians of the Southwest" exhibit; it conveys the cultural traditions and contemporary lifestyles of ten Native American peoples of Arizona and northern Mexico. Temporary exhibits are offered, too. A gift shop sells books and Native American crafts. The **Arizona History Museum** *(949 E. 2nd St., tel 520/628-5774, www.arizonahistoricalsociety.org, closed Sun.)* brings the territorial years to life. Not part of the university, it lies just west of the campus, across Park Avenue. (Park in the garage one block west on Second Street.)

**Tucson Museum of Art & Historic Block**
- 199 C2
- 140 N. Main Ave.
- Closed Mon.
- 520/624-2333
- $$
- www.tucsonmuseum ofart.org

**University of Arizona Visitor Center**
- 199 C2
- 811 N. Euclid Ave. (NW corner of Euclid Ave. & University Blvd.)
- 520/621-5130
- Closed Sat.–Sun.
- www.arizona.edu

## EXPERIENCE: Gaze Heavenward!

Astronomy continues to generate intense enthusiasm among both amateur and professional observers in this part of the state. Couple a telescope (there are plenty of them hereabouts) with dependably stellar weather, and the night sky is yours. Begin the experience at the **Flandrau Science Center** on the University of Arizona campus for astronomy exhibits, planetarium shows (Hector Vector Star Projector does the honors) and, yes, a chance to look through a telescope on observatory nights. The **Tucson Amateur Astronomy Association** *(www.tucsonastronomy.org/)* has regular meetings open to the public and an engaging website with news and places to visit. For a look at cutting-edge astronomy, take a tour of nearby **Kitt Peak** (see p. 217) and **Whipple Observatory** (see p. 221).

David Tineo's vivid "Nuestras Raices Humanas" (Our Roots) graces the Tucson Museum of Art. This is but a small detail.

observatory programs; the website is a good source of local astronomy news and information on planetarium shows. Some evenings, the public gets to use the facility's 16-inch telescope.

Regional and exotic flora appear in an array of beautiful settings, including a tropical greenhouse, in **Tucson Botanical**

The **University of Arizona Museum of Art** *(tel 520/621-7567, http://artmuseum.arizona.edu, closed Mon.),* part of the Fine Arts Center in the northwestern part of the campus, features Renaissance, later European, American, and contemporary art. Occasional visiting shows. (Visitor parking is north across Speedway.)

The **Center for Creative Photography** *(tel 520/621-7968, www.creativephotography.org),* just southeast of the art museum, showcases some of the world's greatest photographers, among them Richard Avedon, Ansel Adams, Paul Strand, and Edward Weston. The center has a research library and small gift shop.

On the east side of campus at University Boulevard and Cherry Avenue, **Flandrau Science Center** *(tel 520/621-7827, www.ua sciencecenter.org)* has a world-class mineral museum and nighttime

**Gardens.** Chances are you will find something of interest at this acclaimed urban oasis of 16 gardens, where environmental stewardship is key. Plantings range from cactuses and succulents to an exhibit of Native American crops and a xeriscape (dry) garden. If you bring children with you, be sure to visit the memorable children's discovery garden. Themed areas feature gardens devoted to irises, wildflowers, and plants that attract butterflies. Pick up a self-guiding brochure; tours and classes are offered on some days. The gardens have a small art gallery and a gift shop, teahouse, and café; staff organize seasonal events and sales. ■

**Tucson Botanical Gardens**

🅰 199 D2

✉ 2150 N. Alvernon Way

☎ 520/326-9686

💲 $$

www.tucson botanical.org

# Walking Tucson's History

This itinerary gives insight into the lives of Spaniards, Mexicans, and Anglos in early Tucson. Beginning in El Presidio Historic District, the site of the 1775 presidio, the tour then loops south to the Barrio Histórico District. Guided tours are scheduled at the Tucson Museum of Art and the Sosa-Carillo-Frémont House Museum.

The exquisitely tiled dome of the Pima County Courthouse adds vibrant color to downtown.

Start the walk at the **Tucson Museum of Art & Historic Block ❶** (see pp. 196–197) at 140 North Main Avenue. You can park in the museum's lot west across Main (the entrance is on Paseo Redondo) or in one of the other parking lots nearby. The museum doesn't open until 10 a.m. (noon on Sundays), so you may prefer to wait until the end of your walk to go inside.

    **Old Town Artisans,** in an 1862 adobe across Meyer, carries Southwestern arts and crafts. From the northwest corner of the historic block, cross Washington to the **Sam Hughes House** *(not open to the public).* Hughes came to Tucson for his health, then became

**NOT TO BE MISSED:**

Tucson Museum of Art & Historic Block • Pima County Courthouse • St. Augustine Cathedral • El Tiradito • Sosa-Carillo-Frémont House

an important businessman and developer. He moved into the house in 1864 and expanded it considerably to accommodate his 15 children.

    North one block and across Main, the 1900 **Steinfeld Mansion,** with its Spanish mission-style architecture of brick and stucco,

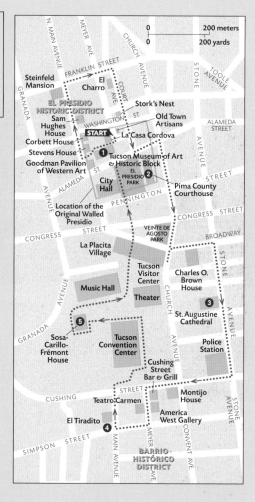

See also area map p. 199
► Tucson Museum of Art &
  Historic Block
⏱ Half a day
↔ 3.3 miles
► Tucson Museum of Art &
  Historic Block

shows how the wealthy lived in Tucson at the beginning of the 20th century.

French stonemason Jules le Flein came to Tucson in the 1890s to work on the St. Augustine Cathedral; then, in 1900, he built his house on Court Avenue—now **El Charro** Mexican restaurant, founded by Flein's daughter Monica in 1922—of dark stone from Sentinel Peak. The adobe **Stork's Nest,** one block south, was Tucson's first maternity ward.

Continue south on Court, turn left on Alameda, then go right on Church to the domed 1928 **Pima County Courthouse** ❷, a colorful mix of Moorish, Spanish, and Southwestern architecture. A small exhibit of the original presidio wall lies inside the Assessor-Treasurer office (turn left from the front courtyard).

Two blocks farther south on Church, you can take a break at the small **Veinte de Agosto Park,** which commemorates the founding of the presidio on August 20, 1775. An equestrian statue of General Francisco "Pancho" Villa stands in the center. You may wish to stop by the **Tucson Visitor Center** across Broadway in La Placita Village.

From the park, head east one block on Broadway past the **Charles O. Brown House,** now El Centro Cultural de Las Americas, built on Jackson in 1858 and extended to Broadway between 1868 and 1877. Around the corner

and two blocks south on Stone, you'll reach the 1896 **St. Augustine Cathedral** ❸, remodeled in the late 1920s with an attractive sandstone facade styled after the Cathedral of Querétaro in Mexico. Look for Southwestern elements along with religious designs.

Turn right after the Police Station (check out the John Dillinger exhibits in the lobby) onto Cushing and pass the **Montijo House,** built by a Mexican ranching family in the 1860s, then remodeled in Victorian style in the 1890s. Joseph Ferrin ran a store in the late 1800s in what is now the **Cushing Street Bar & Grill.**

The big rodeo parade of La Fiesta de los Vaqueros relies entirely on muscle power.

**INSIDER TIP:**

Step inside Tucson's re-created Presidio Walls (Washington St. and Church Ave.) and come face to face with an 18th-century scene from this Spanish colonial town.

—VERA MARIE BADERTSCHER
*National Geographic contributor*

Around the corner on Meyer is the **America West Gallery** *(closed Sat.)*, in a building dating from around the 1880s; you can go inside to see the collection of exotic antiques from around the world and primitive art. **Teatro Carmen,** across the street, opened in 1915 as a Spanish-language theater.

El Tiradito ❹, or the Wishing Shrine, marks the grave of young Juan Oliveras. He was caught having an affair with his mother-in-law, and his father-in-law killed him in 1880. On account of his sins, Juan couldn't be buried in consecrated ground, so people laid him to rest here, lit candles, and prayed for his soul. A custom developed that if a candle lit on the grave burned down to its base, the candle lighter's wish would be granted.

Follow the sidewalk around the Exhibit Hall and Arena of the Tucson Convention Center to the **Sosa-Carillo-Frémont House** ❺ *(151 S. Granada Ave., tel 520/628-5774, call for hours)*. The Carillo family built this adobe residence around 1880 on land purchased from the Sosas, then frequently hosted the fifth territorial governor, John C. Frémont, during his visits to Tucson. A self-guided tour explains architectural details of the house, including the five types of ceilings. From the Frémont House, walk up the steps alongside the Music Hall to a small park, then turn left (north) through La Placita Village—modern shops and offices styled to look like a Mexican village. Continue across two footbridges to **El Presidio Park,** where Spanish soldiers drilled and held fiestas two centuries ago. From here, the Tucson Museum of Art & Historic Block is just a short stroll north.

# More Places to Visit in Tucson

## De Grazia's Gallery in the Sun

Arizona artist Ettore "Ted" De Grazia died in 1982, but his gallery remains open as a museum. Born in the Morenci mining district, De Grazia was fascinated by the colors and cultures of the Southwest. Though best known for his paintings, he used a variety of other media and even wrote several books. Wander through the gallery's various rooms to see just how De Grazia employed these techniques. Don't miss the 1950s open-roof Mission in the Sun. Local artists exhibit in the Little Gallery from November through April. From downtown, head east 4 miles on Broadway; turn left and go 6 miles north on Swan Road. *www.degrazia.org* 199 D3 ✉ 6300 N. Swan Rd. ☎ 520/299-9191 or 800/545-2185

## Reid Park Zoo

Come here to meet both the big African animals and some lesser celebrated creatures, such as anteaters. The South American loop has a walk-in aviary among its dozen exhibits. Vegetation from many lands provides natural habitats for the animals. From downtown, go east 3.5 miles on 22nd Street; the entrance is on the north between Country Club Road and Alvernon Way. *www.tucsonzoo.org* 199 D2 ☎ 520/791-4022 $ $$

## Tohono Chul Park

As its Tohono O'odham name (meaning "desert corner") suggests, Tohono Chul Park allows you to enjoy the desert in the city. Nature trails weave through 49 acres, where you're likely to see birds and other wildlife. A variety of plants grow in themed gardens, including an ethno-botanical garden, a hummingbird garden, and one designed to especially interest children. A wall beside the demonstration garden explains the geology of the Santa Catalinas. Art shows in the Exhibit House reflect Southwestern and Mexican themes. From the junction of Oracle and Ina Roads in northwest Tucson, head west one block on Ina, then turn north (right) at the first light. *www.tohonochulpark .org* 199 C3 ✉ 7366 N. Paseo del Norte ☎ 520/742-6455 $ $$

The adobe Mission in the Sun, De Grazia's inviting sanctuary, is dedicated to Our Lady of Guadalupe.

# West Tucson

For a scenic drive out of town, head west over Gates Pass (cars only—the road isn't suitable for RVs or vehicles with trailers). It's a fine start to a day trip that takes in the rugged Tucson Mountains and worthy attractions aplenty, including the outstanding Arizona–Sonora Desert Museum, Saguaro National Park, and Old Tucson Studios.

A cyclist speeds down from Gates Pass into the Avra Valley, an enclave of local treasures.

**International Wildlife Museum**

🅰 199 C2

✉ 4800 W. Gates Pass Rd. (Road is fine for large vehicles coming from Tucson)

☎ 520/629-0100

💲 $$

www.thewildlife museum.org

Closest to the city, 5 miles west of I-10 on Gates Pass Road, is the **International Wildlife Museum.** Taxidermists have prepared and mounted mammals, birds, and insects of more than 400 species, displayed here in dioramas and natural-looking settings. A 30-foot "mountain" forms the centerpiece for the wild sheep and goats. Dazzling butterflies and beetles show the beauty of the insect world. A nocturnal exhibit re-creates life on a desert evening. You can also see and learn about unusual wildlife, such as rare birds-of-paradise from Papua New Guinea and passenger

pigeons, once abundant in the United States but now extinct. Whatever your age, try out the touch and interactive exhibits.

Unless you have a large rig, head west on Gates Pass Road over the pass, where a scenic overlook on the right is worth a stop. About 11 miles from Tucson, turn left on Kinney Road, then left again in less than a mile for **Old Tucson Studios,** which replicates the town's Wild West years. The site started out as a movie set for the Columbia Pictures film *Arizona* in 1939 and has hosted hundreds of movie and television features since. Adobe and frontier buildings

INSIDER TIP:

**Well under a mile round-trip, Saguaro National Park's Signal Hill Trail provides access to dozens of petroglyphs—rock art left by the Hohokam people some 2,000 years ago.**

—JEANINE BARONE
National Geographic Traveler
*magazine writer*

line the dusty streets, where visitors come to watch gunfighters in blazing battles. Enjoy the hilarious entertainment in the Grand Palace Saloon, a large theater with stage shows. Then settle down to watch movie clips in Rosa's.

Take a stagecoach or trail ride, hop on a carousel, pan for gold, and experience the Iron Door Mine. A narrated train ride around Old Tucson is a good introduction to the site's history and layout. Special events take place, such as haunted evenings around Halloween.

If you continue northwest about 5 miles on Kinney Road from the junction with Gates Pass Road, you will come to **Saguaro National Park (West)**, where the Red Hills Visitor Center introduces you to Sonoran Desert life and various activities here. The nearby **Cactus Garden Trail** identifies plants along a short path. The half-mile **Desert Discovery Nature Trail,** northwest of the visitor center, loops through cactuses on a bajada—the gentle slope between mountain and plain favored by desert plants. Both trails are paved and wheelchair accessible.

Other trails pass through nearby washes and hills, including 4,687-foot Wasson Peak; ask for a map and descriptions at the

**Old Tucson Studios**
- 198 B2
- ✉ 201 S. Kinney Rd.
- ☎ 520/883-0100
- 💲 $$$$

www.oldtucson.com

**Saguaro National Park West**
- 198 B3
- ✉ 2700 N. Kinney Rd.
- ☎ 520/733-5158
- 💲 $$$

www.nps.gov/sagu

---

## EXPERIENCE: The Cowboy Life

Join the cowboys and cowgirls to herd cattle and participate in other ranch life at a working cattle ranch. Or simply head out on a trail ride if you prefer. After a day in the saddle, you dine on tasty Western fare, then bed down in comfortable lodging.

**Williams Family Ranch** (P.O. Box 3855, Wickenburg, AZ 85358, tel 928/308-0589; www.williamsfamilyranch.com) lets you join in day-to-day cattle work such as moving cattle to new pastures, branding calves, looking after horses, and seasonal roundups in the desert hills 16 miles (and an hour's drive) from Wickenburg—northwest of Phoenix. Families and clubs can arrange day rides and cookouts. It's too hot in summer, so the season runs from September through May.

**Price Canyon Ranch** (P. O. Box 39, Rodeo, NM 88056, tel 520/558-2383 or 800/727-0065, www.pricecanyon.com) nestles up against the Chiricahua Mountains in the southeastern corner of Arizona. You can join the cowboys on regular work such as patrolling the ranch boundaries and checking the water lines or seasonal chores including roundups, branding and weaning cattle, and moving herds to new pastures. The ranch is also a great spot for bird-watching, stargazing, and hiking. The ranch accepts guests in spring and autumn, the most pleasant times of year.

## The Majestic Saguaro: Reaching for the Sky

The giant of the cactus world starts out small and takes its time. The babies develop from a pinhead-size black seed, require protective shade, and may reach only a quarter of an inch in their first year. Most don't make it; as seedlings they are vulnerable to birds, rodents, and other foraging animals. They produce their first flowers and fruit at about 30 years, when they are just a few feet high. Arms may begin to appear around age 75. The largest specimens can have half a dozen arms or more, weigh 8 tons, tower 50 feet high, and live more than 150 years.

White blossoms appear on evenings in late spring, then fade the following day.

Both Tohono O'odham and wildlife savor the red fruit, which ripens in June and July.

Desert Botanical Garden (see p. 153) in Phoenix displays the towering saguaro cactus (*Carnegiea gigantean*) in one of the world's finest collections of desert plants. Saguaro National Park (see pp. 205–206) honors its namesake by protecting an estimated 1.6 million saguaro in two sections, the Rincon Unit east of Tucson and the Tucson Mountain District west of the city. At these places, you not only get to admire saguaros in their different stages of growth, but learn more about this amazing plant through exhibits and interpretive programs.

visitor center. The 5-mile Bajada Loop Drive, northwest of the visitor center, winds through pretty countryside past saguaro cactuses, places to picnic, overlooks, and trailheads; you will be driving mostly on graded dirt.

Along the way, you can hike the 0.8-mile round-trip **Valley View Overlook Trail** up a ridge for a broad panoramic view of the Avra Valley. Farther along, **Signal Hill Petroglyphs Trail** (a half-mile round-trip) ascends from Signal Hill Picnic Area to a rock art site.

### Arizona–Sonora Desert Museum

The excellent exhibits here—in a mix of zoo, natural history museum, and botanical garden—help reveal the life of the Sonoran Desert. The range of flora and wildlife comes not just from Arizona but also from the Mexican state of Sonora and

the Gulf of California. There's a lot to see both indoors and out on the 21-acre grounds; you may decide to stay longer than you'd intended.

The orientation area just inside the entrance introduces the museum and posts the day's special events: wildlife demonstrations, talks, tours, and which flowers are in bloom. Docents on the grounds offer informal presentations.

Natural-looking enclosures and environments provide homes for most of the wildlife here. A cave reproduction in the **Earth Sciences** area contains amazingly realistic chambers filled with stalactites and stalagmites, along with salamanders and other cave life; the mineral gallery nearby displays superb specimens.

Vegetation in the **Mountain Woodland** area creates the setting for mountain lion, black bear, Mexican wolf, white-tailed deer,

INSIDER TIP:

The Arizona–Sonora Desert Museum Art Institute offers workshops in painting, photography, and more. What a thrilling way to experience the magic of the desert.

—SHEILA BUCKMASTER
National Geographic Traveler
magazine *editor at large*

to spot the nearly invisible fence enclosures). In the **Riparian Corridor,** underwater viewing ports let visitors look at otters playing and beavers working in their pools and streams. Coati, with their pointed snouts and long tails, explore their streamside habitat nearby, while desert bighorn sheep display balancing skills as they scramble up rocky ledges.

In the **Life Underground** exhibit, nocturnal animals and insects find protection from the desert's temperature extremes.

**Arizona–Sonora
Desert Museum**

🅰 198 B2

✉ 2021 N. Kinney Rd. (14 miles W of I-10 on Speedway Blvd./ Gates Pass Rd.; large vehicles use Ajo Way & Kinney Rd. from I-19)

☎ 520/883-2702

💲 $$$

**www.desertmuseum
.org**

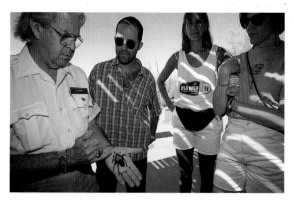

A docent shows a tarantula to Arizona–Sonora Desert Museum visitors.

and other large animals found at elevations between 4,000 and 7,000 feet. Both upper and lower levels give views of the feline species in the dens of **Cat Canyon,** while prairie dogs socialize in their colony at the **Desert Grassland** area. Reptiles include strikingly beautiful rattlesnakes and Gila monsters. Tarantulas, scorpions, and other arthropods put in appearances too.

A stroll along the half-mile Desert Loop Trail takes you to homes of coyote and javelina (try

A walk-in aviary lets you get close to desert birds. Look carefully— they are well camouflaged. You can join hummingbirds in another walk-in aviary. Back near the park entrance, amphibians and endangered fish such as the Colorado squawfish and Gila topminnow have a home.

More than 1,200 species of desert plants add to the beauty of the grounds, including the many members of the cactus family identified in the **Cactus Garden.** Small gardens focus on the flora sought out by various types of pollinators.

You will also be treated to expansive views across the Avra Valley to Kitt Peak (6,875 feet), home to important astronomical observatories (see p. 217), and the sacred Baboquivari Peak (7,730 feet). Both these spots fall within the Tohono O'odham Indian Reservation. The **Gallery at the Desert Museum** hosts changing art exhibitions.

An early start is recommended to enjoy the short-lived cool of the morning, see the animals at their most active, and have enough time for a visit. A hat, sunscreen, and good walking shoes will be appreciated (the trails total nearly 2 miles).

On summer Saturdays from June through September, the museum stays open late so that you can experience desert life—its sights, sounds, and smells—in the evening. (The exception is the aviaries, which remain off-limits in the evening so the birds can roost undisturbed.) There is a choice of restaurants and snack bars, or you can picnic at tables on the southwest side of the parking lot. ■

**INSIDER TIP:**

**Dress for hiking when you head off to the Arizona–Sonora Desert Museum. Two miles of paths weave through 21 acres— home to more than 300 animal species.**

—LINDSEY SMITH
*National Geographic contributor*

**Hummingbirds buzz around the Arizona–Sonora Desert Museum in search of their favorite flowers.**

# North Tucson

So great is the range of vegetation and climate along the way that a journey through the Santa Catalina Mountains has been likened to a drive from Mexico to Canada. The cool forests of fir and aspen on the north-facing slopes above 8,000 feet seem a world away from the saguaro of the desert below.

On the south side of the **Santa Catalina Mountains,** water dances down the streambed of **Sabino Canyon,** bringing life and color to the desert. Come to admire the sparkling pools, lush greenery, wildlife, and rugged canyon scenery (see sidebar p. 210). Just outside the **Sabino Canyon Visitor Center,** the quarter-mile-loop Bajada Nature Trail identifies desert plants. Shuttle buses *(tel 520/749-2327, $$)* make frequent narrated trips from here through the canyon. No cars are permitted in the canyon; cyclists can ride only in early morning and evening hours on certain days.

A hiker takes stock at Windy Point in the Santa Catalinas.

## Catalina Highway

The journey from Tucson up the paved, 25-mile-long Catalina Highway/Sky Island Byway takes about an hour—more if you stop to enjoy the many mountain panoramas en route. Palisades Visitor Center at mile 19.9 is open most weekends and on some weekdays.

The chairlift at **Mount Lemmon Ski Valley** *(tel 520/576-1400)* takes skiers up the slopes in winter, sightseers in the summer. From about May to October you can hike to the summit of **Mount Lemmon** (9,157 feet) from Mount Lemmon Ski Valley or nearby trailheads in about 1.5 miles one way. Ask someone to point out one of the trailheads,

or take the lift up and walk down. A network of trails leads to ridges and canyons from many trailheads; expect to encounter steep and strenuous hiking on most of these.

## Catalina State Park

You can explore the western foothills of the Santa Catalinas in Catalina State Park, 14 miles north of downtown Tucson off Arizona 77. Hiking trails, picnic areas, and campgrounds help you make the most of the desert and mountain scenery, and there are great opportunities to see wildlife, such as javelina, desert mule deer, Gambel's quail, and red-tailed hawk on the Nature Trail and the Birding Trail (each a 1-mile loop).

**Sabino Canyon Visitor Center & Santa Catalina Ranger District, Coronado National Forest**

🗺 199 E2

✉ 5700 N. Sabino Canyon Rd., Tucson, AZ 85750 (13 miles NE of downtown Tucson)

☎ 520/749-8700

**www.fs.fed.us/r3/coronado**

## Catalina State Park

🏞 199 D4

✉ 11570 N. Oracle Rd.

☎ 520/628-5798

💲 $$ day use, $$$$–$$$$$ camping

www.azstateparks.com

## Biosphere 2

🏞 199 D4

✉ Ariz. 77 near Milepost 96.5

☎ 520/838-6200

💲 $$$$

www.b2science.org

Romero Ruin Interpretive Trail climbs a ridge on a loop measuring about three-quarters of a mile to reach the ruins of a Hohokam village and the site of a mid-19th-century ranch.

## Biosphere 2

Farther north off Arizona 77, experience the world in a different way at Biosphere 2. Aimed at increasing humankind's understanding of how our planet (Biosphere 1) operates, scientists and engineers built the world's largest greenhouse; it covers more than 3 acres. Inside the sealed structure are five biomes, or self-sustaining

INSIDER TIP:

**Given the amount of walking entailed in a visit to Biosphere 2, carry lots of water, and avoid the hottest summer afternoons.**

—VERA MARIE BADERTSCHER
*National Geographic contributor*

giant "lungs" outside allowed the greenhouse to breathe by compensating for changes in atmospheric pressure. Enthusiasts saw it as a step toward rescuing humans from impending ecological ruin. The Biospherians lasted out the two years, but various problems arose and little scientific work was accomplished. In 1996, Columbia University took over and redirected the operation toward research. Now University of Arizona scientists conduct research on earth sciences, including the consequences of global climate change.

First, take in the video and exhibits in the visitor center. Guided tours depart for a trip into Biosphere 2. It's a beautiful sight—glass-paneled walls soaring into the sky supported by a maze of interior trusses. After a look at the Biospherians' living quarters, you'll walk through several biomes, then descend into the "Technosphere," where 2 acres of machinery control the climate above. The tour concludes with a look inside one of the lungs—followed, if you like, by a stop at the ocean-viewing gallery on your own. ■

---

## Seven Falls—An Oasis Outside Tucson

**Waterfalls cascade from pool to pool at the end of one of the prettiest hikes in the Tucson area. The 4.8-mile-round-trip trail goes up Bear Canyon and crosses a creek seven times. See the falls on the left. Elevation gain is 550 feet. From Sabino Canyon Visitor Center, hikers can follow a trail 1.7 miles east or hop on the Bear Canyon Shuttle to the trailhead. Important note: Around the Seven Falls pools the rocks are very slippery.**

---

ecosystems: rain forest, desert, savanna, marsh, and ocean.

The first crew—four women and four men—entered Biosphere 2 through an air lock on September 26, 1991. Their mission was to work and conduct research for two years in the facility's self-contained environment. The team enjoyed access to a garden and livestock as well as a computer center and living quarters. Two

# East Tucson

Take the Old Spanish Trail out of Tucson to see the magnificent cactuses in the other half of Saguaro National Park, in the foothills of the Rincon Mountains. Aviation enthusiasts can head out on I-10 and trace the history of flight at the Pima Air & Space Museum. If you have time, continue to drive southeast just a few more miles to experience the subterranean wonders of Colossal Cave.

Saguaro National Park East's Douglas Spring Trail offers views of Tucson and the Santa Catalinas.

The saguaros in **Saguaro National Park (East),** the larger and older section of the two parks (see pp. 205–206), tend to be very young or very old. Before these lands were protected, woodcutters and grazing cattle had trampled young plants and removed the necessary nursery trees that would have shaded them. Find out more about the ecology, geology, plants, and wildlife of the Sonoran Desert at the visitor center just inside the park entrance. The Cactus Garden just outside identifies a variety of plants. To see more of the park, drive or bike the **Cactus Forest Drive,** a scenic 8-mile loop. After driving 2.2 miles from the visitor center, you can turn left to Mica View Picnic Area, named for 8,666-foot Mica Mountain, visible to the east. In another 0.3 mile on the drive, you'll reach the start of the Desert Ecology Trail, a paved quarter-mile loop with explanations as to how plants and wildlife

**Saguaro National Park (East)**

🗺 199 E2

✉ 3693 S. Old Spanish Trail

☎ 520/733-5153

💲 $$$

**www.nps.gov/sagu**

## Colossal Cave Mountain Park

⚑ 199 F1

✉ 22 miles SE of Tucson off Old Spanish Trail, or 7 miles N from I-10 Exit 279

☎ 520/647-7275

$ $ park entry, $$$ cave tour

**www.colossalcave .com**

interact and adapt. Freeman Homestead Nature Trail begins near the end of the drive. On this 1-mile loop through giant saguaro and a mesquite woodland, signs tell of homesteading in the desert.

A 128-mile trail network weaves across the desert, up ridges, and through the canyons of the Rincon Mountains. Trails also climb to the heights from adjacent Coronado National Forest. You can camp at designated sites *(backcountry permit available at visitor center)*. Rangers can be

form little enclosures open on one side), the interior is now dry and a very pleasant 70°F year-round. Regular tours leave frequently and last 45 to 55 minutes, with about half a mile of walking. You'll be descending, then climbing six-and-a-half stories on steps, though at a leisurely pace. Your guide will tell of the local geology, the history of the cave, and a story of outlaws who once hid out here and may have left $60,000 in gold concealed somewhere. In the mid-1930s the Civilian Conserva-

Pima Air & Space Museum looks back with many an aircraft legend.

consulted on conditions for both hikers and equestrians.

Continuing southeast for 12 miles from Saguaro will bring you to **Colossal Cave Mountain Park.** Although water once seeped through limestone cracks to create the cave's stalactites, stalagmites, flowstone, helictites, and boxwork (flat crystals that

tion Corps constructed the stone buildings and overlook near the cave entrance and the flagstone paths inside the cave. Ladder Tours take you off the normal route with helmets and flashlights to explore the cave; call ahead to make a reservation.

**La Posta Quemada,** also in Colossal Cave Mountain Park, is a

INSIDER TIP:

To see natural flyers: Go to the tall cotton- woods at the Nature Conservancy's Pata- gonia–Sonoita Creek Preserve (see p. 230), hummingbird central.

—TIM VANDERPOOL
*National Geographic News
contributor*

120-year-old working ranch with a museum, hiking trails, horseback riding *(tel 520/647-3450)*, library, and café. Exhibits describe the cave's formation, its resident life, and some of the prehistoric arti- facts found inside. Displays explain the area's history and ranch life. A per-vehicle fee collected at the park entrance covers the ranch, picnicking, and camping; you must arrive before the park closes at 5 p.m.

More than 250 historic aircraft spread over 75 acres at the **Pima Air & Space Museum** illustrate the spectacular advances in avia- tion. Rare and unusual planes can be seen here, too. A narrated tram ride circles the grounds and intro- duces the aircraft; you can hop on and off at stops along its route.

Inside the entrance, a full-size reproduction of the 1903 Wright Flyer marks the beginning of the story of controlled flight. Most planes come from the military's World War II years and the jet age that followed. Civilian, helicopter, and space exhibits round out the collection. You'll see famous fighters and gleaming B-17,

B-24, and B-29 bombers from the World War II era, along with memorabilia and photos of the men who flew them. Jet aircraft illustrate the evolution from early models to the F100 series and thence to the amazingly fast SR-71 Blackbird, one of which flew coast to coast in less than an hour. Huge transports and B-52 bombers impress with their size. Presidents John F. Kennedy and Lyndon B. Johnson flew on the VC-118A/ DC-6A on display here.

Narrated **AMARG (Aero- space Maintenance and Regeneration Group) Tours** take you by bus to see the rows of planes and helicopters in the vast aircraft storage area at nearby Davis-Monthan Air Force Base. Tours (about 1 hour) begin at the museum on weekdays. ∎

**Pima Air & Space Museum**

🅰 199 D1

✉ 6000 E. Valencia Rd. (12 miles SE of downtown; 2 miles E from I-10 Exit 267)

☎ 520/574-0462

💲 Museum: $$$
AMARG tour: $$

**www.pimaair.org**

---

**EXPERIENCE:
Outside in the City**

Wide-open vistas make Tucson a fine place to explore on foot or bicycle. Downtown is full of parks and historic districts; try the **Tucson historical walking tour** (see pp. 201–203) for a mix of history, art, and parks. The University of Arizona campus (see pp. 197–198) offers pleasant strolls with opportunities to delve into art, archaeology, history, and science. You're never far from nature—**Tohono Chul Park** offers native desert life, **Reid Park Zoo** (see p. 203) brings in the exotic, and **Tuc- son Botanical Gardens** (see pp. 198–199) has plenty of both. Birders thrill to sight- ings of migratory and resident species at ponds of the **Sweetwater Wetland** on the west side of the city and at **Agua Caliente Park** in the northeast; *www.tucsonaudubon .org* lists guided bird walks.

# Desert Adaptation

**The Sonoran Desert covers much of central and southern Arizona, extending beyond the state's boundaries into southeastern California, the western half of the Mexican state of Sonora, and most of Baja California. It is unique among North American deserts in that it boasts two rainy seasons.**

Although the coastal range of California blocks most Pacific Ocean storms, some winter ones have enough strength to arrive as gentle showers. No mountains obstruct the way from the south, so when moisture blows in from the Gulf of California during late summer, rain can fall in heavy, spotty bursts.

Plants have developed many tricks to survive heat and droughts. Many annuals and ephemerals produce tough seeds that can wait years for rain. When it comes, they quickly complete their cycle—growth, bloom, and seed—before wilting away. For some species, the entire process takes just a matter of weeks, turning the desert into an explosion of color. Perennials survive by remaining dormant during droughts. The whiplike ocotillo, for example, takes advantage of irregular rains by leafing out and blooming, then reentering dormancy within a period of a few weeks—a cycle that can be repeated five times in a year.

To help reduce water loss, leaves are often tiny. Phreatophytes such as the mesquite tree seek out water underground with extremely long roots; 80-foot lengths have been recorded. Cactuses and similar plants soak up water from a shallow root system and transfer it to their expandable tissue. Spines provide shade and reflect heat; a thick, waxy skin also help cactuses retain fluids. The creosote bush's tiny leaf pores close during the day to retain moisture and open at night to capture it. Its unpleasant smell and taste repel most browsing animals, and its double root

Paloverde

Ocotillo

Cactus wren

Kangaroo rat

Coyote

Teddybear cholla

Roadrunner

Gila monster

Organ pipe cactus

Rattlesnake

Javelina

system—shallow for rainfall, deep for ground water—is ideal for changing conditions.

Like plants, desert animals have adapted to baking heat and shortage of water. Most simply avoid the intense summer sun. Birds may fly on to cooler climates after breeding in late winter or early spring. Some reptiles, rodents, bats, and larger animals such as foxes and skunks spend the day in underground burrows or dens. Many are nocturnal. Lizards manage during the day by scampering from one piece of shade to the next. The huge ears of jackrabbits cool their blood quickly as they rest in shady spots. The well-adapted kangaroo rat doesn't need to drink water because it metabolizes dry seeds. Insects obtain the water they need from plants. In turn they provide food and fluids for birds, mammals, reptiles, and even other insects.

Gila woodpecker

Saguaro cactus

Elf owl

Ironwood tree

Prickly pear cactus

Mesquite

Desert tortoise

Gambel's quail

Hedgehog cactus

Globe mallow

Bighorn sheep

Lupine

Gold poppy

# South Tucson

Two important 20th-century technologies are the focus of a trip south out of Tucson on I-19. On a journey that begins with mining machinery and ends at the former site of an apocalyptic nuclear warhead, contemplative travelers can reflect on the nature of progress.

This Titan II missile served exclusively for training purposes.

## Asarco Mineral Discovery Center

- 📍 195 E2
- ✉️ 12 miles S of Tucson off I-19 Exit 80
- ☎️ 520/625-7513
- 🕐 Closed Sun.–Mon.
- 💲 $$ tour, museum free

www.mineral discovery.com

## Titan Missile Museum

- 📍 195 E1
- ✉️ 25 miles S of Tucson; follow signs off I-19 to Duval Mine Rd.
- ☎️ 520/625-7736
- 💲 $$

www.pimaair.org

Copper ore comes out of large open-pit and underground excavations among the terraced white hills southwest of Tucson. To learn more about the mining industry or see the mine in action, stop by the **Asarco Mineral Discovery Center.** Exhibits and short videos illustrate the uses of copper and how miners find and extract it. Tours take you to the edge of the Mission Mine pit, 1,500 feet deep and up to 2.5 miles across, where giant cranes load 320-ton trucks. Next you enter the mill to see the machinery that grinds and concentrates the ore to 28 percent copper.

Although the formerly top-secret site has been deactivated, you may feel apprehension on entering the **Titan Missile Museum,** knowing from 1963 to 1982 a fully fueled missile with a nuclear warhead stood ready for launch. A tour begins with a video that shows crews at work and a missile roaring into the sky. You then head outside to see support equipment, the massive silo cover, rocket engines, and a Titan II missile. Wearing a hard hat, you descend the metal stairs, pass through blast doors, and enter a control room where your guide runs through the launch sequence. A cable-filled corridor leads to the silo for a close look at the missile, which can't help but prompt thoughts of awe and horror at the devastation a launch most certainly would have wreaked. ■

# Tohono O'odham Nation & Kitt Peak

In the heart of the Sonoran Desert southwest of Tucson and far away from any life-sustaining rivers, the Tohono O'odham (pronounced *TAH-ho-no ah-tomb*) have thrived for centuries. They have come to know the land and its springs so well that they can garden and harvest wild foods in an environment others would find uninhabitable.

The new **Tohono O'odham Nation Cultural Center & Museum** provides insight into the lives of this people. Exhibits reveal aspects of their language, food, government, and land.

## INSIDER TIP:

March is wildflower time. The pullout just west of the road to Kitt Peak Observatory offers fine photo-ops for desert-flower fans.

—VERA MARIE BADERTSCHER
*National Geographic contributor*

Two dozen telescopes dot the summit of **Kitt Peak** (6,875 feet). You can drive up to the Kitt Peak National Optical Astronomy Observatory and take a guided or self-guided tour. A video and exhibits illustrate the nature of light and explain how astronomers use it to unravel the mysteries of the cosmos. The gift shop sells Tohono O'odham crafts.

Three Kitt Peak telescopes have viewing galleries—the slanted, partly underground McMath-Pierce Solar, the 2.1-meter (84 inch), and the

huge Mayall 4-meter (158 inch). If you stop at the picnic area 1.5 miles before the summit, you'll see the larger of two radio telescopes.

The Nightly Observing Programs use telescopes near the visitor center to observe the heavens; an Advanced Observing Program is offered for amateur astronomers; make reservations for these. Bring drinks and food, as they aren't available here. Take note: There aren't any gas stations, either. ∎

## Unknown Origin

Are the Tohono O'odham descended from the prehistoric Hohokam? Conquistadores called them Papago (tepary bean eater), a somewhat derisive term used until recent times. Name aside, in 1853, the Gadsden Purchase cut through their lands; tribal leaders are still trying to resolve land issues. Several thousand Tohono are now isolated on the Mexican side; the 25,000 members on the Arizona side continue to speak their native language.

**Tohono O'odham Nation Cultural Center & Museum**

- ✉ From Sells, drive 9 miles S on BIA 19, then turn left 0.3 mile on Fresnal Canyon Rd.
- ☎ 520/383-0201
- ⏲ Closed Sun. & holidays

**Kitt Peak National Optical Astronomy Observatory**

- 🅰 195 E2
- ✉ 56 miles SW of Tucson via Ariz. 86 and Ariz. 386; the last 12 miles are on a paved and well-graded mountain road
- ☎ 520/318-8726
- 💲 Free for visitor center & self-guided tour, $ tour, $$$$$ Nightly Observing Program

**www.noao.edu/kpno**

# Organ Pipe Cactus National Monument

The rough-hewn mountains and gentle valleys here along the Mexican border support a wonderfully diverse display of Sonoran Desert plants. Far from any major city, this land has a feel of remoteness and inspires the pleasure of solitude.

Flowers briefly color the harsh terrain of Cabeza Prieta National Wildlife Refuge.

Start at the Kriss Eggle Visitor Center for an excellent introduction to the area. Interpretive programs run January through March here and in the campground amphitheater. A paved nature trail at the visitor center identifies important components of the desert ecosystem. A warm climate allows organ pipe cactus, elephant trees, and other rare flora to flourish here. You can easily recognize organ pipe cactus by its 5 to 20 branches curving up from a point near the ground. It can grow as high as 23 feet and is second in size only to the saguaro in the United States.

Three easy hiking trails begin at the year-round developed Twin

Peaks Campground: **Palo Verde Trail,** an easy 1.5-mile path, connects Twin Peaks Campground with the visitor center and is pet friendly; **Desert View Nature Trail,** a 1.2-mile loop, goes up a ridge for views; and the 4.2-mile round-trip **Victoria Mine Trail** leads to a historic silver mine. Evenings and mornings are best for wildlife spotting.

There is a small primitive campground for tenters; you will need to obtain a permit from the visitor center. Five miles south of the visitor center in Lukeville, you'll find a store, restaurant, and gas station.

Two scenic drives weave through the rocky hills and desert flora. You may wish to bring a picnic as well as plenty of water; no supplies are available along the way. Cyclists are welcome on these drives. **Puerto Blanco Drive** heads northwest from the visitor center to a picnic area, five miles each way, with stops along the way for far-reaching views and helpful interpretive signs. Across the highway from the visitor center, the 21-mile-loop **Ajo Mountain Drive** positions you for a close look at the flora and geology in the foothills of the range crowned by Mount Ajo (4,808 feet) with its volcanic rock of yellow, red, and brown. This entire area is wetter than most of the Sonoran Desert, which accounts for the lush seasonal flora. Much of the rain (about 8 inches annually) falls in winter and summer. **Arch Canyon Trail,** at Stop #13, is an easy 1.5-mile round-trip. The **Bull Pasture/ Estes Canyon** route (Stop #15) climbs about 800 feet on a 4.1-mile loop.

Note: Before planning a trip, be sure to check with visitor center staff or the website to find out the status of roads and trails in the monument. ■

**Organ Pipe Cactus National Monument**

🅰 194 C2

✉ 120 miles W of Tucson on Ariz. 86, then 22 miles S on Ariz. 85

☎ 520/387-6849

💲 $$

www.nps.gov/orpi

**Cabeza Prieta National Wildlife Refuge**

✉ 1611 N. 2nd Ave., Ajo, AZ 85321

☎ 520/387-6483

🕐 Office closed Sat.–Sun.

www.fws.gov/south west

## Along the Devil's Highway

Native Americans, Spanish missionaries and explorers, and California gold seekers used the Devil's Highway (El Camino del Diablo), connecting the town of Caborca in Sonora, Mexico, with the Colorado River 250 miles away. The going could be brutal, especially in summer. Inexperienced travelers died when they ran out of water between the infrequent springs in some of the Sonoran Desert's driest regions. Bring a map or atlas and you can retrace the heart of this route with a four-wheel-drive vehicle, supplies, and a permit from the Cabeza Prieta National Wildlife Refuge visitor center *(1611 N. Second Ave., Ajo, AZ 85321, tel 520/ 387-6483, closed Sat.–Sun.),* which also has wildlife exhibits and a large selection of video programs. Allow at least two days to cross the refuge on the roads between Ajo and Wellton; distance is 124 miles one way, 59 miles in the refuge.

If you'd like a taste of Cabeza Prieta, drive to Charlie Bell Pass in the Growler Mountains, just 20 miles (two hours) west of Ajo. High-clearance two-wheel-drive vehicles can make this trip. With luck, you may see pronghorn on the plains and desert bighorn sheep in the mountains. The road ends at the pass, where you can hike down the other side or up into the hills.

# Mission San Xavier del Bac

The "white dove of the desert," as this church is known, has called to pilgrims and other devout followers for more than 200 years. Jesuit priest and explorer Eusebio Francisco Kino trekked across the harsh landscape from Mexico in 1692 to minister to Indians at the farming village of Bac. Kino named the mission he founded after his patron saint, a Jesuit missionary in Asia.

**Mission San Xavier del Bac**

🅰 195 E2

✉ 10 miles S of downtown Tucson; follow signs from I-19 Exit 92

☎ 520/294-2624

💲 Donation

**www.sanxavier mission.org**

A chapel served early converts, but the mission community often lacked a resident priest. O'odham revolts in 1734 and 1751 damaged the mission, and raiding Apache caused hardships. The Franciscans built the present adobe church from 1783 to 1797. Artists from Mexico filled the interior with statues of saints, elaborate ornamentation, and murals, creating a folk-art style. Luxuries were out of the question, so painters textured the main altar to resemble marble and drew chandeliers on the upper walls. Workers never completed the east bell tower and other parts of the church.

Padre Kino would be pleased to see the results of his faith. The mission is one of the few that has served its original purpose from Spanish times to the present. O'odham, Hispanic, and Anglo worshipers join for the Sunday Masses and other ceremonies. Unless a service is taking place, you are welcome to enter.

The **mission museum** on the east side of the church illustrates the early history and life of the mission; it also displays furnishings, vestments, and art.

A walk around the grounds takes you to a former mortuary chapel to the west and up to a copy of the Grotto of Lourdes in a small hill to the east. ■

The faith of Franciscan missionaries and local O'odham created this masterpiece from desert soil.

# Santa Rita Mountains

The forested slopes of Mount Wrightson (9,453 feet) tower high above the desert 38 miles to the south of Tucson. Spring-fed Madera Canyon is famed among birders, especially mid-March to mid-September; more than 240 species, including many hummingbirds, have been identified here. Sightings of trogon, a parrot-like bird from Mexico, are eagerly sought.

Desert grasslands and shrubs give way to mesquite groves, then oak, juniper, cottonwood, and Arizona sycamore along the paved road into **Madera Canyon.** Short paved loops on the right near the entrance offer an easy walk and wheelchair access from Proctor Parking Area and Whitehouse Picnic Area.

Elegant trogons such as this female arrive from Mexico in late spring to breed in southeast Arizona's wooded canyons.

**INSIDER TIP:**

**From spring to fall along the Mexican border southeast of Tucson, the air erupts into a hyperkinetic gallery as humming-birds converge.**

—TIM VANDERPOOL
*National Geographic News contributor*

The road ends 2 miles up Madera Canyon at Mount Wrightson Picnic Area, where hikers can head for the summit on the **Old Baldy Trail** (5.4 miles one way) or the **Super Trail** (8.1 miles one way). From the top, you can enjoy a panorama that takes in much of southern Arizona and some of Mexico.

An easier option from road's end is to meander down Madera Canyon on the **Nature Trail.**

Interpretive signs line the trail as it descends 2.7 miles to the Amphitheater trailhead. You could continue hiking along the creek to Proctor Parking Area in 4.4 miles total one way. Many people enjoy the 5.8-mile **Bog Springs Loop.** It starts from Madera Picnic Area, about halfway up the canyon, and gains 1,600 feet in elevation.

The **Whipple Observatory Visitor Center** provides an intro-duction to the astronomy work done atop nearby 8,500-foot Mount Hopkins. From mid-March through November you can join a six-hour tour *(reservations required)* for a very scenic drive up the mountain to see the tele-scopes and panoramic views. ∎

**Nogales Ranger District, Coronado National Forest**
✉ 303 Old Tucson Rd., Nogales, AZ 85621
☎ 520/281-2296
🕐 Closed Sat.–Sun.
**www.fs.fed.us/r3/coronado**

**Whipple Observatory Visitor Center**
🗺 195 E1
✉ 11.5 miles SE of I-19 Exit 56
☎ 520/670-5707
🕐 Closed Sat.–Sun.
💲 $$ tour, visitor center free
**www.cfa.harvard.edu/facilities/flwo**

# Tubac

Now a thriving artists' colony with the motto the "Place Where Art and History Meet," the town of Tubac goes back to 1752, when the Spanish built the Tubac presidio (fort), the first European settlement in what is now Arizona.

**Tubac**

 195 E1

**Visitor information**

✉ Tubac Chamber of Commerce, P.O. Box 1866, Tubac, AZ 85646

☎ 520/398-2704

www.tubacaz.com

**Tubac Center of the Arts**

✉ 9 Plaza Rd.

☎ 520/398-2371

🕐 Call for hours

💲 Donation

www.TubacArts.org

**Tubac Presidio State Historic Park**

✉ Burruel St. & Tubac Rd.

☎ 520/398-2252

🕐 Call for hours

💲 $

www.azstateparks.com

After the United States bought southern Arizona from Mexico in the Gadsden Purchase of 1854, American prospectors and adventurers streamed in to search for old Spanish mines and hit rich silver ore. Tubac boomed, but the good times came to an abrupt halt in the early 1860s when troops stationed there headed east to fight the Civil War. The town began its transformation into the Tubac of today when an art school opened in 1948. About a hundred studios and galleries now display such work as paintings, prints, glassware, ceramics, wood carvings, jewelry, and batiks.

**Tubac Center of the Arts** exhibits work by local, regional, and national artists. Staffers organize a performing arts series, children's programs, lectures, and workshops.

**Tubac Presidio State Historic Park** recounts the history of the people who lived in Tubac during various periods. You can enter an underground excavation to see a foundation and part of a wall of the presidio. Models and artifacts illustrate how the town developed. The printing press used in 1859 for the first newspaper in what is now Arizona is here (you can buy a reproduction of the first issue). Other sights include the 1885 schoolhouse and 1920s church, both successors to ones built in the 1700s, and the state park itself—Arizona's first, opened in 1959. ∎

## Taking Home Artful Creations

Wide-ranging selections of art and handmade works make Tubac a good place to explore. In the studios, you can meet local painters, jewelers, sculptors, potters, and other artisans. You'll also see imports from Mexico. When it's time to take a break, drop by the bookstore or one of the restaurants. There's a bed-and-breakfast in town, too. Everything's within easy walking distance, including Tubac Center of the Arts and Tubac Presidio State Historic Park, both worth a visit.

# Tumacácori National Historical Park

The great adobe ruin of Tumacácori testifies to the devotion and difficulties of early O'odham and Spanish residents. A basic shade ramada served as a church when Father Kino first visited the O'odham here in 1691. Mission work continued over the following century, but the present church was not begun until 1800.

A museum model shows how the church at Tumacácori once looked. Compare this scene with the present-day interior.

**Tumacácori National Historical Park**

- 195 E1
- 48 miles S of Tucson near I-19 Exit 29
- 520/398-2341
- $

www.nps.gov/tuma

Franciscan father Narcisco Gutierrez intended to build a structure as splendid as San Xavier del Bac (see p. 220), but work had not quite finished 22 years later when the Mexican government took over from Spain and cut the funding. Mexican missionaries assisted from time to time, but Apache raids eventually made life too difficult. The last residents packed up in 1848 and moved north to San Xavier del Bac.

Tumacácori fell into ruin before it received protection as a national monument in 1908. The museum displays some of the original **santos**—wooden statues of saints. A video introduces life in the mission, and exhibits illustrate the architecture and history. The mission was far more than just the church, as you will see from the model and self-guided tour of the grounds. Walk through the church's baptistry, sanctuary, and sacristy and continue outside to the cemetery and its mortuary chapel, then to a granary, courtyard, lime kiln, ruins of the priests' quarters, and the foundations of an earlier church.

For a hike with a sense of history, take the **Juan Bautista de Anza National Historic Trail.** It follows the Santa Cruz River 4.5 miles one way to Tubac, crossing the river twice. The trail is named for the captain who led colonists to California in 1775–1776 and founded San Francisco. ■

# Huachuca Mountains

Miller Peak tops this range of canyons and alpine forests southeast of Tucson. Scenic drives climb partway, but only trails continue to the 9,466-foot summit in Miller Peak Wilderness. Two sites commemorate the region's history: Fort Huachuca (wa-CHOO-ka) Museum, near the north end of the mountains, and Coronado National Memorial, at the south end.

**Huachuca Mountains**

🅰 195 F1

**Visitor information**

✉ 3020 E. Tacoma St., Sierra Vista, AZ 85635

☎ 800/228-3861

www.visitsierravista .com

**Sierra Vista Ranger District, Coronado National Forest**

✉ 5990 S. Hwy 92, Hereford, AZ 85615

☎ 520/378-0311

🕐 Closed Sat.–Sun.

www.fs.fed.us/r3/ coronado

**Coronado National Memorial**

✉ 4101 E. Monte- zuma Canyon Rd. Hereford, AZ 85615

☎ 520/366-5515

www.nps.gov/coro

Of the U.S. Army forts established during the Indian wars, only **Fort Huachuca** continues as a military base. In 1877, Capt. Samuel Marmaduke Whitside chose the site for its commanding view of the San Pedro Valley and for the abundance of timber, game, and water in the mountains. It served as the advance headquarters in the campaign to capture the for- midable Apache leader Geronimo. When the Apache were finally subdued in 1886, the fort took up the job of patrolling the Mexican border. Today, the Army tests electronics and other gear and runs an intelligence school here. **Fort Huachuca Museum** *(Hungerford & Grierson Aves., tel 520/533-5736, donation)* has a large collection of photos, Native American and Army memorabilia, and period rooms. Nearby, the **Army Intelligence Museum** *(open some hours)* illustrates the

Army's art of spying. The Nature Conservancy looks after **Ramsey Canyon Preserve** *(tel 520/378- 2785, www.nature.org/arizona)* a 380-acre wildlife sanctuary on the east side of the Huachucas. As many as 14 hummingbird species visit from spring to early autumn. **Carr Canyon Road** ascends 7.8 miles up the east side of the Huachucas to spectacular overlooks at an elevation of 7,200 feet. **Reef Historic Trail** passes near old mine and mill sites in a 0.75-mile loop from the far end of Reef Townsite Campground; signs explain the mining history. The drive begins 7.5 miles south of Sierra Vista on Arizona 92 between Mileposts 328 and 329. Only the first 1.5 miles are paved, but cars can usually make the trip if the road is dry. The Sierra Vista Ranger Station, half a mile north from the Carr Canyon turnoff, has recreation information. ■

## Coronado National Memorial: Backstory & Hikes

Although Francisco Vásquez de Coronado never did find gold in 1540, he's seen as the leader of the first major European expedition in the Southwest. A video and exhibits at the visitor center tell the story. You can also learn about wildlife and flora here. **Coronado Cave Trail** leads to a cave in a 1.5-mile round-trip hike. Bring two

flashlights and water. Drive 3 miles west (the last two are unpaved) to **Montezuma Pass** for a panorama of Arizona and Mexico. For even better views, hike the 0.75-mile round-trip trail from the pass to 6,864-foot Coronado Peak; the 3.1-mile (one-way) **Joe's Canyon Trail** (1,345-foot elevation gain) also ends at the peak.

# EXPERIENCE: Make Your Way on the Arizona Trail

On this stretch of more than 800 miles, you'll leave the roar of traffic far behind to experience Arizona's incredibly diverse and beautiful landscapes. You'll cross cactus-strewn deserts, craggy mountain ranges, densely wooded plateaus, and enter the heart of the Grand Canyon on a route that connects the Mexican border in the far south with the Utah border in the far north.

Travels bring history to life as you pass old mining claims in the foothills of the **Santa Catalina Mountains** northeast of Tucson, prehistoric cliff dwellings near **Roosevelt Lake** east of Phoenix, paths where Basque sheepherders once drove sheep in the **Mazatzal Mountains** southwest of Payson, and the stagecoach road north of **Flagstaff** that was used by early travelers to reach the **Grand Canyon.** Today's exploration options include hiking or riding a horse, mule, or a mountain bike. It is important to note that in wilderness areas—including the Grand Canyon—mechanized travel is prohibited.

A cyclist pedals the Arizona Trail in the company of tall saguaros.

## The Route

Unlike other major long-distance trails that follow a single geographic feature, the Arizona Trail crosses many. In the south you'll ascend a series of "sky islands," isolated mountain ranges completely surrounded by desert—the Huachucas, Santa Ritas, Rincons, and Santa Catalinas. Legends of lost gold mines haunt the **Superstition Mountains;** from here you'll drop to vast Roosevelt Lake before heading up the Mazatzal Mountains in the center of Arizona. Sheer cliffs of the **Mogollon Rim** mark the next major ascent. From Flagstaff, you'll skirt volcanoes of the San Francisco Peaks and head for Grand Canyon National Park. Here you'll descend to the river on the South Kaibab Trail and climb out the other side on the North Kaibab Trail. The going then becomes relatively easy and you'll get another perspective of the Grand Canyon from the **East Rim Viewpoint** area before the last leg to the Utah border.

## Getting Started

Handily, the trail is divided into 43 passages, ranging in length from 8.3 to 33.4 miles, beginning in **Coronado National Memorial** in the south and ending atop the Kaibab Plateau in the north. Spring and autumn are good times to go; in winter, you can hit the trail in sections of lower desert. In the north, if winter and early spring snowfalls have been abundant, you can cross-country ski and snowshoe along the trail's higher stretches. You'll find route details, newsletters, notes on trail repairs and restrictions, and useful links at the official website (www.aztrail.org). The website also lists maps and books , including *Arizona Trail: The Official Guide* by Tom Lorang Jones and the Arizona Trail Association. Contact the Arizona Trail Association (P.O. Box 36736, Phoenix, AZ 85067, tel 602/252-4794, e-mail: ata@aztrail.org) for more information.

# Tombstone

Tombstone is the real thing—a Wild West mining town that survived booms, busts, and some of the territory's most notorious gunslingers. Stroll down the boardwalks past 19th-century saloons, ride a stage, and watch a reenactment of the shootout at the O.K. Corral. The old town of Tombstone lies 70 miles southeast of Tucson.

"A Bird in a Gilded Cage," the hit song about ladies of the night, was written here in Tombstone.

**Tombstone**

🅰 195 G1

**Visitor information**

✉ Tombstone Visitor Center, Allen & 4th Sts. (P.O. Box 995), Tombstone, AZ 85638

☎ 520/457-3929 (visitor center) or 888/457-3929 (Chamber of Commerce)

**www.tombstone chamber.com**

When prospector Ed Schieffelin ventured out this way in 1877, Army troops told him that his own tombstone was the only thing he'd find in the rattlesnake-ridden country, inhabited by hostile Apache. Schieffelin traveled alone and staked his first silver claim as Tombstone. The town sprang up just two years later and grew to be one of Arizona's most important.

Hard-working miners and prospectors found their entertainment here; it was said that saloons and gambling halls made up two of every three buildings. Law and order didn't come easily at first as Apache, defending their land,

and crooks, along with political corruption, gave the place its notoriety. Fires twice raged through Tombstone, but it was flooding of the mines in 1886 that nearly undid the town. But the "town too tough to die" hung on, though it ceased to be a county seat and much of its population moved on. Many buildings from the early days still stand on or near Allen Street. Desperadoes and lawmen fight blazing gun battles in historical re-enactments; ask at the visitor center for details. Stagecoaches on Allen Street offer short narrated tours.

Exhibits at **Tombstone Courthouse State Historic Park** (3rd & Toughnut Sts., tel 520/457-3311) introduce the Native Americans, prospectors, pioneers, cattlemen, lawmen, and women who lived here. Displays tell of the fateful day, October 26, 1881, when Doc Holliday and the Earps, seeking to enforce the law, shot it out with the free-spirited Clanton cowboys near the O.K. Corral. Mining exhibits show how ore was dug out and assayed. Upstairs are the former Cochise County Attorney's office and the courtroom where many a trial unfolded. A gallows outside the 1882 redbrick courthouse spelled the end of the road for some.

Over on Allen, between Third and Fourth Streets, you can step into the **O.K. Corral** to see life-size statues that depict the famous

INSIDER TIP:

In early spring, Tombstone's huge Lady Banksia rose tree at the Rose Tree Museum comes into fragrant bloom; mid-April is Rose Festival time.

—LINDSEY SMITH
*National Geographic contributor*

gunfight. A daily reenactment takes place nearby. Other sights include a reconstructed photographer's studio, old stables, carriages, and a cozy shack from the red-light district. At **Historama** next door, movies and animated scenes illustrate major events in Tombstone's history. The 1879 **Crystal Palace Saloon** serves beverages in its beautifully restored interior at the corner of Allen and Fifth Streets.

Ed Schieffelin allegedly suggested the name for the town's newspaper. Drop into the **office of the** *Epitaph,* on Fifth around the corner from the Crystal Palace, to pick up your own *Epitaph.*

Doors never closed during the first eight years at the 1881 **Bird Cage Theatre.** The marvelously preserved interior of this combined dance hall, theater, saloon, brothel, and gambling house retains its stage, gambling tables, and rare circus posters.

The gift of a rose plant to a homesick bride in 1885 has grown so much that it shades an 8,000-square-foot courtyard at the **Rose Tree Museum** (*5th*

*& Toughnut Streets*). The museum also has pioneer exhibits and period rooms. The 1882 **St. Paul's Episcopal Church** at Third and Safford Streets is Arizona's oldest Protestant church. You can usually take a look inside and see the ship's lamps and stained-glass windows.

Grave markers on **Boot Hill,** just off the highway on the north edge of town, tell about life in early Tombstone. Ed Schieffelin requested a different kind of burial: "It is my wish, if convenient, to be

## EXPERIENCE:
## Good Enough Mine
**Prospector Ed Schieffelin filed a claim for the Good Enough Mine in 1879, finding that the rich silver ore met with his satisfaction. It was his second of 19 mines in this part of the world. Now it is open for tours, and you can descend into the passageways that snake underneath Tombstone and get a sense of the experience of the miners who once dug out ore here. The Good Enough Mine Underground Tour runs daily; check 520/255-5553 for hours.**

buried in the dress of a prospector, my old pick and canteen with me, on top of the granite hills about three miles westerly from the city of Tombstone, Arizona, and that a monument such as prospectors build when locating a mining claim be built over my grave ... under no circumstances do I want to be buried in a graveyard or cemetery." Tombstone's first prospector rests under the **Schieffelin Monument,** in a lonely spot 2.3 miles west of town on Allen Street. ■

# Bisbee

Tucked into canyons of the Mule Mountains 24 miles south of Tombstone, Bisbee still has much of its early 20th-century character. It rode the wave of copper mining, meeting the needs of the new electrical industries and leaving an architectural legacy of splendid Victorian houses and substantial commercial buildings.

In this view from above the Queen Mine, mineral-rich hills squeeze Bisbee into narrow canyons.

**Bisbee**

195 G1

**Visitor information**

Bisbee Visitor Center, #2 Copper Queen Plaza (P.O. Box 1642, Bisbee, AZ 85603)

520/432-3554 or 866/224-7233

**www.discoverbisbee .com**

The history of Bisbee began more than a hundred million years ago, when molten rock deep within the earth expelled enormous quantities of steam and hot water. The acidic, mineral-rich solutions gradually replaced overlying limestone with copper-iron sulfides. Early prospectors looking for silver were disappointed; some established copper claims nonetheless.

In 1880, Judge DeWitt Bisbee and some San Francisco financiers bought the rights. The judge never visited the town named for him. The city grew rich and built up a fine business district. The miners fared less well: When they went on strike in 1917, more than

a thousand were rounded up at gunpoint and shipped out of the state in boxcars. Working conditions improved, but copper prices ruled the town's economy. Work in the Lavender Pit east of town ceased in 1974, and underground mining ended the following year. Vast quantities of ore remain.

Bisbee's setting and Victorian architecture make it popular with artists, retirees, and visitors. Shops and galleries display jewelry—some with beautiful copper minerals—plus other work. A 5,300-foot elevation gives the town a pleasant climate most of the year.

More than 2,000 miles of mine tunnels run through the

Bisbee district. The **Queen Mine Tour** outfits you with a yellow slicker, hard hat, and lamp to ride a mine car into the workings. With 143 miles of passageways on seven levels, the mine operated for 60 years, closing in 1943. Bring a jacket or sweater; the mine temperature is only 47°F. You'll hear about the mine's history and how the miners used their skills in the stope (work area) and tunnels. Tours last 60 to 75 minutes and depart from the Queen Mine Building south across the highway from downtown. **Lavender Jeep Tours** (*www.lavenderjeeptours.com, tel 520/432-5369*) will take you around old Bisbee and beyond.

For a sense of Bisbee's early years, drop by the **Bisbee Mining & Historical Museum** in the

## INSIDER TIP:

**With its steep streets, the fun-to-walk town of Bisbee (where the desert peters out) is an inviting example of the new Old West.**

—ANDREW NELSON
*National Geographic Intelligent Travel blog writer*

1897 Phelps Dodge General Office Building downtown. Exhibits illustrate the town's development, mining, and local ranching. You'll see some of the 300-plus copper compounds from the area, many sparkling with bright greens or deep blues. The elegant general manager's office reveals the luxury enjoyed by top company officials.

---

## The Bisbee 1000

This annual event on the third weekend of October puts participants more than a step ahead. The Work Projects Administration (WPA) built Bisbee's lengthy staircases during the Great Depression, and the event seeks to preserve them. The course, with 1034 steps at last count, takes in nine staircases and loops around on twisting streets. The Bisbee Visitor Center and website (*www.bisbee1000.org*) have event info and a map. Of course, the steps can be tackled anytime.

---

An affiliate of the Smithsonian Institution, the museum opens its research library to those wishing to delve deeper into history.

Community and family heirlooms are on display in the **Bisbee Restoration Museum** (*37 Main St.*), a former department store. Fifty watering holes in the canyon known as **Brewery Gulch** served the miners until Prohibition turned off the spigots. The **Stock Exchange Bar** upstairs in the 1905 Muheim Block at 15 Brewery Avenue still has the original trading board. Between 1898 and 1915, Swiss immigrant and entrepreneur Joseph Muheim Senior built what is now the **Muheim Heritage House** (*207B Youngblood Hill, tel 520/432-7698, closed Wed.–Thurs.*). Tours tell of family life and of Muheim's many businesses in town.

A pullout on the highway just southeast of town overlooks the **Lavender Pit,** a hole 1,000 feet deep, 0.75 mile wide, and 1.5 miles long. Digging began in 1951 and removed 380 million tons of ore and rock over 23 years. ∎

---

### Queen Mine Tour

✉ Queen Mine Tour Bldg., just south of downtown across Ariz. 80

☎ 520/432-2071 or 866/432-2071

💲 $$$

**http://queenmine tour.com**

### Bisbee Mining & Historical Museum

✉ 5 Copper Queen Plaza

☎ 520/432-7071

💲 $$

**www.bisbee museum.org**

# Chiricahua Mountains

In the southeast corner of Arizona, the dramatic rock spires and cliffs of the huge sky island of the Chiricahuas (cheer-e-KAH-wahs) shelter a variety of wildlife, including javelina, coatimundi, skunk, white-tailed deer, bear, and mountain lion. It's great hiking country—just remain alert.

**Chiricahua National Monument**
- 195 G2
- 120 miles SE of Tucson via I-10, Ariz. 186, & Ariz. 181
- 520/824-3560
- $$

www.nps.gov/chir

**Douglas Ranger District, Coronado National Forest**
- 195 G1
- 1192 W. Saddleview Rd., Douglas, AZ 85607
- 520/364-3468
- Closed Sat.–Sun.

www.fs.fed.us/r3/coronado

Trails in **Chiricahua National Monument** lead you into a maze of pinnacles and balanced rocks. The 8-mile paved **Bonita Canyon Drive** curves up to Massai Point (6,870 feet) for views, a geology exhibit, and short nature trail. **Echo Canyon Trail** begins nearby on a 3.3-mile loop through some spectacular scenery.

Rangers offer tours inside the ranch house at **Faraway Ranch** most days. They tell of the Erickson family, which lived on the ranch for 91 years until 1979. From the 1920s on, the Ericksons ran a guest ranch and promoted the scenery, which led to national monument status for these rock formations.

An unpaved mountain road (usually closed in winter) crosses the Chiricahuas between Chiricahua National Monument and **Cave Creek Canyon,** on the eastern flanks, where bird-watchers come to see the elegant trogon and some 330 other species. Between the two is Onion Saddle (7,600 feet), where you can turn south up another road to a campground and trailhead among tall pines at Rustler Park (8,400 feet). The **Crest Trail** heads south from here into the Chiricahua Wilderness and to the range's highest summit—**Chiricahua Peak** (9,796 feet)—in 5.25 miles one way. Or follow the Crest Trail south 2.5 miles to just inside the wilderness boundary, then turn east about 1.9 miles on the **Centella Trail** to **Centella Point** (9,320 feet). ■

---

## EXPERIENCE: Birding in Southeastern Arizona

The thrill of sighting rare birds makes this region one of the best in the country for bird-watchers. Visits from about April through September offer the best chance of sightings. **Madera Canyon** (tel 520/281-2296, www.fs.fed.us/r3/coronado), an easy 38-mile drive south from Tucson, extends deep into the western Santa Rita Mountains with a variety of habitats. **Patagonia–Sonoita Creek Preserve** (tel 520/394-2400, www.nature.org/arizona), 60 miles southeast of Tucson, is looked after by the Nature Conservancy and famed among birders for its flycatchers, hawks, kingbirds, and hummingbirds. On the Huachucas'

eastern slopes, **Ramsey Canyon Preserve** (tel 520/ 378-2785, www.nature.org/arizona), another Nature Conservancy sanctuary, provides nearly perfect conditions for the hummers and other wildlife; there are guided walks. To the east, **San Pedro Riparian National Conservation Area** (tel 520/439-6400, www.blm.gov/az) protects a long stretch of precious water in a desert valley, drawing more than 350 bird species. **Cave Creek Canyon** (tel 520/364-3468, www.fs.fed.us/r3/coronado), in the eastern Chiricahua Mountains near the New Mexico border, offers a chance to see a trogon and other seldom-seen birds in a very scenic setting.

# Kartchner Caverns State Park

In 1974, when cave explorers Randy Tufts and Gary Tenen discovered this beautiful limestone cave on the east side of the Whetstone Mountains, they dared not publicize their find until the site's protection could be guaranteed. That occurred in 1988, when Kartchner Caverns became Arizona's 25th state park.

Speleotherms (cave features) continue to grow drop by drop in this living cave as they have done for the past 200,000 years. Nearly every type of feature known to exist can be found in the cave, including a few that were first seen here, such as the "turnip shield" and the "bird's-nest" needle quartz formations. A multimedia show in the **Discovery Center** recounts how the explorers found and entered the cave. Exhibits illustrate the formation of the cave and its features. A copy of the Throne Room's 21-foot soda straw stalactite hangs inside. Other exhibits reveal the mysteries of the animal life and include a model of the 80,000-year-old Shasta ground sloth, whose skeleton was discovered by researchers.

The Kubla Khan formation provides the grand finale flourish of the Rotunda/Throne Room Tour.

The park offers two tours, each a half-mile loop on paved trails (no steps); both are very popular and advance reservations are highly recommended. The **Rotunda/Throne Room Tour** goes year-round, but the **Big Room Tour,** which only began in 2003, closes mid-April–mid-October to protect the bats inside. A tram takes you up a hill to the cave entrance, where you pass through an air lock that maintains the 99 percent humidity needed for growth of the cave formations. Temperatures average a comfortable 68°F. Your guide will identify the many types of cave features seen on the 1.5- to 1.75-hour tours.

The rich colors of the features come from hematite, manganese, and organic matter that have seeped in through the ceiling.

Above ground you can wander in the hummingbird garden, hike the 2.4-mile **Foothills Loop Trail,** or head out on the 4.2-mile **Guindani Trail Loop** in adjacent Coronado National Forest. ∎

**Kartchner Caverns State Park**

⛰ 195 F1

✉ Off Ariz. 90, 8 miles S of I-10 Exit 302

☎ 520/586-4100 (information), 520/586-2283 (tour reservations)

💲 $$ (free w/ confirmed tour res.), $$$$ tours

**www.azstateparks.com**

# More Places to Visit in Southern Arizona

This stark Fort Bowie building held the store where soldiers and their wives shopped.

against renegade Apache. After their leader Geronimo surrendered in 1886, the fort was little used; the Army abandoned it in 1894. A self-guided 3-mile round-trip walk passes the ruin of a station used by Butterfield's Overland Mail Company from 1858 to 1861, the post cemetery, the site of the Battle of Apache Pass, and Apache Spring. The walk also takes you near ruins of the site's first fort and the larger second fort, where you'll find a visitor center with a small museum and bookshop. *www.nps.gov/fobo* 🅰 195 G2  ✉ On Apache Pass Rd. (last 0.8 mile is unpaved), 12 miles S of Bowie ☎ 520/847-2500

## Amerind Museum

You might not expect to find an outstanding museum in the middle of the rocky desert, but the Amerind is a jewel worth seeking out. Since 1937, when it was established by amateur archaeologist William Fulton, the foundation has devoted itself to studies of American Indian cultures—hence its name, a contraction of the two words. Set among the massive boulders of Texas Canyon, Spanish-colonial revival buildings house an outstanding collection of artifacts, mostly from the Southwest and Mexico.

The Amerind Art Gallery nearby displays paintings and sculptures by American artists of the 19th and 20th centuries. The Museum Store sells Native American art, crafts, jewelry, and books. Take I-10 Dragoon Exit 318, head southeast for 1 mile, turn left for 0.75 mile. *www.amerind.org* 🅰 195 G2  ✉ 64 miles E of Tucson, off I-10 bet. Benson & Willcox ☎ 520/586-3666  🕐 Closed Mon. 💲 $$

## Fort Bowie National Historic Site

Ruins mark the site of an Army fort that guarded the strategic Apache Pass during the Indian wars. It began as a primitive camp in 1862 after Apache ambushed troops and later became a center in the campaigns

## Rex Allen Arizona Cowboy Museum

Rex Allen's (1920–1999) talent for playing the guitar and singing took him from his family's homestead near Willcox into the recording business. Allen went on to star in the 1950 film *Arizona Cowboy* and in other movies, as well as television shows. Here, in an early 1890s building on the original main street of Willcox, you can see his sequined cowboy suits, guitars, saddles, movie posters, and a buggy used in the television series *Frontier Doctor.* A park across the street features his statue and a memorial to his faithful horse, Koko.

A few doors north of the museum, the Apache leader Geronimo once shopped at the 1880 **Willcox Commercial Store,** Arizona's oldest commercial building still selling clothes and other goods at its original location. Around the corner at 127 E. Maley Street, the **Chiricahua Regional Museum & Research Center** *(tel 520/384-3971, closed Sun.)* has displays on the area's land and people. Go south on Railroad Avenue to the restored 1880 **Southern Pacific Depot** *(closed Sat.–Sun.)* to see some exhibits. *www.rexallenmuseum.org* 🅰 195 G2 ✉ 150 N. Railroad Ave., Willcox ☎ 520/384-4583 or 877/234-4111  💲 $

# Travelwise

An easy-to-spot hot-air balloon drifts over Sedona.

# TRAVELWISE

## PLANNING YOUR TRIP

### When to Go

You can enjoy your visit to Arizona in any month of the year. Sunshine prevails year-round, but to avoid extremes of temperature, simply adjust your elevation according to season, between the cooler mountains and plateaus of the north and the warmer deserts to the south. Summer is the time to head to the high country, where the world's largest ponderosa pine forest extends across much of the state; highs typically run in the 70s and 80s. At the same time the deserts get so hot that you'll feel you're in an oven. Highs in the low 100s are common and can exceed 110°F, leaving visitors wondering how people survived in this part of the United States before air-conditioning. (Some of the museums and pioneer houses explain how Native Americans and early settlers coped.)

Thunderstorms rumble over Arizona's landscape in late summer, drenching some areas while leaving adjacent ones dry; that's when drivers and backcountry travelers need to watch for flash floods. Another series of storms, gentler this time, arrives in winter, bringing ski resorts to life in the mountains and awakening desert plants. "Snowbirds"—visitors from the north—flock to the desert then to enjoy delightful weather with highs in the 70s.

If you head to the high country in summer and the low in winter, you'll find not only more comfortable temperatures, but also more festivals and events. Make room reservations. In spring and autumn you can enjoy visiting the entire state, with lower prices and greater availability of accommodations.

## Festivals

### January

**Fiesta Bowl Game** University of Phoenix Stadium, Glendale, early Jan., tel 480/350-0900, www.fiestabowl.org. Holiday fun (see December, p. 236) culminates with this football classic.

**Scottsdale Celebration of Fine Art** Scottsdale, mid-Jan.–late March, tel 480/443-7695, www.celebrateart.com. More than 100 artists—many of whom can be seen at work—gather for this giant exhibition. It's held in the big white tents off N. Scottsdale Road at the 101 Loop.

### February

**Tucson Gem, Mineral & Fossil Showcase** Tucson, first 2 weeks, tel 520/624-1817 or 800/638-8350, www.visitTucson.org/gemshow. Many shows run during the event, including the very popular Tucson Gem & Mineral Show on the final weekend.

**Cochise Cowboy Poetry and Music Gathering** Sierra Vista, usually 1st full weekend, tel 520/249-2511, www.cowboypoets.com, attracts artists and fans for a weekend of both free and ticketed performances.

**World Championship Hoop Dance Contest** Phoenix, 1st or 2nd weekend, tel 602/252-8848, www.heard.org. Native Americans will astound you with their skill at the Heard Museum.

**Phoenix Open Golf Tournament** Phoenix, last week Jan.–early Feb., tel 602/870-0163, www.phoenixopen.com. PGA players compete.

**Arizona Renaissance Festival** Apache Junction, early/mid-Feb.–late March/early April, tel 520/463-2700, www.royalfaires.com/arizona. Enter a 16th-century world of costumed actors and jousting knights who will entertain you with drama, comedy, stories, and songs from a dozen stages. Make a day of the festival, which runs weekends and Presidents' Day at a site off US 60 southeast of Mesa.

**Flagstaff Winterfest** Flagstaff, tel 928/774-4505, www.flagstaffchamber.com. Flagstaff celebrates the winter season with ski competitions, cultural events, arts and crafts, sports, and family games.

**Accenture Match Play Championship** Tucson, www.worldgolfchampionships.com. Top golf pros compete in this PGA tourament.

**La Fiesta de los Vaqueros** Tucson, late Feb., tel 520/741-2233 or 800/964-5662, www.tucsonrodeo.com. Cowpunchers and their fans gather for rodeo action. The Tucson Rodeo Parade is said to be the longest nonmotorized one in the world.

**Parada del Sol Parade and Rodeo** Scottsdale, last 2 weeks, tel 480/990-3179, www.paradadelsol.org. A pro rodeo and several dances accompany the world's longest horse-drawn parade.

**Sedona International Film Festival** Sedona, last week, tel 928/282-1177, www.sedonafilmfestival.com. Movie enthusiasts gather to see new movies and to attend a workshop.

### March

**Cactus League Spring Training** Phoenix area, tel 480/827-4700 or 800/293-0071, www.cactusleague.com or www.visitmesa.com/spring-training/. Baseball fans watch major-league teams warm up for the season in a series of practice and exhibition games.

**Heard Museum Guild Indian Fair & Marketplace** Phoenix, 1st full weekend, tel 602/252-8848, www.heard.org. More than 700

Native American artists display their works, available for purchase, along with music, dance, and food.

**M.C.A.S. Yuma Air Show** Yuma, late Feb.–late March, tel 928/783-0071 or 800/293-0071, www.yumaairshow.com. Pilots and skydivers take to the air above the Marine Corps Air Station.

**Scottsdale Arts Festival** Scottsdale, 2nd weekend, tel 480/994-2787, www.scottsdaleperformingarts.org. Art exhibitions and performances, with children's activities, take place on the Scottsdale Civic Center Mall.

**Tucson Festival of Books** Tucson, mid-month, www.tucsonfestivalofbooks.org. Renowned authors offer talks, interviews, and book signings at this free event on the University of Arizona campus.

**St. Patrick's Day Parade** Sedona, March 17 (or nearest Sat.), tel 928/204-2390, www.sedonamainstreet.com. Fans of the Irish bring out the green.

**Midnight at the Oasis Car Show** Yuma, 1st weekend, tel 928/783-0071 or 800/293-0071, www.midnightattheoasis.net. Beautiful and unusual vehicles on display. Bands give concerts.

**Fourth Avenue Street Fair** Tucson, tel 520/624-5004, www.fourthavenue.org. Entertainers, craftspeople, artists, and food vendors create a festival atmosphere. The event is repeated in early December.

## April

**Easter Pageant** Mesa, 2 weeks preceding Easter, tel 480/654-1077, www.easterpageant.org. This continually popular event takes place at the Mormon Church's Arizona Temple. It is said to be the world's largest annual outdoor Easter pageant, with a cast of over 400.

**Maricopa County Fair** Phoenix, tel 602/252-0717, www.maricopacountyfair.org. Entertainment,

carnival rides, animals, and exhibits draw crowds to this big event.

**Tucson International Mariachi Conference** Tucson, mid to late April, tel 420/838-3908, www.tucsonmariachi.org. Bands play this traditional form of Mexican music to appreciative audiences.

**Pima County Fair** Tucson, late April, tel 520/762-9100, www.pimacountyfair.com. There are seemingly countless fun things to see and do, including circus events, concerts, carnival rides, exhibits, and livestock shows.

**Verde Valley Birding & Nature Festival** Cottonwood, last full weekend, tel 928/282-2202, www.birdyverde.org. Field trips and other programs explore the diverse natural world in the Verde Valley.

## May

**Cinco de Mayo** Tucson, weekend closest to 5th, tel 520/624-1817 or 800/638-8350. Folk dancers, musicians, artists, and food vendors commemorate Mexico's 1862 victory over the French.

**Phippen Western Art Show & Sale** Prescott, Memorial Day weekend, tel 928/778-1385, www.phippenartmuseum.org. Some 150 artists come to Courthouse Plaza for a juried arts show.

## June

**Sharlot Hall Museum Folk Arts Fair** Prescott, 1st full weekend, tel 928/445-3122, www.sharlot.org. Costumed actors bring the territorial years to life demonstrating woodworking, churning, spinning, weaving, cowboy cooking, and entertainment.

**Sedona Taste** Sedona, 2nd Sun., tel 928/282-0122. Sample fine wines and food prepared by top chefs.

**Pine Country Pro Rodeo** Flagstaff, 3rd weekend, tel

888/681-3556, www.pinecountryprorodeo.com. Top rodeo cowboys provide plenty of thrills.

**High Country Warbirds Fly-In** Valle (north of Williams), tel 928/635-1000, www.planesoffame.org. Famous aircraft from WWII and other eras take to the skies. A car show runs as well.

## July

**Small Town 4th of July** Williams, tel 928/635-1418 or 800/863-0546, www.williamschamber.com. A parade, BBQ, ice cream social, and other family activities celebrate the Fourth.

**Prescott Frontier Days** Prescott, July 4th week, tel 928/445-3103 or 800/358-1888, www.worldsoldestrodeo.com. Cowboys have been celebrating Independence Day with rodeos here since 1888. The action with professional rodeo cowboys begins in late June and lasts through the July 4th holiday. Prescott Frontier Days Parade—one of Arizona's biggest—rolls through downtown on the Saturday nearest July 4. Other festivities include dances, a concert, Whiskey Row race, fun runs, golf tournament, rodeo queen coronation, and fireworks.

**July 4 Celebration** Flagstaff, tel 928/774-9541 or 800/842-7293. A parade, the Pioneer Days Festival, the Hopi Festival of Arts and Culture, an arts and crafts show, and fireworks celebrate both Independence Day and the legendary naming of Flagstaff.

**Arizona Highland Celtic Festival** Flagstaff, 3rd full weekend, tel 928/556-3161 or 800/842-7293, www.nachs.info. The celebration relives the heritage of Brittany, Cornwall, Ireland, the Isle of Man, Scotland, and Wales with bagpipers, dancers, athletic demonstrations. Traditional food adds a tasty note.

**White Mountain Native American Art Festival**

Pinetop-Lakeside, 3rd full weekend, tel 928/367-4290 or 800/573-4031, www.pinetoplakesidechamber.com. Artisans from across the Southwest gather to show their work, along with dances, music, and food.

**Arizona Cardinals Training Camp** Flagstaff, usually late July–mid-Aug., tel 928/774-9541 or 800/842-7293, www.azcardinals.com. Most practice sessions of this NFL team at Northern Arizona University are open to visitors.

## August

**Navajo Festival of Arts and Culture** Flagstaff, 1st full weekend, tel 928/774-5213, www.musnaz.org. Experience the Navajo "Beauty Way" philosophy through artists, storytellers, dancers, and musicians.

**White Mountain Bluegrass Music Festival** Pinetop-Lakeside, 2nd full weekend, tel 928/367-4290 or 800/573-4031, www.pinetoplakesidechamber.com. Musicians play lively music among the pines.

**Payson Rodeo** Payson, 3rd weekend, tel 928/474-4515 or 800/672-9766, www.paysonrimcountry.com. Local rodeo fans claim this is the world's oldest continuous rodeo—since 1884. A parade accompanies the professional rodeo thrills.

**Arizona Cowboy Poets Gathering** Prescott, 3rd weekend, tel 928/776-2000 (ticket office), www.azcowboypoets.org. Poems and songs recall life in the saddle.

## September

**Navajo Nation Fair** Window Rock, early Sept., tel 928/871-6647, www.navajonationfair.com. Navajo and visitors gather for a rodeo, parade, powwow, carnival, and Miss Navajo Pageant.

**Coconino County Fair**

Flagstaff, Labor Day weekend, tel 928/679-8000, 928/774-9541, or 800/842-7293. The large fair features livestock, entertainment, exhibits, a carnival, and demolition derby.

**Grand Canyon Music Festival** Grand Canyon Village, tel 928/638-9215 or 800/997-8285, www.grandcanyonmusicfest.org. Experience the broad diversity of chamber music in a series of concerts atop the South Rim.

**Fall Artisans Festival** and **Run to the Pines Car Show** Pinetop-Lakeside, last full weekend, tel 928/367-4290 or 800/573-4031, www.pinetoplakesidechamber.com. Art, cars, and more in the high country for the last big celebration of the summer season.

**Flagstaff Festival of Science** Flagstaff, late Sept.–early Oct., tel 928/774-9541 or 800/842-7293, www.scifest.org. The ten-day festival celebrates the excitement of science with talks by top scientists, interactive exhibits, and field trips.

**Andy Devine Days** Kingman, last weekend of Sept., tel 928/753-6106 or 866/427-7866, www.kingmanrodeo.com. A parade, PRCA rodeo, and other events honor Kingman's favorite son.

## October

**Fort Verde Days** Camp Verde, 2nd weekend, tel 928/567-9294. The cavalry returns for drills and reenactments. Festivities include a parade, arts and crafts, bull riding, kids carnival, music, and dances.

**Arizona State Fair** Phoenix, mid-Oct.–early Nov., tel 602/252-6771, www.azstatefair.com. Concerts, contests, rides, and prize livestock.

**Helldorado Days** Tombstone, 3rd weekend, tel 520/457-3929 or 888/457-3929, www.tombstonechamber.com. Three days of reenactments, street entertainment, kids carnival, and a parade

celebrate Tombstone's rip-roaring 1880s heritage.

**Apache Jii (Day) Celebration** Globe, 3rd weekend, tel 928/425-4495 or 800/804-5623, www.globemiamichamber.com. Various tribes perform songs, dances, and stories. More than 100 booths offer Native American arts and crafts, demonstrations, and food.

**London Bridge Days** Lake Havasu City, mid-Oct., tel 928/208-1251, www.newlhcmainstreet.com. A parade, entertainment, kids' activities, and food celebrate the famous bridge's dedication.

## November

**Yuma Colorado River Crossing Balloon Festival** Yuma, weekend before Thanksgiving, tel 928/783-0071 or 800/293-0071, www.caballeros.org. Hot-air balloons fill the skies.

## December

**Christmas City** Prescott, Nov.–Dec., tel 928/445-2000 or 800/266-7534, www.prescott.org. Its Christmas parade, courthouse lighting, music, and exhibits have earned Prescott the name "Arizona's Christmas City."

**Fourth Avenue Street Fair** Tucson, tel 520/624-5004, www.fourthavenue.org. Artists and craftspeople display their work while entertainers and food booths provide diversions.

**Fiesta Bowl Parade** Phoenix area, late Dec. or early Jan, tel 480/350-0900, www.fiestabowl.com. A parade, the National Band Championship, a block party, and sporting events lead up to the big game (see also January, p. 234).

## What to Take

Because of the low humidity, temperatures can swing drastically at any time of year; dressing in layers is the best way to adapt. Comfortable clothes and sturdy walking shoes will add to your enjoyment. Arizonans tend to dress informally. Only a handful of restaurants in the state expect men to wear ties, and a few Western-style restaurants even prohibit them, as is sometimes evident from the snipped-off ends tacked onto the ceiling! The bola tie, a cord held by a clasp typically made of silver with inlaid minerals, is the preferred neckwear; bolas are sold at many jewelry and gift shops.

A hat and sunblock will help fend off the dazzling sun. You're unlikely to encounter biting insects, but a few canyons have them in summer; repellent comes in handy.

## Further Reading

Both city sights and outdoors are covered in several regularly revised, comprehensive state or regional guidebooks. Guides for hikers include *100 Classic Hikes in Arizona* (2007) and *Exploring Arizona's Wild Areas* (2002) by Scott S. Warren, *Hiking Grand Canyon National Park* (2006) by Ron Adkison, and *Sedona's Top 10 Hikes* (2008) by Dennis Andres.

For descriptions and maps of great bike rides, try *Mountain Biking Arizona Guide: Fat Tire Tales & Trails* (2005) by Cosmic Ray. *A Field Guide to the Grand Canyon* (1996) by Stephen Whitney identifies plant and animal life. *A Natural History of the Sonoran Desert* (1999) by the Arizona-Sonora Desert Museum reveals the surprising diversity of this arid realm. Natural history buffs should take a look at Barbara Kingsolver's *High Tide in Tucson* (1996) and Gary Paul Nabhan's *The Desert Smells Like Rain: A Naturalist in O'Odham Country* (2002).

*House of Rain: Tracking a Vanished Civilization Across the American Southwest* (2008) by Craig Childs is a fascinating exploration

of the ancestral Puebloan people. John Wesley Powell's account of his epic 19th-century boat trips through the Grand Canyon, *The Exploration of the Colorado River and its Canyons* (1895), is widely available in reprints. A first-hand account of frontier Arizona is *Vanished Arizona* (1911) by Martha Summerhayes. *Arizona Ghost Towns and Mining Camps* (2005) by Philip Varney will help you find and appreciate these places.

Aspects of Native American cultures are explored in *Left-Handed Son of Old Man Hat: A Navajo Autobiography* (1938) recorded by Walter Dyk and available in reprints, and also in the illustrated *The Enduring Navaho* (1994) by Laura Gilpin, *Hopi* (2009) by Susanne and Jake Page, and *Art of the Hopi* (2009) by Jerry and Lois Essary Jacka.

The Old West comes alive in the many novels of **Zane Grey.** Passionate environmentalist Edward Abbey wrote *The Fool's Progress: An Honest Novel* (1988), loosely based on his own life.

## Getting to Arizona
### By Air

Sky Harbor International Airport, conveniently located for Phoenix, Tempe, and Scottsdale, provides the most connections to the rest of the country and beyond *(tel 602/273-3300, www.phxskyharbor .com)*. Phoenix-Mesa Gateway Airport *(tel 480/988-7600, www .phxmesagateway.org)*, on the city's southeast side, offers connections to a sprinkling of small cities in the West and Midwest.

Major carriers also serve Tucson International Airport in the southeastern part of the state *(tel 520/573-8000, www.tucsonairport .org)*. Flights to and from Tucson airport may cost more, so shop around. Both airports are well served by rental car agencies, taxis,

and local buses.

**Grand Canyon's Airport**
*(tel 928/638-2446, www.grand canyonairport.net)* is the next busiest, though most of the flights here are in smaller aircraft and originate in Las Vegas, Nevada.

### By Train

Amtrak *(tel 800/872-7245, www .amtrak.com)* runs two luxury trains across the state, connecting Los Angeles with New Orleans, Chicago, and other points to the east. The *Southwest Chief* goes through the north of the state and runs daily in both directions via Kingman, Williams Junction, Flagstaff, and Winslow. The *Sunset Limited* goes across southern Arizona only three times weekly in each direction via Yuma, Maricopa, Tucson, and Benson.

### By Bus

Greyhound *(tel 800/231-2222, www.greyhound.com)* has several routes in Arizona and connects with smaller bus companies. Arizona Shuttle *(tel 520/795-6771 or 800/888-2749, www.arizonashuttle .com)* connects Grand Canyon, Williams, Flagstaff, Sedona, Camp Verde, Phoenix, and Tucson.

## GETTING AROUND
### By Car

Most people find their own vehicle the handiest way of getting around Arizona. Public transport is generally useful only between the cities and within Phoenix and Tucson. Additionally, the Grand Canyon National Park has shuttle services on the South Rim to alleviate traffic congestion.

Many rental-car agencies compete for your business; you may be able to rent an RV or a 4WD vehicle as well. Advance reservations can help get the lowest rate. You'll need insurance; check to see if your personal policy or credit card provides coverage before paying extra. Major agencies include: **Alamo** (tel 877/222-9075, www .alamo.com), **Avis** (tel 800/331-1212, www.avis.com), **Budget** (tel 800/527-0700, www.budget.com), **Dollar** (tel 800/800-3665, www. dollar.com), **Hertz** (tel 800/654-3001, www.hertz.com), **Thrifty** (tel 800/847-4389, www thrifty.com).

## By Air
Within Arizona, commuter flights radiate out of Phoenix to Tucson, Flagstaff, and Yuma, and perhaps other destinations. Costs are high, but you're likely to enjoy good views.

## Other Options
Gray Line Tours (tel 520/622-8811or 800/276-1528, www.gray linearizona.com) provides day and overnight excursions out of Tucson. Senior citizens can check out the many educational tours in Arizona provided by Exploritas—formerly Elderhostel (tel 978/323-4141 or 800/454-5768, www.exploritas.org).

## PRACTICAL ADVICE
### Maps
Statewide maps are widely available at tourist offices and bookstores. The AAA Indian Country Guide Map provides exceptional coverage of northern Arizona and the Four Corners region; it's also available in stores. The Benchmark Arizona Road & Recreation Atlas shows much greater detail than most similar publications and has back roads, shaded relief, public land designations, GPS grids, and recreation information.

Each of Arizona's national forests has one or more maps that will help in navigating back roads and in finding trailheads and other points of interest. The Bureau of Land Management has a good map of

the Arizona Strip in the far north; it's recommended if you plan to explore the backcountry there. Hikers have a choice of topographic map scales; the 1:24,000 (7.5-minute) series has the most detail.

## Safety
Arizona's crime rate is low. You're unlikely to have problems if you are aware of natural hazards and take care with your gear. Even the downtowns of the big cities are considered safe at night, but it is still wise to use common sense and pay attention.

Natural hazards may present problems: Flash floods sometimes obstruct highways after storms; just wait for the water to go down, which normally happens quite quickly. Dust storms can block visibility so badly that it is best to pull off the road (turn off lights so as not to confuse other drivers)—these can last from a few minutes to several hours.

## Taxes & Tipping
A sales tax of between 7 and 10 percent is added to the bill at most motels, hotels, resorts, commercial campgrounds, restaurants, shops, as well as some attractions. Tax is not usually added to prices at federal, state, or Native American sites and campgrounds. Taxi drivers, bartenders, and waiters who provide table service expect a tip of 15 to 20 percent.

## Travelers with Disabilities
Airlines, ground transport, newer motels and hotels, restaurants, parks, and public buildings often have facilities for people with mobility difficulties. You can call ahead with special needs and requests. Tourist offices may have advice and literature too. Access-Able Travel Source

(P.O. Box 1796, Wheat Ridge, CO 80034, tel 303/232-2979, fax 303/239-8486, www.access-able.com) provides up-to-date information to help people with disabilities enjoy safer, worry-free journeys.

## Vistor Information
The Arizona Office of Tourism's visitor center (1110 W. Washington St., Suite 155, Phoenix, AZ 85007, tel 602/364-3700 or 866/891-3640 to request printed information, fax 602/364-3701, www.arizona guide.com) is open Mon.–Fri., 8 a.m.–5 p.m. Information is also available at Arizona's many local tourist offices and at the Painted Cliffs Welcome Center just off I-40 Exit 359, near the New Mexico border.

## Websites
The Arizona Office of Tourism's excellent website (www.arizona guide.com) has travel information in addition to links to visitor bureaus and chambers of commerce. For the Grand Canyon, try Grand Canyon National Park's website (www.nps.gov/grca) and the commercial site (www.thecan yon.com). Also helpful are the big-city websites (www.flagstaffari-zona.org, www.visitphoenix.com and www .visittucson.org).

## Emergencies
### Emergency Number
Dial 911 (or the number posted on the telephone) for police, ambulance, and fire emergencies.

## Health
For nonemergency medical care, a doctor's office or a clinic will have lower costs than a hospital emergency room.

# Hotels & Restaurants

**Accommodations in Arizona range from world-famous resorts and guest ranches with excellent recreation facilities in spectacular settings, through an abundance of good-value motels, both mid-range and bargain-priced, to youth hostels. The accommodations described here lie close to the attractions listed in this book or are destinations in themselves.**

## Accommodations

Peak times are late winter and early spring in the desert areas and summer weekends in the high country. Reserve ahead. That goes for Grand Canyon accommodations year-round. Across the state, weekends and holidays tend to be busiest and often cost more. During the off-season, you can sometimes check into a resort for as little as half the peak-season rate. Many travelers find the lowest prices with major online services such as Hotels.com *(www.hotels.com)*, Expedia *(www.expedia.com)*, Travelocity *(www.travelocity.com)*, Orbitz *(www.orbitz.com)*, Priceline.com *(www.priceline.com)*, and Hotwire.com *(www.hotwire.com)*.

Smaller inns and bed-and-breakfasts often prohibit smoking or restrict it to outdoors. All accommodations on these pages offer non-smoking rooms, if they're not entirely non-smoking, and all restaurants listed are non-smoking (partly thanks to a recent state law). You'll find free or validated parking nearly everywhere.

## Hotels & Motels

The major chains have become very popular—you're likely to find your favorites in the cities and larger towns. Chains include: **Best Western** *(tel 800/780-7234, www.bestwestern.com)*, **Comfort Inn** *(tel 877/424-6423, www.comfortinn.com)*, **Days Inn** *(tel 800/329-7466, www.daysinn.com)*, **Econo Lodge** *(tel 877/424-6423, www.econolodge.com)*, **Hilton** *(tel 800/445-8667, www.hilton.com)*, **Holiday Inn** and **Holiday Inn**

**Express** *(tel 800/465-4329, www.holidayinn.com)*, **Marriott** *(tel 888/236-2427, www.marriott.com)*, **Motel 6** *(tel 800/466-8356, www.motel6.com)*, **Radisson** *(tel 888/201-1718, www.radisson.com)*, **Ramada Inn** *(tel 800/272-6232, www.ramada.com)*, **Rodeway Inn** *(tel 877/424-6423, www.rodeway.com)*, **Super 8** *(tel 800/800-8000, www.super8.com)*.

Historic hotels take you back in time. The grand hotels, well worth a visit to the lobby even if you're staying elsewhere, include El Tovar on the Grand Canyon's South Rim, Grand Canyon Lodge on the North Rim, La Posada in Winslow, the Hassayampa Inn at Prescott, and the Copper Queen Hotel in Bisbee. Modest historic hotels have character, too, such as the Weatherford in Flagstaff and the Congress in Tucson, but loud music from the bands downstairs can make sleep difficult at these two!

Older motels, long since bypassed by interstates and freeways, can be fine and often have bargain rates. They're numerous on segments of Route 66 in towns across northern Arizona and on old highways through cities in the rest of the state. The key to happiness in these independents is to check the room before handing over money—not all give refunds if you change your mind. Staying at family-owned motels not only saves money but also helps preserve these disappearing pieces of Americana.

## Bed and Breakfasts

Hosts offer a personal service and comfortable rooms both in the cities and out in the countryside.

Because a B&B reflects the owner's personality, it's worth asking about the establishment's policies and features. Reservation agencies can be a big help in matching you with a proprietor who has similar interests. The agencies also know of small bed-and-breakfasts that have no advertising or listings elsewhere. Mi Casa Su Casa *(P.O. Box 950, Tempe, AZ 8528, tel 480/990-0682 or 800/456-0682, www.azres.com)* has many places statewide and beyond. Arizona Trails Travel Services *(P.O. Box 18998, Fountain Hills, AZ 85269, tel 480/837-4284 or 888/799-4284, www.arizonatrails.com)* also offers listings statewide and beyond; adventure tours can be arranged, too. Arizona Association of Bed & Breakfast Inns *(www.arizona-bed-breakfast.com)* provides information about its members.

## Guest Ranches

Staying on a ranch gives you the opportunity to view the scenery from horseback. Guest ranches provide a mix of Old West atmosphere and resort comforts. The Arizona Dude Ranch Association *(P.O. Box 603, Cortaro, AZ 85652, www.azdra.com)* is a good source.

## Campgrounds

By pitching a tent or parking an RV, you can stay in some of the most beautiful places in Arizona. You have thousands of choices. Commercial campgrounds offer the most amenities—hookups, showers, laundromats, and recreation facilities. Arizona State Park campgrounds tend to be the best deal—they have most of the services of a commercial campground plus some great locations near lakes or mountains. National Park Service, Forest Service, and Indian campgrounds tend to have just the basics—a picnic table, a place to park, and a toilet or outhouse; water may be available, but only occasionally will showers be nearby.

Dispersed camping is an option on much of the national forest, Bureau of Land Management, and national recreation area lands. This takes a bit more work—you have to check regulations, bring water, carry a shovel for burying waste, and find a suitable spot away from towns, highways, developed recreation areas, and sole water sources (used by wildlife and stock). Check for fire restrictions—you may need a campfire permit. During dry periods, smoking, campfires, and even entry to certain areas of forests may be prohibited. The benefits of dispersed camping can be tranquility rarely experienced in established campgrounds, cost savings, and the freedom to come and go as you please.

## Credit Cards
Abbreviations: AE (American Express), DIS (Discover), MC (MasterCard), and V (Visa).

## Restaurants
It is always a good idea to call ahead to resort and other fine-dining restaurants for dinner reservations and to check on dress codes. Arizonans enjoy ethnic food, too, and you'll rarely be far from a Mexican or Chinese restaurant. Other cuisines abound in the larger cities, especially those with universities.
    L = lunch   D = dinner

The hotels and restaurants listed here are grouped first according to their region, then listed alphabetically within their price category.

State law prohibits smoking in restaurants and bars, with some exceptions. For disabled access, it is best to call the establishment to verify the extent of their facilities. A key to symbols in this section appears on the back-cover flap.

## ■ GRAND CANYON COUNTRY

### GRAND CANYON VILLAGE (SOUTH RIM)

**Reservations.** You can make reservations for all lodging inside the park on the South Rim and Phantom Ranch through Xanterra South Rim, 6312 S. Fiddlers Green Circle, Suite 600N, Greenwood Village, CO 80111, tel 888/297-2757 or 303/297-2757 (advance reservations), 928/638-2631 (same-day reservations), fax 303/297-3175, www.grand canyonlodges.com.

### SOMETHING SPECIAL

#### 🏨 EL TOVAR HOTEL
**$$$–$$$$$**
RESERVATIONS See above. Since 1905, El Tovar has offered the finest accommodations and dining in the park. The lobby's cathedral ceiling, handmade furniture, fireplace, and pine-log walls greet you as you enter this rustic yet elegant lodge. Rooms—no two alike—range from small to spacious; all have private baths. Four suites have canyon views.
ⓘ 78 🅿 🅢 🕭 All major cards

#### 🏨 BRIGHT ANGEL LODGE
**$–$$$$$**
RESERVATIONS See above. Some of the cabins offer canyon views and fireplaces. The early 1890s Buckey O'Neill Suite cabin is one of the oldest buildings in the park. Rooms inside the

lodge come as private bath, shared bath, or no bath. This popular spot on the rim near the Bright Angel Trailhead offers a snack bar, mule rides desk, and two restaurants (no reservations).
ⓘ 138 🅿 🕭 All major cards

#### 🏨 THUNDERBIRD & KACHINA LODGES
**$$$**
RESERVATIONS See above. The contemporary design doesn't fit with the historic buildings nearby on the rim, but these lodges offer comfortable rooms in a convenient location. Second-story canyon-side rooms have views yet cost only a bit more than those in back.
ⓘ 104 🅿 🕭 All major cards

#### 🏨 MASWIK LODGE
**$$–$$$**
RESERVATIONS See p. 240. Back in the woods from the rim, travelers have a choice of accommodations: small cabins or two types of motel rooms.

---

🏨 Hotel  🍴 Restaurant  ⓘ No. of Guest Rooms  🪑 No. of Seats  🅿 Parking  🕒 Closed  🛗 Elevator

Cafeteria.
ⓘ 278 🅿 🄢 (Maswik North)
🄲 All major cards

### 🏨 YAVAPAI LODGE
**$$–$$$**
RESERVATIONS See above.
Largest of the lodges within
the park, Yavapai has two
types of motel rooms and a
cafeteria. It's a mile east of
Bright Angel Lodge and set
back from the rim.
ⓘ 358 🅿 🄢 (Yavapai East)
🄲 All major cards

### 🍴 EL TOVAR DINING ROOM
**$$$–$$$$**
TEL 928/638-2631 EXT. 6432
Canyon views complement
fine service and food in the
El Tovar Hotel (see p. 240)
restaurant. The menu offers
regional and continental
dishes. Dinner reservations,
required, can be made up to
30 days in advance (6 months
with an El Tovar Hotel room
reservation).
🛏 250 🅿 🄢 🄲 All major cards

## INNER GORGE

### 🏨 PHANTOM RANCH
**$–$$**
RESERVATIONS See p. 240.
You can hike or ride a mule
down to these rustic stone
cabins near the sparkling
Bright Angel Creek at the
bottom of the Grand Canyon.
Mule rides include cabin
accommodations, while hikers
normally stay in the dormi-
tory (separate for men and
women). Evaporative coolers
fend off the summer heat.
The ranch-style dining room
offers breakfast, box lunches,
and a choice of stew, vegetarian, or steak dinners. During
the day the dining room
offers snacks for sale. Advance
reservations required for both
accommodations and meals.
ⓘ 13 🄲 All major cards

## TUSAYAN

Nine miles south of Grand
Canyon Village, this busy
tourist village has many places
to stay, restaurants, an IMAX
theater, and a nearby airport.

### 🏨 BEST WESTERN GRAND CANYON SQUIRE INN
**$$$–$$$$$**
TEL 928/638-2681 OR
800/622-6966
FAX 928/638-2782
**www.grandcanyonsquire
.com**
The inn offers large modern
rooms and suites, two dining
rooms, a sports bar, and many
amenities—bowling, pool, spa,
sauna, exercise room, and
video arcade. The **Coronado
Room** has fine dining nightly;
the main dining room offers
breakfast and lunch.
ⓘ 250 🅿 🄢 🄢 🄲 🄴
🄲 All major cards

### 🏨 GRAND HOTEL
**$$$–$$$$$**
TEL 928/638-3333 OR
888/634-7263
FAX 928/638-3131
**www.grandcanyongrandhotel
.com**
The rustic stone-and-timber
exterior encloses an indoor
pool and spa, and comfortable
hotel rooms with South-
western art. Some rooms
have balconies. A musician,
cowboy singer, or band often
entertains in the Canyon Star
Restaurant & Saloon.
ⓘ 121 🅿 🄢 🄢 🄢
🄲 All major cards

### 🏨 CANYON PLAZA RESORT
**$$$–$$$$**
TEL 928/638-2673 OR
800/995-2521
FAX 928/638-9537
**www.grandcanyonplaza.com**
There's Southwest style in spa-
cious rooms, most with patios
or balconies. A spacious atrium

houses the restaurant (buffet
and full-service menu) and
Wintergarten Lounge. Relax in
indoor and outdoor spas and
an outdoor pool.
ⓘ 232 🅿 🄢 🄢 🄴 🄲 All
major cards

## NORTH RIM

## SOMETHING SPECIAL

### 🏨 GRAND CANYON
### 🍴 LODGE
**$$–$$$**
TEL 480/337-1320 OR
877/386-4383 (ADVANCE RES.),
928/638-2611 (SAME-DAY AND
RESTAURANT RES.)
FAX 480/998-7399
**www.grandcanyonlodgenorth.
com**
Motel rooms and three types
of cabin have a wonderful
location amid the ponderosa
pines. The splendid main lodge
has huge windows facing the
sublime immensity of the
Grand Canyon. Amenities in-
clude a mule rides desk, snack
bar, post office, and saloon.
Diners at the Lodge receive
rimside seats and memorable
food (dinner reservations
required). These are the only
accommodations within the
park on the North Rim, so
reserve well in advance.
ⓘ 214 🅿 🕐 Closed mid-Oct.–
mid-May 🄲 All major cards

### 🏨 JACOB LAKE INN
**$$–$$$**
JUNCTION OF US 89A & ARIZ. 67
TEL 928/643-7232
FAX 928/643-7235
**www.jacoblake.com**
Accommodations at this inn
in the Kaibab National Forest
consist of 26 cabins (summer
only), 12 motel rooms, and 24
hotel rooms.
ⓘ see text above 🅿
🄢 (hotel rooms) 🄲 AE,
MC, V

🄢 Air-conditioning  🄢 Indoor Pool  🄢 Outdoor Pool  🄴 Health Club  🄲 Credit Cards

### KAIBAB LODGE
**$$–$$$**
ARIZ. 67
TEL 928/638-2389 IN SEASON
www.kaibablodge.com
Rustic cabins and modern rooms 18.5 miles north of Bright Angel Point nestle amid trees beside a meadow in the Kaibab National Forest. The main lodge's great room has high beamed ceilings and a beautiful stone hearth. The restaurant serves breakfast, lunch, and dinner.
🛏 32 🅿 🕑 Closed early Nov.–mid-May 🏧 AE, MC, V

## PAGE

### LAKE POWELL RESORT
**$$$–$$$$**
100 LAKESHORE DR.
TEL 928/645-2433 OR
800/528-6154
FAX 928/645-1031
www.lakepowell.com
On the shore of Lake Powell, the lodge offers boat tours and a variety of boat rentals. Half the rooms overlook the water (best views in the west wing). The restaurant's curved glass wall provides diners with a panorama of Lake Powell.
🛏 348 🅿 🕑 🏊 🛗 🏧 All major cards

### COURTYARD BY MARRIOTT
**$$$**
600 CLUBHOUSE DR.
TEL 928/645-5000 OR
800/851-3855 (RES. ONLY)
FAX 928/645-5004
Spacious accommodations, views of Lake Powell (some rooms), and adjacent Lake Powell National Golf Course make this a top choice for many. Pepper's restaurant has continental fare with Southwest flair.
🛏 153 🅿 🕑 🔄 🏊 🛗 🏧 All major cards

### BEST WESTERN ARIZONA INN
**$$**
716 RIM VIEW DR.
TEL 928/645-2466 OR
800/826-2718
FAX 928/645-2053
www.bestwesternarizona.com
Half of the rooms at this modern motel have a grand panorama of Lake Powell; other rooms are a tad cheaper. 🛏 103
🅿 🔄 🕑 🏊 🛗 🏧 All major cards

### LU LU'S SLEEP EZZE MOTEL
**$–$$**
105 8TH AVE. & ELM
TEL 928/608-0273 OR
800/553-621
www.lulussleepezzemotel.com
This little motel in Page's "historic district," lined with apartments dating from the time of the construction of Glen Canyon Dam, has attractively renovated rooms.
🛏 4 🅿 🕑 🏧 MC, V

### KEN'S OLD WEST RESTAURANT
**$–$$**
718 VISTA AVE.
TEL 928/645-5160
This cowboy steak house serves steak, prime rib, chicken, and seafood. A Western band performs many nights.
🍴 285 🅿 🕑 🔄 Closed L & Sun.–Tues. winter 🏧 All major cards

## PEACH SPRINGS

### HUALAPAI LODGE
**$$**
900 ROUTE 66
TEL 928/769-2230 OR
888/255-9550
FAX 928/769-2372
www.grandcanyonwest.com
The modern lodge is a good base for visiting the western Grand Canyon. Arrange river trips here and obtain information on overlooks and the drive into the canyon. Peach Springs is at the midpoint on the longest remaining section of old Route 66.
🛏 60 🅿 🔄 🕑 🏊 🛗 🏧 All major cards

## ■ NORTHEASTERN ARIZONA

## CAMERON

### CAMERON TRADING POST MOTEL
**$$–$$$**
TEL 928/679-2231 OR
800/338-7385
FAX 928/679-2501
www.camerontradingpost.com
Southwestern decor at this trading post beside the Little Colorado River. It's a popular stop between the canyon's rims, and with visitors to Navajo and Hopi lands. Excellent restaurant.
🛏 66 🅿 🕑 🏧 All major cards

## CANYON DE CHELLY & CHINLE

### HOLIDAY INN
**$$**
TEL 928/674-5000 OR 800/HOLIDAY
FAX 928/674-8264
Most of the rooms have a balcony or patio and face a shaded courtyard. It's located near the mouth of Canyon de Chelly on the road from Chinle. A full-service restaurant prepares American and Navajo cuisine (lunch only on weekdays except winter).
🛏 108 🅿 🕑 🔄 🏊 🛗 🏧 All major cards

### THUNDERBIRD LODGE
**$$**
TEL 928/674-5841 OR
800/679-2473
FAX 928/674-5844

www.tbirdlodge.com
Cottonwood trees and lawns surround the lodge buildings near the mouth of Canyon de Chelly. Rooms have Navajo art and decor. The original 1896 trading post is now a cafeteria that serves American and Navajo food. Canyon tours depart from the lodge.
ⓘ 74 🅿 🔄 🏧 All major cards

## KAYENTA

### 🏨 HAMPTON INN
### $$$
US 160
TEL 928/697-3170 OR
800/426-7866
FAX 928/697-3189
Large rooms have Southwestern style. The restaurant serves a continental breakfast to guests only and then is open for lunch and dinner. This is a good base for exploring Monument Valley and Navajo National Monument.
ⓘ 73 🅿 🔄 🏊 🏧 All major cards

## MONUMENT VALLEY

## SOMETHING SPECIAL

### 🏨 THE VIEW HOTEL
### $$$-$$$$$
MONUMENT VALLEY TRIBAL PARK
TEL 435/727-5555
FAX 435/727-4545
www.monumentvalleyview.com
For location, this hotel in Monument Valley Tribal Park is the top choice. Each room has a private balcony, where you can take in the magnificent scenery by day and stars at night. The restaurant serves Navajo and American food. Monument Valley Trading Post has a large selection of Navajo rugs among its Native American crafts and artwork.
ⓘ 96 🔄 🅿 🔄 🎽 🏧 AE, DIS, MC, V

### 🏨 GOULDING'S LODGE
### 🍴 $$$
TEL 435/727-3231
FAX 435/727-3344
www.gouldings.com
The modern rooms each have a balcony. See historic exhibits in the original trading post. The restaurant prepares American and some Navajo dishes. Just north of the Arizona border on US 163, then west 1.5 miles.
ⓘ 62 🅿 🔄 🏊 🎽 🏧 All major cards

## SECOND MESA

### 🏨 HOPI CULTURAL
### 🍴 CENTER INN
### $$
TEL 928/734-2401
FAX 928/734-6651
www.hopiculturalcenter.com
Modern rooms provide the only accommodations on the Hopi reservation. Sample authentic Hopi food, such as *paatupsuki* (pinto beans and hominy soup) and *tsili' ngava* (pinto beans and ground beef in a chili sauce). For breakfast, try the blue corn pancakes. American favorites served, too.
ⓘ 33 🅿 🔄 🏧 All major cards

## WINDOW ROCK

### 🏨 QUALITY INN NAVAJO
### NATION CAPITAL
### $$
48 W. HWY. 264
TEL 928/871-4108 OR
800/662-6189
FAX 928/871-5466
Guest rooms have Navajo decor; the restaurant serves Navajo and American cuisine.
ⓘ 56 🅿 🔄 🏧 All major cards

### 🏨 NAVAJOLAND DAYS
### INN & SUITES
### $-$$
392 W. HWY. 264
TEL 928/871-5690 OR
800/329-7466

FAX 928/871-5699
An indoor pool and spa are features of this motel in St. Michaels, 3.4 miles west of Window Rock.
ⓘ 73 🅿 🔄 🏊 🎽 🏧 All major cards

## ■ NORTH-CENTRAL ARIZONA

## COTTONWOOD

### 🏨 BEST WESTERN
### COTTONWOOD INN
### $$-$$$
993 S. MAIN ST. (JCT. OF ARIZ. 89A & ARIZ. 260)
TEL 928/634-5575 OR
800/350-0025
FAX 928/634-5576
Comfortable, centrally located motel has free breakfast for guests; a Mexican restaurant serves dinner.
ⓘ 77 🅿 🔄 🏊 🏧 All major cards

### 🍴 BLAZIN' M RANCH
### $$$
OFF 10TH ST.
TEL 928/634-0334 OR
800/937-8643
Cowboy food is followed by cowboy songs and skits. It's great fun and popular with children. Reservations recommended, especially for the veggie dinner.
🍴 280 🅿 🕐 Schedule varies with the season 🏧 AE, MC, V

### 🍴 NIC'S ITALIAN STEAK &
### CRAB HOUSE
### $-$$
925 N. MAIN ST. (IN OLD TOWN)
TEL 928/634-9626
Nicole serves seafood, Tuscan-style grilled steaks, ribs, chicken, veal, and pasta for dinner in a dimly lit space. No reservations.
🍴 85 🔄 🏧 MC, V

## FLAGSTAFF

## SOMETHING SPECIAL

### INN AT 410
**$$$–$$$$**
410 N. LEROUX ST.
TEL 928/774-0088 OR
800/774-2008
FAX 928/774-6354
www.inn410.com
Each of the rooms in this
beautifully restored Craftsman-
style bungalow has a different
theme and all have fireplaces.
Gourmet breakfasts.
9 P 🅿 MC, V

### LITTLE AMERICA
**$$–$$$$**
2515 E. BUTLER AVE.
TEL 928/779-7900 OR
800/352-4386 (RES. ONLY)
FAX 928/871-5466
www.littleamerica.com/
flagstaff
Rooms and suites have balconies at this large hotel just
off I-40. The **Western Gold
Dining Room** offers American
and Continental cuisine.
247 P 🅿 All major
cards

### ABINEAU LODGE BED & BREAKFAST
**$$$**
10155 MOUNTAINAIRE RD.
TEL 928/525-6212 OR
888/715-6386
FAX 928/255-5577
www.abineaulodge.com
Located beside a meadow in
the ponderosa pines south of
Flagstaff, the inn offers a sauna,
hiking, biking, and peace and
quiet. Full breakfast served
family-style.
9 P 🅿 All major cards

### RADISSON WOODLANDS HOTEL
**$$$**
1175 W. ROUTE 66
TEL 928/773-8888 OR
800/333-3333 (RES. ONLY)
FAX 928/773-0597
www.flagstaffwoodlands
hotel.com
In perhaps the most elegant
hotel in Flagstaff, you'll find
many amenities, including two
good restaurants, the Sakura
with Japanese cuisine and the
**Woodlands Café.**
183 P 🅿 All
major cards

### ARIZONA MOUNTAIN INN
**$$–$$$**
4200 LAKE MARY RD.
TEL 928/774-8959 OR
800/239-5236
FAX 928/774-8837
www.arizonamountaininn.com
Bed-and-breakfast suites and
rustic cabins set amid ponderosa pines south of town.
20 P 🅿 All major cards

### HOTEL MONTE VISTA
**$–$$$**
100 N. SAN FRANCISCO ST.
TEL 928/779-6971 OR
800/545-3068
FAX 928/779-2904
www.hotelmontevista.com
In the heart of town, this 1927
hotel has been restored to its
original grandeur. Rooms and
suites come in many sizes.
46 P 🅿 All major cards

### HORSEMEN LODGE
**$$–$$$**
8500 N. HWY. 89
TEL 928/526-2655
www.horsemenlodge.com
Join the locals at this popular
dinner spot, 3 miles north of
the Flagstaff Mall, for steak, ribs,
chicken, trout, and seafood.
180 P 🅿 Closed L & Sun.
🅿 All major cards

### JOSEPHINE'S
**$$–$$$**
503 N. HUMPHREYS ST.
TEL 928/779-3400
www.josephinesrestaurant.com
A modern American bistro with
fine service in a restored 1911
house near downtown. Brunch
on Sat. and Sun. in warmer
months.
70 P 🅿 Closed Sat.–Sun.
L in winter, Sun. D in winter-
🅿 All major cards

### PASTO
**$$–$$$**
19 E. ASPEN AVE.
TEL 928/779-1937
www.pastorestaurant.com.
Enjoy Italian cuisine in a casual
fine-dining setting in a historic
building downtown.
100 🅿 Closed L & Sun.
(open daily in summer) 🅿 All
major cards

### COTTAGE PLACE
**$$**
126 W. COTTAGE AVE.
TEL 928/774-8431
www.cottageplace.com
This elegant restaurant serves
Continental cuisine in a 1909
bungalow on the south side
of downtown.
40 P 🅿 Closed Mon.–
Tues. 🅿 DIS, MC, V

---

### PRICES

**HOTELS**
An indication of the cost of a
double room in peak season
is given by $ signs.

| | |
|---|---|
| **$$$$$** | Over $280 |
| **$$$$** | $200–$280 |
| **$$$** | $120–$200 |
| **$$** | $80–$120 |
| **$** | Under $80 |

**RESTAURANTS**
An indication of the cost of
a three-course meal without
drinks is given by $ signs.

| | |
|---|---|
| **$$$$$** | Over $80 |
| **$$$$** | $50–$80 |
| **$$$** | $35–$50 |
| **$$** | $20–$35 |
| **$** | Under $20 |

---

🏨 Hotel  🍴 Restaurant  ⓘ No. of Guest Rooms  ➕ No. of Seats  P Parking  🕐 Closed  ⬛ Elevator

## HIMALAYAN GRILL
$–$$
801 S. MILTON RD., UNIT A
TEL 928/213-5444
The wonderful flavors of India
include tandoori chicken (marinated in yogurt and spices,
then baked in a clay oven)
and *malai kofta* (cheese and
vegetable dumplings in a rich,
creamy sauce and garnished
with nuts). Or try the Tibetan
specialties. Dinners offer set
meals as well as the menu. At
lunch (brunch on Sun.) choose
from the buffet or menu.
🍴 70 ❄ 🅿 ⏰ Closed Sun. &
Sat. L winter ❖ All major cards

## GALAXY DINER
$
931 W. ROUTE 66
TEL 928/774-2466
This fun diner has photos of
movie stars and 1950s decor.
The honest American food
includes great breakfasts and
serious desserts.
🍴 195 🅿 ❄ ❖ All major
cards

## KACHINA DOWNTOWN
$
522 E. ROUTE 66
TEL 928/779-1944
Mexican food with attrac-
tive decor on the east side
of downtown. Open for
breakfast.
🍴 252 🅿 ❄ ❖ All major
cards

## SALSA BRAVA
$
2220 E. ROUTE 66
TEL 928/779-5293
www.salsabravaflagstaff.com
Well-prepared Mexican
favorites and homemade salsa
satisfy diners in the informal
restaurant on the east side
of town.
🍴 192 🅿 ❄ ❖ All major cards

# JEROME

## SOMETHING SPECIAL

### 🏨 JEROME GRAND HOTEL
$$$–$$$$$
200 HILL ST.
TEL 928/634-8200 OR
888/817-6788
FAX 928/639-0299
www.jeromegrandhotel.com
Opened in 1927 as the United
Verde Hospital and renovated
as a hotel in 1996, this land-
mark offers seven categories
of rooms. Its mile-high perch
above the Verde Valley
provides stunning views. Enjoy
them from **The Asylum** *(tel
928/639-3197)* while dining on
New American cuisine.
🛏 25 🅿 ❄ ❖ DIS, MC, V

# PAYSON

## 🏨 MAJESTIC MOUNTAIN INN
$–$$$
602 E. HWY. 260
TEL 928/474-0185 OR
800/408-2442
FAX 928/472-6097
www.majesticmountaininn.com
The modern mountain-lodge
architecture makes this an
enjoyable place to stay. You
have a choice of standard,
deluxe, and luxury rooms.
🛏 50 🅿 ❄ 🏊 ❖ All major
cards

## 🏨 CHRISTOPHER CREEK LODGE
$$–$$$
23 MILES E OF PAYSON ON
ARIZ. 260
TEL 928/478-4300
www.christophercreeklodge
.com
Motel rooms and cabins in
woods beside the creek.
🛏 24 🅿 ❖ All major cards.

# PRESCOTT

## SOMETHING SPECIAL

### 🏨 HASSAYAMPA INN

$$–$$$$
122 E. GURLEY ST.
TEL 928/778-9434 OR
800/322-1927
FAX 928/445-8590
www.hassayampainn.com
Since opening its doors in 1927
as Prescott's finest hotel, the
Hassayampa has continued to
be one of the top places in town
to stay. The elegant lobby with
its painted ceiling and the attrac-
tive rooms and suites recall the
era of the grand hotel.
🛏 67 🅿 ❄ ❖ 🏋
❖ All major cards

## 🏨 HOTEL VENDOME
$$–$$$
230 S. CORTEZ ST.
TEL 928/776-0900 OR
888/468-3583
FAX 928/268-2844
www.vendomehotel.com
This beautifully restored small
inn dates from 1917. It lies on a
quiet street just one block from
Courthouse Plaza and boasts
rooms that have floral linens
and antique fixtures.
🛏 21 🅿 ❄ ❖ All major cards

## 🏨 HOTEL ST. MICHAEL
$–$$
205 W. GURLEY ST.
TEL 928/776-1999 OR
800/678-3757
FAX 928/776-9802
www.stmichaelhotel.com
On the corner of Gurley and
Montezuma, you're right on
Whiskey Row in this 1900 hotel.
This block of Monte-zuma
became known as Whiskey Row
because of the many saloons
here. Some are still in business
(see the Palace p. 246). Rooms
in the hotel come in many sizes.
Bistro St. Michael is a popular
spot for a coffee or a meal.
🛏 68 ❄ ❖ All major cards

## MURPHY'S
$$–$$$
201 N. CORTEZ ST.
TEL 928/445-4044

www.murphysrestaurants.
com
The high-ceilinged dining
room in an 1890 mercantile
building provides a great setting for salmon, catfish, prime
rib, mesquite-grilled steak,
and more.
🔲 205 🔲 🔲 All major cards

### 🍴 PALACE
$$–$$$
120 S. MONTEZUMA ST.
TEL 928/541-1996
www.historicpalace.com
Thirsty patrons have strolled
up to the magnificently ornate
Brunswick bar for 120 years.
They even carried the bar
across the street to safety
during the 1900 fire. The
dining room offers an Old
West atmosphere for steaks,
prime ribs, pasta, and seafood
dinners with Southwestern
style. Entrees are prepared
with glazes such as honey,
Dijon mustard, or Merlot, or
marinated and served with
staples like baked or mashed
potatoes, or salads.
🔲 234 🔲 🔲 All major cards

### 🍴 PEACOCK ROOM
$$–$$$
122 E. GURLEY ST.
TEL 928/778-9434 OR
800/322-1927
www.hassayampainn.com
The dining room of the Hassayampa Hotel has a 1920s
elegance for American and
Continental choices.
🔲 50 🅿 🔲 🔲 All major cards

### 🍴 ROSE
$$–$$$
234 S. CORTEZ ST.
TEL 928/777-8308
www.theroserestaurant.com
An elegant setting in a
Victorian house sets the mood
for fine dinners with northern
Italian and other cuisines. Veal
is a specialty, or you choose
from the pasta, chicken, duck,
steak, lamb, and seafood.

🔲 44 🅿 🕀 Closed Mon.–
Tues. 🔲 🔲 All major cards

## SEDONA

## SOMETHING SPECIAL

### 🏨 ENCHANTMENT
### 🍴 RESORT
$$$$$
525 BOYNTON CANYON RD.
TEL 928/282-2900 OR
800/826-4180
FAX 928/282-9249
www.enchantmentresort.com
Enchantment's magical red-
rock setting west of Sedona
charms its guests. Hiking and
the many resort activities can
keep you busy by day, followed
by fine dining and stargazing in
the evening. Native American
cultures influence the adobe-
style casitas, resort activities,
and spa treatments. The
two restaurants offer superb
food and spectacular canyon
views from both indoor and
patio tables (see Yavapai
Restaurant p. 247). The spa
not only provides many types
of therapies and activities, but
also has accommodations and
a restaurant on its grounds.
Camp Coyote organizes activities for children.
🛈 236 🅿 🔲 🔲 🔲 🔲
🔲 All major cards

---

### 🏨 AMARA HOTEL
### 🍴 $$$$–$$$$$
100 AMARA LANE
TEL 928/282-4828 OR
800/815-6152
FAX 928/282-4825
www.amararesort.com
With a minimalist decor, this
stylish boutique hotel has
a pretty setting amid the
greenery of Oak Creek. A full-
service spa pampers guests.
Hundred Rox Restaurant (tel
928/340-8859) prepares
California-inspired Italian cuisine. Shopping and restaurants
of uptown Sedona are just

steps away.
🛈 100 🅿 🔲 🔲 🔲 🔲 🔲 All
major cards

## SOMETHING SPECIAL

### 🏨 L'AUBERGE DE SEDONA
### 🍴 $$$–$$$$$
301 L'AUBERGE LANE
TEL 928/282-1661 OR 800/272-6777
FAX 928/282-1064
www.lauberge.com
A romantic getaway, this
French-style country inn has an
idyllic setting under sycamores
beside Oak Creek. One- and
two-bedroom cottages have
wood-burning fireplaces and
covered porches. Lodge rooms
feature French decor and a patio
or balcony. L'Auberge (see p.247)
is one of the finest restaurants
in Arizona.
🛈 89 🅿 🔲 🔲 🔲 🔲 All
major cards

### 🏨 BEST WESTERN
### ARROYO ROBLE HOTEL
### & CREEKSIDE VILLAS
$$$–$$$$$
400 N. HWY. 89A
TEL 928/282-4001 OR
800/773-3662
FAX 928/282-4001
www.bestwesternsedona.com
The five-story main building has
good views from most rooms.
You can also stay down beside
Oak Creek in a two-bedroom
villa. All rooms and villas have a
balcony or patio.
🛈 65 🔲 🔲 🔲 🔲 🔲 All
major cards

### 🏨 JUNIPINE RESORT
$$$–$$$$$
8 MILES N ON HWY. 89A
TEL 928/282-3375 OR
800/742-7463
FAX 928/282-7402
www.junipine.com
In Oak Creek Canyon, each
"creekhouse" has two bedrooms,
baths, and fireplaces and a
kitchen. Or you can rent them
as one-bedroom, one-bath units.
The Junipine Café & Grill serves

---

🏨 Hotel  🍴 Restaurant  🛈 No. of Guest Rooms  🔲 No. of Seats  🅿 Parking  🕀 Closed  🔲 Elevator

Southwestern and Continental cuisine.

**[i] 41 [P] [&] All major cards**

### [hotel] RADISSON POCO DIABLO RESORT
$$$–$$$$$
1752 S. HWY. 179
TEL 928/282-7333 OR
800/395-7046
FAX 928/282-2090
www.radissonsedona.com
Modern rooms, some with fireplaces and spas, overlook landscaped grounds beside Oak Creek. Guests enjoy tennis courts, a nine-hole golf course, and **T. Carl's** restaurant (Southwestern cuisine).

**[i] 137 [P] [S] [pool] [health] [&] All major cards**

### [hotel] APPLE ORCHARD INN
$$$–$$$$
656 JORDAN RD.
TEL 928/282-5328 OR
800/663-6968
FAX 928/204-0044
www.appleorchardbb.com
Each of the luxurious guest rooms has a different Old West theme. Guests also enjoy a gourmet breakfast, cooling pool, and a hot tub.

**[i] 7 [P] [S] [&] All major cards**

### [hotel] SKY RANCH LODGE
$–$$$
1105 AIRPORT RD.
TEL 928/282-6400 OR
888/708-6400
FAX 928/282-7682
www.skyranchlodge.com
You'll find one of the best views in town here atop Airport Mesa. The lodge has a variety of rooms and cottages, priced according to views and amenities such as fireplaces, decks, and kitchenettes.

**[i] 94 [P] [S] [pool] [&] AE, MC, V**

### [rest] L'AUBERGE
$$$$–$$$$$
L'AUBERGE DE SEDONA
301 L'AUBERGE LANE
TEL 928/282-1661
www.lauberge.com
Elegant surroundings set the stage for magnificent French dishes, including the popular tasting menu, available with wine pairings. Breakfast and lunch are served too. Enjoy creekside dining May–September.

**[fork] 50 (plus 50 creekside) [P] [S] [&] All major cards**

### [rest] RENÉ AT TLAQUEPAQUE
$$$–$$$$
336 HWY. 179
TEL 928/282-9225
www.rene-sedona.com
Great American and Continental lunches and dinners are served daily in an elegant dining room and on Patio Azul.

**[fork] 90 [P] [S] [&] AE, MC, V**

### [rest] YAVAPAI RESTAURANT
$$$–$$$$
525 BOYNTON CANYON RD.
TEL 928/282-2900 OR
800/826-4180
Panoramic views of Boynton Canyon accompany the New American cuisine, which you can enjoy for breakfast (buffet available), lunch, and dinner. The nearby Tii Gavo (Havasupai for "gathering place") offers Southwestern fare in a casual setting. Both have patios.

**[fork] 140 [P] [S] [&] All major cards**

### [rest] DAHL & DILUCA RISTORANTE ITALIANO
$$$
2321 W. HWY. 89A
TEL 928/282-5219
www.dahlanddiluca.com
Chefs prepare central and northern Italian cuisine nightly with homemade pasta and other tasty offerings such as vitello Botticelli (veal and prawns in a Marsala mushroom sauce).

**[fork] 100 [P] [clock] Closed L [S] [&] All major cards**

### [rest] COWBOY CLUB
$$–$$$
241 N. HWY. 89A
TEL 928/282-4200
www.cowboyclub.com
Western decor accentuates the "high desert cuisine." The menu has something to please everyone; if you're feeling adventurous, try the cactus fries with prickly pear sauce or buffalo tenderloin topped with brandy peppercorn cream sauce. Open nightly, the Silver Saddle Dining Room features an upscale "rustic and romantic" experience.

**[fork] 120 [P] [S] [&] All major cards**

### [rest] SEDONA AIRPORT RESTAURANT
$$–$$$
AIRPORT MESA
TEL 928/282-3576
www.sedonaairportrestaurant.com
Small planes taking off and landing provide entertainment while diners enjoy entrees such as sizzling fajitas or pecan-crusted halibut with mango cream sauce. Breakfast also served.

**[fork] 81 [P] [S] [&] DIS, MC, V,**

## WILLIAMS

### [hotel] GRAND CANYON RAILWAY HOTEL
$$$–$$$$
235 N. GRAND CANYON BLVD.
TEL 928/635-4010 OR
800/843-8724
FAX 928/635-2180
www.thetrain.com
This modern hotel blends in with the adjacent 1908 depot, where the Grand Canyon Railway trains depart for the Grand Canyon. The large lobby and spacious rooms have a Southwest decor. Spenser's Pub displays an impressive 19th-century bar.

**[i] 297 [P] [S] [S] [pool] [health] [&] All major cards**

[S] Air-conditioning [pool] Indoor Pool [pool] Outdoor Pool [health] Health Club [&] Credit Cards

### 🏨 SHERIDAN HOUSE INN
$$$
460 E. SHERIDAN AVE.
TEL 928/635-9441 OR
888/635-9345
www.grandcanyonbedand
breakfast.com
This large house on a pine-
forested hillside offers visitors
a home-style atmosphere.
Guests enjoy a gourmet break-
fast, hiking, and many extras.
🛏 7 🅿 🍽 All major cards

### 🏨 THE RED GARTER BED
& BAKERY
$$-$$$
137 W. RAILROAD AVE.
TEL 928/635-1484 OR
800/328-1484
www.redgarter.com
The saloon in this 1897
Victorian Romanesque-style
building downtown serves
drinks, food, and tasty pastries.
A madam and her ladies once
entertained guests in the
bordello rooms upstairs, now
converted to a bed-and-break-
fast with 1890s decor.
🛏 4 🅿 🍽 Closed mid-
Dec.–mid-Feb. 🍽 DIS, MC, V

### 🍴 CRUISER'S CAFÉ 66
$$-$$$
233 W. ROUTE 66
TEL 928/635-2445
www.cruisers66.com
At this 1930s former gas sta-
tion, you can fill up on family
fun and thick juicy burgers,
barbecued ribs, and sizzling
fajitas. The imaginative Route
66 decor includes antique
gas pumps and automobile
paraphernalia.
🍴 100 🍽 🍽 May close L in
winter 🍽 All major cards

### 🍴 PANCHO
MCGILLICUDDY'S
$-$$
141 W. RAILROAD AVE.
TEL 928/635-4150
www.panchomcgillicuddys
.com
The Mexican menu includes

some American favorites.
Musicians entertain on summer evenings.
🍴 125 🍽 All major cards

### 🍴 ROD'S STEAK HOUSE
$-$$
301 E. ROUTE 66
TEL 928/635-2671
www.rods-steakhouse.com
Traditional Western food like
fine mesquite-broiled steaks,
barbecued ribs, broiled trout,
and seafood is served here,
along with homemade soups,
yeast rolls, and pies.
🍴 150 🍽 🍽 Closed Sun.
🍽 All major cards

## ■ WESTERN ARIZONA

### KINGMAN

### 🏨 BEST WESTERN KINGS
INN & SUITES
$$-$$$
2930 E. ANDY DEVINE AVE.
TEL 928/753-6101 OR
800/750-6101
FAX 928/753-6192
The modern motel offers
spacious rooms, mini-suites,
and suites.
🛏 101 🅿 🍽 🍽 🍽 All
major cards

### 🏨 HUALAPAI MOUNTAIN
PARK
$-$$$
HUALAPAI MOUNTAIN RD.
TEL 928/681-5700 OR
877/757-0915
www.mcparks.com
Cabins are tucked away in the
mountains of this county park
14 miles southeast of King-
man. All have kitchenettes and
most have either a fireplace or
woodstove, but you need to
bring your own bedding and
kitchenware. Make reserva-
tions for summer weekends.
🛏 19 🅿 🍽 DIS, MC, V

### 🏨 HOTEL BRUNSWICK

$-$$
315 E. ANDY DEVINE AVE.
TEL 928/718-1800
FAX 928/718-1801
Beautifully restored, this 1909
hotel offers rooms decorated
with quilts and antiques. Of
the 24 rooms, 15 have private
baths. **Brunswick Bistro** (see
below) offers fine dining, and
**Mulligan's Bar** is a good place
to relax.
🛏 24 🍽 🍽 🍽 All major cards

### 🍴 BRUNSWICK BISTRO
$$$-$$$$
315 E. ANDY DEVINE AVE.
TEL 928/718-1800
This attractive restaurant in the
Hotel Brunswick serves Ameri-
can and Continental cuisine.
🍴 54 🍽 🍽 Closed L Sat.–Sun.
🍽 All major cards

### 🍴 MATTINA'S
RISTORANTE ITALIANO
$$-$$$
318 OAK ST.
TEL 928/753-7504
www.mattinasristorante.com
The owner takes great pride

in his steaks, as well as the chicken, seafood, and pasta dishes. Photos of famous mobsters decorate one dining area, and those of Frank Sinatra and his Rat Pack grace another.
🏠 90 🔄 🕐 Closed L, & Sun.–Mon. 🈺 AE, MC, V

## LAKE HAVASU CITY

### 🏨 NAUTICAL INN
**$$$–$$$$$**
1000 MCCULLOCH BLVD. N.
TEL 928/855-2141 OR
800/892-2141
FAX 928/453-5808
www.thenautical.net
All of the rooms have lake views and a private patio or balcony. Amenities include a restaurant with everything from wraps and pizza to steaks and seafood, a waterside bar, and on-site watercraft rentals. The inn lies beside an 18-hole golf course on the island, reached via London Bridge.
🛏 139 🅿 🔄 🏊 🈺 All major cards

### 🏨 HEAT HOTEL
**$$–$$$$$**
1420 MCCULLOCH BLVD. N.
TEL 928/854-3018 OR
888/898-4328
FAX 888/868-4328
www.heathotel.com
At this stylish contemporary hotel, you'll enjoy views of the water and London Bridge; each of the rooms and suites has a private balcony or patio.
🛏 25 🅿 🔄 🈺 All major cards

### 🏨 LONDON BRIDGE RESORT
**$$–$$$$$**
1477 QUEENS BAY
TEL 928/855-0888 OR
800/624-7939
FAX 928/855-5404
www.londonbridgeresort.com
The size and English-style architecture of this resort near London Bridge set it apart. All units are timeshares, but

the studios and one- and two-bedroom units are often available for rent. Guests congregate around the three pools and spa or at one of the restaurants. It's worth stepping inside the elegant lobby to see a replica of the ornate Gold State Coach. The 1762 original has conveyed all of the British monarchs since George III to their coronations in Westminster Abbey.
🛏 122 🅿 🔄 🔄 🏊 🈺 All major cards

### 🍴 SHUGRUE'S
**$$–$$$$**
ISLAND MALL
TEL 928/453-1400
www.shugrues.com
You cross London Bridge to reach Shugrue's and diners enjoy views of the grand structure while feasting on steaks, seafood, or pasta. Specialties include rack of lamb, Bombay chicken, and garlic-crusted halibut. Shugrue's also runs the nearby Barley Brothers Brewery.
🏠 130 🅿 🔄 🈺 All major cards

## PARKER

### 🏨 BLUEWATER RESORT
### 🍴 & CASINO
**$$$–$$$$**
11300 RESORT DR.
TEL 928/669-7000 OR
888/243-3360
FAX 928/669-7075
www.bluewaterfun.com
The rooms and suites here all have balconies or patios and overlook the Colorado River. A huge atrium shelters four pools, spa, and waterfalls. Rates drop considerably on weekdays. The **Feast** offers a choice of buffet or menu offerings. The **River Willow Restaurant** features fine dining in the evening.
🛏 200 🅿 🔄 🔄 🏊 🈺 AE, MC, V

### 🏨 HAVASU SPRINGS RESORT
**$$$–$$$$**
2581 HWY. 95
TEL 928/667-3361
FAX 928/667-1298
www.havasusprings.com
On Lake Havasu, 16 miles north of Parker and 20 miles south of Lake Havasu City, this resort offers three motels, apartments, RV park, restaurant, nine-hole golf course, and swimming beaches.
🛏 44 🅿 🔄 🏊 🈺 All major cards

## YUMA

### 🏨 BEST WESTERN INNSUITES
**$$–$$$$**
1450 S. CASTLE DOME AVE.
TEL 928/783-8341 OR
800/922-2034 (RES. ONLY)
FAX 928/783-1349
http://yuma.innsuites.com
Guests enjoy large studios and suites, a breakfast buffet, and many amenities.
🛏 166 🅿 🔄 🏊 🏊 🈺 All major cards

### 🏨 LA FUENTE INN & SUITES
**$$–$$$$**
1513 E. 16TH ST.
TEL 928/329-1814 OR
800/841-1814
FAX 928/343-2671
www.lafuenteinn.com
Rooms and suites at this attractive Spanish-colonial inn face a courtyard.
🛏 96 🅿 🔄 🏊 🏊 🈺 All major cards

### 🍴 JULIEANNA'S PATIO CAFÉ
**$$–$$$**
1951 W. 25TH ST. (1 BLOCK S OF 24TH ST. VIA 19TH AVE.)
TEL 928/317-1961
www.julieannaspatiocafe.com
A romantic spot for candlelight dining inside or on the

garden patio. You can dine on steak, prime rib, rack of lamb, chicken, seafood, and pasta. Lunch offers lighter fare. 55 inside, 100 patio, 200 tent P Closed Sun. All major cards

### GARDEN CAFÉ
$
250 S. MADISON AVE.
TEL 928/783-1491
This charming café beside the Sanguinetti House Museum downtown is a pleasant spot for breakfast, lunch, or Sunday brunch, surrounded by gardens and serenaded by birds from nearby aviaries.
20 inside, 120 outside Closed Mon. & summer AE, MC, V

## SOUTH-CENTRAL ARIZONA

### MESA

### PHOENIX MARRIOTT MESA
$$$–$$$$
200 N. CENTENNIAL WAY
TEL 480/898-8300 OR
888/236-2427
FAX 480/964-9279
www.phoenixmarriottmesa.com
The 12-story hotel has comfortable rooms with good amenities, restaurant, and bar.
275 P All major cards

### SAGUARO LAKE RANCH RESORT
$$$–$$$$
13020 BUSH HWY.
TEL 480/984-2194
FAX 480/380-1489
www.saguarolakeranch.com
Overlooking the Salt River northeast of Mesa, this rustic resort makes a great base for horseback riding, hiking, mountain biking, boating, kayaking, fishing, and 4WD

tours. Resort offers an American plan with three meals during the cooler months and bed and breakfast rooms the entire season.
25 P Closed late May–early Sept. All major cards

### CROWNE PLAZA SAN MARCOS GOLF RESORT
$$–$$$$
1 SAN MARCOS PLACE, CHANDLER
TEL 480/812-0900 OR
800/528-8071
FAX 480/963-6777
www.sanmarcosresort.com
In 1913, this was your only choice for a full-service Arizona resort. Today's guests enjoy the old Arizona charm, along with fine dining, golf, course, swimming, and tennis.
295 P All major cards

### ROCKIN' R RANCH
$$$
6136 E. BASELINE RD.
TEL 480/832-1539
www.howdyshow.com
Enjoy a good feed of cowboy food followed by a musical stage show. Open Saturdays and some weekdays, depending on the season.
700 P Call for reservations & times All major cards

### PHOENIX

### ROYAL PALMS RESORT & SPA
$$$$$
5200 E. CAMELBACK RD.
TEL 602/840-3610 or
800/672-6011
FAX 602/840-6927
www.royalpalmshotel.com
Spanish-mission architecture, courtyards, and enclosed gardens create a restful atmosphere. Antiques and tasteful design grace the luxurious rooms, casitas, and

suites. Alvadora Spa provides Mediterranean-inspired treatments. T. Cook's (see p. 251) prepares exceptional cuisine.
119 P All major cards

## SOMETHING SPECIAL

### ARIZONA BILTMORE
$$$$–$$$$$
24TH ST. & MISSOURI AVE.
TEL 602/955-6600 OR
800/950-0086
FAX 602/381-7600
www.arizonabiltmore.com
Frank Lloyd Wright inspired many of the architectural details of this lavish resort, opened in 1929. You may choose a standard room, resort room, villa suite, or even higher levels of service at the Ocatilla boutique hotel on the grounds. Guests enjoy the landscaping, restaurants, eight pools (one with a 90-foot waterslide), two 18-hole golf courses, tennis courts, children's activities, and a health spa/athletic club. The central location is handy for sightseeing and shopping. Wright's Restaurant specializes in contemporary American cuisine, while Frank & Albert's serves up American classics.
740 P All major cards

### HYATT REGENCY PHOENIX
$$$–$$$$$
122 N. 2ND ST.
TEL 602/252-1234 OR
800/233-1234
FAX 602/254-9472
http://phoenix.hyatt.com
Rooms and suites here in the heart of downtown have a Southwest decor. The Compass (see p. 251) restaurant has an unbeatable panorama.
696 All major cards

### 🏨 HOLIDAY INN EXPRESS PHOENIX DOWNTOWN
**$$$**

620 N. 6TH ST.
TEL 602/452-2020 OR
877/424-6423
FAX 602/252-2909
The inn has a convenient location on the northeast side of downtown.
ⓘ 90 🅿 🔁 🆂 🏊 🏋 🅲 All major cards

### 🏨 QUALITY INN & SUITES
**$$$**

202 E. MCDOWELL RD.
TEL 602/528-9100 OR
800/776-5560
FAX 602/258-7259
The hotel offers a choice of standard rooms or suites in a location near museums and other downtown attractions.
ⓘ 48 🅿 🔁 🆂 🏊 🅲 All major cards

### 🍴 VINCENT ON CAMELBACK
**$$$$**

3930 E. CAMELBACK RD.
TEL 602/224-0225
www.vincentsoncamelback.com
Guests savor French-inspired Southwestern cuisine in a French country atmosphere. The adjacent Vincent Market Bistro offers lighter fare and specialty groceries.
🍴 200 🅿 🆂 🅲 Closed Sun. & Mon.–Tues. June–Sept.
🅲 All major cards

### 🍴 CHRISTOPHER'S $$$–$$$$

2502 E. CAMELBACK RD.
TEL 602/522-2344
www.christophersaz.com
Chef Christopher and his team prepare such delights as wild mushroom soup and smoked-truffle-infused filet mignon. The French-inspired fare is served in the sleek main dining room, Crush Lounge, and on the patio. Located in Biltmore Fashion Park.

🍴 75 inside, 25 patio 🅿
🆂 🅲 All major cards

### 🍴 COMPASS
**$$$–$$$$**

HYATT REGENCY PHOENIX
122 N. 2ND ST.
TEL 602/440-3166
Dine on American and Continental cuisine and enjoy views of the mountain-ringed Valley of the Sun by day and the twinkling lights at night. Arizona's only revolving restaurant is on the 24th floor of the Hyatt Regency Phoenix.
🍴 130 🆂 🅲 Closed Sun. L
🅲 All major cards

### 🍴 T. COOK'S
**$$$–$$$$**

ROYAL PALMS RESORT & SPA
5200 E. CAMELBACK RD.
TEL 602/808-0766
www.royalpalmshotel.com
Superb Mediterranean-inspired food in a romantic setting makes this a special place. Breakfast and Sunday brunch too.
🍴 308 🅿 🆂 🅲 All major cards

### 🍴 COUP DES TARTES
**$$$**

4626 N. 16TH ST.
TEL 602/212-1082
www.nicetartes.com
In a cozy house a couple of blocks south of Camelback Road chefs perpare country French cuisine along with other fine fare. No alcohol on the menu, but you are welcome to bring your own beer or wine.
🍴 40 🅿 🆂 🅲 Closed L Sat.–Sun. & D Sun.–Mon.
🅲 All major cards

### 🍴 GREEKFEST
**$$–$$$**

1940 E. CAMELBACK RD. (NW CORNER OF CAMELBACK & 20TH ST.)
TEL 602/265-2990
www.thegreekfest.com
Greek and Byzantine flavors

entice diners at this popular restaurant.
🍴 120 🅿 🆂 🅲 Closed Sun.
🅲 All major cards

### 🍴 ELIANA'S
**$**

1627 N. 24TH ST.
TEL 602/225-2925
Delicious El Salvadoran food features plantains and stuffed tortillas. The chile rellenos are stuffed with meat, potatoes, and cheese.
🍴 80 🅿 🆂 🅲 Closed Sun.–Mon. 🅲 All major cards

### 🍴 VEGETARIAN HOUSE
**$**

3239 E. INDIAN SCHOOL RD.
TEL 602/264-3480
A long, varied Chinese menu, but everything is strictly 100 percent vegetarian.
🍴 70 🅿 🆂 🅲 Closed Sun.–Mon. 🅲 All major cards

## SCOTTSDALE

### 🏨 THE BOULDERS RESORT 🍴 & GOLDEN DOOR SPA
**$$$$$**

34631 N. TOM DARLINGTON DR. (16 MILES N OF DOWNTOWN)
TEL 480/488-9009 OR
800/553-1717
FAX 480/488-4118
http://theboulders.com
Casitas and villas in elegant Southwestern decor nestle among granite boulders. The resort has two 18-hole golf courses, a driving range, three pools, tennis courts, trails, and the Golden Door Spa. Dining options include the refined, yet rustic, **Latilla Room** serving classic American food with contemporary regional flavors.
ⓘ 221 🅿 🆂 🏊 🏋 🅲 All major cards

## SOMETHING SPECIAL

### 🏨 THE PHOENICIAN
### 🍴 $$$$$

6000 E. CAMELBACK RD.

---

🆂 Air-conditioning 🏊 Indoor Pool 🏊 Outdoor Pool 🏋 Health Club 🅲 Credit Cards

TEL 480/941-8200 OR
800/888-8234
FAX 480/947-4311
www.thephoenician.com
The 250 landscaped acres
here at the foot of Camelback
Mountain showcase one of
the world's most luxurious
resorts. The spacious rooms,
casitas, and suites have a host
of amenities. Guests can fill
their days with the 27-hole
golf course, tennis garden, nine
pools, waterfalls, fitness center,
and health spa. Children will
enjoy the 165-foot waterslide
and special activities. Savor
Italian cuisine at **Il Terrazzo**
or steakhouse classics at **J&G
Steakhouse**.
🚹 643 🅿 🚫 🔄 ♿ 📺 🚫 All
major cards

---

🏨 **MONDRIAN**
🍴 **SCOTTSDALE**
**$$$$–$$$$$**
7353 E. INDIAN SCHOOL RD.
TEL 480/308-1100 OR
800/697-1791
FAX 480/308-1200
www.mondrianscottsdale.com
This stylish vision of modern
glamour provides a restful
haven downtown. **Asia de
Cuba Restaurant** fuses Asian
and Cuban cuisine.
🚹 194 🅿 🚫 🔄 ♿ 📺
🚫 All major cards

🍴 **SUSHI ON SHEA**
**$$–$$$**
7000 E. SHEA BLVD.
TEL 480/483-7799
www.sushionshea.com
Sushi, teriyaki, sukiyaki, and
noodle dishes are served
in a contemporary setting.
🪑 89 🅿 🚫 🚫 All major cards

🍴 **MALEE'S ON MAIN**
**$$**
7131 E. MAIN ST.
TEL 480/947-6042
www.maleesthaibistro.com
Tasty gourmet Thai cuisine
in Old Town Scottsdale.

🪑 150 🅿 🚫 🔄 Closed Sun.
L in summer 🚫 All major
cards

🍴 **SUGAR BOWL**
**$**
4005 N. SCOTTSDALE RD.
TEL 480/946-0051
www.sugarbowlscottsdale
.com
Sweet tooths will be in heaven
at this old-fashioned ice-cream
parlor that also serves home-
style American food.
🪑 140 🚫 🚫 All major cards

# TEMPE

🏨 **TEMPE MISSION PALMS
HOTEL**
**$$$$**
60 E. 5TH ST.
TEL 480/894-1400 OR
800/547-8705
FAX 480/968-7677
www.missionpalms.com
The large guest rooms have
a contemporary decor. Suites
add a living room.
🚹 303 🅿 🔀 🚫 ♿ 📺
🚫 All major cards

🏨 **TWIN PALMS HOTEL**
**$$–$$$**
225 E. APACHE BLVD.
TEL 480/967-9431 OR
800/367-0835
FAX 480/303-6602
www.twinpalmshotel.com
This seven-story hotel is adja-
cent to Arizona State Univer-
sity and Mill Avenue. Guests
can keep fit with privileges at
the ASU recreation facilities.
🚹 140 🅿 🔀 🚫 ♿ 📺
🚫 All major cards

🏨 **AMERICA BEST VALUE
INN TEMPE/ASU**
**$–$$**
1005 E. APACHE BLVD.
TEL 480/968-7871 OR
800/831-4667 (RES. ONLY)
FAX 480/968-3991
www.americasbvi-tempe-asu
.com

This motel is located just east of
Arizona State University.
🚹 90 🅿 🚫 ♿ 🚫 All major
cards

🍴 **HOUSE OF TRICKS**
**$$$–$$$$**
114 E. 7TH ST.
TEL 480/968-1114
www.houseoftricks.com
Bob and Robin Trick offer
creative American food in a
restaurant converted from a
pair of Craftsman bungalows.
Most customers head for the
shaded patio.
🪑 70 (plus 80 outside)
🅿 🚫 🔄 Closed Sun. & part
of Aug. 🚫 All major cards

🍴 **PITA JUNGLE**
**$**
1250 E. APACHE BLVD.
TEL 480/804-0234
www.pitajungle.com
Tasty Mediterranean and Amer-
ican dishes including falafel,
wood-fired pizzas, and spicy
mango shrimp are served at
this healthful restaurant. Vege-
tarians will find plenty of choices.

---

See website for other Arizona locations.

🛏 90 🅿 ❄ 💳 All major cards

## WICKENBURG

### 🏨 FLYING E GUEST RANCH
### $$$$$
2801 W. WICKENBURG WAY

TEL 928/684-2690 OR
888/684-2650

FAX 928/684-5304

www.flyingeranch.com

Cowboys still work cattle across a nearby spread. Guests enjoy the informal Western atmosphere where they ride horses, relax around the pool, hike in the hills, or socialize in the lodge. Rooms, which come in different sizes, have Western furnishings. Rates include family-style meals.

🛏 17 🅿 ❄ 💦 🏋 🕒 Closed May–Oct. 💳 MC, V

### 🏨 KAY EL BAR GUEST RANCH
### $$$$$
RINCON RD. (BOX 2480, WICKENBURG, AZ 85358)

TEL 928/684-7593 OR
800/684-7583

FAX 928/684-4497

www.kayelbar.com

The adobe buildings of this early 1900s ranch give it an Old West feel. Guests can ride, hike, or enjoy the pool and hot tub. There's a choice of historic lodge rooms, a cottage, and the larger Casa Grande room. Everyone dines family-style.

🛏 12 🅿 💦 🕒 Closed early May–mid-Oct. 💳 MC, V

### 🏨 RANCHO DE LOS
### 🍴 CABALLEROS
### $$$$$
1551 S. VULTURE MINE RD.

TEL 928/684-5484 OR
800/684-5030

FAX 928/684-2267

www.sunc.com

The most elegant of the guest ranches round Wickenburg,

it offers an 18-hole golf course as well as horseback riding, tennis, swimming, spa services, and children's programs. Rooms and suites have a Southwest decor. The restaurant prepares American and Continental cuisine; it's open to the public (reservations required) and you'll need to dress up for dinner (jacket for men).

🛏 79 🅿 ❄ 💦 🏋 🕒 Closed early May–early Oct. 💳 MC, V

### 🏨 BEST WESTERN RANCHO GRANDE
### $$
293 E. WICKENBURG WAY

TEL 928/684-5445 OR
800/854-7235

FAX 928/684-7380

www.bwranchogrande.com

This centrally located motel has Spanish colonial-style architecture and a choice of room sizes.

🛏 78 🅿 ❄ 💦 💳 All major cards

## ▦ EASTERN ARIZONA

## ALPINE

### 🏨 TAL-WI-WI LODGE
### $–$$
40 COUNTY RD. 2220

TEL 928/339-4319

FAX 928/339-1962

www.talwiwilodge.com

This rustic lodge, 3 miles north of Alpine, is a good base for exploring the surrounding mountain and forest country. Some of the rooms have a hot tub or woodstove.

🛏 20 🅿 💳 MC, V

## HOLBROOK

### 🏨 WIGWAM MOTEL
### $
811 W. HOPI DR.

TEL 928/524-3048

FAX 928/524-9335

Have you slept in a wigwam

lately? This modest motel from the late 1940s has become a Route 66 icon, thanks to its unusual architec-ture. Inside the cozy interiors, you'll find one or two double beds and original hickory furniture. A small museum displays Indian artifacts and petrified wood. Vintage cars on the grounds add to the nostalgic feeling.

🛏 15 🅿 ❄ 💳 MC, V

### 🍴 MESA ITALIANA RESTAURANT
### $$
2318 NAVAJO BLVD.

TEL 928/524-6696

Don't be put off by the plain exterior, but follow your nose inside for flavorful Italian and American dishes; there's a wine list, too.

🛏 60 🅿 ❄ 🕒 Closed L Sat.–Sun. 💳 All major cards

## HON-DAH

### 🏨 HON-DAH RESORT
### $$–$$$
777 HWY. 260 (AT HWY. 73)

TEL 928/369-0299 OR
800/929-8744

FAX 928/369-7504

www.hon-dah.com

The immense lobby and spacious rooms and suites are sure to impress. The smoky casino may not. Restaurants offer fine dining and some buffets, including a big Sunday brunch.

🛏 128 🅿 ❄ 💦 💳 All major cards

## PINETOP-LAKESIDE

### 🏨 LAKE OF THE WOODS
### $$–$$$
2244 W. WHITE MTN. BLVD.

TEL 928/368-5353

FAX 928/368-5350

www.lakeofthewoodsaz.com

Cabins of many sizes and styles nestle under the pines near the resort's private lake; all have fireplaces and cooking facilities. Take a canoe or rowboat out

on the lake. The resort has two Jacuzzis.
**(i)** 33 **P** 🅢 🅖 MC, V

## 🍴 CHARLIE CLARK'S STEAKHOUSE
$$$
1701 E. WHITE MTN. BLVD.
TEL 928/367-4900 OR
888/333-0259
www.charlieclarks.com
In business since 1938, this popular restaurant specializes in steak, prime ribs, and seafood.
**+** 300 **P** 🅢 🅖 All major cards

## SAFFORD

## 🏨 QUALITY INN & SUITES
$$–$$$
420 E. HWY. 70
TEL 928/428-3200 OR
877/726-2328
FAX 928/428-3288
www.visitsafford.com
Some of the rooms have spa tubs or you can go for a suite.
**(i)** 102 **P** 🖨 🅢 🅖 🅥 🅖 All major cards

## WINSLOW

## SOMETHING SPECIAL

## 🏨 LA POSADA
$$–$$$
303 E. 2ND ST.
TEL 928/289-4366
FAX 928/289-3873
www.laposada.org
Architect Mary Colter not only designed this great railroad hotel, she created a story behind it, suggesting that it was a grand 18th-century Spanish hacienda. Arched halls, antiques, a ballroom, rustic furniture, and exotic gardens helped create the effect. Staying here, you felt as though you were the personal guest of a Spanish don. When the hotel opened in 1930, Winslow was a crossroads of the West—a major stop on transcontinental railroad, airline, and highway routes. The hotel closed

in 1959, a victim of the decline in railroad passenger traffic, and lay forgotten for four decades. Now it's welcoming guests again. The **Turquoise Room** (see below) serves fine meals. Even if you're not staying at the hotel, it's worth taking the self-guided tour of the public areas.
**(i)** 45 **P** 🅢 🅖 DIS, MC, V

## 🍴 TURQUOISE ROOM
$$–$$$
LA POSADA
303 E. 2ND ST.
TEL 928/289-2888
www.theturquoiseroom.net
Menus change frequently, but chef/owner John Sharpe serves Southwestern fare and such specials as filet mignon wrapped in applewood-smoked bacon on a bed of red caboose-mashed potatoes with wild mushroom sauce.
**+** 100 **P** 🅢 🅖 All major cards

## ◼ SOUTHERN ARIZONA

## AMADO

## 🏨 REX RANCH
$$$
131 AMADO MONTOSA RD.
TEL 520/398-2914
FAX 520/398-8229
www.rexranch.com
The peaceful setting south of Tucson is great for bird-watching or as a base for Tubac, Tumacacori, and the Santa Rita Mountains. The ranch offers a full-service spa and arranges horseback riding and mountain biking. The restaurant serves European and Southwestern cuisine.
**(i)** 32 **P** 🅢 🅖 All major cards

## BISBEE

## 🏨 COPPER QUEEN
$$$

11 HOWELL AVE.
TEL 520/432-2216
FAX 520/432-3819
www.copperqueen.com
The Copper Queen Mining Company built this four-story hotel in 1902 and it's still impressive today. The restaurant serves American and Italian food.
**(i)** 52 🖨 🅢 🅖 All major cards

## 🏨 BISBEE GRAND HOTEL
$$–$$$
61 MAIN ST.
TEL 520/432-5900 OR
800/421-1909
www.bisbeegrandhotel.com
Richly decorated Victorian rooms carry you back to the romance of the 1890s. A café and saloon downstairs add to the atmosphere with a high pressed-tin ceiling and an 1880s bar from Tombstone. **(i)** 13 🅖 All major cards

## 🏨 SCHOOL HOUSE INN BED & BREAKFAST
$$
818 TOMBSTONE CANYON
TEL 520/432-2996 OR
800/537-4333
FAX 520/432-3134
www.schoolhouseinnbb.com
Spacious rooms in a 1918 brick school building; a full breakfast is included.
**(i)** 10 **P** 🅖 All major cards

## 🏨 CALUMET & ARIZONA GUESTHOUSE
$–$$
608 POWELL ST.
TEL 520/432-4815
www.calumetaz.com
Once a guesthouse for officials of the Calumet & Arizona Mining Company, this 1906 house and an adjacent building now offer eight rooms (four with private bath), cooked-to-order breakfasts, guest kitchen, and free Internet.
**(i)** 8 **P** 🅖 MC, V

## DOUGLAS

### 🏨 GADSDEN HOTEL
**$–$$$**

1046 G AVE.
TEL 520/364-4481
FAX 520/364-4005
www.hotelgadsden.com

The amazing lobby of this grand hotel, built in 1907, has faux marble columns decorated with gold leaf supporting a vaulted ceiling that has stained-glass skylights. A white marble staircase sweeps up past a Tiffany stained-glass mural. More than 200 cattle brands cover the walls of the Saddle and Spur Tavern. The restaurant serves American and Mexican food.

🛈 130 🅿 🔁 ❄ 🪟 All major cards

## PEARCE

### 🏨 SUNGLOW GUEST RANCH
**$$$$–$$$$$**

14066 S. SUNGLOW RD. (OFF TURKEY CREEK RD.)
TEL 520/824-3334 or
866/786-4569
FAX 520/824-3176
www.sunglowranch.com

In the western foothills of the Chiricahua Mountains, the ranch offers birding, hiking, astronomy, outdoor swimming pool, and trail rides. Casitas, all with patios, are decorated in Southwestern style; larger units have a fireplace and living room. The dining room is open to the public by reservation for Saturday dinner.

🛈 9 🅿 🏊 🪟 All major cards

## SANTA RITA MOUNTAINS

### 🏨 SANTA RITA LODGE
**$$**

TEL 520/625-8746
FAX 520/625-1956
www.santaritalodge.com

Nestled in the woods of Madera Canyon at an elevation of 5,000 feet, the lodge is a great base for bird-watchers, hikers, and other outdoor lovers. Both cabins and rooms are cozy with wood-paneled walls (in cabins) and kitchenettes.

🛈 12 🅿 ❄ 🪟 MC, V

## SASABE

### 🏨 RANCHO DE LA OSA
**$$$$$**

TEL 520/823-4257 OR
800/872-6240
FAX 520/823-4238
www.ranchodelaosa.com

Near the border village of Sasabe, 66 miles from Tucson, this historic ranch offers horseback riding, pool, whirlpool, birding, biking, and miles to roam. Art and Mexican antiques decorate the colorful interiors of the adobe buildings.

🛈 18 🅿 🏊 🪟 MC, V

## TOMBSTONE

### 🏨 BEST WESTERN LOOKOUT LODGE
**$$–$$$**

781 N. HWY. 80
TEL 520/457-2223 OR
877/652-6772
FAX 520/457-3870
www.bestwesterntombstone
.com

Views from the large rooms take in the surrounding desert and the Dragoon Mountains.

🛈 40 🅿 ❄ 🏊 🪟 All major cards

### 🏨 TOMBSTONE BOARDING HOUSE
**$$**

108 N. 4TH ST.
TEL 520/457-3716 OR
877/225-1319

Two 1880s adobe houses in a quiet neighborhood offer comfortable rooms and a strong sense of history. The Wild West action on Allen Street lies just two blocks south. Rates include full breakfast. **Lamplight Room Restaurant** offers fine dining with both American and Mexi-can menus.

🛈 5 🅿 🪟 MC, V

## TUCSON

## SOMETHING SPECIAL

### 🏨 ARIZONA INN
**$$$$$**

2200 E. ELM ST.
TEL 520/325-1541 OR
800/933-1093
FAX 520/881-5830
www.arizonainn.com

First opened in 1930, the inn combines old Arizona charm and modern amenities. Gardens create a peaceful refuge amid the pink adobe buildings. Spacious rooms contain period furniture, some made by dis-abled World War I veterans. The lounge has piano music nightly. A tasting menu is offered nightly, and you can finish it off with homemade ice cream, such as the ginger cappuccino.

🛈 96 🅿 ❄ 🏊 🏊 🪟 All major cards

### 🏨 CANYON RANCH
**$$$$$**

8600 E. ROCKCLIFF RD.
TEL 520/749-9000 OR
800/742-9000
FAX 520/749-7755
www.canyonranch.com

You can experience top-quality treatment and fitness programs at this health spa near Sabino Canyon. Packages of four nights or longer include luxurious rooms, healthy gourmet meals (no alcohol), and an extensive roster of spa services.

🛈 180 ❄ 🏊 🏊 🪟 🪟 All major cards

### 🏨 RITZ-CARLTON DOVE MOUNTAIN
**$$$$$**

15000 N. SECRET SPRINGS DR.
TEL 520/572-3000 OR
800/241-3333 FAX 520/572-3001
www.ritzcarlton.com/dove
mountain

Dove Mountain offers a luxury resort experience in the Tortolina Mountain foothills, 20 miles northwest of Tucson, in Marana. Rooms and casitas reflect the surrounding desert in their design and materials. Guest enjoy views, spa treatments, and a long list of amenities. The resort is a great place for hiking and star-gazing or relaxing beside one of the three pools. The 27-hole golf course is designed for world-class competition. Kids will have fun on the four-story waterslide and other activities just for them. Four informal dining options serve American and Southwestern favorites.

🛈 253 ⬛⬛⬛⬛⬛ All major cards

### 🏨 LOEWS VENTANA
### 🍴 CANYON RESORT
**$$$–$$$$$**
7000 N. RESORT DR.
TEL 520/299-2020 OR
800/234-5117
FAX 520/299-6832
www.loewshotels.com
This luxurious oasis beneath the rugged Santa Catalina Mountains features two 18-hole golf courses, two pools, waterfall, tennis, health spa, and a lively kids club. The spacious rooms all have balconies.

🛈 398 ⬛⬛⬛⬛⬛ All major cards

## SOMETHING SPECIAL

### 🏨 TANQUE VERDE GUEST
### RANCH
**$$$$$**
14301 E. SPEEDWAY BLVD.
TEL 520/296-6275 OR
800/234-3833
FAX 520/721-9426
www.tanqueverderanch.com Guests enjoy both the height of luxury and the great outdoors at the foot of the Rincon Mountains, 10 miles east of Tucson. Riders and hikers can head into the nearby

Saguaro National Park or Coronado National Forest. Many of the large rooms and casitas have fireplaces and shaded patios, but don't expect a TV. The ranch offers riding stables, pools, tennis, exercise room, saunas, and children's programs, as well as a nature center, trails, and wildlife observation areas.

🛈 74 ⬛⬛⬛⬛⬛⬛⬛ All major cards

### 🏨 EL PRESIDIO BED &
### BREAKFAST INN
**$$$**
297 N. MAIN AVE.
TEL 520/623-6151 OR
800/349-6151
FAX 520/623-3860
www.bbonline.com/az/elpresidio
Antiques and art decorate the guest rooms of an 1880s adobe house in El Presidio Historic District. Just a short stroll from restaurants and the Tucson Museum of Art.

🛈 4 ⬛⬛⬛ MC, V

### 🍴 JANOS
**$$$–$$$$**
WESTIN LA PALOMA RESORT
3770 E. SUNRISE DR.
TEL 520/615-6100
www.janos.com
French-inspired Southwestern cuisine is served here. **J Bar,** right next door, offers less expensive Latin American and Caribbean food ($$, same telephone).

🍴 140 ⬛⬛⬛ Closed L & Sun. ⬛ DIS, MC, V

### 🍴 KINGFISHER
**$$$**
2564 E. GRANT RD.
TEL 520/323-7739
www.kingfishertucson.com
Fresh seafood is the star, but you'll also find meat and vegetarian dishes.

🍴 180 ⬛⬛⬛ Closed L Sat.–Sun. ⬛ All major cards

### 🍴 LA FUENTE
**$$**
1749 N. ORACLE RD.
TEL 520/623-8659
www.lafuenterestaurant.com
A garden setting provides an enjoyable spot for Mexican dining. Mariachi or other bands serenade evening diners. Brunch on Sundays and a choice of buffet or light lunch the rest of the week.

🍴 350 ⬛⬛⬛ All major cards

### 🍴 EL CHARRO
**$–$$**
311 N. COURT AVE.
TEL 520/622-1922
www.elcharrocafe.com
Sonoran Mexican food has been satisfying diners here in this historic stone house since 1922. Call or check the website for other Tucson locations.

🍴 200 ⬛⬛ All major cards

### 🍴 LA COCINA
**$**
201 N. COURT AVE.
TEL 520/622-0351
Good Southwestern and other cuisines rejuvenate at the Old Town Artisans shopping plaza. Dine in the courtyard or inside.

🍴 70 ⬛⬛ Closed D ⬛ AE, MC, V

### 🍴 GOVINDA'S NATURAL
### FOOD BUFFET
**$**
711 E. BLACKLIDGE DR.
TEL 520/792-0630
www.govindasoftucson.com
Excellent vegetarian food served buffet-style. Dining rooms are small, but there's an attractive patio. A Hare Krishna community runs this restaurant, so no alcohol is allowed. Brunch on Sundays.

🍴 25 inside, 30 outside ⬛⬛⬛ Closed L Mon.–Tues. & D Sun.–Mon. ⬛ MC, V

# Shopping in Arizona

Arizona artists translate the hues of earth and sky in countless ways, and the arts and crafts that you'll see tend to reflect the cultures and landscapes of the Southwest. Navajo and Hopi, the most prolific artisans of Arizona's many tribes, incorporate sacred symbols into their ceramics, weavings, woodcarvings, and other work. Colorful Mexican crafts entice visitors to shop in border towns.

## ■ GRAND CANYON COUNTRY

### General Supplies

**Canyon Village Marketplace** South Rim (S of visitor center), tel 928/638-2262. Huge store, good for books, camping supplies, film, groceries, clothing, and souvenirs; there's a deli, too. Smaller general stores in the Grand Canyon area are in Tusayan and at Desert View.

**Marble Canyon Lodge** Marble Canyon, tel 928/355-2225. A convenience store, Native American crafts, as well as supplies for camping, river running, and fishing.

### Arts, Crafts, & Souvenirs

You'll find a gift shop almost everywhere you turn in Grand Canyon Village and Tusayan on the South Rim of the Grand Canyon. Also, many Navajo families sell their work at tiny roadside stalls along Ariz. 64 between Cameron and Desert View. The largest cluster is at a viewpoint of the Little Colorado River between Mileposts 285 and 286.

**Hopi House** South Rim just E of El Tovar, 928/638-2631, ext. 6374. An outstanding selection of Native American art on two floors of a pueblo-style building, opened in 1905.

### Regional Books & Maps

**Grand Canyon Association shops** South and North Rims, tel 928/638-2481 or 800/858-2808, www.grandcanyon.org. Large selection of canyon books, maps, videos, music, posters, and postcards on the South Rim at Canyon View Information Plaza, Verkamp's Visitor Center, Kolb Studio, Yavapai Observation Station, Tusayan Museum, and Desert View. Another shop is on the North Rim in the Grand Canyon Lodge complex, near Bright Angel Point.

**Carl Hayden Visitor Center** Glen Canyon Dam, tel 928/608-6404, www.glencanyonnha.org. The shops here and at Navajo Bridge (near Lees Ferry) carry regional and nature books, maps, posters, videos, music, and postcards.

## ■ NORTHEASTERN ARIZONA

### General Supplies

Trading posts on the Navajo and Hopi reservations often sell groceries and other everyday items. See, for example, Cameron Trading Post (below) and Van's Trading Company (see p. 258).

### Arts, Crafts & Souvenirs

You'll have many opportunities to buy directly from the Navajo and Hopi in this region. Navajo usually sell from roadside stalls. Hopi have small shops in their villages and sometimes sell out of their homes—look for signs. Both tribes also have large cooperative stores. See "Native American Arts" (pp. 38–41).

**Cameron Trading Post** US 89, Cameron, tel 928/679-2231 or 800/338-7385, www.cameron tradingpost.com. A huge sales floor in the main building has almost any kind of souvenir a traveler could wish for; groceries are sold, too. Most of the museum-quality Native American art is in a two-story building in front.

**Goulding's Trading Post** Monument Valley, Utah (just N of Arizona border on US 163, then W 1.5 miles), tel 435/727-3231, www.gouldings.com. The sales gallery offers many fine Native American pieces.

**Hopi Arts & Crafts** Second Mesa (W of Hopi Cultural Center), tel 928/734-2463. The Silvercrafts Cooperative Guild offers a great selection of silver inlay work and other Hopi art. You can often see silversmiths at work.

**Hubbell Trading Post National Historic Site** Ganado, tel 928/755-3475, www.nps.gov/hutr. This historic trading post hasn't changed much over the years. Navajo still drop in to trade. You can pick up canned goods, clothing, or shop for superb rugs and jewelry.

**Navajo Arts & Crafts Enterprise Shops** in Cameron (tel 928/679-2244), Chinle (tel 928/674-5338), Kayenta (tel 928/328-8120), and Window Rock (tel 928/871-4090), www.gonavajo.com. This business has been promoting and selling high-quality work by Navajo artisans since 1941.

**Thunderbird Lodge** Canyon de Chelly National Monument, tel 928/674-5841 or 800/679-2473, www.tbirdlodge.com. Large gift shop offering high-quality work.

**Tsakurshovi** 1.5 miles E of Hopi Cultural Center, Second Mesa, tel 928/734-2478. A little trading post, packed with high-quality Hopi work. Good selection of arts and crafts, including kachina dolls, plus books and Native American music. The owners are full of advice on visits to the Hopi lands. **Tuba Trading Post** Tuba City (1 mile N of US 160), tel 928/283-5441. Good selection of Native American artistry in an attractive building. The trading post dates from 1870 and the unusual two-story octagon was added in 1920. **Van's Trading Company** US 160, W of Tuba City, tel 928/283-5343. This large trading post sells Native American arts and crafts, groceries, and just about everything else.

### ◼ NORTH-CENTRAL ARIZONA

## Arts, Crafts, & Souvenirs

**The Artists Gallery** 17 N. San Francisco St., Flagstaff, tel 928/773-0958, www.flagstaff artistsgallery.com. More than 40 local artists exhibit at this gallery in Flagstaff's historic downtown. The website has details on the First Friday Art Walk.
**Coconino Center for the Arts** 2300 N. Fort Valley Rd., Flagstaff, tel 928/779-2300, www.cultural partners.org. Spacious galleries behind the Pioneer Museum host art exhibits and concerts. Some pieces are for sale. Call or check the website; the center some-times closes between exhibitions.
**Garland's Indian Jewelry** 4 miles N of Sedona on Ariz. 89A, tel 928/282-6632, www.garlands jewelry.com. The Oak Creek Canyon gallery specializes in Native American jewelry, though you'll also find Hopi kachinas and other work.
**Garland's Navajo Rugs** 411 Ariz. 179, Sedona, tel 928/282-4070, www.garlandsrugs.com. This shop claims to have over 5,000 rugs, plus other Native American work.
**Hillside Sedona** 671 Ariz. 179, Sedona, tel 928/282-4500, www.hillsidesedona.net. Sculpture gardens decorate this group of

galleries and restaurants.
**Museum of Northern Arizona** 3101 N. Fort Valley Rd., Flagstaff (3 miles NW of downtown Flagstaff), tel 928/774-5213, www.musnaz.org. A large gift shop sells top-quality Native American art and crafts. A series of annual cultural festivals offer a chance to meet artists and purchase their work. The bookstore has an excellent choice of Native American and nature books.
**Sedona Arts Center** N. Hwy. 89A at Art Barn Rd., Sedona, tel 928/282-3809 or 888/954-4442, www.sedonaartscenter.com. Galleries display works by both emerging and well-known artists. There's a gift shop as well. The center organizes art classes, workshops, and field trips.

## Books

**Bookmans** 1520 S. Riordan Ranch St. (off S. Milton Rd.), Flagstaff, tel 928/774-0005, www.book mans.com. In addition to books there are magazines, music, games, and software. Internet café and free wireless Internet.
**Hastings Books Music & Video** 1540 S. Riordan Ranch St., Flagstaff, tel 928/779-1880. South of Bookmans, this large store offers both new and used titles.
**The Worm Book & Music Store** 6645 Ariz. 179, Suite C-1, Factory Outlet Mall, Village of Oak Creek, tel 928/282-3471, www.sedonaworm.com. A great selection of regional and new age titles, general reading, hiking maps, and music. Internet café and free wireless Internet.
**The Worm Book & Music Store** 128 S. Montezuma St., Prescott, tel 928/445-0361. Regional, general reading, and used books plus maps.

## Shopping Centers

**Flagstaff Mall** 4650 N. Hwy.

89, Flagstaff, tel 928/526-4827, www.flagstaffmall.com. More than 80 shops, including Dillard's, and a food court.
**Tlaquepaque** 336 Hwy. 179, Sedona, tel 928/282-4838, www.tlaq.com. Shady courtyards, flowers, fountains, and Spanish-colonial architecture create a lovely setting for shops, restau-rants, and regional art.

### ◼ WESTERN ARIZONA

## Arts, Crafts, & Souvenirs

**Algodones, Mexico** tel 928/783-0071 or 800/293-0071 (Yuma Visitors Bureau), www.losalgo dones.com. This Mexican town offers good shopping for crafts just 8.5 miles from Yuma. Head west 6.5 miles into California on I-8, and then turn south 2 miles at the Algodones/Andrade Exit. There's parking just before the border, then it's only a short walk to the shops.

### ◼ SOUTH-CENTRAL ARIZONA

## Arts, Crafts & Antiques

**Old Towne Shopping District and Historic Catlin Court Shops** Around Glendale Ave., E of 59th Ave., Glendale. Antiques shops and specialty stores attract shop-pers to this area of downtown Glendale, northwest of Phoenix. The Historic Catlin Court Shops, many in Craftsman bungalows, offer shops and galleries just to the north in the four blocks east of 59th Ave. between Myrtle and Palmaire Avenues. Cerreta Candy Company whips up sweet attrac-tions and tours, 5345 W. Glendale Ave., tel 623/930-9000, www.cerreta.com.
**Old Town Scottsdale** Main St. & Brown Ave., Scottsdale, www.scottsdalecvb.com. Porch-front shops sell Native American work, cowboy and other Western art,

crafts, and Western clothing. Many restaurants, too. The Main Street Arts & Antiques District runs west of Old Town along Main St. and First Avenue. More galleries, boutiques, and restaurants lie northwest of Old Town on Fifth Avenue and in the Marshall Way Arts District. Scottsdale Gallery Association (www.scotts dalegalleries.com) provides listings of member galleries, a map, and details on the Scottsdale Art Walk, every Thursday 7-9 p.m.

## Books
**Bookmans** 8034 N. 19th Ave., northern Phoenix, tel 602/433-0255, and 1056 S. Country Club Dr., Mesa, tel 480/835-0505, www.bookmans.com. These large stores offer all manner of media along with free wireless Internet.
**Changing Hands Bookstore** 6428 S. McClintock Dr., C-101, Tempe, tel 480/730-0205, www.changinghands.com. Excellent selection of new and used books; the store hosts many events.

## Outdoor Equipment
**REI** 1405 W. Southern Ave. at Priest, Tempe, tel 480/967-5494, www.rei.com. (Another branch at 12634 N. Paradise Village Pkwy. West in Paradise Valley, tel 602/996-5400.) REI has an excellent selection of outdoor recreation gear, plus clinics.

## Shopping Centers
**Arizona Mills** 5000 Arizona Mills Circle, Tempe, tel 480/491-7300, www.arizonamills.com. Movie theaters (including a giant-screen Imax), restaurants, and a game arcade in an outlet mega-mall.
**Biltmore Fashion Park** E. Camelback Rd. & 24th St., Phoenix, tel 602/955-8400, www.shop biltmore.com. Macy's, Saks Fifth Avenue, and dozens more. Plus restaurants.

**Borgata of Scottsdale** 6166 N. Scottsdale Rd., Scottsdale, tel 602/953-6538, www.borgata .com. Towers and archways styled after 14th-century San Gimignano in Italy grace this elegant center.
**El Pedregal Festival Marketplace** 34505 N. Scottsdale Rd., Scottsdale, tel 480/488-1072, www. elpedregal.com. A festival atmosphere adds to the fun of visiting this center, which offers boutique shopping and restaurants.
**Metrocenter** 9617 N. Metro Pkwy., Phoenix (just W of I-17 Dunlap and Peoria Ave. exits), tel 602/997-2641, www.metro centermall.com. In northwestern Phoenix and handy to I-17, this huge mall offers several department stores, a movie theater, and more than 160 specialty shops and eateries.
**Scottsdale Fashion Square** 7014 E. Camelback Rd., Scottsdale, tel 480/945-5495, www.fashion square.com. More than 225 stores, including Neiman Marcus. There's a cinema and plenty of places to grab a bite or meal.

## ▪ EASTERN ARIZONA
### Arts, Crafts, & Souvenirs
**Jim Gray's Petrified Wood Company** Hwy. 77 & 180, Holbrook, tel 928/524-1842, www.petri fiedwoodco.com. Huge store at the southern edge of town, on the way to the south entrance of Petrified Forest National Park. An impressive array of petrified wood, agates, crystals, and fossils.

## ▪ SOUTHERN ARIZONA
### Arts, Crafts, & Souvenirs
**Nogales, Mexico** The Nogales-Santa Cruz Chamber of Commerce provides advice on shopping in Mexico at 123 Kino Park, Nogales, tel 520/287-3685, www.thenogaleschamber.com.

Mexican artists and craftspeople turn out an astonishing array of work, sold at shops a short stroll from the U.S.–Mexico border. Park at one of the pay lots on the Arizona side of Nogales. Mexican salespeople speak English and accept U.S. dollars. Shop around and bargain; at least ask for a discount! Popular items include embroidered clothing and leather goods. A passport, passport card, or other valid travel document is required to re-enter the United States; see www.travel.state.gov.
**Old Town Artisans** 201 N. Court Ave., Tucson, tel 520/623-6024 or 800/782-8072, www .oldtownartisans.com. Galleries in an 1850s adobe building contain works by Native American, Mexican, and Western artists.

## Books
**Bookmans** 1930 E. Grant Rd., Tucson, tel 520/325-5767; 3733 W. Ina Rd., Tucson, tel 520/579-0303; and 6230 E. Speedway Rd., Tucson, tel 520/748-9555, www.bookmans.com. Books, magazines, music, free wireless Internet.
**Singing Wind Bookshop** (near Benson from I-10 Ocotillo, Exit 304, turn N 2.3 miles on Ocotillo Rd.; turn right on Singing Wind Rd. for half a mile), tel 520/586-2425. A bookstore on a ranch! It's a good idea to call ahead; Singing Wind is usually open 9 a.m.–5 p.m daily.

## Shopping Centers
**Foothills Mall** 7401 N. La Cholla Blvd., Tucson, tel 520/219-0650, www.shopfoothillsmall.com. Specialty shops, outlet stores, 15-screen movie theater, food.
**Tucson Mall** 4500 N. Oracle Rd., Tucson, tel 520/293-7330, www .tucsonmall.com. More than 200 department and specialty stores, food court, and restaurants.

# Entertainment

Outdoor events usually follow the seasons to take advantage of the desert's winter sun and the high country's summer breezes. Indoors, you can enjoy music and theater all year, especially in the cities. Sports fans can visit rodeos, watch the Cactus League Spring Training, or see games by pro and college teams.

## ■ GRAND CANYON COUNTRY

**Grand Canyon IMAX Theater** Tusayan, tel 928/638-2468, www .explorethecanyon.com. Frequent showings of the *Grand Canyon: IMAX Movie,* with images of the canyon—its wildlife and history. **Navajo Village Heritage Center,** 1253 Coppermine Rd., Page, tel 928/660-0304, www.navajo village.com. Navajo demonstrate crafts, explain about the culture, serve a traditional dinner, and tell stories. April–Oct.

## ■ NORTH-CENTRAL ARIZONA

**The Museum Club** 3404 E. Route 66, Flagstaff, tel 928/526-9434, www.museumclub.com. This Route 66 roadhouse has hosted generations of country music bands and their fans. Today's owners have added additional popular musical styles to the mix. Inside the log building (a former trading post): a Route 66 exhibit, dance floor, and gleaming 19th-century bar. **Northern Arizona University** Flagstaff, tel 928/523-5661 or 888/520-7214, www.nau.edu. NAU Theater, music, dance, and sporting events on campus; the university also hosts the Flagstaff Symphony (*www.flagstaffsym phony.org*). **Prescott Fine Arts Association** 208 N. Marina St., Prescott, tel 928/445-3286, www.pfaa.net. The association sponsors plays, musicals, and concerts; gallery. **Yavapai College** 1100 E. Sheldon St., Prescott tel 928/445-7300, www.yc.edu. A mix of concerts, plays, and events on campus.

## ■ SOUTH-CENTRAL ARIZONA

**Arizona Opera** Phoenix, tel 602/266-7464, www.azopera .com. Productions staged Oct.– April at Symphony Hall, Phoenix Convention Center. **Ballet Arizona** Phoenix, tel 602/ 381-1096 (box office), 381-0184 (administration), or 888/322-5538, www.balletaz.org. Classical and modern works at Symphony Hall and Orpheum Theatre. **Cricket Pavilion** 2121 N. 83rd Ave., Phoenix, tel 602/254-7200, www.cricket-pavilion.com. This 20,000-seat amphitheater hosts big-name music shows. **ASU Gammage** Arizona State University, Tempe, tel 480/965-3434 (box office), www.asugam mage.com. Varied offerings of theater, dance, and concerts in a Frank Lloyd Wright building. **Herberger Theater Center** 222 E. Monroe St., Phoenix, tel 602/252-8497 (box office) or 602/254-7399 (administration), www.herbergertheater.org or www.aztheatreco.org. Arizona Theatre Company and other groups stage musicals and plays. **Phoenix Symphony** 1 N. 1st St., Suite 200, Phoenix, tel 602/495-1999 or 800/776-9080, www .phoenixsymphony.org. Concerts in Symphony Hall and the Orpheum Theatre in Phoenix and Scottsdale Sept.–May. **Phoenix Theatre & Cookie Company** 100 E. McDowell Rd., Phoenix, tel 602/254-2151, www .phxtheatre.org. The group offers a variety of performances for adults plus children's programs. **Scottsdale Center for the Performing Arts** 7380 E. 2nd St., Scottsdale, tel 480/994-2787, www.scottsdaleperformingarts .org. Theater performances, comedy acts, contemporary art shows, and special events.

## ■ SOUTHERN ARIZONA

**Arizona Theatre Company** 330 S. Scott Ave., Tucson, tel 520/622-2823 (box office) or 520/884-8210 (administration), www.aztheatreco.org. The company peforms in the restored 1927 Temple of Music & Art. **Gaslight Theatre** 7010 E. Broadway Blvd., Tucson, tel 520/886-9428, www.thegaslighttheatre .com. Dastardly villains fight heroes over helpless heroines in old-style melodramas. **Tucson Convention Center** (TCC) 260 S. Church Ave., Tucson, tel 520/791-4101, www .tucsonaz.gov/tcc. The Music Hall, Leo Rich Theatre, and Arena host many events. Performing groups include: **Arizona Friends of Chamber Music,** tel 520/577-3769, www.arizona chamber-music.org; **Arizona Opera,** tel 520/293-4336, www.azopera .com; **Ballet Arizona,** tel 888/322-5538, www.balletaz. org; and **Tucson Symphony,** tel 520/882-8585, http://tucson symphony.org. **University of Arizona,** Tucson, tel 520/621-3341 (UA Presents), tel 520/621-1162, (Fine Arts), www .arizona.edu. Plays and concerts are performed on campus.

# Activities

Arizona's outdoors offers the grandeur of deep canyons and vast open spaces, lush alpine forests, and unusual desert life. There are ski slopes for winter and water sports for hot summer's days. Hiking and camping are a great way to get close to nature, or you can sign up for tours of the skies, the back roads, the rivers, or the lakes.

## ■ GRAND CANYON COUNTRY

### Guided Hikes & Tours

**Grand Canyon Field Institute**
P.O. Box 399, Grand Canyon, AZ 86023, tel 928/638-2485 or 866/471-4435, www.grand canyon.org/fieldinstitute. Small groups explore on day hikes, river trips, and pack trips.

### River Running

**Colorado River Discovery**
50 S. Lake Powell Blvd., Page, tel 928/645-9175 or 888/522-6644, www.raftthecanyon.com. Motorized rafting through Glen Canyon. Half-day trips go at least once daily except in winter. Full-day rowing trips, spring and autumn.
**Hualapai River Runners**
Hualapai Lodge Peach Springs, tel 928/769-2219 or 888/255-9550, www.grandcanyonwest.com. The Hualapai tribe offers one- and two-day motorized raft trips through the lower Grand Canyon from Diamond Creek, followed by a helicopter ride to Grand Canyon West. Mid-March–Oct.

### Scenic Flights over the Grand Canyon

Fixed-wing and helicopter flights go year-round from the airport just south of Tusayan on the South Rim. Shortest helicopter flight: to the North Rim and back.
**Air Grand Canyon** tel 928/638-2686 or 800/247-4726, www.airgrandcanyon.com. Cessnas.
**Maverick AirStar Helicopters** tel 928/638-2622 or 800/962-3869, www.maverickhelicopter.com.
**Grand Canyon Airlines** tel 928/638-2359 or 866/235-9422, www.grandcanyonairlines.com. High-wing Twin Otters.
**Grand Canyon Helicopters** tel 928/638-2764 or 800/541-4537, www.grandcanyonhelicoptersaz.com

### Trail Rides

For more than a century, sure-footed mules have carried people in and out of the Grand Canyon. Riders need to be able to control their mules, mount and dismount without assistance, and be prepared for long hours in the saddle. Check carefully the list of requirements. Show up before the check-in time or you could lose your space. From the South Rim, riders go on 3-hour trips to Abyss Overlook and on overnight excursions to Phantom Ranch at the bottom of the canyon. On the North Rim: a one-hour ride, half-day excursion to Uncle Jim's Point, and half- or full-day trips down the North Kaibab Trail.
**South Rim mule rides: Xanterra South Rim,** P.O. Box 699, Grand Canyon, AZ 86023, tel 303/297-2757 or 888/297-2757, www.grandcanyonlodges.com. Rides go year-round; you can make reservations months in advance. For last-minute spots, **Bright Angel Lodge,** tel 928/638-3283.
**Apache Stables** Just outside the South Entrance, tel 928/638-2891, www.apachestables.com. Trail and wagon rides weave through the forest near the South Rim, March–Oct.
**North Rim mule rides: Grand Canyon Lodge** (near Bright Angel Point), tel 928/638-9875 (mid-May–mid-Oct.) or 435/679-8665 (before June 1); www.canyonrides.com. Reservations recommended.
**Allen's Outfitters** (tel 435/644-8150), just outside the park, runs hourly, day, and pack trips mid-May–early Sept. from the North Rim; year-round in Kanab.

## ■ NORTHEASTERN ARIZONA

### Guided Hikes & Tours

**Monument Valley Navajo Tribal Park** Navajo guides operating at the visitor center (tel 435/727-5874) show you the backcountry. Travel on horseback, by foot, or in a vehicle for as short or as long as you'd like. Pack trips offered too (bring food and camping supplies). Vehicle tours can also be arranged through Goulding's Lodge and the motels at Kayenta.
**Canyon de Chelly National Monument** tel 928/674-5500. Ask at the visitor center for a Navajo guide or information on tours that take visitors into the sheer-walled canyons on horseback, on foot, or in vehicles.
**Hopi Country** Hopi guides, tel 928/206-7433 or 800/774-0830, www.hopitours.com. Tours led by Hopi to traditional villages, artists, rock art, and historical sites.
**Thunderbird Lodge** tel 928/674-5841 or 800/679-2473, www.tbirdlodge.com. Popular half- and full-day vehicle tours into the canyons.

## ■ NORTH-CENTRAL ARIZONA

### Horseback Riding

**A Day in the West** Sedona: tel 928/282-4320 or 800/973-3662, www.adayinthewest.com.
**M Diamond Ranch** (Sedona Red

Rock Jeep Tours) tel 928/282-6826 or 800/848-7728, www.redrockjeep.com.
**Trail Horse Adventures** Cottonwood, tel 928/634-5276 or 866/958-7245, www.trailhorseadventures.com.

## Scenic Flights
**Northern Light Balloon Expeditions** Sedona tel 928/282-2274 or 800/230-6222, www.northernlightballoon.com. Hot-air balloons in the early morning.
**Red Rock Biplane Tours** tel 928/204-5939 or 888/866-7433, www.sedonaairtours.com. Fly in an open-cockpit biplane. Fixed-wing and helicopters, too.

## Skiing & Chairlifts
**Arizona Snowbowl** tel 928/779-1951, www.arizonasnowbowl.com. Chairlifts take skiers up the San Francisco Peaks. In summer, views of northern Arizona.

## Tours & Excursions
**Earth Wisdom Jeep Tours** tel 928/282-4714 or 800/482-4714, www.earthwisdomtours.com. Trips reveal red rock beauty.
**Open Road Tours** tel 800/766-7117 or 602/997-6474, www.openroadtours.com. Around Flagstaff, Grand Canyon, Sedona, and other spots.
**Prescott Historical Tours** tel 928/445-4567, or 928/830-1813. Tours led by a costumed guide.
**Sedona Red Rock Jeep Tours** tel 928/282-6826 or 800/848-7728, www.redrockjeep.com. Scenics and archaeological sites.

## ■ WESTERN ARIZONA
### Boat Tours
**Black Canyon River Adventures** Hacienda Hotel & Casino on US 93 near Boulder City, Nevada, tel 702/294-1414 or 800/455-3490, www.blackcanyonadventures.com. Raft trips down the

Colorado from Hoover Dam.
**Bluewater Jetboat Tours** Lake Havasu City, tel 928/855-7171 or 888/855-7171, www.coloradoriverjetboattours.com. Head into Topock Gorge.
**Yuma River Tours** tel 928/783-4400, www.yumarivertours.com. Jet boat and sternwheeler cruises on the Colorado from Fisher's Landing, near Yuma.
*Desert Princess* tel 702/293-6180, www.lakemeadcruises.com. Through Lake Mead from near Boulder Beach, Nevada.

## Canoeing
**Jerkwater Canoe Company** Topock, tel 928/768-7753 or 800/421-7803, www.jerkwatercanoe.com. Tours, rentals, and shuttles along the lower Colorado River.

## ■ SOUTH-CENTRAL ARIZONA
### Ballooning
**Unicorn Balloon Company of Arizona** tel 480/991-3666 or 800/755-0935, www.unicornballoon.com. Flights near Scottsdale.

## Horseback Riding
Many stables arrange lessons, cookouts, and overnight trips.
**MacDonald's Ranch** North Scottsdale, tel 480/585-0239, www.macdonaldsranch.com.
**Papago Stables** Papago Park tel 480/966-9793, www.papagostables.com.
**O.K. Corral Stables** tel 480/982-4040, www.okcorrals.com.
**Ponderosa Stables** tel 602/268-1261, www.arizona-horses.com. Rides in South Mountain Park.

## River Running
**Desert Voyagers** tel 480/998-7238, www.desertvoyagers.com. Go year-round.
**Salt River Recreation** tel 480/984-3305, www.saltrivertubing

.com, offers summer tubing on the Salt River near Phoenix. The Salt River Canyon Wilderness north of Globe has thrilling white water in the spring: **Salt River Rafting** tel 800/425-5253, www.raftthesalt.com; **Mild to Wild** tel 800/567-6745, www.mild2wildrafting.com; **Wilderness Aware Rafting** tel 800/462-7238, www.inaraft.com.

## Tours & Excursions
**Arrowhead Desert Tours** Phoenix, tel 602/942-3361, www.azdeserttours.com. Backcountry tours into the rugged desert.
**Wild West Jeep Tours** Scottsdale, tel 480/922-0144, www.wildwestjeeptours.com. Backcountry tours.

## ■ EASTERN ARIZONA
### Horseback Riding
**Snowy Mountain Stables** Sunrise Park Resort, tel 928/735-7449. A variety of rides in summer, sleigh rides in winter.

## Skiing & Chairlifts
**Sunrise Park Resort** tel 928/735-7669 or 800/772-7669, www.sunriseskipark.com. More than 65 ski runs. Season: Nov.–April. Scenic sky ride offered late May–Oct.

## ■ SOUTHERN ARIZONA
### Tours & Excursions
**Gray Line Tours** Tucson, tel 520/622-8811 or 800/276-1528, www.graylinearizona.com. Day trips around Tucson and multiday excursions to the Grand Canyon.
**Mount Lemmon SkyCenter** Tucson, tel 520/626-8122, http://skycenter.arizona.edu. See the heavens from atop Mt. Lemmon.
**Trail Dust Adventures Jeep Tours** Tucson, tel 520/747-0323, www.traildustadventures.com.

# INDEX

## ILLUSTRATIONS CREDITS

National Geographic

# TRAVELER
# Arizona

**Published by the National Geographic Society**

John M. Fahey, Jr., *President and Chief Executive Officer*

Gilbert M. Grosvenor, *Chairman of the Board*

Tim T. Kelly, *President, Global Media Group*

John Q. Griffin, *Executive Vice President; President, Publishing*

Nina D. Hoffman, *Executive Vice President; President, Book Publishing Group*

**Prepared by the Book Division**

Barbara Brownell Grogan, *Vice President and Editor in Chief*

Marianne R. Koszorus, *Director of Design*

Barbara A. Noe, *Senior Editor*

Carl Mehler, *Director of Maps*

R. Gary Colbert, *Production Director*

Jennifer A. Thornton, *Managing Editor*

Meredith C. Wilcox, *Administrative Director, Illustrations*

**Staff for This Book**

Sheila Buckmaster, *Project Editor*

Kay Kobor Hankins, *Art Director*

Jane Sunderland, *Text Editor*

Connie D. Binder, *Indexer*

Michael McNey and Mapping Specialists, *Map Production*

Al Morrow, *Design Assistant*

Brittany R. Brown, Lawrence M. Porges, Matt Propert, Sally Younger *Contributors*

**Manufacturing and Quality Management**

Christopher A. Liedel, *Chief Financial Officer*

Phillip L. Schlosser, *Vice President*

Chris Brown, *Technical Director*

Nicole Elliott, *Manager*

Rachel Faulise, *Manager*

Robert L. Barr, *Manager*

**National Geographic Traveler: Arizona (Fourth Edition)**
**ISBN: 978-1-4262-0713-6**

First edition: Edited and designed by AA Publishing (a trading name of Automobile Association Developments Limited, whose registered office is Norfolk House, Priestley Road, Basingstoke, Hampshire, England RG24 9NY. Registered number: 1878835).

Drive maps drawn by Chris Orr Associates, Southampton, England

Illustrations drawn by Maltings Partnership, Derby, England

Sonoran desert illustration by Ann Winterbotham

The National Geographic Society is one of the world's largest nonprofit scientific and educational organizations. Founded in 1888 to "increase and diffuse geographic knowledge," the Society works to inspire people to care about the planet. It reaches more than 325 million people worldwide each month through its official journal, *National Geographic*, and other magazines; National Geographic Channel; television documentaries; music; radio; films; books; DVDs; maps; exhibitions; school publishing programs; interactive media; and merchandise. National Geographic has funded more than 9,000 scientific research, conservation and exploration projects and supports an education program combating geographic illiteracy. For more information, visit nationalgeographic.com.

For more information, please call 1-800-NGS LINE (647-5463) or write to the following address:

National Geographic Society
1145 17th Street N.W.
Washington, D.C. 20036-4688 U.S.A.

Visit us online at www.nationalgeographic.com

For information about special discounts for bulk purchases, please contact National Geographic Books Special Sales: ngspecsales@ngs.org

For rights or permissions inquiries, please contact National Geographic Books Subsidiary Rights: ngbookrights@ngs.org

ISSN: 1536-8629 (2001 edition)
ISBN: 0-7922-7899-2 (1st edition)
ISBN: 0-7922-3888-5 (2nd edition)
ISBN: 978-1-4262-0228-5 (3rd edition)

The information in this book has been carefully checked and to the best of our knowledge is accurate. However, details are subject to change, and the National Geographic Society cannot be responsible for such changes, or for errors or omissions. Assessments of sites, hotels, and restaurants are based on the author's subjective opinions, which do not necessarily reflect the publisher's opinion.

Printed in China
10/TS/1

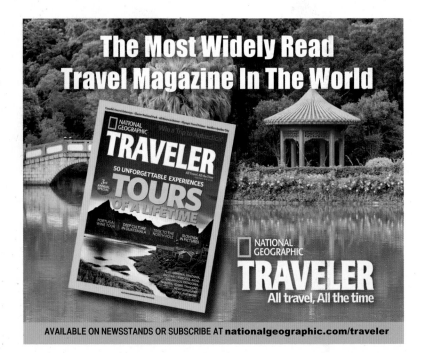